T0341849

The Pleasures of Contamination

TEXTUAL CULTURES: THEORY AND PRAXIS

H. Wayne Storey, editor

The Pleasures of Contamination

EVIDENCE, TEXT, AND VOICE
IN TEXTUAL STUDIES

David Greetham

INDIANA UNIVERSITY PRESS

Bloomington & Indianapolis

This book is a publication of

Indiana University Press
601 North Morton Street
Bloomington, IN 47404-3797 USA

www.iupress.indiana.edu

Telephone orders 800-842-6796
Fax orders 812-855-7931
Orders by e-mail iuporder@indiana.edu

© 2010 by David Greetham
All rights reserved

No part of this book may be reproduced
or utilized in any form or by any means,
electronic or mechanical, including
photocopying and recording, or by
any information storage and retrieval
system, without permission in writing
from the publisher. The Association of
American University Presses' Resolution
on Permissions constitutes the only
exception to this prohibition.

∞ The paper used in this publication
meets the minimum requirements of
the American National Standard for
Information Sciences—Permanence
of Paper for Printed Library
Materials, ANSI Z39.48-1992.

Manufactured in the United
States of America

Library of Congress Cataloging-
in-Publication Data

Greetham, D. C. (David C.), [date]-
  The pleasures of contamination :
evidence, text, and voice in textual
studies / David Greetham.
    p. cm. — (Textual cultures:
theory and praxis)
  Includes bibliographical
references and index.
  ISBN 978-0-253-35506-5 (cl : alk. paper)
— ISBN 978-0-253-22216-9
(pb : alk. paper) 1. Criticism, Textual.
2. Intertextuality. 3. Influence
(Literary, artistic, etc.) I. Title.
  P47.G73 2010
  801'.959—dc22

                           2009052649

1 2 3 4 5 15 14 13 12 11 10

FOR ROBIN

Contents

Preface

As the introduction describes more fully, this book has been in composition for several years and marks a concentration on the theme of *contamination* that has been long developing in my writing. Thus, while the motivation, organization, and purpose of the book are all new, some of the content has grown out of earlier work. The first chapter, "Truthiness in an Age of Contamination," and the epilogue, "The Limits of Contamination," have been composed especially for this book, and all of the other chapters have been thoroughly revised and updated with current references. Inevitably, in all book production (perhaps especially in scholarly collections), there is a gap between the completion of composition and actual publication. For example, the "Truthiness" chapter, which derives its title from Stephen Colbert's accurate critique of the administration of George W. Bush having deliberately promoted *faith* over *fact,* might appear to depend on the events of a particular period (now mercifully behind us). But the chapter does provide a wide range of other examples from film, TV movies, newspapers, popular and classical music, fashion photography, sculpture, painting, performance pieces, comic strips, cartoons, video games, YouTube, legal decisions, and so on. And while the Bush regime did exemplify one of the more morally dubious aspects of contamination, the lessons that (one hopes) its misprisions will have taught us should provide a permanent warning against the abuse of language, science, evidence, and much else that it embodied.

Acknowledgments

In such a wide-ranging (and long-aborning) book, I have inevitably benefited from, and relied on, the work of numerous scholars and colleagues. The names in "Works Cited and Consulted" record the most obvious of these debts, but I have also had the advantage of unrecorded input from faculty and graduate students at the City University of New York Graduate Center and elsewhere. My close friends David Gordon, Jack Hall, the late Speed Hill, and Gerhard Joseph have responded, sometimes with bemusement, more often with real insight, to various chapters in this book. I have also made much use of the scholarly work of colleagues from other disciplines, for example, Leo Treitler, Allan Atlas, and Richard Kramer from the CUNY Graduate Center's music program. Moreover, various administrators at the CUNY Graduate Center have given me the necessary institutional support to work on the book: President William P. Kelly and English executive officer Steven Kruger are just the two most obvious. Most of these essays would not have been written without the institutional and intellectual hospitality of colleagues from other universities, including George Bornstein of the University of Michigan; Marilyn Deegan of King's College, London; Paul Eggert of University College, Canberra; Neil Fraistat of the University of Maryland; Andrew Gurr, formerly of Reading University; John Hollander of Yale University; Seth Lerer of Stanford University; Jennifer Lewin of the University of Kentucky; Elizabeth Bergmann Loiseaux of the University of Maryland; the late Donald F. McKenzie of Oxford University; Margaret Sankey of the University of Sydney; Robert D. Sattlemeyer of Georgia State University; Peter L. Shillingsburg of Loyola University, Chicago; Tom Shippey of St. Louis University; Kathryn Sutherland of Oxford University; Richard Utz of Tübingen University; and Marta Werner of D'Youville College—inevitably, only a partial list.

For the record, earlier versions of the chapters appeared as follows: "The Resistance to Philology," in *The Margins of the Text,* ed. D. C. Greetham (Ann Arbor: University of Michigan Press, 1997), 9–24; "Contamination and/of Resistance," in *Never Again Would Birds' Song Be the Same: New Essays on Early Modern and Modern Poetry in Honor of John Hollander,* ed. Jennifer Lewin (New Haven, Conn.: Yale University Press/Beinecke Library, 2002), 189–205; "Textual Forensics," in *PMLA* 111 (Jan. 1996; a special issue, *Status of Evidence*): 32–51; "Facts, Truefacts, Factoids; or, Why Are They Still Saying Those Things about Epistemology?" in *The Text as Evidence: Revising Editorial Principles (A Hermeneutics of External Evidence),* ed. Andrew Gurr and Philippa Hardman, a special issue of *Yearbook of English Studies* 29 (1999): 1–23; "Who's In, Who's Out: The Cultural Poetics of Archival Exclusion," in *The Poetics of the Archive,* ed. Paul J. Voss and Marta L. Werner, a special issue of *Studies in the Literary Imagination* 32.1 (2000): 1–28; "Phylum-Tree-Rhizome," in *Reading from the Margins: Textual Studies, Chaucer, and Medieval Literature,* ed. Seth Lerer, a special issue of *Huntington Library Quarterly* 58 (1996): 99–126; "Is It Morphin Time?" in *Electronic Text: Investigations in the Method and Theory of Computerized Textuality,* ed. Kathryn Sutherland (Oxford: Clarendon, 1997); "'"What Does It Matter Who Is Speaking,' Someone Said, 'What Does It Matter Who Is Speaking'?"'" in *The Editorial Gaze,* ed. Paul Eggert and Margaret Sankey (New York: Garland, 1997); "Romancing the Text, Medievalising the Book," in *Medievalism in the Modern World: Essays in Honor of Leslie J. Workman,* ed. Richard Utz and Tom Shippey (Amsterdam: Brepols, 1998), 409–31; "The Philosophical Discourse of [Textuality]?" in *Reimagining Textuality,* ed. Neil Fraistat and Elizabeth Loiseaux (Madison: University of Wisconsin Press, 2002), 31–47; "The Telephone Directory and Dr. Seuss: Scholarly Editing after *Feist v. Rural Telephone,*" in *Editing the Literary Imagination,* a special issue of *Studies in the Literary Imagination* 29 (1996): 53–74.

This book would never have gotten off the ground without the inspiration, collegiality, and several interventions of my good friend and colleague H. Wayne Storey of Indiana University, who is the editor of both *Textual Cultures* and the textual series of which *Contamination* is the first volume. Similarly, production of the book has depended very much on the help of Jane Behnken, music and humanities editor at Indiana University Press, and on the wise and deft input from copyeditor Merryl Sloane. And this book would not have been as visually interesting without the generosity of Elliott Arkin, whose provocative sculpture appears on the cover, and of space coyote, whose Calvin and Hobbes "deviant art" cartoon illustrates the chapter "Truthiness."

My final acknowledgment is much closer to home. My son, Alex Greetham, has participated in the digital manipulation of the original sources for the book and, as an enthusiastic geek, has provided me with several contemporary references to bring the text up to date as well as the video game morph in chapter 9. My assistant, Melissa Phruksachart, produced the names index. And, at numerous moments in the research, editing, and production of *Contamination*, my partner, Robin Berson, has generously given the psychological and practical support without which none of this would exist. To her, I dedicate this book.

The Pleasures of Contamination

Introduction

This book wrote itself. That is, for the last few years I have been writing various essays for various circumstances, and very much after the event began to realize that, whatever the occasion, a particular thread had been running through them—and this thread was *contamination*. Whether the topic was ostensibly "evidence" or "archives" or "genetics"—all with some sort of "textual" significance—the means used to address it always seemed to call on this underlying theme of "contamination." This should not have been surprising for, as the new opening essay demonstrates, we are living in an age of contamination, where one mode of discourse (political, religious, musical, philosophical, and so on) leaks into or infects another, so that we experience both at the same time. When the voice boxes of Barbie dolls and G.I. Joes were deliberately exchanged for "political" purposes (so that the girls unwrapping their new dolls heard them yelling "Attack!" "Vengeance is mine!" and "Eat lead, Cobra!" and the boys found their war heroes demanding "Will we ever have enough clothes?" "Let's go shopping," and "Let's plan our dream wedding!"), clearly the cultural images and sexist roles of the two figures had contaminated one another, doubtless much to the consternation of the children receiving them (see Firestone 1993 and the chapter "What Does It Matter Who Is Speaking?").

This contamination was planned (by the so-called Barbie Liberation Movement) as a way of highlighting the gendered stereotypes of the toys that we give our children to play with. The infection of one expectation by another had an overt social purpose, and inevitably hit the newspapers.

But contamination is not always so easily defined, although different groups may recognize that something strange has happened. Thus, when Shostakovich suddenly introduces the famous theme from the overture

1

of Rossini's *William Tell* into his Fifteenth Symphony, it will be obvious to all listeners that some sort of "intervention" has occurred (the famous melody just doesn't "fit" into the symphony), but to some it will seem obvious that what is contaminating the Shostakovich is not Rossini but the theme from *The Lone Ranger* television series. Given that the symphony has many other such contaminating incursions (the "Fate" motif from Wagner's *Ring* is introduced "seriously" before being turned into a waltz-like development that undermines the portentousness of the original Wagner), we could easily place the Rossini "quote" into the pattern of Shostakovich's technique for his symphony: *except*—there will presumably be some listeners who hear *only* the theme from *The Lone Ranger*, some who hear *only* the Rossini, and some who hear *both,* the one filtered through the other. What did the original Russian audience for the Fifteenth hear, or a contemporary American one? Had *The Lone Ranger* yet made a cultural incursion in Russia? Was the Rossini familiar to this same audience, given the dearth of Russian performances of *William Tell* (but not necessarily of the overture)? What did Shostakovich *intend?* Is *The Lone Ranger/William Tell* invasion serious, ironic, comical, and what is therefore its intended effect?[1] Does it even matter what Shostakovich intended, given that we are talking about a *cultural* phenomenon, of the variable reception of a "mixed" discourse?

This question is just one of many addressed in this book, most specifically in the chapter "What Does It Matter Who Is Speaking?" The questions are many because the opportunities for experiencing and examining the function of contamination are many. While contamination has always been a part of our cultural experience (it is, for example, a major issue in the transmission and editing of classical and medieval texts), it may be that we are living in a period when there is a proliferation of contamination, almost to the point where it becomes an expected part of discourse, especially political, and that the contours of this contamination can be best viewed under the wide auspices of current theories and practices of interdisciplinary textuality.

The Pleasures of Contamination thus aims to put such textual issues at the center of an ongoing debate involving philosophy, law, history, music,

---

1. Whenever I have played this section of the symphony to my graduate students or at conferences, the result (in America) has always been the same: laughter.

film, religion, and other modes of expression, with a cast of characters ranging from Frank Sinatra to Dr. Seuss to the U.S. Supreme Court and involving particle accelerators, telephone books, forensic science, and, of course, literature—all seen with the cultural pressures and contexts in which they appear. But with the focus on the various manifestations of contamination, this collection is very different from my earlier *Textual Transgressions: Essays toward the Construction of a Biobibliography,* in which I aimed to show how the production of scholarly work was reflective of a personal narrative, involving (one hopes) some intellectual growth and many contradictions and changes of mind; its organization more or less followed a chronological narrative. There is a narrative of sorts to *Pleasures of Contamination,* in which each part of the subtitle, "Evidence, Text, and Voice in Textual Studies," is drawn upon, but it is schematic, not chronological.

The main title itself is an example of contamination, since the "pleasures" invoked are in part an *hommage* to Roland Barthes's *The Pleasure of the Text* (a work in which the exploration of the multiplicity of "textual"—i.e., "textile"—threads becomes both obsessive and even orgasmic). *Contamination* offers no orgasmic pleasure of the sort promised by Barthes's *jouissance,* although one of its main themes is sexuality as an example of contamination—the mixing of male and female—especially as that figure has been (mis)used in textual genealogy (see the chapter "Phylum-Tree-Rhizome"). But *Contamination* does provide the interwoven threads, the co-option of pieces of various disciplines, various discourses, that have been a major underpinning for my career since at least the 1979 founding of the deliberately interdisciplinary Society for Textual Scholarship and the publication of its journal, *Text,* which, very appropriately, has now been renamed *Textual Cultures: Texts, Contexts, Interpretation.* That *Pleasures of Contamination* should be the first monograph in a series accompanying *Textual Cultures* is, I hope, both logical and auspicious.

I do recognize that any title with *Contamination* as one of its main elements is going to be seen as deliberately provocative, for contamination is generally thought of as something unseemly, dangerous, or improper, and certainly not a quality that one should be endorsing or taking pleasure in, even with the reference to Barthes. But I believe that this book will show how contamination may be seen as normative, healthy, and necessary: a textual (and human) condition to be celebrated rather than condemned.[2] However, I acknowledge that the timeliness of this book does depend upon the recent proliferation of contamination in public discourse, which often has an agenda much less laudable than that of the Barbie Liberation Movement.

While the presence (and exposure) of contamination can be positively seen as a renewed and revitalized interest in textuality itself, it is clear that contamination has been (ab)used in a new and dangerous way in the twenty-first century, an issue that is taken up in the opening chapter, "Truthiness in an Age of Contamination." We are living in a culture in which contamination (especially as it relates to evidence, text, and voice) has acquired a particularly powerful, even ominous, presence. The single most contentious issue of the Bush administration was the contamination (for good or ill, to achieve specific results) of "evidence" in order to justify, prosecute, and then deny the realities of the war in Iraq (see Rich 2006; Ricks 2006; Suskind 2008; and, more generally, Gore 2007). From the erroneous (mis)reporting of the "evidence" of "weapons of mass destruction" by Judith Miller of the New York Times and others, to the disputed (and carefully contaminated) "evidence" that Iraq was behind the attacks of September 11, 2001, and had tried to buy yellowcake uranium from Niger, to the flagrant co-option of overtly ideological considerations in the hiring and firing of U.S. prosecutors, a global public has been made aware of the rhetoric of what we may call "facticity" (or, as I do in one of the chapters, "facts," "truefacts," "factoids"). Similarly, the presence (or absence) of "voice" has acquired an especially resonant cultural significance in the repeated issue of tape recordings by Osama Bin Laden, by the hectoring at the trials of Saddam Hussein and Slobodan Milosevic, and by the belated "confessional" of Robert McNamara (1995) that "we were wrong, terribly wrong" in Vietnam.[3] Such related cultural problems as the suppression (or invention) of ideologically or religiously inspired

---

2. A brief coverage of the technical/textual meaning of "contamination" and its relations with the similar, and often confused, meaning of "conflation" occurs as the introduction to the chapter "Contamination and/of Resistance."

3. This change of mind was parodied in the New Yorker (Buckley 1995) as "Doing the Mc-Namara," with such historical figures as Idi Amin Dada and Jack the Ripper apologizing for their crimes. This moment of reassignation of the term "McNamara" thus contaminated the earlier straight reference in the Simon and Garfunkel song "A Simple Desultory Philippic (or How I Was Robert McNamara'd into Submission") (1969); see chapter 8.

"evidence" in what are presented as "scientific" studies on, for example, global warming or stem-cell research; the contamination of professional medical reports by the payments by pharmaceutical companies to the doctors producing such ostensibly objective studies; and, in general, the contamination (and suppression) of *fact* by *faith* in the Bush administration (see Michaels 2008; Manjoo 2008)—these are just further examples of how contamination in the presentation of evidence has become a well-known (even an expected) feature of our culture.

While I do not feel that the book need be read as a narrative, there is an organizational sequence that I think does most justice to the theme. This organization moves from the opening chapter on current contamination to a section on the status of philology (once thought to be an objective, "pre-hermeneutic" discipline) and contamination, incorporating a discussion of forensics and evidence. The next part addresses contaminated texts in various fields, including biological models and digital morphing, and the concluding section deals with the various contaminations of voice (including those Barbie dolls and G.I. Joes; see "What Does It Matter Who Is Speaking?") and the multivocalic nature of medieval and postmodern text production. This arrangement also has the advantage of presenting together several chapters that were originally intended to be seen (and read) as pairs or parts of the same argument but have so far not appeared in their intended order and, I would guess, have not been encountered by the same intended readers.[4] While there is inevitably some overlap in this method (and often the same seminal works are cited in the arguments in different chapters), I believe that this sequence will organize the case for and about contamination in a logical and persuasive manner.

Thus, the essays in the "Evidence" part begin with "The Resistance to Philology," which takes up Paul de Man's stance that philology is "pre-critical" and argues that all forms of textual criticism are inevitably hermeneutic and rhetorically contaminated. This section then moves on to

---

4. For example, the chapter "Contamination and/or Resistance" was written as a companion piece to "The Resistance to Philology"; the chapter "Facts, Truefacts, Factoids" was a follow-up to the essay "Textual Forensics" and included some materials that, because of space considerations, could not be presented in the first essay; and the two essays "Romancing the Text, Medievalizing the Book" and "The Philosophical Discourse of [Textuality]?" approach serially the issue of medieval and postmodern authorial and socialized voice. In some cases, I had included a brief summary of the arguments of the first essay in each pair as a link to the second; I have retained some of these links in the current collection, since I assume that some readers will dip into the book as a series of independent essays.

"Contamination and/of Resistance," which maintains that contamination is an essential element in all resistance to orthodox thought and practice. The next pair in the section is "Textual Forensics"—an examination of forensics (i.e., the rhetorical formulation of the rules of evidence), suggesting that all such evidence is culturally contaminated—and "Facts, Truefacts, Factoids; or, Why Are They Still Saying Those Things about Epistemology?" which takes up Rorty's attack on epistemology (v. Susan Haack) and argues that evidence is a very slippery concept, even in philology, and that the "facts" of evidence depend on the rhetorical position of the writer/speaker.

The "Text" part begins with "Who's In, Who's Out: The Cultural Poetics of Archival Exclusion," a discussion, partly based on Derrida's *Archive Fever*, of the cultural power of the archive, especially in the (Freudian) suppression of certain types of evidence, ranging from Cole Porter to computer spell-check programs to the Roman Catholic suppression even of *debate* on certain issues (e.g., women in the priesthood). The next chapter in this section, "Phylum-Tree-Rhizome," addresses the function of the hierarchical "tree" arrangement of, for example, genetics and textual descent (thus rigorously anti-contamination) versus the nonhierarchical "rhizome" (and thus contaminated) concept derived from plant biology and Deleuze and Guattari's discussion of evidentiary ambiguity. The final chapter in this part, "Is It Morphin Time?" examines a graphic series of digital illustrations (deriving ultimately from Ovid and Spenser and encompassing such contemporary phenomena as the Power Rangers, the *Terminator* movies, and video games by way of Calder, Goya, and Magritte), all showing the playfulness of various cultural images in their attitudes toward the supposed singularity of identity, authority, and ontology.

The final section, "Voice," begins with ""'What Does It Matter Who Is Speaking,' Someone Said, 'What Does It Matter Who Is Speaking'?""" a wide-ranging discussion (from Barbie dolls to Shakespeare) of the function of voice (or the lack of same) in determining the evidentiary status of speech, which takes up the challenge posed in a Beckett citation (used by Foucault), especially in contaminated or ambiguous speech. This section continues with the paired chapters "Romancing the Text, Medievalizing the Book," an analysis of the Romantic notion of the single, authoritative, "originary moment" in the creation of texts versus the multivocalic, contaminated authoriality of medieval book production, and "The Philosophical Discourse of [Textuality]?" which, playing on the positivist arguments of Habermas toward disambiguation, argues that the appropriate philosophical approach for contemporary textuality is not the single utterance and utterer, but the multiple (and sometimes contradictory) nature of evidence. The part concludes with "The Telephone Directory and Dr. Seuss: Scholarly Editing after *Feist v. Rural Telephone*," an examination of the legal and textual implications of several twentieth-century copyright decisions as they impinge on questions of Romantic originality, authority, and voice, including a discussion of the contemporary cultural phenomenon of the neologistic language of Dr. Seuss as a celebratory attitude toward "new" voices and utterances in contamination.

I do not claim that my book is overtly political or that it attempts a resolution of any of the specific issues surrounding contamination; rather, it is appearing during a period when the reading public's consciousness about this contamination of evidence is particularly acute. In some of the chapters, I do draw examples from contemporary events, for example, the presence or absence of the Bruno Magli shoes in the two trials of O. J. Simpson, with their two very different results (see "Facts"), and the cancellation of the superconducting super collider (SSC) that might have provided evidence for a unified field theory and its replacement by the still (as of this writing) not fully tested LHC (large Hadron collider) at the European Organization for Nuclear Research (CERN; see Overbye 2009 and the discussion in "Facts"); but my polemical purpose is, perhaps paradoxically, to challenge the prevailing view of contamination as dangerous and to propose that, in textual as in various other of the human sciences, we need contamination to survive. For example, in the essay "Phylum-Tree-Rhizome," I make what is (to me) the obvious argument that the so-called genealogical method of stemmatics is mapped upside down, since in nature, family (i.e., sexual) filiation results from the combination or, yes, the "contamination" of two sets of genes to produce an individual offspring, as opposed to the parthenogenesis of stemmatics. This is perhaps a trivial (or, as Joyce might put it, a *quadrivial*) point, but it demonstrates the probing and what I hope is the unsettling nature of my argument in this book. One of my earliest essays was called "A Suspicion of Texts" (and was written for a "popular" audience; 1987b). That "suspicion" runs through every part of this current book, and it will therefore

(I trust) engage not just textual scholars, not just academics, but all those who might wonder why a Cole Porter song should have its lyrics changed from "a sniff of cocaine" to "the purfume from Spain" (see "Who's In, Who's Out"), or why some recent research in historical linguistics might show that German is a "bastard," "hybrid" language, an idea that could clearly not have been given voice during the Third Reich (see "Phylum").

So, maybe, this book is political after all, if by that we mean all of the pressures, congruencies, and dissociations that occur within a greatly expanding polis. In the past, textual scholars have been notorious for building themselves redoubts, safe havens where "objective" research could be conducted free from the constraints of time and place: the famous Center for Editions of American Authors' "definitive" editions could claim to stand outside the moment of their making, "monuments of unageing intellect." My aim in this book, as in most of my other work, is to break open the redoubts, to allow one field to contaminate another, and thus to celebrate the pleasures of contamination.

ONE

Truthiness in an Age of Contamination

Contamination has got a bad name, and yet we do it and recognize it all the time. Journalists, newspaper editors, filmmakers, painters, digital geeks, cartoonists, and other contributors to current media rely on the fact (and inference) of contamination to make meaning. Consider the *New York Times* science article by Natalie Angier (2008), entitled (by her or an editor at the newspaper) "Who Is the Walrus?" The article itself is a perfectly straightforward, if deliberately playful and ironic, account of the nature and plight of walruses. But that title would alert anyone familiar with the music of the Beatles that what appears to be simply a direct question depends for its suggestive power on the line "I Am the Walrus" by John Lennon. In fact, Ms. Angier specifically alerts her readers to this external influence, noting that "walruses remain perversely, lumpishly obscure, known mostly for their sing-song linkage with a carpenter, an eggman and goo goo joob" (4), where the reference to "eggman" brings in another part of the Beatles lyrics for "I Am the Walrus." This outside interference from another medium has already been signaled by Angier's having pointed to Lewis Carroll's "Walrus and the Carpenter" from the second *Alice* book (which is itself the reference imported by Lennon) and then to the Beatles refrain of "goo goo g'joob." It is more than likely that most contemporary readers would make the Carroll connection even if the Beatles, and then Angier, had not already made it for them (see further at http://en.wikipedia.org/wiki/I_Am_the_Walrus).

In this example, the external text behind the title "Who Is the Walrus?" is reinforced and confirmed by the later incorporation of the three-fold layers of meaning. This is what contamination does; and we are pleased by it, particularly when we can congratulate ourselves on having correctly identified the layers. In the technical lexicon of textual criticism, *contamination* is this sort of confluence whereby an external or precedent text invades the composition (consciously or unconsciously) of the current text. It is thus distinct from *conflation,* in which two separate texts, often of equal status or significance, together produce a third derivative text. Back in the medieval scriptorium, contamination could occur when a scribe was producing/copying one text, but with his mind and memory under the influence of another text, so familiar that it did not have to be physically present to infiltrate the current production. Conflation, however, usually suggested that both texts were open to the scribe's view, and that he moved back and forth from one to the other. Contamination is seditious, ironic, fun, sometimes invisible, and a sign of the human mind at work; conflation is, by comparison, rather ponderous, deliberate, and not nearly as interesting. We do not need to assume that Natalie Angier had the text of the Beatles or of Lewis Carroll in front of her to produce her contaminated text; she can rely on, and play with, the cultural suggestiveness of the figure of the walrus and her own memory.

But contamination can often be more complex, and perhaps less visible, than the walrus example. To stick with the *New York Times:* on the same date as the Angier article (May 20, 2008), there appeared a review of a concert by the Metropolitan Opera Orchestra conducted by Valéry Gergiev, in a program of works by Mussorgsky. Perhaps predictably, the editor (or possibly the reviewer, Allan Kozinn) titled the review "A Dark and Stormy Night, Played for All Its Drama" (Kozin 2008: E1). Fair enough, given that Mussorgsky's *Night on Bald Mountain* was on the program, in the starker, less civilized version by Mussorgsky himself rather than in the familiar Rimsky-Korsakov reorchestration. Of course, those of us brought up on Snoopy's attempts to type out the great canine novel (every version of which begins with "It was a dark and stormy night") presumably enjoyed the ironic undercutting of the frightening Mussorgsky by the review title's invocation of *Peanuts.* But the layers do not end there, for unwittingly or otherwise, Snoopy was himself co-opting the (in)famous beginning of the Bulwer Lytton novel *Paul Clifford* (1830), which has had the unfortunate history of having even its title submerged by the opening line, so that the current *Oxford Dictionary of Quotations* (2004) lists the line not under Bulwer Lytton or his novel but in the separate category of famous "Opening Lines." We need not know of Snoopy's reading habits to recognize the contamination that is occurring when he begins his novel, and we are certainly not expected to make a correct allusion to *Paul Clifford* (in the way that Angier might reasonably expect us to incorporate the Beatles and Lewis Carroll). Which of these layers are lurking in the title of the review? In this case, it hardly matters, because of the free cultural availability of the phrase.

But the Kozinn review of Mussorgsky sets up yet another opportunity for contamination, by simply noting that the program also included *Pictures at an Exhibition,* in the Ravel orchestration that Kozinn characterizes as "cinematic" as opposed to Mussorgsky's solo piano "line drawings," a deft distinction derived from yet another medium. In making such a distinction, Kozinn was doubtless relying at least in part on a listener/reader's awareness of the two versions, and we do not need to speculate that Kozinn had already seen a contaminated version of the title of the Mussorgsky/Ravel in the May 18 magazine section of the same newspaper. In the feature rather archly called "The Medium," Virginia Heffernan (or, again, an editor) co-opts the Mussorgsky/Ravel in an article called "Pixels at an Exhibition: Art, Mystery and the Meaning of YouTube" (2008: 20). We might groan at the facility of this co-option of the external, though we can do this only if we can congratulate ourselves on being already aware of the Mussorgsky/Ravel; but unlike both the Kozinn and the Angier articles, there is no further textual reinforcement in Heffernan's piece, which takes no additional advantage of the precedent text in the body of her account of the Kitchen Gallery's invitation to "art-world figures" to use YouTube as "a supply store, slag heap or rag-and-bone shop" (20). This lack of reinforcement makes the contamination of "Pixels" by the precedent *Pictures* even more egregious, and thus perhaps more likely that the co-option was made not by Heffernan herself but by a smart-ass editor. This editor would of course have to assume that readers of the Sunday *Times Magazine* had a similar range of cultural reference as those reading the Kozinn review two days later; otherwise, the title might look amusing, but would be essentially a dead end, without the contamination that makes it work.

Perhaps a more straightforward example of the sort of contemporary cultural infiltration of one text by another (again from the *New York Times* and again involving the Beatles) is another headline, "I Got the News Instantaneously, Oh Boy," over an article by Tim Arango (2008: WK3).

Like the Angier "Walrus" piece, the editorial headline assumes some familiarity in the readers' minds with the opening line of "A Day in the Life," the last track on *Sgt. Pepper's Lonely Hearts Club Band*—"I read the news today oh boy." But, unlike the Angier, there are no further references in the article itself to anything that might reinforce this connection. Moreover, it is telling that it is primarily the apparently throwaway expression "oh boy" that confirms the lurking presence of the Beatles line, for the first part of the title is, of course, a *mis*-citation ("I read" becomes "I got"). This tangle may make the evidence for contamination more tenuous than in the other examples, and that is precisely my point: the use (almost the expectation) of minor pieces of contamination like this demonstrates just how ubiquitous the technique has become. In this case, a reader unfamiliar with *Sgt. Pepper* could still make good sense of the article (though perhaps regarding the "oh boy" as gratuitous). But the combination of the *form* of the first part of the headline with that very interjection provides a nudge to knowing readers, and even those not specifically recognizing the source of the intrusion will be alert to something strange in the headline. Contamination can, by the disjunction it usually creates, thus show symptoms of its presence even to an audience long removed from the contaminating documents, just as those Continental manuscripts ultimately derived from Insular scripts can betray paleographic symptoms of their origins even when no Insular exemplar is extant (see Greetham 1994: 275, 282–83, for further discussion of this phenomenon).

I recognize that subjecting four pieces from the *New York Times* to such an analysis can easily be regarded as bringing too much rhetorical argument to these relatively harmless exercises. It is perhaps the equivalent of explaining a joke. If it needs explanation, it's not a joke. If the contamination needs uncovering, then it has failed as contamination. Not quite, for the very ubiquitousness of such familiar tropes in current media is emblematic of the theme of this chapter, and this book. Maybe we are indeed so accustomed to the layering, so inured to it, that we no longer need to register this ubiquitousness. Obviously, I think otherwise: the omnipresence of contamination, and its being taken for granted as almost a tic, is a characteristic of an age in which the unsullied, pure text, devoid of interpenetrations by other texts, is chimerical. Clearly, there has always been contamination of one sort or another, and it has given the various pleasures that will be described in this book. But there is another side to contamination, a more ominous cultural expectation that there are layers—of deceit, deception, prevarication—in our public discourse that are dangerous to the moral coherence of our society. The "play" of Angier, Kozinn, and Heffernan is relatively harmless. But what of types of contamination that could continue to reinforce the negative connotations of the term?

A perhaps ambiguous example is the criticism that arose after the fashion magazine *Vogue* (the epitome of high-end, expensive couture) did a shoot in India using as "models" the poor and the underprivileged rather than the usual glamorous and rich. One shot was of a man modeling a Burberry umbrella costing $200, another was of a peasant child wearing a $100 Fendi bib, when 456 million Indians live on less than $1.25 a day. *Vogue* clearly intended the contamination of high fashion by placing it in an incongruous setting, but the sociopolitical effects of that decision caused some negative responses. As reported in Timmons (2008: C5), "How does one sell something like a $1,000 handbag in a country where most people will never amass that sum in their lives, and many are starving? The answer is not clear cut, though *Vogue*'s approach may not be the way to go." This is a polite way of saying the contamination was culturally harmful (to *Vogue*'s image, if nothing else), and the discrepancy between model and outfit created an unacceptable gap. This gap might be regarded simply as a matter of style (in the sense of one way of making a statement—in any medium—rather than another), going back to the original meaning of *style* as derived from the "stylus" or pen, which could produce different strokes depending on the way it was held. Such discrepancies or gaps in style are familiar, and some might seem more gratuitous than others.

Thus, when Wagner introduced post-*Tristan* harmonics and chromaticism for the *Venusberg* music of the 1861 Paris version of the 1845 early lyrical *Tannhäuser*, even a listener not experienced in Wagnerian opera would have been alerted by the shift: one style invades (contaminatoo) the style of the rest of the work: it sounds strange. Such incursions are, of course, among the staples of style variation in music and other arts. A number of postmodern composers have indeed made such stylistic contaminations a major feature of their work. Peter Maxwell Davies, for example, embeds various Renaissance forms into his opera *Taverner* (1972)—as does Britten in the opera *Gloriana* (1953)[1]—and Davies's *St. Thomas Wake* (1969) combines a suite of foxtrots (played in 1920s instrumentation) together with a pavane by John Bull. His opera *Resurrection* (1987) includes various parts for a rock ensemble. In his realizations of earlier (especially Renaissance) music, Davies gradually plays on the period disjunction by beginning in a relatively straightforward, "authentic" style and then contaminating this ground with modern harmonics, so that it is not always clear where the stylistic incursion takes off. Sometimes, the filter of contaminating/contaminated styles can be even more complex, as when Corigliano uses not only Mozart's *Le Nozze di Figaro* (1786) as a source but then filters Mozart through Rossini (*Il Barbiere di Siviglia*, 1816) and Strauss (*Der Rosenkavalier*, 1911) in some of the ensemble pieces of *The Ghosts of Versailles* (1991). Who is contaminating whom? When done as pastiche, this sort of co-option (in music and other arts) is often regarded as one of the primary characteristics of postmodernism (see Greetham 1993a).

But, if such artistic contamination is indeed almost the norm, and we may recognize that we live in an age of contamination, where does "truthiness" fit into this system, and does it generally have positive or negative connotations? Is truthiness pernicious in a way that walruses, the Beatles, Peter Maxwell Davies, and the rest are not?

The term was invented by Stephen Colbert on October 17, 2005, in the premiere of his late-night *Report*. As quoted by Farhad Manjoo (2008: 188–89), Colbert used the term to distinguish between "two camps whose philosophies could never reconcile—those who *think* with their *head*" and those who "*know* with their *heart*." In the role of a "blowhard TV pundit" modeled on Bill O'Reilly of the Fox network, Colbert impersonates a "*knower*," for whom "truthiness" is "the quality of a thing *feeling* true without any evidence suggesting it actually [is]." This formulation is ultimately derived from the Thomist concept of *quidditas*, the "thingness" of a concept, but whereas Aquinas used the strictures of Aristotelian logic to demonstrate this *quidditas*, the Bush administration had no truck with

---

1. In the example of *Gloriana*, it is perhaps ironic that until recently it was only the most overt "Renaissance" aspects of the opera that succeeded (as an independent suite, *Courtly Dances*), while the opera itself initially failed.

either Scholastic or Enlightenment reason and, as Al Gore shows in his chronicle of the "assault on reason" (2007), continually put a faith-based "feeling" ahead of any logical argument. Throughout this book, Gore documents the increasing disparity between faith and fact, especially regarding the actual conditions of the lead-up to and prosecution of the war in Iraq. Gore, along with other critics of the war and of other aspects of the Bush/Cheney foreign policy, sees this tension in terms of a phenomenological *gap*, a disjunction between one perception of reality and another. There is ample justification for this formulation, from Donald Rumsfeld's dictum that "we will impose our reality on them" (see Suskind 2008: 380) to the deliberate suppression of information from Tahir Habbush, the head of Iraq's intelligence organization, that Saddam Hussein had already destroyed all his weapons of mass destruction years before the Bush/Cheney White House decided to proceed with an invasion that they *knew* (with the powers of reason) was unjustified, but that they *felt* to be right anyway. As Colbert put it: "If you *think* about it, maybe there are a few missing pieces to the rationale for war. But doesn't taking Saddam out *feel* like the right thing, right here in the gut[?]" (as reported in Manjoo 2008: 189).

This model—the gap, the missing pieces, the disjunction between faith and reason—would appear to describe a policy in which truthiness (as defined by Colbert) dictates actions and beliefs. But I think another way of perceiving the faith/reason collocation is to map the relationship between the two discourses as one in which the access to the "real" is via (not in spite of) a filter of "belief," so that the rival discourse of truthiness contaminates and invades the domain of mere fact, the recognition of which is always a product of, not the cause of, faith. We should recall that the reason the Inquisitors refused to look through Galileo's telescope to view the supposed moons of Jupiter was not because they thought the reality of the moons would *not* be supported by the empirical evidence of the telescope, but quite the opposite: they thought that this evidence would be observable but would be a product of mere sensory perception, which was unreliable and positively disturbing to the precedent faith that the moons could not really be there. When evidence supplied to the Bush administration might have undermined the faith-based determinations, then this evidence had to be suppressed, bracketed, buried. Gore and others might be right that a fissure will open up between Colbert's "two camps," but the reason such a gap becomes significant is that empiricism is suspect in the face of belief, and belief (manifested as truthiness) therefore contaminates the other discourse.

This model is one narrative thread running through David Michaels's *Doubt Is Their Product* (2008), where the history of the suppression of fact-based research by the Bush administration is told very much in terms of a series of contaminations. Thus, describing the activities of the "Traditional Values Coalition," Michaels notes that, while the National Institutes of Health (NIH) had been "more insulated from politicization" (206) in previous years, under Bush, the traditional values group was given its head, and, using a "hit list of agency grantees who were studying prostitution, substance abuse, homosexuality, or sexually transmitted diseases" (ibid.), the coalition influenced the House of Representatives to bring in a vote that fell just two votes short of defunding such research, even though the studies had already been approved by the NIH process of peer review. The lesson? As Michaels puts it, "researchers who focus on areas like sexual behavior . . . [will] have to avoid the wrong research questions [and] will be forced to abandon certain areas of investigation that hold great promise for public health" (ibid.).

Another way that the faith-based agenda can contaminate fact-based scientific research is by determining the mode of access to this research. Librarians across the country protested against the decision (April 2008) of the Popline medical database administered by the Johns Hopkins University to remove *abortion* as a searchable term for those accessing the 360,000 records kept in the university's database, a database funded by public money through the Agency for International Development (see Pear 2008). Of course, once the deliberate suppression of the research term was discovered by the outraged librarians, Hopkins did the right thing (out of embarrassment?) and restored the term, after having previously told the librarians at the Medical Center of the University of California, San Francisco, that "'abortion' was no longer a valid search term" (Pear 2008). The rhetorical contortions of the Popline managers to explain away the contamination of science by faith would have been risible, if they had not been (temporarily) effective. Debra L. Dickson of Popline had "suggested" that, instead of using "abortion" as a search term, librarians could have used such euphemisms as "fertility control, postconception" or "pregnancy, unwanted." Such manipulations were invoked *after* the research had already been done and documented, demonstrating that every stage of the production of "fact" is now susceptible to contamination by "faith." And this concentration on faith over fact was observable throughout the Bush presidency, as when a group calling itself Family, Faith and Freedom distributed a DVD entitled *George W. Bush: Faith in the White House,* which cast Bush as a prodigal son with "the moral clarity of an old-fashioned biblical prophet" (see Rich 2006: 144–45, quoting Kirkpatrick 2004).

While the invasions of supposedly fact-based empirical data by the ideological requirements of faith were characteristic of the Bush years as a whole, it is undoubtedly in the rationalization and prosecution of the Iraq war that the technique of contamination can be most disturbingly revealed. Even the methods of military strategy have come to be seen as the contamination of one medium by another. Ricks (2006: 75–76) notes that the PowerPoint planning for war rather than using formal written memoranda was symptomatic of simplification through the use of an inappropriate medium. "That reliance on slides rather than formal written orders seemed to some military professionals to capture the essence of Rumsfeld's amateurish approach to war planning" (75). It is obviously absurd to suggest that Bill Gates was responsible for the debacle in Iraq, and yet, as documented by Ricks, it was Rumsfeld's reliance on PowerPoint slide shows ("the clearest manifestation of OSD's [Office of the Secretary of Defense] contempt for the accumulated wisdom of the military profession"—Col. Andrew Bacevich, quoted in Ricks 2006: 75) that turned what was a very complex operation into a simplistic series of visuals, later treated by Jenny Holzer as precisely that—"exhibits" in a sideshow to her enormous *Projections* performance piece (2008) in the cavernous Massachusetts Museum of Contemporary Art in North Adams.

Moreover, the use of domestic political requirements to justify or promote military events (and the reporting thereof) gravely affected all stages of the war. As Rich notes:

> [It was] [a]ll too predictable that even when the administration was forced into rebuilding Iraq, it would time every pivot point, from the creation of a constitution to the scheduling of elections, to deadlines dictated by Rove's political goals at home (whether a State of the Union speech or a domestic election), rather than to the patience-requiring realities of a post-Saddam government. (2006: 222)

Similarly, the Cheney decision to ignore the protests of British intelligence and to move in prematurely on the still-undeveloped plotting to blow up aircraft on the London–New York route was based primarily on the need to have some "positive" news of American success for the midterm elections. As it turned out, the British had been correct, and Cheney's precipitate move resulted in the collapse of the case for the prosecution. As reported later by John F. Burns and Elaine Schiolino, "the case was hampered from the beginning, prosecutors said, by an investigation that was cut short . . . and by problems with introducing evidence in courtrooms" (2008: A1).

In perhaps the most famous (ab)use of a military operation, the dramatic "reenactment" on network television (and the reconstitution of the facts on the ground by political needs) consciously constructed a *Saving Jessica Lynch* narrative at odds with what actually happened, and thereby obviously sought to co-opt the successful Spielberg World War II film, *Saving Private Ryan,* that would create what Rich calls "the Mona Lisa of Operation Iraqi Freedom" (2006: 109).

While such contamination of narrative by political expediency is clearly not limited to the prosecution of this particular war, there is little to compare historically with the suppression of known "facts" about weapons of mass destruction (WMD) to justify a course of action that had long been predetermined. As Sir Richard Dearlove, head of the British Secret Intelligence Service tells Suskind about the infamous Downing Street Memo: "Bush wanted to remove Saddam, through military action, justified by the conjunction of terrorism and WMD. But the intelligence and facts were being fixed around the policy" (Suskind 2008: 189). Bush, Cheney, and Blair certainly knew that the claim of WMD was false, but needed it for the initial prosecution; it was later superseded by other post facto rationales when the WMD failed to materialize.

Even in the on-the-ground practicalities of warfare, the Bush policies relied upon other sorts of contamination, perhaps most notoriously in both the no-bid contracts awarded to companies associated with Cheney and the related use of corporate mercenaries, to the extent of there being over 20,000 "private shooters" by 2006, costing over $1 billion. Of course, military history is full of such mercenaries, but in the case of the Iraq war, these corporate mercenaries were a liability, not an asset. As reported by U.S. Marine colonel T. X. Hammes to Ricks (2006): "Fundamentally, the bodyguards' mission differed from that of the U.S. military. The contractor was hired to protect the principal. He had no stake in pacifying the country. Therefore, they often ran Iraqis off the road, reconned by fire, and generally treated locals as expendable." "They scared the hell out of me. These shooters. You'd see them in the gym. Steroids, tension, and guns are not a good mix" (Ricks 2006: 371). Financial at-home considerations dictated the actual conduct of part of the war, to the embarrassment of the U.S. military.

There is clearly no end to this recital of contaminations and abuses. While the most damning may be the forging of the so-called Habbush letter, which was dictated by the White House to prove (retroactively) that Saddam Hussein had indeed been in collusion with Al Qaeda and had tried to purchase weapons-grade uranium (see Suskind 2008: 380), it is perhaps in the corruption of the U.S. judicial process that the long-term effects of the contaminations will be experienced. Just one case: Candace Gorman, a civil rights lawyer, had been representing Abdul Hamid al-Ghizzawi, a designated "enemy combatant" held at Guantánamo for six years without charge or trial. Discovering that her client had been exonerated in one hearing only to be recharged on the basis of "new evidence," with persistence she managed to get access to this supposed new evidence. What she found both appalled and enraged her. There was no new evidence. "[T]hey're saying evidence is new when it's not. All that happened was they took old evidence and then stamped the word *classified* on it. The only thing that's new is the stamp" (reported to Suskind 2008: 101). Through such machinations, the country had lost what Suskind, Rich, Ricks, and others regard as the "moral authority" it had previously been able to assert and use. The contamination of evidence and the contamination of the operations of warfare by political and ideological expediency have meant that the international standing of the United States is in grave disrepair.

And that the same intrusive expediency was still at work was shown when it was discovered that an anonymous "editor" ("YoungTrigg"), a confessed volunteer for the John McCain presidential campaign, had made thirty "edits" to the Wikipedia article on Alaska governor Sarah Palin in the twenty-four hours prior to the announcement of her selection as the Republican vice presidential nominee. The record of the infiltration was made possible through WikiScanner (see http://wikiscanner

.virgil.gr), a website created by Virgil Griffith to detect contamination of an article by outside editors, even anonymous ones. Amazingly, Young Trigg claimed no conflict of interest, but was later listed as "retired" after another editor, "Ferrylodge," toned down the glowing entries. Yes, Wikipedia is an open source to be approached with some skepticism, but this sort of "editing" is a sign that contamination is alive and well in politics.[2]

Since I have included the "nonsense" of Lewis Carroll in this survey of contemporary contamination, it is fitting that this section on the dangerous interventions during the Bush years should again cite Carroll, but this time in the words of a U.S. court. As reported on July 1, 2008, "With some derision for the Bush administration's arguments, a three-judge panel said the government contended that its accusations against the defendant should be accepted as true because they had been repeated in at least three secret documents" (Glaberson 2008: A1). The court compared this sort of repeated falsity to the absurd declaration of a character in the Lewis Carroll poem *The Hunting of the Snark:* "'I have said it thrice: What I tell you three times is true.' This comes perilously close to suggesting that whatever the government says must be treated as true" (as reported in the decision of the Court of Appeals for the District of Columbia Circuit).

And, while it may be disconcerting to the national psyche to admit this, even a revered object like the manuscript of the Declaration of Independence on display in the National Archives (the subject of a glitzy, fanciful movie thriller—*National Treasure*—in 2004) is technically a contaminated text. Supposedly written on July 4, 1776, this document was in fact commissioned by Congress later that summer (and presumably done by hand to make it seem more authentic) and backdated to July 4, that is, it was forged. But print copies of the now-lost (if ever extant) original Declaration had been in circulation *before* the National Archives manuscript, and the archives version must have depended on one or another of these 200 prints, of which 25 still exist. It is not the free-standing "original"

---

2. Such corporate giants as Diebold, Amgen, Pfizer, Walmart, and ExxonMobil have been "edited," usually to improve the image of the corporation. The fact that Bob Jones University has had more "edits" (over a hundred) to its Wikipedia entry than any other American educational institution is clearly not a reflection of its intellectual prominence (Harvard and Princeton each have had one, and Yale none) but of its politically charged identity as a result of its dating and clothing and racial codes (and the fact that George W. Bush made an important ideological speech there).

document we might like it to be, but a contaminated version most likely based on a second-generation copy (see Widmer 2008).

This sorry history of contamination of documents, databases, legal evidence, and so on can hardly be thought of as giving the sort of pleasure promised by this book; that, I hope, will emerge more forcefully in the chapters to follow. But I cite them here to demonstrate that, even though these contaminations would appear to undermine the rationale for the Iraq war, the holding of prisoners at Guantánamo, and so on, that potential undermining has (as of this writing) produced no significant reaction, apart from various books and articles. George W. Bush remained in power throughout these exposures, the war grinds on, and there are still prisoners being held in Guantánamo without charge or legal proceeding. To be cynical about these exemplary instances of different sorts of contamination, I might just admit that the years of the Bush presidency have provided a rich trove for the study of the cultural phenomenon; but while I do believe that those eight years have been especially productive of one medium, set of principles, or rhetorical strategies invading and "corrupting" the status and substance of others, surely the ubiquitousness of contamination must lead us to accept that we have become less concerned with the preservation of the singularity of discourse, that we almost expect the edges to be blurred, the incursive influence of one discourse over another, and the combination of horror and delight in our living in a world of "mixed media."

And so, to demonstrate that there is still delight, I introduce three pleasurable examples of cultural contamination. The website Deviant Art (www.deviantart.com) is almost entirely devoted to this sort of play on mixed identities, mixed media, and is wonderfully illustrated by the artist space coyote, who produced some delightful layering in a Calvin and Hobbes cartoon. This cartoon obviously depends upon our recognition that there were historical figures called "Calvin" and "Hobbes" (together with a rough sense of what they looked like). But the contaminated illustration also demands that these two figures now invade the graphic template of the *Calvin and Hobbes* comic strip, in which Calvin is a short, irrepressible six-year-old boy and Hobbes his stuffed tiger (who appears "live" only in Calvin's presence). The comic strip is thus the "ground" for this display and the philosopher/theologians the "figure," forcefully introduced into a precedent framing. Ideally, an appreciative reader of

FIGURE 1.1. space coyote's contamination of the "historical" characters Calvin and Hobbes with their avatars in the popular comic strip. *Reproduced by permission of the artist.*

space coyote ought to be familiar with both the ground and the figure, and a reader/viewer who knew only one or the other would come away with a very different (and limited) understanding.

The Calvin and Hobbes example, while certainly an illustration of contemporary contamination, might also be viewed as conflation (as defined above): both media are simultaneously present. But this is not quite a case of both producing a *tertium quid* but rather of one medium being viewed and made particularly meaningful by being experienced *through* the other. Contamination is thus a sort of phenomenological filter (like a filter on a camera) in which the original lens now sees otherwise as a result of the presence of the filter.

From Calvin and Hobbes, I turn to the Muppets, and to a particular scene in *The Muppet Movie,* the wedding of Kermit and Miss Piggy. The story line has been prepared by numerous previous Muppet shows in which Miss Piggy has tried to "snag" Kermit into matrimony. Now, at last, it seems to be happening. There is to be a musical on stage, during which there will be an enactment of a marriage ceremony—in other words, that sort of performative speech act (e.g., on stage) that Austin's theory of "sincere" or "constative" utterances would bracket as "parasitic" or "insincere." But we are forewarned that something strange is happening in this scene by the presence of such characters as Big Bird and Bert and Ernie in the audience: that is, figures/identities co-opted from another sort of reality—*Sesame Street,* not *The Muppet Movie.* Then, as the onstage ceremony is about to begin, Kermit looks a little anxious and expresses some concern about whether this scene is really in the script of the musical (and thus fiction) or is a "real" ceremony that just happens to be occurring on a stage. Miss Piggy gives one of her nervous laughs and just shrugs: noncommittal. But the most disturbing, most "contaminated" part of the scene occurs when a *human* priest (not a Muppet) appears to conduct the service: he is the only human on stage, all the others being in the audience. This of course makes Kermit even more anxious as the priest concludes the marriage vows. With the officiating presence of this human, we never do know whether Miss Piggy and Kermit are really married (at last) or have just "played" the scene, and it is the contamination of the Muppets by the sole human that raises doubts. These doubts were later raised anew on the death of the actor who played the priest. In his obituary, it was noted that he was indeed a "real" priest, but had often been asked to play the *role* of a priest in movies. In his vestments and serious demeanor, we (and Kermit) might ask which of his roles he was playing in *The Muppet Movie,* a question for which there is no satisfactory answer, whether or not one is using Austin's theory of speech acts.

This sort of contamination by crossover is prevalent in the online and gaming community of teenagers and geeks (and combinations thereof). For example, while the main gaming consoles for the most part retain some integrity, under special circumstances a character/avatar from one can leak into another. For example, in the video game *Soul Calibur IV*, characters such as Darth Vader (from the PS3 console) and Yoda (from the Xbox 360)—both of them, of course, originally from *Star Wars*—show up. Similarly, the very popular *Super Smash Brothers Brawl* (for the Wii) uses Snake (from *Metal Gear Solid*) and *Sonic the Hedgehog* (from the *Sonic* games). And *Marvel vs. Capcom* uses both Spiderman from Marvel and Ryu from the *Street Fighter* series, on the Sega console *Sega Dreamcast*. And in the increasingly popular remix series on YouTube, the genres of movies can be moved from one class to another (for example, from family movie to horror and vice versa). To my mind, the most successful of these remixes is the *Scary Mary* horror film version of the Disney *Mary Poppins* (at www.youtube.com/watch?v=2T5_oAGdFic), where through a clever reshuffling of clips from the original and the introduction of captions such as "the fog rolls in . . . and she appears" and "hide your children," with some appropriately "creepy" music, we experience what is clearly the trailer for a very frightening movie (and thus perhaps a little more faithful to the original *Mary Poppins* book than was the sugar-coated Disneyfica-tion). Similarly, at http://www.youtube.com/watch?v=bkoX5Ebtt78&fea ture=related, the sensitive portrayal of autism in *Rainman* is remixed as a thriller. It is perhaps easier to go in this direction (comedy/family film to horror/thriller) than the other direction, although *Shining* (not *The Shin-ing*, itself an interesting comment on the significance of the definite ar-ticle) at www.youtube.com/watch?v=KmkVWuP_sOo&feature=related almost succeeds, as a few tender moments between the maniacal Jack and his family turn the film into a Romantic comedy—and again, using *only* clips from the original movie. The attempt to turn *The Matrix* into a story of "lost love" at www.youtube.com/watch?v=EsNyiB2J1Gk&feature=rel ated also almost succeeds, though with clearly more recalcitrant material. A more problematic example is the remix of two different films, at www .youtube.com/watch?v=P1xpwcFi6r4&feature=related, where the com-edy/thriller *Night at the Museum* is mixed with scenes from the Holocaust drama *Schindler's List,* to disturbing effect. (A more direct, and possibly less offensive, remix of *Schindler's List* as a "Romantic comedy" is at www .youtube.com/watch?v=17dpK61bsqs.) The sort of remix typified by the *Night at the Museum/Schindler's List* example begins to move away from contamination (where a superficial "figure" is undermined by an invasive "ground") into conflation, since both *Night at the Museum* and *Schindler's*

List compete for the same generic space. Similarly, the remix of *The God-father, The Return of the King, Rocky,* and *Apocalypse Now* at www.youtube .com/watch?v=ajZflZMXEpM&feature=related produces a conflation rather than a contamination, even though it is described as a "mashup," and even though *The Godfather, Rocky,* and *Apocalypse Now* contribute only audio voiceovers and music. The popularity of these remixes is yet another testimony to electronic media being especially hospitable to fur-ther experiments in contamination, involving a questioning of genre, character, and performance arising from the demonstrable crossing of boundaries, of one medium, one reality, invading and contaminating another. If the Muppets' priest had been just another Muppet and not a human, or if Mary Poppins had not become a child-molesting ghoul, we would not have been surprised—and we would have missed a lot of the fun.

And that is what I believe contamination can do: it can give pleasure, which will be celebrated in the rest of this book. The cover for this book, with an illustration by Elliott Arkin, demonstrates both the delight and the horror: taking off from the well-known Norman Rockwell triple self-portrait, it achieves one sort of recognition by this simple correlative. But the fact that the subject (both artist and model) is now faceless, in a version of the voluminous burqa, adds a disturbing layer of recognition to the "nonportrait." It is no surprise that Arkin's stimulus for his *Triple Non Portrait* was the riots and threats issued against both Denmark and the press (especially cartoonists) on the newspaper publication of a se-ries of satirical cartoons of Muhammad. Arkin both adopts the layer of anonymity created by the burqa and at the same time gives it a special and clear "identity" in the context of the Rockwell self-portrait (and the various other self-portraits, e.g., of Dürer, that are part of both the cultural history and the citation present of the Rockwell).

So it is still true that contamination has a bad name, and true that the Bush presidency provided all too many examples of the cross-fertilization that all contamination depends on. Nonetheless, I hope that the remain-ing chapters in this book, while accepting that we do indeed live in an age of contamination, will show what various pleasures can be drawn from its operations.

The Contamination of Evidence

PART ONE

Consideration of Evidence

TWO

The Resistance to Philology

Students of corrupt textual transmission will probably have already spotted that my title, "The Resistance to Philology," is a conflation of the titles of two essays by Paul de Man: "The Return to Philology" and "The Resistance to Theory," published as companion pieces (1986). It is a purposeful conflation, and its results embody the problem with which all textual scholars are confronted: an institutional resistance to philology, just as de Man was confronted with an institutional resistance to theory in the early 1980s. In the first of these essays, de Man recounts his experience in Reuben Brower's course "The Interpretation of Literature" at Harvard in the 1950s, in which Brower insisted that students "were not to say anything that was not derived from the text they were considering. They were not to make any statements that they could not support by a specific use of language that actually occurred in the text" (de Man 1986b: 23). This constraint on interpretation should be familiar to those textual critics who have tried to follow G. Thomas Tanselle's injunction always to look in "the text itself" for meaning and thus for intention (1976: 179). But de Man regards this "mere" (i.e., "close" or "text-based") reading as "deeply subversive to those who think of the teaching of literature as a substitute for the teaching of theology, ethics, philosophy, or intellectual history" (1986b: 24), and he claims that Brower's approach, obviously deriving from the practical criticism of I. A. Richards and other formalist critics, was of a piece with the "turn to theory" in the 1970s and early 1980s, which de Man sees as a "return to philology, to an examination of the structure of language prior to the meaning it produces" (ibid.). So much for Tanselle's injunction. I have severe reservations about this claim (see

Greetham 1999b: 5), but my demurral is not based on de Man's thesis that
the pre-semantic, pre-hermeneutic philological model for theory denies
what he calls an "ethical function to literature" (1986b: 25)—the common
charge against theory made by critics such as Walter Jackson Bate (1982)
and Alvin Kernan (1990).[1] Rather, my "resistance" to de Man's conflation
of theory and philology is that such a conflation falls into the trap of cir-
cumscribing philology, and thus the bibliographical and textual research
that characterizes its current operations in the scholarly world, by the
foundationalist and positivist (i.e., pre-hermeneutic) requirements that so
many literary critics seem to accord to bibliography and textual study and
that have led us to the current marginalized condition of textual study in
the academy. For example, while sensibly questioning whether philology
can ever be "prior to literary and cultural interpretation" (Culler 1990: 52),
as de Man would have it, Jonathan Culler still regards his own promotion
of what he calls "antifoundational" philology as somehow inimical to, or
in sharp contrast to, the present functioning of philology as a "scientific"
enterprise. He dreams of a philology that would show how "philological
projects rely uncritically on literary and cultural conceptions that come
from the domains of thought that are supposedly secondary" (Culler
1990: 50)—a division between primary and secondary that is another
figure for the condition of estrangement or schism[2] that has brought us
to this pass. Richard Lanham (1989: 110) in a conference[3] and publication sponsored by the Modern Language Association (MLA) and the
Ford Foundation, charged that textual critics ought to abandon their
claims for positivist, definitive print editions and instead acknowledge
that text could be electronically manipulable, fragmented, versionist,

1. See esp. "The Tree of Knowledge: Literature's Presence in the Social World," in which
Kernan claims that, because of the ravages of various contemporary theoretical dispensa-
tions, "literature is in the process of losing a place in the knowledge tree and therefore in
danger of breaking up in the social world" (1990: 202).

2. The figure of an ideological/religious schism between literary criticism and bibliographical studies has become almost a staple of discussion in those fields—indeed, overcoming it
was the basic purpose of the series in which this essay was originally published. Examples
occur in McGann 1984, 1985; Bornstein 1991; Cohen 1991.

3. The MLA/Ford Foundation conference, "The Future of Doctoral Study in English,"
Wayzata, Minn., 1986.

and, well, "critical." Paradoxically, so great was Lanham's own faith in
the definitiveness of print that he retained the charge unmodified in the
published version of his paper, even though the discussion after his conference presentation made it quite clear that such textual critics as Hans
Walter Gabler, John Miles Foley, Michael Warren, Gary Taylor, Donald
H. Reiman, and a host of Franco-German geneticists had already put into
practice Lanham's prescriptions for us, practices of which Lanham was
clearly ignorant. De Man, Culler, and Lanham were thus laboring under
an outmoded view of the philological model that textual critics as diverse
as Jerome McGann, D. F. McKenzie, and Tanselle have frequently called
into question: witness Tanselle's insistence, on the one hand, that it is
a delusion to think that textual scholarship is pre-hermeneutic, or that
it "merely prepares the way for scholarly criticism and is not itself part
of the critical process" (Tanselle 1981c: 50) and, on the other, that the
old collocation of bibliography and science will not withstand scrutiny
(Tanselle 1974).[4]

But we have to acknowledge that this collocation is deeply entrenched
institutionally, that bibliographical and textual research and writing are
typically regarded as different in nature from other forms of text production, and that a textual or bibliographical book is indeed thought of as pre-
hermeneutic, or noncritical, by our colleagues, our students, and those
administrators who have charge of our promotion, tenure, and salary. It
is no betrayal of confidence, and was certainly no news to members of the
MLA Division on Methods of Literary Research, who heard a much earlier version of this essay, that the title of the conference session in which
it was presented ("But It's Not a Book!") comes from the experience of
Gerald MacLean, in whose home institution a scholarly edition or a bibliography was counted as exactly one-half of a "real" book in personnel and
budget committee decisions, and that a former chair of my department
would regularly go through an applicant's curriculum vitae, checking
off the publications that were "notbooks." This peculiarly structuralist,
semiotic bibliographical universe, in which a book is known by what it
is not (a "biblieme" perhaps?), is part of a general cultural resistance to

---

4. See my further commentary on this issue of the epistemological relations between bibliography and science in the "Textual Forensics" chapter of this volume.

philology that is all too easily documented.[5] Some years ago, C. H. Sisson (1979) spoke forcefully for the marginalization of textual/bibliographical study when, in a review of an edition of Pound for the *Times Literary Supplement,* he pronounced that "the prestige of fiddling with minute variants and bibliographical details should be low. It is, intellectually, the equivalent of what is done by clerks everywhere, labouring to pay [earn?] wages and to feed computers. Such things hold the world together" (616). Such disdain for the apparently "mechanical" and the "clerical"—a desire to see their operations as different in kind from genuine criticism or scholarship—is rarely stated as bluntly as in Sisson's review, but there is a long tradition of critical hostility to the philological edition, perceived as that which, according to Lewis Mumford (1968) and Edmund Wilson (1968), puts editorial "barbed wire" between author and reader, preventing the reader from getting direct access to the text. Indeed, an important rhetorical aim of Wilson's case against the "fruits of the MLA" (those editions sponsored through the Center for Editions of American Authors [CEAA]) is that there is a professional, "professorial" *trahison des clercs,* a conspiracy by the "clerisy" of the professoriate to use the mumbo jumbo of supposedly scholarly method to deny the amateur (like himself) any role in the transmission of the canonical texts of American literature. Wilson's conspiracy theory was doubtless colored by the fact that his own proposal for a user-friendly uniform edition of that literature, based on the Pléiade editions of French literature, had been turned down by the National Endowment for the Humanities (NEH), which decided to fund CEAA directly. And there is an obvious irony in NEH's having later ceased such direct support and having been a major contributor to the

---

5. While the citations of antibibliographical sentiment reprinted here date from the late 1970s, when I was presenting my paper "Critics and Scholars" at various universities in Canada and the United States, the positions espoused were seen to be replicated in critical reviews of editing and textual scholarship in a number of more recent publications. For example, Gerald Graff (1992: 354) maintains that "the declining status of textual editing" (once "the staple of doctoral dissertations") is symptomatic of a general decline in positivist and "detailed" scholarship and is a result of its being "discounted as positivistic." He commends an "alliance with theory . . . to reverse the downward fortunes of editing." I contend that this argument falls into the "territorial fallacy" (that theory and bibliography take place in different parts of the academic and intellectual map and must be imported or exported into each other's native *Heimat*). See my critique in 1999b: 18. See also my account of nationalist antibibliography in "Getting Personal/Going Public" (1995a) and my article "Textual Imperialism" (1997c).

Pléiade-like Library of America (1982–), but his designation (throughout "The Fruits of the MLA") of *professor* and *professorial* as the most polemical of his terms of abuse emphasizes the gentleman amateur's dismay at the professionalization and institutionalization of editing. And it is this fear—that the technicalities and arcane vocabulary of scholarly editing had denied a role to the amateur and that large-scale, multivolume editions of the canonical authors demanded heavy institutional investment—that led John Gross (1979) to the nostalgic wish for "earlier, simpler days" in his review of the Cambridge Lawrence:

> A true collected edition at last, then, and one fitted out with all the accoutrements of sound scholarship—fully annotated, with every source conscientiously cited and with the texts (as far as one can judge) scrupulously transcribed. How could anyone interested in Lawrence fail to welcome such an undertaking? And yet I must admit that, faced with the first volume, I also felt a pang of affection for earlier, simpler days. The Huxley collection, and the Harry T. Moore collection for that matter, were books, to be bought and read through; with the Cambridge edition we are in the presence of a Project: all the more incongruous in the case of the early letters, since so many of them show the young Lawrence and his friends conducting their own informal—and intense—literary education, seizing books in whatever cheap edition or reprint they could afford. By contrast, the Cambridge editors are inescapably involved in the task of bringing literature off the streets and into the library or the seminar room. (17)[6]

This desire that the edition should somehow be compatible with, or even "look like," its subject, that a youthful, bibliographically rough-hewn author should not be constrained by the "apparatus" of dry-as-dust modern scholarship, was promoted with even greater critical fervor in Paul Delany's review of the same Lawrence volume:

> The editorial commentary arouses more mixed feelings. It is sharply incongruous to see Lawrence's vital personality so cribbed and confined by the scholarly apparatus; he would, of course, have detested the whole enterprise—though that need not be a final criticism of such posthumous tributes. In any case, Professor Boulton has labored devotedly to provide us with chronologies, maps of every place Lawrence went, lists of his college textbooks, glosses on Midlands slang and thousands of other facts. Too many, I suppose, for some tastes and most purses. (Delany 1979: 44)

---

6 See also Ross and Jackson (1995) and Greetham (2010) for further accounts of the Cambridge Lawrence.

Gross's affections for earlier belletristic modes of textual scholarship becomes here an attack on the very rationale for modern bibliographical scholarship. One of Fredson Bowers's favorite informal definitions of responsible textual critics was that they should put all their cards on the table, but Delany would apparently have preferred them to keep some of their cards up their sleeves. Gross is similarly concerned about overt display: "the actual editing is very good: the notes are informative without being fussy, the textual apparatus is decently unobtrusive" (Gross 1979: 17). The loaded vocabulary of this damning with faint praise ("without being fussy," "decently unobtrusive") suggests that an edition is the more decorous if its scholarly pudenda have been kept out of sight. The suspicion of editorial plenitude and the desire for an epistemological or visual fit between edition and subject meet in Rosemary Dinnage's review for the *New York Review of Books* of Morton Cohen's edition of the Lewis Carroll letters:

> The standard of editing is modern and extravagantly good. The twenty years' labor was supported by money from six prestigious American endowments. Fifty-eight librarians, curators, archivists, and keepers receive acknowledgment, and there is another couple of pages of names of guides and advisers. The edition has a chronology, family tree, and bibliography (fortunately selective), and there are biographical notes, which must have involved much toil, for almost every recipient. . . . If these were the letters of a novelist, philosopher, or poet of world stature they could not be more ceremoniously and impeccably presented—indeed there are writers of world stature who have never been paid the compliment of an edition like this. But Carroll is, when all is said and done, the author of a couple of classic children's books. (Dinnage 1979: 10)

This is damning not with faint praise but with critical eulogy. If only Cohen had turned his obvious editorial talents to the work of a real writer, instead of a minor Oxford don's part-time scribbling. There is no argument here over the discipline of textual criticism itself, no quibbling over vital personalities being confined or old, friendly editions being superseded. And yet, in one sense, the reaction is even more dangerous to the status of textual scholarship, for it assumes that editing, commenting, and annotating are a chore, an activity nobody with any professional self-esteem would indulge in for pleasure. This notion is hinted at in the other reviews, in which, for example, Sisson's "clerks" and Delany's "labored devotedly" imply a similar doggedness, but the "toil" that lies at the center of Dinnage's comments is more telling, since it is seen as misdirected. Delany detects almost a perverseness in the Cambridge Lawrence's having foisted all this unnecessary material on Lawrence lovers, whereas Dinnage admires Cohen's tenacity over twenty years but finds it difficult to reconcile with the limited merits of its object. Textual scholarship becomes almost a masochistic experience, undertaken only for the greater good of deserving or undeserving authors.

One might object that this is no more or less than textual critics have been claiming for a century and more: that their labors were to allow the text "to speak for itself" and that in this claim they were aligning themselves with one of the central theses of nineteenth-century criticism in general, expressed in Matthew Arnold's famous dicta that the critic should attempt to cultivate "disinterestedness" in order to "see the object as in itself it really is" ("Function of Criticism") and to avoid the "personal fallacy" that might make our "affinities, likings, and circumstances . . . overrate the object of our interest" ("Study of Poetry"). The sublime assurances of this "impersonalist" criticism, when married to the technical sureties seemingly conferred on scholarship by Lachmannian stemmatics or historical and analytical bibliography, have meant that textual scholarship has, to the outside observer, retained its nineteenth-century positivism long after such claims have been given up, or even thought desirable, in other parts of the academic map.

But the schism is not wholly of others' making: textuists have in part contributed to it, by the use of a seemingly forbidding, arcane, technical vocabulary and methodology in such areas as descriptive and analytical bibliography and by continued appeals to the definitive, the positivistic, and the permanent in some forms of scholarly editing: so, for example, the "critical" edition of the Anne Frank Diary was published (with much public acclaim) several years after the 1989 publication of the "definitive" edition by the Dutch Institute of War Documentation; neither edition is, in fact, complete or definitive.[7] All too many of us have tried in the past to assert a moral, and certainly a cultural, superiority over the ephemeral,

---

7. I am grateful to Laurie Bley for detailing the inadequacies of both editions ("The Many Many Diaries of Anne Frank: From Variorum to Monument," seminar paper, CUNY Graduate School, 1997).

prejudice-bound interpretations of our colleagues and have wanted our text productions to be regarded as cultural monuments and thus as permanent, as positivist, as definitive, in other words, as noncritical, or nonhermeneutic. Is it any wonder that the noncritical chickens might have come home to roost and that what was once an epistemological virtue has now become an institutional liability? There are doubtless good reasons for this determination of difference and for both our having embraced it and our now being branded by it: for example, descriptive and analytical bibliography, like any other account of complex physical states, requires a similarly complex terminology, and one can understand the psychological and the financial temptations to claim definitiveness for a textual edition. Put bluntly, authority so defined as definitiveness is almost a requirement in securing foundation or federal funding, for no bureaucrat is likely to loosen the purse strings for an editorial project that admits, even celebrates, its critical bias and its likely ephemerality. And no man but a blockhead (not even for money) would spend decades working on a scholarly edition if it could be superseded at any moment. But, if scholarly editing and scholarly editions were truly definitive and timeless and not a product of their cultural assumptions and cultural practices—of what Clifford Geertz (1983, esp. "Local Knowledge: Fact and Law in Comparative Perspective," 167–234) calls "local knowledge"—then Erasmus would not have felt it necessary to replace Jerome's Vulgate (1516, 1969), or Johnson (1765, 1768) and Theobald (1740) to reedit Shakespeare after Pope (1723–1725, 1728), or John Kidd to question Hans Walter Gabler's "definitive" *Ulysses* (1984, 1986) and to produce his own "Dublin edition."[8] Under this principle of local knowledge, perhaps de Man is justified, given his inevitable cultural myopia and the moment of his inscription, to see (in "The Resistance to Theory") "historical and philological facts as the preparatory condition for understanding" (1986a: 4), and perhaps he is equally correct historically in seeing the link (via logic) between the trivium and the quadrivium to be "a clear instance of the interconnection between a science of the phenomenal world and a science of language conceived as

---

8. This Dublin edition has never appeared, though Kidd has been threatening it on and off for years. The legal—and personal—problems in bringing out any edition of Joyce are laid out in Max 2006 and put in context in Greetham 2010.

a definitional logic, the pre-condition for a correct axiomatic-deductive, synthetic reasoning" (1986a: 13). De Man would presumably have been quite comfortable on those promotion committees I have mentioned, sorting out the books from the nonbooks and critical sheep from bibliographical goats. The logic of his own analysis thus plays out of this "definitional" precondition (in which foundational philology seems securely based) into the larger claims that grammar-based systems (derived from the first component of the trivium) are nonthreatening because they are "in the service of logic" (14)—the last component—and that perceived threats occur to the relationship between theory and phenomenalism only when the tropical dimension, that associated with rhetoric (the middle component) rather than with grammar, begins to assert itself: in other words, when "text-producing functions" rather than "extra-linguistic generalisation" (15) become the dominant mode of a theoretical discourse. It thus follows that, for de Man's model of theory (a pre-referential, text-based, linguistic one), "the resistance to theory is in fact a resistance to reading" (ibid.) and certainly to the sort of circumscribed, nonreferential, "rhetorical" reading that Reuben Brower practiced.

For as long as scholarly editing and bibliography could be regarded primarily (or even solely) as analogous to grammatical rather than to rhetorical modes of discourse, as productions that promoted the logical connection (i.e., the connection via logic) between the theoretical and phenomenological worlds, then editing and bibliography could indeed be "philological" in the restricted sense that Culler assumes for our traditional practices. The problem with this formulation is (I believe) that, just as criticism under poststructuralism became tropical and linguistic rather than extralinguistic and referential, so too did the operations of textual criticism become equally rhetorical and therefore just as threatening to the imputed pre-hermeneuticism that de Man and Culler, in their different ways, observe for philology. Or, rather, as Gary Taylor has convincingly demonstrated, the rhetorical medium in which textual criticism had always conducted its business, despite a long-standing attempt to pass off its rhetoric as a grammar, now became available for rhetorical rather than (or as well as) grammatical, or logical, analysis. As Taylor puts it: "the fact did not change; we just saw it differently. Or rather, the problem did not change; but we phrased it differently" (1988: 53; see also

Taylor 1994: 19–59, for an account of the various rhetorical responses to Taylor and Wells's Oxford Shakespeare). Taylor uses this description of change to draw textual criticism into the Kuhnian model of changes in scientific perception (1970), itself simply one version (via Kuhn's theory of discourse and reception) of the history of the transmission and reformulation of logical systems: "Revolutions in science, like revolutions in editing, depend upon rhetoric, upon the ability of a clique of adherents to persuade a majority of potential practitioners" (Taylor 1988: 33). The inevitable problem, which Taylor resolutely faces, is that this substitution of a rhetorical for a grammatical (i.e., linguistic rather than logical) system at a specific moment in cultural history runs the risk of "turning a discussion of the rhetoric which pervades our discourse into a defense of a particular point of view" (53)—that is, to mistake rhetoric for grammar, or (in the language of speech act theory) to confuse the performative with the constative. De Man had done no less in asserting, as a rhetorical necessity in his moment of theory, that philology had indeed been viewed as grammatical but that the pre-hermeneutic qualities of that grammar now rendered it (in the poststructuralist, linguistic dispensation) emblematically theoretical. It is this ploy that I am now rejecting and yet rejecting it via Taylor's caveat about rhetoric as imputed authority.

The institutional, cultural problem in my formulation for both Taylor's and de Man's assumptions about rhetoric and grammar is in the word *now*. For, in the decade or so following de Man's critique of philology and theory, it is tellingly, perhaps painfully, obvious that poststructuralism, and thus the now that went along with de Man's timing of his promotion of rhetoric over grammar, and linguistics over reference, ceased to be the dominant discourse while, on the contrary, the constative and extralinguistic began to intrude quite forcefully on our profession's deliberations.

This itself is no longer news. In the plangent tones of his MLA presidential address of 1986 ("The Triumph of Theory"), J. Hillis Miller noted that his definition of "theory" (the very language-based structure endorsed by de Man and, for textual criticism, by Taylor) had been co-opted or invaded by historicizing extralinguistic movements (cultural studies, gender studies, and so on) that to Miller seemed to have disenfranchised theory. "Literary study in the past few years has undergone a sudden, almost universal turn away from theory in the sense of an orientation toward language as such and has made a corresponding turn toward history, culture, society, politics, institutions, class and gender conditions, the social context, the material base" (1986: 283).

If what Miller and a typical "literary" convention program in the twenty-first century have to say is true—and I think it would be foolish to deny it as a statistical reality—then the rhetoric-based vehicle of textual criticism that Taylor prescribed for us in 1988 has long been superseded, and we are back in that interstitial, logic-based location between the trivium and the quadrivium, a position that in former days had given peculiar privilege to textual criticism as the arbiter between "the text itself" (the language-based trivium) and the phenomenological world (the nonverbal quadrivium of number [mathematics], space [geometry], motion [astronomy], and time [music]), whether in annotation, glossing, or the establishment of authorial (or anybody else's) intention. But what does this shift in philological positioning mean at this now, and can we textuists take advantage of the shift to resituate ourselves as other than the "other," other than the "not-a-book"? Can we get promoted again now that cultural studies and gender studies have sent poststructuralism off with its pre-hermeneutic tail between its legs?

The local answer, using the text productions of local knowledge, is probably yes, the moment is propitious. Marion Wynne-Davies, under feminist auspices, produced a gendered edition of Chaucer's *Clerk's Tale* and *Wife of Bath's Tale* just six years after Miller's MLA address, and Ann Thompson, now co–general editor of the "new" *New Arden,* laid down feminist (i.e., extralinguistic) protocols for the editing of Shakespeare (in the volume in which the first version of this essay appeared).[9] And, as Brenda Silver (on gendered adaptation), Gerald MacLean (on class), William Andrews (on "minority" texts), Jonathan Goldberg (on gay textuality), and Jonathan Bate and Sonia Massai (on the politics of adaptation) forcefully demonstrated in the "discourse" section of the same volume, there are enormous challenges in thinking about textuality from one of the current constative, extralinguistic positions (such as race, gender, or

---

9. See also the discussion of gendered editing in chapter 10 of Greetham 1999b.

class). And the same could be said for the much larger project of actually producing editions that embody the social textual criticism of McGann, McKenzie, and others, of which Gerald MacLean's editing of Restoration poetry (1987a, 1987b, 1995) is just one possible manifestation.

Now, it could be argued (I have argued it myself: 1999b, esp. 211–212) that these apparently concessive gestures to the nonlinguistic turn are just as rhetorical, and therefore just as nongrammatical, as were the supposedly pre-hermeneutic philologies espoused by de Man and carried out by (say) the text-centered productions of the Center for Scholarly Editions and the Center for Editions of American Authors. In fact, the rhetorical model, as long as it can be perceived as itself a social production (something that both de Man and the CEAA editors barely recognized), is observable at almost any stage in the history of editing and bibliography, from the decision of Kallimachos to exclude the Torah on ethnic grounds from his otherwise "comprehensive" *Pinakes* (while including the menus and erotic delights of banquets given by Alexandrian courtesans; see Blum 1991, esp. 103) down to the political, Germanist assumptions about race, national origins, and social constraint in the "standard," "philological" Klaeber edition of *Beowulf* (see McGillivray 1994a).

So, the larger rather than the local answer may not be just to redirect our editorial and bibliographical practices to political, social, gendered, and racial ends that now happen to be fashionable (and about which we may feel at the very least suspicious and cautious) but, rather, to undertake the much more difficult job of both self-interrogation and proselytizing that will (1) persuade us that, while trying very hard not to persuade, that is in fact what we have been doing in our bibliographies and editions, and (2) help us to convince others, particularly those whose professional position gives them the power to distinguish between the "real" book and the nonbook, that editing can never be pre-hermeneutical because it is already embedded, as a cultural artifact, in the hermeneutic circle and that such apparently new movements as "personalist criticism"[10] are already

---

10. The term is widely used in much contemporary literary criticism, especially by feminist theorists (see esp. Miller 1991). It is adopted for bibliography by Donald H. Reiman (1993) in order to "humanize the study of modern manuscripts by citing personal experiences and characterizing individuals involved in the anecdotes" (xi–xii). The concept provides the narrative and the rationale for my *Textual Transgressions* (1998).

documented in our editions, whether we still cling to their definitive pretensions or not. This latter tack will require some loss of face and loss of credibility for those philologists who still like to think of themselves as pre-hermeneutic; it will require that we abandon both James L. W. West III's hope for "invisibility" (1994a) and what Talbot Donaldson (1970: 105) derisively called the "editorial death-wish." It will require that (in the words of Stanley Fish 1995: 208; 1989b: 482) philologists identify themselves as members of the species *homo rhetoricus* rather than *homo seriosus*,[11] but I cannot see that any other admission—an admission of sameness rather than of difference—is ever going to lead to the general reincorporation of textual and bibliographical study into the academic and scholarly world.

I have argued elsewhere (1993a, 1994) that this shift in Linnaean, or species, identification may be forced upon us anyway, for the 1991 unanimous Supreme Court *Feist* decision,[12] allowing the resale of nonprotectable historical "fact" in the white pages of the telephone directory, might well render the very claim of scholarly "grammatical" definitiveness a publishing liability rather than a virtue. Under *Feist*, the more an edition (especially a clear-text edition of the typical CSE/CEAA type) promotes its historical definitiveness, the more it pretends to be pre-hermeneutic, the less protectable it becomes. One of the ironies of this decision might thus be that "inclusive text" editions (those in which the editorial "presence," "intrusion," or "constraint" are avowedly made part of the textual page—rather than seen as pudenda to be discreetly hidden in the back of the book) could be the more easily protectable because the "text itself" (historical fact) cannot practically be photocopied separately from the editorial barbed wire (the "property" of the editor). It is ironic that, by acknowledging our textual and bibliographical research as contingent, local, and ephemeral—in other words, as personal criticism, or local knowledge—we may be better able not only to protect it under the copyright law's endorsement of Romantic originality, but also to convince our colleagues and peers that what we produce really are books, not nonbooks

---

11. Fish adopted the terms from Lanham 1976, esp. 1, 4.

12. See also *CCC Information Services, Inc. v. MacLean Hunter Market Reports, Inc.* (1994). And see Greetham 1997c and "The Telephone Directory and Dr. Seuss" in this volume.

or half-books. William Hazlitt is reputed to have claimed that "it is utterly impossible to convince an Editor that he is a nobody" (quoted in Epstein 1993: 9)—a challenge that the academy has clearly tried to meet, for we seem to have become nobodies producing nonbooks. But, if a combination of the *Feist* decision, personalist criticism, local knowledge, and the post-hermeneutic dispensation can make us textually dangerous again,[13] then perhaps the loss of philological face will have been worth it.

---

13. Even the antibibliographical Sisson has to confess that "the future—even a little, with this [Pound] volume, the present—is with the indexers and the bibliographers" (1979: 616), and he admits that, despite his reservations about editing in general, "this volume . . . is something which all under a compulsion to keep their Pound material up to date must certainly possess."

THREE

Contamination and/of Resistance

Some years ago, I wrote a polemical, take-no-prisoners introductory piece to a collection I was editing, *The Margins of the Text*.[1] While the resulting volume, with essays by such luminaries as Jonathan Goldberg on gay textualities ("Under the Covers with Caliban"), Ann Thompson and Brenda Silver on some varieties of feminist editing ("Feminist Theory and the Editing of Shakespeare: *The Taming of the Shrew* Revisited" and "Whose Room of Orlando's Own? The Politics of Adaptation," respectively), and William L. Andrews ("Editing 'Minority' Texts"), advanced the study of various fields considerably, my own impassioned leadoff, which I playfully called "The Resistance to Philology," seems to have been folded into my general thesis for the conflation, indeed even the contamination, of

---

1. To nontextuists, the polemic may seem an unexpected, almost improper mode of discourse, though anyone who has seen Tom Stoppard's *The Invention of Love*, on A. E. Housman, the most celebrated and influential textual critic of his time, will recognize that the plaintive, rustic nostalgia of *A Shropshire Lad* was replaced by an aggressive irony in his textual essays, especially in the sardonic tones of "The Application of Thought" (1921, 1961, 1988). Indeed, it might be argued that the polemic is the primary discourse of textual criticism, from Jerome onward, in that scholarly editors often justify themselves by attacks on precursor editors, whose inadequate or misrepresentations of their texts become the rationale for one's own work. Jerome J. McGann, in one of the most influential essays of the late twentieth century ("Monks," 1985), in his own polemic finds that the apparently objective, apparently scholarly, apparently timeless editions produced by Fredson Bowers in the previous generation were emblematic of the polemical edition. McGann has even disavowed his own monumental edition of Byron on ideological as well as methodological grounds— all of which may seem passing strange in the light of my next note, but that is precisely the point of much of my work: there is a conflict being waged for the very soul of textualism.

textual theory and literary hermeneutics, and it is that "folding" (indeed "invagination")[2] that forms one of the threads in this chapter.

"The Resistance to Philology" essay had arisen out of an MLA panel I had organized earlier on "Race, Class, and Gender in Scholarly Editing," just three of the several nonlinguistic issues that the central tradition of textuality had preferred not to confront. The resulting *Margins of the Text* volume (part of the Michigan series Editorial Theory and Literary Criticism, instituted by George Bornstein) divided the study of "margins" into two classes: the margins of discourse (those social, nonlinguistic forces that were not supposed to be admitted into editorial protocols) and the bibliographical margins (titling, marginalia, glossing, and commentary) that had, of course, always been a part of the "whole book," but had been undervalued—in fact, generally ignored—during the hegemony of the Greg-Bowers-Tanselle school of concentration on the New Critical/ New Bibliographical formalist "text itself." My own contribution was to interrogate (in the "discourse" section) Paul de Man's thesis that this very focus on the text itself was of a piece with the turn to theory in the 1970s, which de Man saw as a "return to philology, to an examination of the structure of language prior to the meaning it produces" (1986b: 24). I argued that de Man's agenda or hope that "historical and philological facts [should be] the preparatory condition for understanding" (ibid.: 4) was illusory, and reinforced that too widely held assumption that philol-

---

2. I use *invagination* in the common Derridean sense of a linguistic double embedding and continual recontextualizing of types of discourse, a figure that will inform much of this chapter on contamination. See, for example:

> Invagination is the inward refolding of *la gaine* [sheath, girdle], the inverted reapplication of the outer edge to the inside of a form where the outside then opens a pocket. . . . Like the meaning [of] "genre" or "*mode,*" or that of "corpus" or the unity of a "work," the meaning of version, and of the unity of a version, is overrun, exceeded, by this structure of invagination. (Derrida 1979: 97, 102)

That quoted essay, I believe (from my position on the margins), imitates (or parodies) in its very textual appearance the dual form of the page of a scholarly edition, with "text" above and "commentary" or "apparatus" below, in reduced type (see Greetham 1999b, 1991b, for a fuller commentary on what I perceive as Derrida's failure to exploit the figural and parodic interpenetrations of his two discourses). I also use invagination in the connotational sense of Irigaray's "When Our Lips Speak Together" in *This Sex Which Is Not One* (1985), a textual "speaking" only accomplished by the doubling of the two pairs of lips of the vulva.

ogy was "non-hermeneutic," and thus the products of philology in such monuments to "fact" as scholarly editions were not critical and therefore not "real" books. My polemic was mounted not so much against de Man and his thesis but against those textuists who resisted both the theory and the practice of hermeneutics (taking refuge in that very pre-hermeneutic grammar that de Man postulated for philology) and thus ghettoized scholarly editing and textualism institutionally and culturally. I claimed instead that scholarly "philologists" had to acknowledge that (like Joyce's famous comment that his work was not only "trivial," but "quadrivial" as well) philology was also rhetorical and not merely "in the service of logic" (de Man 1986a: 14); that is, textuists had to become "textually dangerous" again, even if this meant the "loss of philological face," for otherwise we would continue to be "nobodies producing nonbooks" (Greetham 1997d: 20).

I had already alerted the reader to the technical as well as the more general senses of both conflation and contamination[3] by the apparent simplicity of my title. But of course there are different classes of "alert" readers: my title depended for its conflation and/or contamination on the forceful yoking of two essays by de Man, "The Resistance to Theory" and "The Return to Philology," and thus on a reader's familiarity with de Man's work (though I will admit that I explicated the yoking since that was one of the themes of the piece). Brenda Silver's similar act (1997) of making strange bedfellows depended on a differently alert reader, one who not only knew that both *Orlando* and *A Room of One's Own* were by Woolf (the first slotted into the second) but, as the essay itself demonstrated, that both works had recently been themselves contaminated by being edited by other hands for different media—film, television, and

---

3. *Contamination*, strictly speaking, refers to the memorial infiltration of one text by another: say, a copyist might be ostensibly following the text in witness *x*, but with a prior familiarity with witness *y* will unconsciously(?) allow variants from this precedent *y* into the resulting text, *z*. *Conflation* is properly reserved for the deliberate construction of *z* by an active and presumably hermeneutic or evaluative criticism of the variants contained in the two texts *x* and *y*, which lie before the copyist in this active misprision of the documentary authority of either one in the service of some greater good: authorial intention, social reception, and so on. As is quite appropriate, however, the two terms are often conflated (or even contaminated).

stage production. Silver, I think, made her contaminations work harder than I did mine (and she did have the advantage of fairly recent performative versions of her two texts).[4]

All of this may seem to either the culture critic or the bibliographer to be much ado about (almost) nothing, for the art (and craft) of both contamination and conflation are a staple of contemporary discourse, from the posters on bus shelters and the ironic covers of the *New Yorker* and other magazines, to television and virtually every form of modern/ postmodern media reception: hence this book.[5] As has been often noted, even something as monumental as Philip Johnson's AT&T Building in New York is a conflation (for those who know their architectural history) of the Gothic cathedral at street level, the Chippendale grandfather clock at the pediment, and the stark geometrism of essentialist modernism (the perfected extruded cube) in the middle. When one adds to this mix an awareness of the career of the building's designer, from modernist to postmodernist architect, the canny reader of the intertextualities of this monument (and I use the term very deliberately, since I believe that in some way it is indeed Johnson's public manifesto of his own biography) will undoubtedly feel a sense of "mastery" over the apparent irreconcilables of the cultural icon. Case apparently closed.

But while even the most strict and pure bibliographer of the most positivist days of philology would surely not suggest that the disparate elements of the AT&T Building be reconstructed to form a "text that never was" (the Holy Grail of eclectic editing of the Greg-Bowers-Tanselle dispensation), immutable in its Platonic ideality, with texts existing in

---

4. Such conflation and contamination might almost be a staple of Silver's work as, for example, in her essay "Who's Afraid of Virginia Woolf: Part II" (1991), which subsumes Albee's play as its "already written" precursor text.

5. Such a cross-citational ethic is, I believe, a perfect manifestation of the very etymology of text as "textile" (see the historical references in my "[Textual] Criticism," 1991b, esp. n. 19), with the continual contest being between this Barthesian meaning and what might appear to be its exact opposite, text as authority—particularly in relation to the scriptures— as something fixed and determinate. Moreover, I have posited textual criticism as the exemplary site for a terminological and methodological interdisciplinarity, with the important qualification that textual criticism deforms and reinvents the terms it co-opts from other disciplines, making them do other than they would in their home disciplines (Greetham 1993a, in response to Stanley Fish 1989a).

what have sometimes been conveniently designated as the "linear" media
(literature, music, and so on) as opposed to the "spatial" (painting, sculpture, architecture) being more hospitable in their very ontology to the
incursions of eclecticists, idealists, social receptionists, and other brands
of the current textual potpourri, one is given pause by this overly neat
dichotomy and by its most quoted embodiment in Bateson's provocative question (1961: 67–77), "If the *Mona Lisa* is in the Louvre, where is
Hamlet?"[6]

That artful question, relying on the singularity and non-iterability of
the spatial art work[7] as against the linguistic or notational abstraction of

---

6. This question has been widely cited by, for example, James L. McLaverty (1984b) in his
argument that the materiality and spatial properties Pope specifically undertook for the
Dunciad Variorum are not simply the surface accidentals of the work, but its very seman
tic coding, and thus its meaning. Note also that McLaverty's essay is yet another with a
deliberately contaminated title, positing itself against the several, nonmaterial "modes of
existence" examined in René Wellek and Austin Warren's *Theory of Literature* (1956), and,
perhaps even more tellingly, that McLaverty nowhere in his own essay feels it necessary to
acknowledge the intertextual play, any more than did Silver in "Who's Afraid" (1991).

7. On the iterability problem in textuality, see, for example, Joseph Grigely 1991, where, for
instance, he denies that the "work is . . . equivalent to the sum of its texts . . . whether those
texts are authorized or not," claiming instead that, since a work (of literature) cannot be
"finished," and since "its boundaries are not prescribed," there can be only a "series of texts
that comprise [the work's] polytext" (176). The major statement on the ontology of textual
repetition (especially as it relates to textuality and, inferentially, to editing) remains Walter
Benjamin's "The Work of Art in the Age of Mechanical Reproduction" (1968), though see
also Gilles Deleuze, *Difference and Repetition* (1968), which lays out a thesis very similar to
that in this essay on contamination and conflation:

> Modern Life is such that, confronted with the most mechanical, stereotypical rep-
> etitions [I will admit that I am uncertain whether Deleuze intends a bibliographical
> contamination in this phrase, which finds emblematic historical exemplification in
> the shift from hot type, which although participating in a "mechanical" process is
> still literally manual in its composition, and the stereotype, in which the mechani-
> cal achieves its most significant textual shift, having also major cultural ramifica-
> tions; see Dooley (1992), where the social and economic commodification of an au-
> thor like George Eliot can be charted by the shift from hot type to stereotype in the
> setting of her novels], inside and outside ourselves, we endlessly extract from them
> little differences, variations, and modifications. Conversely, secret, disguised, and
> hidden repetitions, animated by the perpetual displacement of a difference, restore
> bare, mechanical, and stereotypical repetitions, within and without us. In simu-
> lacra, repetition already plays upon repetitions, and difference already plays upon
> differences. Repetitions repeat themselves, while the differenciator differenciates
> itself. The task of life is to make all these repetitions coexist in a space in which dif-
> ference is distributed. (Deleuze 1968: ix)

the linear (that is, *Hamlet* would somehow still "exist," even if it were to be found nowhere specifically, even if all concrete manifestations of the authoritative work were to disappear, whereas the single-state ontology of the painting or sculpture is contained and defined by its formal properties), begs far too many questions than can be answered here: for example, what is an authority, what is a work, a text, a manifestation? And these questions have been the subject of much debate in textual circles since the late twentieth century.[8] But it would be a safe generalization to note that, since then, the focus of much textual attention has shifted from the text *qua* text (the "linguistic codes") to, on the one hand, the materiality of its medium and mode of production and, on the other, to the cultural and

---

It is exactly this play and counterplay between open and secret repetitions and differences with which I am concerned in this essay and this book.

But Benjamin's analysis of mechanical reproduction has achieved such a wide-ranging influence that it must be acknowledged as the locus classicus (pre-Derrida's iterability) of textual repetition and the cultural dissemination of this repetition. Thus, while I have some major reservations about Benjamin's theory—in part derived from the social and historical circumstances in which it was composed—and have dealt with them in some detail in my *Theories* (1999b: "Benjamin and Textual Reproduction," 389–97), a few remarks are still necessary for this current essay. For example, as I note in *Theories*, Benjamin bases his historical account on Marx's assumption that the superstructure (the thought and ideology of a culture) will change more slowly than the base (the means of production). Thus it is only several centuries after the invention of mechanical reproduction that we can begin to assess its cultural significance. And, like Deleuze, he acknowledges a difference between simulacra (Benjamin's "replicas"), manmade simulations or imitations of an original, and true *mechanical* reproduction, which he believes begins only with the woodcut, the first infinitely reproducible medium (1968: 218, 243n2). I find Benjamin's reliance on the concept of "infinite reproduction" to be bibliographically and historically naive (see Greetham 1999b: 390), but I do accept that his key concepts of *authenticity, aura, presence, distance, cult, ritual, exhibition, exile, readership, distraction,* and *concentration* are all, to one degree or another, relevant to my current consideration of contamination and conflation. For example, Benjamin's claim that "for the first time in world history, mechanical reproduction emancipates the work of art from its parasitical dependence on ritual. To an ever greater degree the work of art reproduced becomes the work of art designed for reproducibility" (1968: 224) is a concession that the aura of an originary moment of inscription may pass—through mechanical reproduction—to the derived copy, which may be culturally so disseminated that it displaces the original in authenticity. Benjamin can therefore maintain that the fact of an "authentic" print being an ontological absurdity is evidence of a complete reversal of the function of art: freed from ritual, it now becomes political (that is, part of the polis).

8. The two most succinct statements for, on the one hand, the Platonizing/idealist position and, on the other, the materialist/socialized view of text are, respectively, Tanselle 1989 and McGann 1983, which have primarily influenced Anglo-American textual theory, and McKenzie 1986.

social forces at work in both the creation (with an interest in collaboration as paradigm rather than the Romantic figure of the isolated singular author) and the dissemination of textual forms beyond the control of any author and sometimes taking on forms and usages that could never have been envisaged by such an author. As Gary Taylor, co-editor of the Oxford Shakespeare, has often muttered, out-Barthing Barthes, "The author has always been dead."[9]

It may therefore seem paradoxical that contemporary textuality may accept an always-dead author while at the same time beginning to move away from the positivist, technology-driven disappearance of the editor—what Talbot Donaldson (1970) dismissively referred to as the "editorial death-wish"—toward what Donald H. Reiman (1993) has labeled a "personalist bibliography," in parallel with the personalist criticism of some feminist critics, notably Nancy K. Miller, Hélène Cixous (1991), and

---

9. Taylor's work on rhetoric in textuality puts in high relief the double bind de Man constructed in creating a class (for philology) of the pre-hermeneutic, a reading of the trivium as being in the service of logic. For example, Taylor's assertion (1988: 47) that "[t]extual criticism is about rhetoric, rhetoric is about persuasion, persuasion is about audiences" denies any pre-hermeneutic function for foundationalist philology, but instead resituates supposed philological facts as part of a series of social negotiations, so that even his injection of rhetoric becomes ultimately a social construct:

> A textual critic does not worry about promiscuously persuading any possible reader; a textual critic must persuade the readers who matter. We expect our intellectual actions to be judged by a jury of our peers; but who are the peers of a textual critic? The definition of that peerage fluctuates historically, and that fluctuation depends upon the perceived relationship between textual and literary criticism. (Ibid.)

So the relational and reflexive nature of the philological enterprise forbids any firm position in either the trivium or the quadrivium. Indeed, Taylor argues that the editorial production of text can only be a rhetorical strategy—even down to the construction of a table of contents—under which an intentionalist editor commits a form of ventriloquism in moving the authority for the rhetoric elsewhere: to the author. Taylor sees this rhetorical strategy in Foucauldian terms ("to adopt the voice of power is to speak beyond oneself, to ascribe one's powers elsewhere" [Foucault 1980: 93–94; Taylor 1988: 43]). As I note in *Theories* (1999b: 145n5), even a seemingly "positivist" textual critic like Tanselle can recognize that "[i]n the end, all evidence is internal," for sooner or later one reaches a point where there is nothing outside to relate to; that is, no foundationalist philology can provide a pre-hermeneutic grounding; and thus "[w]hat we agree to call historical knowledge is built up by the accretions of individual acts of pattern-finding, some of which invalidate previous acts and some of which confirm and extend them" (Tanselle 1995a: 283). Or, as Taylor might more cynically (or demographically) put it: "the more registered voters who support a textual proposition, the more likely it is to be true" (1988: 47).

Mary Ann Caws (1986). Endorsing and playing on such an enlargement of the biographical presence of the textuist, I have written what (I think) I am pleased to have had reviewed as "the strangest book on text criticism" (Bornstein 1999).

All of which can be read both as a supplement to that first essay on resistance (to which I now provide a further glossarial context in which the clash of discourses may be read—historically, formalistically, psychologically, and so on) and as a textual foreplay on my privileged, editorial empowerment through belatedness by making my two (now three) texts speak otherwise.[10]

Clearly, I make much of the prominence of notes, which may sometimes serve as apparent clarifications or even disquisitions on points made in the "superior" text from which they hang, but may just as frequently be cast as an *adversarius,* a feature of annotation that Heather Jackson (2001) nicely documents in her history and genre study of marginalia, where she adopts the image of marginalia/annotation being a "shouting at" the dead author from John Hollander's poem "The Widener Burying-Ground" (ibid.: 83, 274). I would hope that my own alert reader has concluded,

---

10. This formal property of making the "base" text (again a term conferring privilege on the belated editor, for this base is, like Edmund, to be considered as a "bastard," the improper miscegenation and cohabitation of texts, which the purely moral acts of a Platonizing editor will disambiguate) speak otherwise is one of those potentially figural or parodic elements that I believe Derrida does not exploit fully. I comment:

> Thus, the "lower" ("Border Lines") text is indeed quite properly concerned at first with discussing, allusively and figuratively, the relationship between the commentary/apparatus and "the text itself" above. Noting (in the text of "Living On") that the commentary is usually thought of as "only a textual supplement," an "in other words" for the text proper, Derrida nowhere takes up this frequent theme of the "other words" and applies it to the formal mechanism of an apparatus, which is constructed precisely to find a home for these "other words" of the text. The apparatus is nothing but the text in other words (rejected words).

As I have several times pointed out, however, these rejected words exist in order to be made inferior precisely because at some point in the textual transmission (and most often in the base text), they were regarded as the text speaking properly and not otherwise; otherwise, they would not be present in any witness, and especially not in the "authoritative" base text. No editor has, to my knowledge, invented a reading solely for the purpose of rejecting it, though the orthodox use of Lachmannian stemmatic theory might postulate non-extant misreadings in a medial hyparchetype to account for the transmissional degradation from the purity of the originary moment of composition to the corrupted, contaminated extant form in the insincere witnesses.

through the title, layout, and cross-referencing between "text" and "note," that the shouting at the dead author (de Man in the original "Resistance," myself—the author is always dead, remember, even the author writing here and now—and all texts ever edited or annotated by subsequent editors) is the motivating formal and rhetorical mode of this essay.[11]

---

11. At the moment of this authorial inscription, I am in much the same position as Derrida in his ignored instructions to the editors/compositors of "Border Lines": "My desire [is] to take charge of the Translator's note myself. Let them [the translators] also read this band as a telegram or a film for developing" (a film "to be processed," in English?; 1979: 77–78); "This would be a good place for a translator's note" (79); "to be quoted in its entirety" (135)—none of these authorial instructions to the translator/editor are in fact carried out in the published text. My comment on this apparent malfeasance is "[s]o by what is the authorial will countermanded? Paradoxically, by the translator's desire for fidelity to the text and therefore fidelity to the authorial will. And so here is the double bind" (1991b: 22): the translator is in the long line of descent from those early Benedictine scriptoria in which the exact text was to be rendered warts and all, without additions (even when, as in this case, asked for by the author), deletions, or emendations. Sometimes that desire for literal fidelity can yield wonderfully comic effects, as when the scribe of one of the manuscripts of Hoccleve's *De Regimine Principum,* on realizing that he has inadvertently omitted an entire stanza of his copy-text, subsequently writes out the missing stanza—where else but in the margins?—and then puts a rope around the stanza, and draws in a figure dragging the stanza into its right and "proper" place on the text page. My guess is that most readers have so delighted in this spatial play that they have come to regard the margin as the "proper" place for this particular *mise-en-page,* just as in the Harley manuscript of the same work, Hoccleve has "caused" to be drawn a portrait of Chaucer in the margins, pointing to Hoccleve's text. See Tinkle 1998, in which she admits in the headnotes to the notes (79) that there is some ambiguity as to which word exactly Chaucer's finger is pointing to (or shouting at?), a difference that has substantial implications in calibrating the relationships between text and commentary/margin, image and language, and originating "transdiscursive" author and diligent but subservient disciple (see Foucault 1984, esp. 113–17, where Foucault cites Freud, Galileo, and Marx as examples of "transdiscursive" authors who will not only be "the authors of their own works. They have produced something else: the possibilities of and the rules for the formation of other texts" [114]). I (and obviously Hoccleve) would include Chaucer as a transdiscursive author, and thus a contaminating author, since he does not merely become the "begetter" of other works but also (graphically and substantively) retroactively co-opts and invades the work of his disciple.

   In one early version of this essay, I asked a very obliging editor, Jenn Lewin, to try to use her editorial prerogative to make sure that my annotations would present spatially a "dialogue" with the text page by being set as footnotes (see Tribble 1997) rather than endnotes (for which there is no excuse in these days of computer typesetting), and to try to get the compositor to reflect the typographic distinctions I am inheriting from *The Iconic Page* (Bornstein and Tinkle 1998). But on that occasion, I was told that I should not worry about formatting in general, since the copyeditor would happily take on that burden. Since this concession was offered as a palliative to the overextended author, I took it as an act of courtesy, but of course, in my argument for the shouting at the dead, the dead ought properly to be alive (or present) enough for the reader to see what one is shouting at. I was relieved when Yale house style did not preempt the important spatial and graphical distinctions I

To my mind, there is therefore a link (or perhaps a *rite de passage*) between the currency of textual rhetorics and de Man's nostalgia[12] for a linguistic-based mode of discourse, but one in which, ironically, the "pre-hermeneutic" is its perfected form. This rhetorical swerve is, however, itself a hermeneutic act, a declaration that the ideality of linguistic form is in a moment before the fuller expository mode of composition has been ignited (borrowing from Shelley's "burning coal" image)

---

was trying to make. Indiana house style is not quite as accommodating, though I am still hopeful that the bulk of the shouting across borders will be observed. In any case, I would want the Derridean instructions to be preserved, even if (as in "Border Lines") they are not acted upon. The absence will in this case speak to the ongoing power struggle for control of the text between author and publisher, of which the most egregiously daring I have so far encountered (as editor) has been Randall McLeod's attempt (1991) to repaginate the entire volume of the journal *Text* from the point at which he was demonstrating from the evidence of analytical bibliography that there had been a pagination dislocation in the English translation of *Orlando Furioso*, a "bibliographical disjunct" that he wanted to make materially manifest by simulating it in the repagination of his own essay, which suddenly became a "new" essay with a "new" author (McLeod is continually reinventing himself with pseudonyms—Random Clod [or Cloud or Clovd], Claudia Nimbus, and so on—as he teases out the spatial "meaning" of a material object through his own idiosyncratic typesetting codes).

12. *Nostalgia* might seem a paradoxical term to apply to one of the most critically sophisticated and forcefully interrogative writers of the twentieth century. After all, it was de Man who, in his *Allegories of Reading* (1979), warned most severely against the metaphorical status of the "voice" of the inscribing "author," allying this metaphor along with the "metaphors of primacy, of genetic history, and most notably, of . . . the self" (16), figures that, as I have noted (1999b: 160 and passim), are among the staples of textual criticism. Citing de Man's interest in the *literalization* of metaphor (especially in his brilliant analysis of the "sublime simplicity" with which Archie Bunker's wife, Edith, responds *literally* to Archie's *rhetorical* question "What's the difference?" whether his bowling shoes' laces should be laced over or under ["Semiology and Rhetoric," in de Man 1979: 9; Greetham 1999b: 160n2]), I have, I will admit, made much productive use of de Man's caveats about the construction of a speaking subject out of the *remaniements* of its predicate (especially when these *remaniements* are scribally or compositorially contaminated or conflated); and in the discussion of voice as a metaphor for an absent presence, it is to de Man that I turn:

> [E]ven if we free ourselves of all false questions of intent and *rightfully* [my emphasis] reduce the narrator to the status of a mere grammatical pronoun, without which the narrator could not come into being, this subject remains endowed with a function that is not grammatical but rhetorical, in that it gives voice, so to speak, to a grammatical syntagm. The term *voice*, even when used in grammatical terminology

and of necessity long before the social acts of textual misprision have been committed by those charged with the constructivist act of creating the "contaminated" formal properties of text that Edward Mendelson (1987) has likened to the composite historical and formal syntheses of the medieval cathedral. (My own postmodernist architectural exemplar has usually been the Beaubourg, where the formal properties and elements of the Centre Pompidou are literally turned inside out, as well as

---

as when we speak of the passive, or interrogative, voice is, of course, a metaphor inferring by analogy the intent of the subject from the structure of the predicate (de Man 1979: 18) cited in Greetham 1999b: 160)

One can easily see (or hear?) why de Man was so intent on preserving the integrity (and separation) of "the structure of the predicate" from such metaphorical extensions (or, as I would put it, contaminations) as the subject and his/her voice, but it is in this fear that such a contamination will indeed often (perhaps usually) happen—despite the moral force of his own rhetoric ("rightfully," "reduce the narrator," and so forth)—that de Man is in a sense aligning with pure structural modeling, such as in Paul Maas's horror (*Textual Criticism*, 1958) at the possible bridging of the gap between "semiosis" and "structure," which is alarmingly, even histrionically evident when Maas throws up his hands in despair in acknowledging that "Gegen die Kontamination ist keine Kraut," and, what is even more telling, when Maas admits (on purely technical, structural grounds) that the presence of contamination in the charting of the descent of witnesses is the equivalent of introducing female lines into family trees. See my analysis of this patriarchal prejudice in Greetham 1999b: 478 et seq., where I note that (like de Man?), Maas so relies on the integrity of his grammar of philology that he admits to a desire to recognize "dissident readings" (1958: 8), to afford "[s]ome degree of protection against contamination . . . [that] makes it impossible to hope for a clear-cut solution" (ibid.). From Turing's box down to contemporary studies of chaos and complexification, the distinction that de Man worries about (via Archie Bunker's shoes) between Yeats's "dancer" and the "dance," between pure structure and impure (because contaminated) semiosis, puts de Man's desire for a foundationalist, grammatical philology in some very good company, both textual and scientific: Greg's *Calculus* (1927); Dearing's *Principles* (1974); and Quentin's *Essai* (1926)—among others—have all sought, through symbolic logic or algebraic formulas, to fortify structure against semiosis, an issue that the modeling theorems of complexification also confront (see, for example, Merrell 1998 or Casti 1995). My point is that once it becomes culturally possible for, say, Cerquiglini (1989) to assert that contamination is the normative rather than aberrational state of dissemination (that is, *convergent* not *divergent*) and for this position to be widely embraced by practitioners outside its immediate audience, then the pure grammatical philology that both Maas and de Man, in their different ways, so determinedly wanted to protect, does indeed begin to look, well, nostalgic.

contaminated, with a color-coding[13] of these elements to emphasize the "invagination.")[14]

---

13. To adopt one of Derrida's unfulfilled instructions in the "Border Lines" commentary on "Living On": This note should be read after the longer subsequent note on the Beaubourg; it is thus I think quite fitting that, as a purely linguistic device, color-coding can be used as a phenomenological decoding of the states, or couches, or "guerrilla raids" on the text that Ralph Hanna III (see Middleton 1990) regards any form of interposition through annotation or emendation to be. Indeed, responding to the Anglo-American distaste for, and unfamiliarity with, the complex set of editorial sigla Hans Walter Gabler used on the verso pages of the three-volume "critical and synoptic" edition of *Ulysses* in charting the composition of the "single manuscript text" of that work, in a provocative response to the structuralist nature ("on/off switches") of these sigla, Vicki Mahaffey proposed a color-coded system of states and variants that could overlie the abstract sigla (1991). And I will admit that, in tabulating the manuscript variants of the extant witnesses to Trevisa's *De Proprietatibus Rerum*, I employed a similar system of color-coding to identify each manuscript's swerve from the copy-text, without (of course) any expectation that the august Clarendon Press would ever represent variance through such visual coding. No, it was all rigorously linguistic, not graphic. It is easy to see why such a huge volume as the Trevisa (set in Monotype if one can believe it) could not indulge the expense of color-coding (though color was used from the very beginning by the Gutenberg press and its immediate descendants), but many of the "editions" completed by my graduate students as their final assignment in the required textuality seminar I teach at CUNY have sought out the riches of computer composition on a website or CD-ROM, where the spatial relations can easily assume an even greater significance (and presence) than the purely linguistic.

14. As Ivan Zaknic notes (1983: 23), "All the mechanical services, as well as structural elements, are exposed. It is like a human body with all its organs and systems externalized, including the skeleton. There is something honest and grotesque about this unmasking" (cited in my "Contemporary Editorial Theory," 1993a: 540). Within the fading coal/Gothic cathedral dichotomy of Mendelson's theory of compositional, transmissional, and editorial theory, I place Zaknic's analysis within the broader frame of modernist essentialism versus postmodernist citation (of which Mendelson's cathedral partakes). This is not a matter of a chronological progression, even though my prepositional "from" and "to" might make it seem so, but of a series of stylistic (and thus ontological) swerves. While the inheritance of the Beaubourg is eminently modernist, deriving from Le Corbusier's "twentieth-century museum concept" (the square spiral of 1931), and while its architects have acknowledged their debt to other modernist precursors, including the constructivists, futurists, archigramists, and metabolists, the urban machine actually produced is in conceit and use far removed from the sleek geometrizing associated with Gropius and van der Rohe, where function was totalized and subsumed under the "clear text" of pure form. Repudiating clarity (or at least exemplifying a competing and at first disquieting mode of clarity, where color becomes the taxonomic discriminator, not geometric form, which is placed in the service of color), the Beaubourg's architects promoted instead flexibility and adaptability. There is no point at which this building *begins*, or *ends*, or has a *middle*: it is quite possible to envisage its continual reopening of its own text (that is, its textile qualities, its interweavings)—a figure that I use throughout *Transgressions* as markers for the specific autobiographical crossings of textual boundaries—in an infinite regress of deferral (or, I suppose, spatial difference) that takes the compositional narrative of the accretional cathedral, but then subjects

Inside/outside, difference/repetition, textile/authority, rhetoric/demographics, contamination/conflation, "Living On/Border Lines": in these and many of the other contradictions and crossings of discourse alluded to in this chapter, I hope only to demonstrate that my initial encounter with de Man's model for foundationalist, pre-hermeneutic philology can generate a good many *adnotationes,* and that it is in the play of rhetoric between the *adnotationes* and the (much reduced) *textus* that the anti-discipline of textuality may be most constructively observed. The annotations should indeed constrain and hedge in the "text itself" as well as illuminating and perhaps on occasion clarifying it. The "inferior" footnotes very deliberately contaminate and invade what might be the "superior" narrative of the text. Derrida claims that he has "always been interested in footnotes," and it is to the notes that he will go first when encountering a book (1991: 204), for it is there that the real "discourse" is to be found. By contaminating my text with the exorbitance of the annotation, I have both subjugated it and yet allowed it to participate—as provocateur, as conspirator, as addressee—with a circle of rhetoric that, while it may never hope to be pre-hermeneutic or foundational, may form a sort of ground for more exorbitance.*

---

this narrative to an inside-out reading, a contamination of the outside by the inside. It is very different in historical conceit from the disjunctive joining by a Saussurean rather than Derridean *différence* in the preservation of the bombed-out ruins of the medieval Coventry cathedral, to which is attached (but not incorporated) the modernist museum (with the enormous textile of Graham Sutherland's *Christ in Majesty* over the altar, and the nave full of the several tokens of artistic modernism), which becomes the contemporary "completion of the cathedral" (mis-cited from the *Textual Transgressions* version of "Modernism and Postmodernism").

*An earlier form of the previous chapter, "The Resistance to Philology," was written as the opening to a collection on the margins of the text. The current chapter was always intended as a companion piece to the "Resistance" piece (hence its title), and appeared in very different form in a 2002 *Festschrift* for John Hollander (Greetham 2002).

FOUR

Textual Forenɟicɟ

text ... L. textus ... style, tissue of a literary work, ... that which is woven, web, texture ... **1b.** ... an original or authority ... **2c.** ... the original matter ... **3a.** ... The very words and sentences of Holy Scripture.

OXFORD ENGLISH DICTIONARY

forensic ... pertaining to, connected with, or used in courts of law or public discussion and debate ... **forensics** ... the art or study of argumentation and formal debate.
forensic chemistry ...
forensic medicine ...
forensic psychiatry ...

RANDOM HOUSE DICTIONARY

forensic ... A college exercise, consisting of a speech or ... written thesis maintaining one side or the other of a given question.

OXFORD ENGLISH DICTIONARY

Textual scholarship is an anti-discipline because it does not occupy a permanent or consistent epistemological position and because it has no definable *Fach,* or subject matter. And textual scholarship is a postmodernist anti-discipline because it consists of co-opted and deformed quotations from other fields. Textual scholarship is thus, by its very definition and practice, a nexus of contaminations from elsewhere. Misappropriating concepts and vocabulary from law and jurisprudence, from ethics, philosophy, logic, theology, music, physics, mathematics, statistics, medicine, biology, genetics, sociology, and psychology, textual scholarship is a fragmented pastiche: in the words of Fredric Jameson, a "blank parody" without a central governing figure or even a defined body of knowledge (1991: 17).[1] Textual scholarship thus exemplifies the postmodernist breakdown of the "master narratives" of intellectual discipline. If the paradigm for modernism is, as Clement Greenberg writes (1980a, b), an essentialist, opaque, nonreferential *quidditas* (or "whatness" [Joyce 1964: 213]), textual scholarship is closer to the postmodern, defined by Jameson as a co-option of reference or as paradoxical quotation without a consistent transcendental grounding, without a fixed position from which this co-option can be evaluated.

Accordingly, the status of the raw data from which this anti-discipline draws its conclusions—the character and function of the evidence called on in formulations of empirical and rhetorical proof—may be emblematic of a postmodernist breakdown of the master narrative of evidence itself.[2] What happens to the concepts of cause and effect, to the relations between the inductive, empiricist accumulation (and independent replication) of testable "fact" and the formulation of generative principles of demonstration, in an area of research where the rules for the definition and admissibility of evidence are in flux? One way of approaching this problem is to confront the ambivalent history of textual scholarship and the field's equally ambivalent foundational term, *text.* The definitions quoted at the beginning of this chapter show just two (contradictory)

---

1. Examples of misappropriated terms include *substance* and *accidence,* from theology and philosophy; *calculus of variants,* from mathematics; *distributional analysis,* from statistics; *witness* and *examinatio,* from law; *rules of parsimony* and *rings of probability,* from logic; *sincere* manuscripts, *good* and *bad* quartos, and the motto *lectio difficilior probior est* ("the more difficult reading is the more moral [or honest]"), from ethics. In "Contemporary Editorial Theory" 1993a), I argue that this co-option and lack of center is not "simple imperialism" or the "reflexive distance that textual criticism needs to define itself" but is instead "the very 'construction' . . . of our epistemology: a system of knowledge based on inadequacy, a system of quotation and an annexation without a core of givens" (21).

2. See the wide range of testimony on this large topic in Chandler, Davidson, and Harootunian 1993. The breakdown of the definition or ontology of evidence has been the subject of much debate, in works as diverse as Simon Schama's *Dead Certainties/Unwarranted Speculations,* John Gross's *The Rhetoric of Science,* and John Fowles's "novel" *A Maggot.*

meanings of text from the first appearance of the word in English, in the fourteenth century. *Text* is an "authority," an "original," the word of God, and yet text is also something "woven," a "tissue."[3] As the other quotations suggest, the forensics of text would therefore be both the rhetorical display of the textile "figure in the carpet" (a pattern that varies with different perspectives and rhetorics) and the demonstration of an irrefutable truth about origins and authority, empirical and testable as the hard facts of the physical universe are in the forensic laboratory ("Send the evidence to forensics"). Two sets of ambiguities create manifold possibilities for indeterminacy and confusion.

One of the indeterminacies of textual research is its relation to the disciplines that rely on the discovery and interpretation of evidence. In its attitudes toward, and use of, evidence, is textual scholarship an art, a social science, or a physical science, a combination of the three, or some episteme not directly related to any of these classes of knowledge? The question is an old one, but it will not go away. Despite A. E. Housman's 1921 declaration that "textual criticism is not a branch of mathematics, nor indeed an exact science at all" (as reprinted in Housman 1961: 131) and despite the efforts of even the strictest bibliographers to place fallible human judgment rather than objective empirical demonstration at the center of the textual enterprise (e.g., Tanselle 1974), there remains among some textuists the residual conviction that textual scholarship is an activity separate from criticism and best aligned with the evidentiary protocols of the hard sciences.[4] And the assumption that textual study is positivistic, empirical, and definitive is still all too common among nontextuists.

---

3. Roland Barthes brings out the rich connotations of this etymology. See also Scholes; Gracia, *Metaphysics* and *Theory*; and the chapter "Ontology" in my *Theories of the Text* for further discussion of this ambiguity.

4. The literature on this conflict is enormous. For example, Sebastiano Timpanaro rejects the "metaphysics" of Freudian analysis in favor of textual criticism as science (1976: 78, 87, ch. 7); Eugène Vinaver declares that some work has "raised textual criticism to the position of a science" (1930: 351); Fredson Bowers avers that the social textual theories associated with Jerome McGann use "the language of literary criticism . . . not of strict textual criticism" (1988: 8); Hiroshi Yamashita looks forward to the day when the editing of Japanese literature will become truly a "science"; and in *Scholarly Editing,* a collection of essays I edited, contributors from diverse fields discuss the scientific aspirations of textual study.

The position of an anti-discipline among the disciplines affects, or even determines, the "whatness" of the raw data on which the rhetoric of the field is constructed. Because textual scholarship is found nowhere and everywhere, there is no place for what I designate "textual forensics." If text is both "authority... Holy Scripture" (*textus*) and "tissue" (textile) and if forensics is both the manipulation of argument to sustain a proposal (rhetoric) and the apparently objective, empirical study of the evidence on which this proposal relies for its probity (science), then current theoretical and practical work in textual scholarship should probably be placed at several mutually contradictory positions on an epistemological scale, for each of the definitions and practices can be looked on as a contamination by the others. At one end of the scale is the "Galilean" normative, abstract, and replicatory paradigm of science, and at the other end is the individual, symptomatic, "character"-based prescription for what Carlo Ginzburg calls "venatic lore" (1986: 103). In the following account of textual forensics as contamination, I cover the tension between these poles by addressing first the concept of "everything" in textual evidence, especially in the creation of evidence and in the role of contradictory evidence. I then confront different ways of reading texts for evidence, focusing on debates within bibliography, and investigate the phenomenological distinction between the substance and the accidence of textual evidence. Finally, I pose an epistemological distinction between the replicability of scientific evidence and the symptomatic nature of character and style and interrogate the correspondence between texts and a constative reality outside them.

CONTRADICTORY AND CREATED EVIDENCE: THE PROBLEM OF "EVERYTHING"

The rule of contradictory evidence (Newton's fourth law of reasoning) holds that "in experimental philosophy we are to look upon propositions inferred by general induction from phenomena as accurate or very nearly true, notwithstanding any contrary hypotheses that may be imagined, till such time as other phenomena occur, by which they may be made more accurate, or liable to exceptions" (quoted in Van Doren 1991: 210). This rule has usually been accepted by analytical bibliographers—those who rigorously and empirically investigate the technology of the printed book.[5] But, as Peter Davison shows, the relations between such physical evidence and its rhetorical formulation and interpretation in a forensics (of persuasion) are not necessarily governed by Newton's principle. Davison wrestles with the "hypothetico-deductive" method described in D. F. McKenzie's "Printers of the Mind" (1969) and comes to question the rule of contradictory evidence, which Davison states as follows: "every effort should be made to disprove a conjecture and if a single piece of contradictory evidence—a counter-instance—is thrown up, the conjecture must be abandoned" (1977: 104).[6] Unlike Newton, Davison argues that phenomena (contradictory or otherwise) do not just occur but are created as evidence. He claims that it "is difficult in bibliographic matters to ascertain what evidence 'exists'"—that is, as "scientifically acceptable knowledge." A more accurate description of the procedures of textual forensics, he says, is that "[w]e *find* differences in running titles, in spellings, types; from this we create evidence about compositorial practice; upon this we base our conjectures" (105). The conjecture (the hypothetical forensics) depends on the prior construction of empirical data. But the act of finding in order to create is selective and interpretive, the first stage of a hermeneutics that eventually produces meaning that seems construable directly and unambiguously from the data. The problem is exacerbated when differing hermeneutic protocols produce two or more contradictory meanings from the same selection of data. For example, in an exchange in the *Times Literary Supplement,* Brian Vickers (1993) regards the first ("bad") quarto of *Hamlet* as only a corrupted "memorial reconstruction" of Shakespeare, whereas Graham Holderness and Bryan Loughrey (editors of the quarto, 1993) and Evert Sprinchorn (1994), who

---

5. The location of bibliography within technology (and the consequent reliance on material, testable evidence) appears in the work of John Bidwell and of Allan Stevenson on paper, of Fredson Bowers on the printer's measure (1949–1950) and on running titles (1948–1949), of G. Thomas Tanselle on type damage (1968), of Robert K. Turner Jr. on reappearing type, of Adrian Weiss on reproductions, and of Richard N. Schwab and his collaborators on Gutenberg's ink. But evidence has become equally significant in the social history of bibliography, as in C. Paul Christianson's study of the manuscript book trade and Kate Harris's of book ownership.

6. Note that Davison regards as unauthoritative not just Newton's contrary hypothesis (as does Newton) but also the hard physical counter-instances, the phenomena that Newton accepts as a reason for reformulating the original hypothesis.

reflect Steven Urkowitz's innovative evaluation (1986), find in the text evidence of a direct authorial presence.

Recognizing the insolubility of this conundrum, Jerome McGann declares that the aim of historical criticism, including textual historicism, is not a "[s]trict constructionist" recovery of the "lost phenomena" (the bibliographical evidence) but a "dialogical" and "rhetorical event" (a forensics) that is "invariably multiple" (1993c: 166, 167). In his test case of the variant order of chapters 28 and 29 of Henry James's *The Ambassadors*, McGann argues that true and false interpretations of the evidence cannot be clearly distinguished: "The scandal is that the novel makes no sense no matter which order the two chapters are put in." The bibliographical variance, at first unnoticed and then regarded as error, does not expose an authorial or a production slippage from the truth but rather shows that "both ways of reading the novel are authorized at the bibliographical level" (168).[7]

The dual readings that McGann derives from evidence and the circularity in Davison's prescription for textual forensics respond to what have long been considered major liabilities in the recognition, arrangement, and probity of a work's "textual witnesses"—the successive states of the work, either extant or inferred. For example, the Lachmannian system of genealogical testing uses the concept of error to determine the status of witnesses in their dissemination of textual evidence and thus to position them on a family tree, or stemma. A witness containing an erroneous reading of a preceding witness is placed below the other on the stemma. Thereafter, the error in the lower witness may be used to evaluate the probity of the preceding witness—a perfect case of circular reasoning. Moreover, according to the principle of *eliminatio codicum descriptorum*

---

7. In "The Case of *The Ambassadors* and the Textual Condition," McGann situates his study of the bibliohistorico-hermeneutic crux in James within the general epistemological challenge of contemporary textual study:

> The anomaly of [the] text [of *The Ambassadors*] is an emblem of textuality as such, where endless meaning seems to pour forth from dead letters. We glimpse such endlessness, however, not in the power of spiritual imagination, but in the deathlessness of the material scripts, in the "spirit" of their facticity—in that "positive existence" that Paul de Man, wrongly, thought literary works could never have. (1993b: 165)

See also McGann, "Revision" (1992).

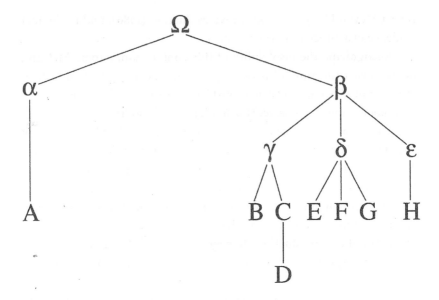

(the elimination of derivative texts), any witness whose testimony derives solely from an extant witness can be disregarded: the testimony is a form of hearsay, with no independent, or even corroborative, authority.

The hermeneutic creation of evidence before the (editing) event is a widespread phenomenon. Thus, most modern editions of *King Lear* do not reference the text of the Nahum Tate version of the play (in which Cordelia marries Edgar and Lear goes into genteel senior citizen assisted living), even though this was the only version of the play performed for well over a century. Similarly, as Thomas L. Berger complains, the front matter of the Shakespeare First Folio (including "The Names of the Princpall Actors in all these Playes") and other mentions of the actors in the folio (e.g., in *Henry IV: Part 2* and *Measure for Measure*) are omitted from

---

FIGURE 4.1. *(above)* A sample stemma from R. J. Tarrant's "Classical Latin Literature," charting the genealogical descent of a text through its extant witnesses, designated by Latin letters, and its non-extant (inferred) witnesses, designated by Greek letters. The lower an item is in the chart, the less its evidentiary value. The extant witnesses B, C, E, F, G, and H, which descend from a single non-extant witness, β, together have the same testamentary status as A alone, because A also derives from one inferred witness. The witness D, which descends solely from an extant witness, can be disregarded, according to the rule of the elimination of derivative texts.

FIGURE 4.2. *(facing)* From the Shakespeare First Folio.

The Workes of William Shakefpeare,

containing all his Comedies, Hiftories, and
Tragedies: Truely fet forth, according to their firft
ORJGJNALL.

The Names of the Principall Actors
in all thefe Playes.

Illiam Shakefpeare.

Richard Burbadge.

John Hemmings.

Auguftine Phillips.

William Kempt.

Thomas Poope.

George Bryan.

Henry Condell.

William Slye.

Richard Cowly.

John Lowine.

Samuell Croffe.

Alexander Cooke.

Samuel Gilburne.

Robert Armin.

William Oftler.

Nathan Field.

John Underwood.

Nicholas Tooley.

William Eccleftone.

Jofeph Taylor.

Robert Benfield.

Robert Goughe.

Richard Robinfon.

Iohn Shancke.

Iohn Rice.

the through-line numbering system in Charlton Hinman's facsimile: to Hinman, "the front matter is not 'text,' quite literally, it does not count. The front matter, the material which authorizes and legitimates the texts which follow, doesn't matter at all. It's not part of the 'text'" (Berger 1993: 196). Even in hypertext editing, where the (inter)textual play is presumably most liberal and comprehensive, the selection of evidence can have specific hermeneutic intentions and results. The editors of the Piers Plowman Archive, a digitized, hypertext presentation of the manuscripts of a highly variant poem, decided to include in their first stage of transcription only the eight manuscripts that most easily permit reconstruction of the hypothetical B archetype and to delay inclusion of two B manuscripts because of their exceptional idiosyncrasy (Duggan 1993, esp. 61n10, 66). George Kane and E. Talbot Donaldson ignored the same two non-normative manuscripts in their print edition of the B text, contending that the manuscripts lacked (authorial) authority. Thus, the desired result determines the sort of evidence that is presented.

In surveying the enormous field of potential evidence, all editors confront the question: under what principles can the evidentiary status of a witness be determined? Or, perhaps more accurate: is it possible to determine evidentiary status without having a desired version of the work in mind? The editor faces a version of Foucault's famous definition of the documentary meaning of "everything" in the construction of the "author-effect":

> Even when an individual has been accepted as an Author, we must still ask whether everything that he wrote, said, or left behind is part of his work. The problem is both theoretical and technical. When undertaking the publication of Nietzsche's works, for example, where should one stop? Surely everything must be published, but what is "everything"? Everything that Nietzsche himself published, certainly. And what about rough drafts of his works? Obviously. The plans for his aphorisms? Yes. The deleted passages and the notes at the bottom of the page? Yes. What if, within a workbook filled with aphorisms, one finds a reference, the notation of a meeting or of an address, or a laundry list: Is it a work, or not? Why not? And so on, ad infinitum. How can one define a work amid the millions of traces left by someone after his death? A theory of the work does not exist, and the empirical task of those who naively undertake the editing of works often suffers in the absence of such a theory. (1984: 103–104)

Where to stop? How to stop? How much information does an editor need to prove positions on such topics as intention, attribution, and style? The guidelines of the MLA Committee on Scholarly Editions, for example, have an even larger definition of *everything* than Foucault does, including "second-party" materials such as letters sent to the author and revisions made by copyeditors, proofreaders, and others besides the author. In an attempt to discern two classes of everything, Japanese editing makes a distinction between *bungaku* collections of literary works, and *zenshu*, "everything written by the author," although both terms imply completeness (Yamashita 1995). In a prescription for variorum editing, Richard Knowles nicely catches the uncertainty about the evidence of everything when he cites R. P. Blackmur ("Use everything"), the skeptic Pyrrho ("Trust nothing"), Richard Rorty ("Decide how well it works"), and Wittgenstein ("Only the exhaustive is interesting") (Knowles 1994: 41).

Recognizing that the evidentiary range in bibliographical research (everything) may be too large and yet too incomplete to allow an editor to use an analogy from science, Davison rejects the hypothetico-deductive method because of its dual assumptions that "all the evidence is theoretically recoverable" and that "such evidence is 'hard' not 'created' evidence" (1977: 105). His specific caveat against the counter-instance clause in this model is that since "what comes down to us can be the exceptional and the illogical" (107), the editor cannot necessarily determine whether extant data were typical or atypical in their original context, and the counter-instance may only be inferable, not demonstrable. The gap between inference and demonstration is crucial to bibliographical and editorial "proofing"—the effort to establish reliable evidence for the incidence of error in a text.[8]

But Davison's recognition of an evidentiary gap between the forensics of hard science and the forensics of the creation and rhetorical manipulation of evidence in textual research is too concessive. In mapping the universe of data collection, he discusses rules of bibliographical evidence in terms of a putative scientific norm for plausibility, which is provable in the physical sciences and not in textual research. The plausibility of any body of knowledge, however, depends directly on its peculiar evidentiary circumstances: what is recoverable and what is lost, what is comprehensive and what is partial. While admitting, even celebrating, the "irrational" and the "exceptional," Davison's design for textual forensics is still based on a comparison in which the inevitable incompleteness of textual evidence makes this forensics inferior to what he regards as the scientific model. Yet even abstract science must make conceptual leaps when direct

---

8. W. Speed Hill and David Shaw address differently the problem of proofing on a statistical basis of limited, even defined, certitude. Hill (1978) postulates a "calculus of error" whereby a form of the law of diminishing returns sets in as the editor attempts to narrow the possible range of error with each successive proofing of the evidence. Shaw (1972) defines a series of "unreliability" factors to indicate the correlation among such data as the number of variant copies extant, the number of sheets printed before a final proof correction, and the percentage of verifiably correct sheets—and thus the degree of certitude—at which the editor should arrive by manipulating these data.

evidence is lacking: the theory of black holes preceded their firm demonstration, and various features of the Einsteinian universe were "proved" empirically long after Einstein had argued that they ought to exist.[9] I am not convinced that there is a single conceptual position, scientific or hermeneutic, empirical or rhetorical, from which bibliographical evidence of the sort Davison confronts can be evaluated. Difference from (or similarity to) a particular discipline does not position textual scholarship on the current epistemological map.

BIBLIOGRAPHICAL DEBATES AND VARIABLES

CONCEPTS OF THE TEXT

The problem of perspective occurs even within bibliography: to what type of bibliographical research should data be attributed—historical? social? technical? D. F. McKenzie, a proponent of a social approach to bibliography, tries to displace John Carter and Graham Pollard's *An Enquiry into the Nature of Certain Nineteenth-Century Pamphlets* (1934, 1983), on the forgeries perpetrated by T. J. Wise, from its usual position within analytical bibliography (the empirical examination of physical books as an aspect of technological history) to social history. Carter and Pollard's book, "informed though it was by the historical evidence of trade documents, paper technology, and type, was seen more as a triumph of analytical bibliography than as an exercise in book history. As the title implies, it reinforced an editorial and bibliophiliac concern for authenticity" (McKenzie 1992: 293–94). McKenzie also chastises such monumental gatherings of bibliographical evidence as W. W. Greg's *Bibliography of the English Printed Drama to the Restoration* (1939–1959) and Harry Carter and Herbert Davis's edition of Joseph Moxon's *Mechanick Exercises on the Whole Art of Printing* for betraying the same "bibliocentric . . . resistance to generality and abstraction" (1992: 294)—that is, for concentrating so much on the technological trees that they cannot see the sociological wood. Of course, McKenzie cannot stand fully outside the ideological

---

9. For example, the direct evidence for the Bose-Einstein condensate (a type of matter, unlike a solid, liquid, or gas, in which atoms lose their separate identities and react as a single structure) was produced only in June 1995, seventy years after Bose and Einstein predicted the existence of the condensate (Browne 1995).

history of the field he comments on, and he speaks necessarily from a particular moment in the evolution of a normative history of the interpretation of evidence. Because of his conviction that "the full range of historical and analytical studies" must be employed to sift the evidence of book history, McKenzie supports "the use of archival evidence to confute many ill-informed assumptions made by analytical bibliographers" (293, 294). G. Thomas Tanselle, however, attempts to incorporate within analytical bibliography the supposed generalities that McKenzie finds only in the social history of the book. Any history of publishing based solely or even primarily on archives and business records is inadequate, Tanselle insists, for it lacks the essential evidence:

> When historians write about printing and publishing firms, they are likely to think of the archives of the firms and any other relevant manuscript materials as the primary evidence; and so they are in some respects. But the printed items themselves also provide information about the bookmaking process, and whenever that information conflicts with the archival record, it must take precedence: the actual books constitute the evidence, whereas printers' and publishers' records contain statements about the books. (1981a: 11)

Thus, Tanselle reverses McKenzie's hierarchy, taking data from the sociology of texts and inscribing this evidence within, or as dependent on, the technological history promoted by analytical bibliography. He co-opts McKenzie's social-based "full range of historical" evidence as merely a subclass of the normative evidence to be found in analytical bibliography; and where the two sets of evidence clash, the book is to be given probative primacy.

Whereas McKenzie interprets this conflict over the status of evidence as an Anglo-American resistance to the general and the abstract, David Shaw dismisses French *bibliologie* in favor of the Anglo-American emphasis on "the internal or archeological examination of the book as evidence for the book and the book trade" ("*La bibliologie*," in Davison 1992: 210).[10] And yet, in the fields of Continental philosophy and the history of the Renaissance, Paul Oskar Kristeller argues for a turn from general theories of history to specificities, particularly in textual history, which

---

10. For further analysis of this conceptual/cultural conflict, see Greetham 1993b, "Textual Imperialism" (1997c), and the chapter "Society and Culture in the Text" in *Theories* (1999b).

must "deal with details, many of them minor, and thus operates . . . on a lower and more modest level" than general history, the domain of laws "valid for all historical or literary developments" (1987: 5). The conflict between Kristeller and McKenzie over the abstract and the general raises larger questions about the position of textual scholarship. Is this field a science on the Galilean model, in which quantification and the repetition of phenomena can be used to determine abstract principles? Or is it one of the pursuits that Carlo Ginzburg labels "evidential and conjectural," in which "the object is the study of individual cases, situations, and documents, precisely because they are individual, and for this reason get results that have an unsuppressible speculative margin" (1986: 106)?

The tension between a textual forensics that is specific, local, and provable and one that is conceptual, general, and speculative is epitomized by the work of Randall McLeod, who has tried to force a technical and epistemological disjunction between the local evidence derivable from analytical bibliography and the generalized evidence resulting from reading, which constructs large-scale meaning from the symbolic codes of a document. In contrast to McGann's insistence on the phenomenological inseparability of linguistic codes (the text itself, or the words) and bibliographical codes (the physical and spatial context in which the text is transmitted), McLeod considers it essential to segregate these two competing forms of evidence, because of the mutual "interference of signals"—that is, the inevitable contamination—they provoke: "I can't I I I I can't simultaneously read I can't *read* a book I can't READ a book and LOOK at it at the same time" (1990: 61). In this passage, McLeod differentiates symbolically the acts of looking at and reading a book ("read" progresses from roman type to italic to italic caps, while "look" is set in bold caps): similarly, he refuses to read the texts of Renaissance books, the better to understand their typographic codes. As he points out: "Renaissance books use different visual codes than ours. And not just neutrally different codes, but pointedly different, because we arrived at our codes by undoing theirs!" (76). In a series of brilliant, though sometimes infuri-

---

FIGURE 4.3. *(facing)* An example of Randall McLeod's determination to avoid reading a text in order to see it. His article "From 'Tranceformations in the Text of *Orlando Furioso*'" includes an upside-down photograph of himself looking at a book in the McLeod Portable Collator, which inverts the text page: "MATURE SCHOLAR SEEKS VISUALLY ARRESTING BOOK NOT TO READ."

through the verso of its leaf, which you are now turning to gaze on. For the light falling over your left shoulder still illuminates the opening that you have not fully closed. Not a single solitary mirror-image word of it departing, glimpsed before it could evenAt first I did very well in the Combray School. I was training to be a textual editor.

The doctor they referred me after it happened the second time—actually a whole battery of them. One of them suggested that the backaches headaches and dreams (and the "behavioural things") were concocted in some way with this missionary position. This person thought up this term. (Would *I* have dreamt of it on *my own?*) That I should left my eye sometimes go right where it wanted to go. Or the other eye. That it was alright for either of them to want to—to do these things on its own. "The book will not be hurt," she quiped. "Let your eyeballs do their things—it's OK," I can recall her quiping and cajollying me encouragingly many times.

So five six years ago I've become as you see me now in that time. You wouldn't mistake me for a textual editor, now, eh? I sought a way to *adapt* my training. (No question of just *chucking* it!) I undertook a systematic MATURE SCHOLAR SEEKS VISUALLY ARRESTING BOOK NOT TO READ, and at last I have chosen Harington's translation of *Orlando Furioso*. Have been looking at copies of first two eds. ever since. (They are like big picture books, but for grownups.) My project is not just not to *read* the *Orlando*, but not to read it *over and over again* until I have a new *way* to read. (I will explain why I gaze at it upsidown in just a minute.)   Photo by Pamela Harris.

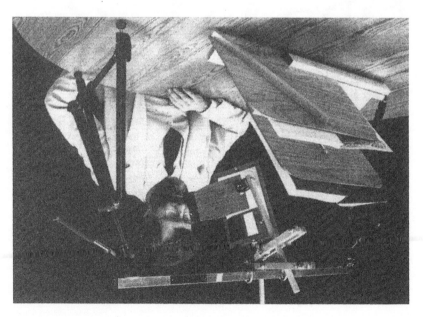

62

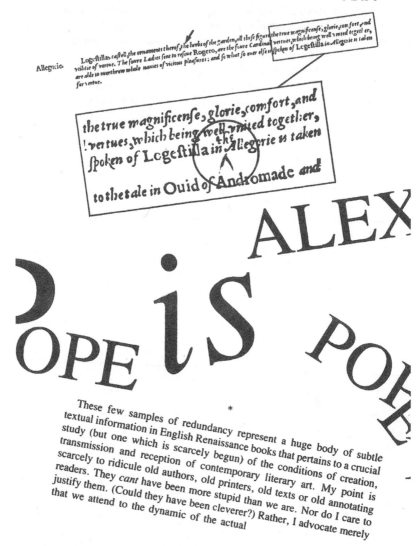

278

TEXT

Allegorie. Logestillas castell, the ornaments therof, the herbs of the garden, all these figures are able to ouerthrow whole masses of vicious pleasures: and so what so euer else is for vertue.

the true magnifcense, glorie, comfort, and vertues, which being well vnited together, spoken of Legestilla in Allegorie is taken to the tale in Ouid of Andromade and

ALEX

POPE is POPE

These few samples of redundancy represent a huge body of subtle textual information in English Renaissance books that pertains to a crucial study (but one which is scarcely begun) of the conditions of creation, transmission and reception of contemporary literary art. My point is scarcely to ridicule old authors, old printers, old texts or old annotating readers. They *cant* have been more stupid than we are. Nor do I care to justify them. (Could they have been cleverer?) Rather, I advocate merely that we attend to the dynamic of the actual

FIGURE 4.4(a–b). *(above and facing)* Pages 278–79 from McLeod's 1991 "Information on Information." The graphic codes suggest that an article ends, but its final words are repeated in the title on the next page, and the substance of the text continues without break in the (apparently) new article, attributed to Random Clovd. Enlarged and fragmented letters and words float across the pages as abstract shapes.

The Dynamic of the Actual

RANDOM CLOVD

> *The struggle for tne text* is *the text.*
> R. Cloud

how texts were writtentransmittedandread in the Renaissance, that we recognize this dynamic not as an airy adjunct to textual study, but as something rooted so deep in texts of the period that it is ineradicable (Unless, of course, you *edit* them.), because, simply, it *is* text.

In the 18th century, when the Editing of Shakespeare As we Know It began, there was no practical means of broadcasting the texts of the Renaissance without a laborious resetting of them, type by type. Inevitably, by sheer weight of numbers and the inaccessibility of original editions (and lack of knowledge about them, in any case), it was modernizing editions that became the standards of reference. In stating these facts of production and use, I dont apologize for an ideology that was also at work, reshaping historic texts for a new market. Not only had the language changed, and taste changed, and the theatre changed—all of which weighed on the editors who, as a class, intervened between the old textual evidence and the new reading public (which had itself changed along with the rest), but also it was generally perceived that there was a role Shakespeare could be made to play in the shaping of contemporary national and class identities. All of these factors and more worked to transform texts.

But the photographic revolution of the 19th century has put our relationship to the printed books of the Renaissance on a technological basis quite different from that of the editorial foundling fathers in the century before. The drynamic world of editing has been slow to realize this fact, and it may take the electronic revolution of our own century to propel it into the 19th. What the photo-facsimile achieved is the exposure of the 18th-century edition and its modern descendants as being in the

ating, articles on bibliographical evidence, McLeod interrupts, prevents, and derails any attempt to impose a linear, consistent, abstract reading on his research. To arrest the eye on the specificity of symbols, he has facsimiles and modern text printed upside down and diagonally; has material printed into and across the gutter and from recto to verso margins; presents an inverted picture of himself "not reading," looking into his "collator in a handbag"; introduces "editorial" marginalia like "Go on. You can trust Randy" (1991: 275); turns pages; begins an article twice, under different pseudonyms; and generally misorders the traditional scholarly format and narrative in a practical, visual demonstration that to "understand" textual "paradox we shall have to pass from a consideration of the . . . words as lexical items to the system of graphic codes in which they function" (1991: 250). These graphic codes are part of the game of detecting—or failing to detect—the evidence:

> But why did I play that game with you, and make you feel stupid because you couldn't find "tne"? (After all, *youre* not stupid.) Because *that* is what it was like to be a Renaissance reader. (And thats what thises say is about?) (1991: leaf between 276 and 277)

McLeod's simulation of Renaissance reading by modern looking makes readers feel stupid because they cannot see the evidence or can see it only as either a lexical or a bibliographical function: weighing evidence of one type disturbs the value of evidence of another type.

McLeod's play on the disturbance caused by the interpreting of bibliographical features visually exemplifies Ginzburg's characterization of philology as a site for the "conjecture" that is essential to a "speculative margin" requiring an individual and interpretive, even quirky, critic and creator of evidence. And yet, as McKenzie insists on the conceptual value of abstraction, Ginzburg maintains that "the abstract notion of text explains why textual criticism, even while retaining to a large extent its divinatory qualities, had the potential to develop in a rigorously scientific direction" (1986: 107). He senses the paradox in the definitions of text: if text is original, authoritative, and scriptural—that is, fixed but not immediately accessible in its concrete form—then it might be susceptible to a Galilean model of the general, in which "for the natural philosopher as for the philologist, the text is a profound, invisible entity to be reconstructed independently of material data" (108). But if text is tissue and web, it needs the critical, "divinatory" qualities of the speculative margin.

SUBSTANCE, ACCIDENCE, AND CRITICAL APPARATUS

The Galilean view of text recalls the work of W. W. Greg and Fredson Bowers, in which an "ideal text" may be non-extant as a documentary, material phenomenon but can be constructed under Platonist principles. According to this concept, a text is composed of two elements: the accidentals, or surface features (punctuation, capitalization, spelling, and so on), and the substantives, or meaning (the words). In the Greg-Bowers theory of "dual [divided] authority," the best evidence for the accidentals comes from an authorial manuscript or early print, in which the surface features are least disturbed by the social transmission (copying or printing) of the text, whereas evidence for the substantives may come from any subsequent stage of transmission in which revision has authority—usually because there is reason to think that the author presided over or carried out the revisions (Greg 1950–1951; Bowers 1978). The result is an eclectic text, a text that never was, which fulfills ideal rules of composition but is constructed under two systems of evidence.

Greg formulated his so-called copy-text rationale, suggesting an evidentiary distinction between substance and accidence, pragmatically in the context of the production conditions of Renaissance drama, in which scribes and compositors indeed might quickly contaminate an author's accidentals. However, through the proselytizing zeal of Bowers and Tanselle, the rationale was exported as a principle into periods and genres undreamed of by Greg—including nineteenth-century American literature (Bowers 1964b), philosophy (Boydston 1991), and even biblical, classical, and medieval literature (Tanselle 1983; Greetham 1988)—and was eventually enshrined in the principles of the MLA's Center for Editions of American Authors. To be replicated in times and places other than the original Renaissance context, Greg's textual protocols had to be turned from a speculative margin into an abstract, Galilean paradigm. The great majority of works that have been awarded seals by the CEAA and its successor, the Committee on Scholarly Editions, have been eclectic, ideal-text editions.[11]

---

11. The current CSE guidelines (reprinted in Barnard, O'Keefe, and Unsworth 2006: 23–46) no longer endorse a specific copy-text theory. This shift resulted from changes in the ideological climate since the heyday of Greg and Bowers, from the 1960s to the 1980s, and shows how evidentiary rules of bibliography are in constant flux.

had a noble boy about a year old, who bore a marvellous resemblance to Mehevi, whom I should certainly have believed to have been the father, were it not that the little fellow had no triangle on his face—but on second thoughts, tattooing is not hereditary. Mehevi, however, was not the only person upon whom the damsel Moonoony smiled—the young fellow of fifteen, who permanently resided in the house with her, was decidedly in her good graces. I sometimes beheld both him and the chief making love at the same time. Is it possible, thought I, that the valiant warrior can consent to give up a corner in the thing he loves? This too was a mystery which, with others of the same kind, was afterwards satisfactorily explained.

189.25–28	had . . . happening. E	had . . . happening. A appeared to be equally at home. AR
190.6	these E	these A those AR
190.15–16	but . . . hereditary. E	but . . . hereditary. A [omitted] AR
190.19–21	I . . . loves? E	I . . . loves? A [omitted] AR

Greg's notion of dual types of evidence was not unopposed, contrasting, for example, with the editorial rationale promoted by Philip Gaskell (1972, 1985: 399–400) and others. In this alternative view, a manuscript is not direct evidence of its author's intentions, since an author submitting a work for publication usually assumes that the accidentals of the manuscript will be changed to conform to house styling. For Greg and Bowers, evidence for intention is psychologistic; for Gaskell, it is social and con-

FIGURE 4.5. (above) Top: Lines 13–22 of page 190 from a clear-text edition of Melville's *Typee* (Hayford, Parker, and Tanselle 1968). Bottom: An excerpt from the list of substantive variants in the back of the book, showing some of the variants for pages 189–90 (354). The reader must consult this list to learn that the editors have, for example, restored large sections cut by the author. The ellipses in the list may refer to anything from a phrase to virtually an entire chapter.

FIGURE 4.6. (facing) Part of an inclusive text ("synoptic") page from an edition of *Ulysses* (Gabler 1984: 18). Through an elaborate system of brackets, raised numerals, and so on, all the witnesses speak at the same time, even when they contradict one another.

He flung up his hands and tramped down the stone stairs, singing out
of tune ⟨in⟩ with a Cockney accent:°
—O, *won't we have a merry time,*
Drinking whisky, beer and wine! °
25 *On coronation,*
Coronation day! °
O, won't we have a merry time
On coronation day! °
    ^⟨Sudden warm sunlight ☒⟩ Warm sunshine ⌐[merry] merrying¬^ over
30 the sea. The nickel shaving-|bowl shone, forgotten, on the ⟨^sunny⟩ parapet.
Why should I bring it down? Or leave it there all day, forgotten friendship?
    He went over to it, held it in his hands awhile, feeling its coolness,
smelling the clammy slaver of the lather in which the brush was stuck. ^⟨☒⟩
So^ I carried the boat of incense then at Clongowes. I am another now and
35 yet the same. A servant too. A server of a servant.

---

22 accent:] s5; accent. aR   24 *wine!*] STET aR; *TD: wine* (tB):1; *wine,* a1   26 *day!*] STET
aR; *TD: day* (tB):1; *day?* a1   28 *day!*] STET aR; *TD: day* (tB):1; *day?* a1

18   I.1 · TELEMACHUS

tractual. McGann's social textual criticism extends the arguments of Gaskell, Donald Pizer (1971, 1985), and James Thorpe (1972, esp. 48) in favor
of the collaborative model of authorship and dissemination by changing
the evidentiary definitions of basic concepts, such as the primary witness
(*Critique,* 1983, 1992). To Greg, Bowers, and the intentionalists, primary
documents are those over which the author might have had some over-
sight, including posthumous documents, such as the Shakespeare First
Folio, that are at least in part based on lost states possibly seen by the
author. But to the social textual critic, any *textus receptus,* no matter how
far removed from a demonstrable authorial intention—indeed, even if it
contradicts such an intention—acquires primary evidentiary status as a
cultural artifact (see, e.g., Pizer 1985: 156–60, on Dreiser) and cannot be
impugned or deemed inadmissible.

    Beyond the evaluation of authorial control over substance and ac-
cidence, eclectic text theory also affects the evidence presented to the
reader. The typical edition gives prominence to a "clear-text" page unsullied by any indication of where and how the evidence for substantives
and accidentals was used in the construction of the ideal text. All such
evidence is buried in lists of variants at the end of the book, together with

evidence for the editor's critical intervention. E. Talbot Donaldson calls the philosophy behind such clear text an editorial "death-wish" (1970: 105)—a desire to conceal the evidence of one's editorial handiwork so that the resulting clueless text acquires transparency and authority, seeming not to depend on the demonstrable intervention of a fallible editor's many choices among often contradictory pieces of evidence. Of course, this death wish has a major advantage: the text can be easily separated from its apparatus and published in a different format for a nonspecialist audience, as has been done with several CEAA/CSE volumes reprinted in the Library of America series. The alternative to clear text is "inclusive text"—pages in which the editorial sigla and apparatus interrupt the reader's linear progression. Editions of Emerson (Ferguson et al.), Wordsworth (Parrish), Yeats (Finneran et al.), and *Ulysses* (Gabler) use inclusive texts.

It is ironic that Donaldson upbraids textual scholars who aim for anonymity, for although his and George Kane's famous edition of the B version of *Piers Plowman* is inclusive, its text carefully marked with every sign of editorial intervention (even notations of expansions of conventional scribal abbreviations), it has been accused of an evidentiary sleight of hand, of seeming to provide evidence while in fact concealing it. For example, Charlotte Brewer charges that Kane and Donaldson's decision to record in the apparatus only the readings that depart from the edited text creates the impression that all other (uncited) witnesses agree with the editors' judgment—an assumption that is frequently unwarranted, given the enormous gaps in the testamentary coverage of this highly variant poem. From the evidence cited in the apparatus, the reader cannot tell "whether Kane and Donaldson's reading originates from [the A or C text] or whether instead, it is the product of the editors' conjectural emendation" (Brewer 1991: 61–62).

This edition provides a complex example of variable testamentary states—and the lack of them—that have to be interpreted continually through fact or inference in the apparatus of recorded variants and textual notes. Unfortunately, few scholars have sufficient interest or competence to navigate the deep waters of apparatus successfully. Jo Ann Boydston, the editor of the complete thirty-seven-volume edition of John Dewey's writings, dolefully reports that, to her knowledge, not a single study of Dewey has ever referred for evidence to the enormous end-of-volume apparatus of rejected variants (1991b: 9). As Davison recognizes:

[T]he problem is that whereas no bibliographer should, traditionally, trust the word of the Archangel Gabriel (on matters bibliographic, that is), most of us, however assiduous we may be in leaving no stone unturned in checking the text with which we are concerned, must take on trust, to some extent at least, the work of others on other texts and problems. (1977: 102)

A critical apparatus, the evidence it contains, and the text constructed from it must thus be taken at face value, not just in the accuracy of the attestations presented in the data, which may become part of the tradition of reporting on the text, but also—more dangerously, as in the Kane-Donaldson edition—in the range of the universe of data deemed relevant to the demonstration of these "self-evident" truths.[12]

REPLICABILITY, SYMPTOMS, AND STYLOMETRICS

This trusting of apparatus points to another major difference between textual scholarship and science in their use of evidence (and experimentation). According to the idealist Galilean paradigm, replicability is vital to the evidentiary truth of a scientific principle (as the failure of replicability in cold-fusion experiments demonstrated some years ago). Kane and Donaldson invoke the principle of replicability when they claim that the only way a critic can systematically challenge their findings is to reedit the text using the same data. Of course, no one—not even Kane and Donaldson—would expect such a procedure to replicate their ideal form exactly. The resulting edition would differ from the original because textual and editorial scholarship, mixing abstraction and the speculative margin, is closer to Ginzburg's prescription for "medical semiotics" than it is to natural science: "The definition of the chosen method [of Hippocratic medicine] depended on the explicit notion of symptom (*semeion*). The Hippocratic school maintained that only by attentively observing and recording all symptoms in great detail could one develop precise 'histories' of individual diseases; disease, in itself, was out of reach" (1986:

---

12. Davison observes that the cumulative force of the tradition of reportage—embedded in the apparatus of variorum and critical editions—invites and yet at the same time discourages a replication of the empirical research that created the tradition (1977). One of the persistent marketing claims for editions is that they are "fresh" ("freshly edited," "based on a fresh examination of the documentary evidence" or on "fresh investigation of the witnesses," and so on) rather than merely inherited. Yet, readers tend to take on trust the basic research of others when it has become traditional.

105). Analogously, the text of *Piers Plowman* or Shakespeare or Homer or the Bible is observable only in its symptoms.

Nonetheless, the symptoms can be described—even quantified—and can be used as evidence for historical reconstructions, with the proviso that symptoms are always partly idiosyncratic and partly systemic and are therefore not perfectly replicable. To be replications, data or their organization into texts must recur in sufficiently alike form, constituting classes or sets. The more specific phenomena are and the more they are products of individual intervention, the less likely replication is. Ginzburg describes a descending scale from the set to the individual when he discusses how a scribe's hand exhibits "character," which betrays identity while still assigning the hand to a class, to what the paleographer calls a script:

> [S]cientific value, in the Galileian [*sic*] sense of the term, decreased abruptly as one passed from the universal "properties" of geometry to "properties common to the century" in writing and then to the "individual properties" of paintings—or even calligraphy.
>
> This descending scale confirms that the real obstacle to the application of the Galileian [*sic*] paradigm was the centrality (or the lack of it) of the individual element in the single disciplines. The more that individual traits were considered pertinent, the more the possibility of attaining exact scientific knowledge diminished. (1986: 111)

This issue of the identifiable properties of a class or an individual can most clearly be shown in attribution studies conducted "symptomatically," at the level of both character and style. What does it mean, for instance, to find that a Continental manuscript bears Insular "symptoms"—that some of its forms show the influence of the rounded or pointed scripts of Ireland or England, famous in the Latin (round) text and the Anglo-Saxon interlinear (pointed) glosses of the Lindisfarne Gospels? These symptoms might confirm the circumstantial—that is, extratextual—historical account asserting that Irish and English monks exported Insular Christianity to Central Europe at such foundations as Bobbio, Fulda, Reichenau, and St. Gall. By this measure of character, present (i.e., surviving) conditions sustain a cultural hypothesis and demonstrate a putative past condition: the existence of Insular manuscripts (now lost) on the Continent, from which the symptoms in extant manuscripts are derived. This reasoning exemplifies the development of what

Ginzburg calls "venatic lore," the "ability to construct from apparently insignificant experimental data a complex reality that could not be experienced directly" (1986: 103). Ginzburg connects this tie of present with past to the forensics of Holmesian detection and to the basic motivation of Freudian psychoanalysis, "a method of interpretation based on discarded information, on marginal data, considered in some way significant" (101).

The marginal, which Ginzburg correlates with calligraphic "flourishes" (1986: 118), plays a similar role in efforts of attribution through style (and stylometrics) in art history, literature, and any other medium in which there is an attempt to move down a descending scale from the ideal of Galilean science to the idiosyncratic, symptomatic level of the individual artist. Ginzburg cites Freud's well-known interest in Giovanni Morelli's method of attribution in painting, which emphasized the involuntary, the inadvertent, and the unintended over the conscious and the striking. According to Freud:

> [Morelli] had caused a revolution in the art galleries of Europe by questioning the authorship of many pictures, showing how to distinguish copies from originals.... He achieved this by insisting that attention should be diverted from the general impression and the main features of a picture, and he laid stress on the significance of minor details.... It seems to me that his method of inquiry is closely related to the technique of psychoanalysis. It, too, is accustomed to divin[ing] secret and concealed things from unconsidered or unnoticed details, from the rubbish heap, as it were, of our observations. (*Moses of Michelangelo*; quoted in Ginzburg 1986: 99)

The connection between psychoanalysis and editing is a staple of current textual theory, as various arguments on authorial intention, the slip, and the error testify.[13] But in attribution studies, the measuring, quantification, and interpretation of the non-Galilean, medical symptom—the individual character—has become crucial to the adjudication of ambivalent documentary evidence. All too often, scholars engaged in such adjudication have looked only for the intentional and the normative. The essays in David V. Erdman and Ephim G. Fogel's *Evidence for Author-*

---

13. See Timpanaro (1976, an anti-Freudian work); Tanselle 1979; McLaverty, "Concept" (1984a) and "Issues" (1991); Greetham, "Slips" (1997b), the chapter "Psychoanalysis of the Text" in *Theories* (1999h), and "Manifestation" (1991a), which encompasses post-Freudian (e.g., Lacanian) models as well.

ship (1966) and in René Wellek and Alvaro Ribeiro's *Evidence in Literary Scholarship* (1979) concentrate on the conscious formation of "style and ideas." Arthur Sherbo's prescriptions on "the uses and abuses of internal evidence" defines this approach:

> Internal evidence divides nicely into two parts, style and ideas. Stylistic considerations include such matters as length and structure of sentences (structure includes antithesis, balance, parallelism, repetition, inversion, etc.), verbal and phrasal likes and dislikes, kind of vocabulary (i.e., Latinate or not, polysyllabic or not, frequency of certain parts of speech, etc.), characteristic imagery, peculiarity of spelling and punctuation . . . range and density of learning and allusions, and parallels of various kinds with known works by the particular writer in question. (1966: 7)

The problem with this formulation is that virtually all its features of attributable style (especially "likes and dislikes," which involve volition) are replicable by others. They are open to copying, influence, and downright forgery—the factors that Morelli's (and Freud's and Holmes's) concentration on the nonvolitional, the "flourish," seek to remove. Erdman recognizes the potential flaw in Sherbo's list when he notes that "[p]arallels can be illusory or coincidental; recognition of the author's signature in characteristic constructional rhythms or in modes of metaphor and metaphysics can be precarious." But he nonetheless concludes that the "combination" of these features "constitutes the most satisfactory internal evidence" (1966: 53); in other words, evidence is quantifiable, and quantification lends it plausibility and then authenticity. But such a view does not resolve the problem posed by Davison and Foucault: how much is "everything," and what specific combination(s) of the components of everything engender(s) meaning?

A more Morellian approach to stylometrics would construct (or test) the author's idiolect—the personal pattern of choices from the available linguistic resources—from neutral or semantically empty terms (function words, pronouns, etc.) and would be particularly wary of a context that might make these units less than neutral. Derek Pearsall and R. A. Cooper (1988) properly chastise a stylometric study of *Pearl* that shows the poem to have a high incidence of "I," "me," "she," and "her" and a low incidence of "he," "him," "they," and "them"; a quick look at the context of *Pearl*—a dialogue between a dreamer/narrator and a vision of a maiden—immediately shows that this pattern is determined by authorial decisions outside the idiolect. Thus, apparently neutral stylometric studies ought to concentrate on unconscious selections within the idiolect, not on the volitional choices favored by Sherbo.

ON INTERNAL AND EXTERNAL, DOCUMENTARY AND CIRCUMSTANTIAL CORRESPONDENCES

Much of the discussion in Erdman and Fogel's *Evidence for Authorship* centers on the disputable relations between the sort of internal, stylometric evidence enlisted by Sherbo and "external evidence" derived from documents that provide information on such matters as date, logistics of creation and reception, and contemporary attribution and that are regarded as closer to the scene of composition than the latter-day textual critic is. Erdman proposes a distinction between the two classes, derived from Coleridge: "Any work which claims to be held authentic, must have had witnesses, and competent witnesses; this is external evidence. Or it may be its own competent witness; this is called internal evidence" ("Intercepted Correspondence"; quoted in Erdman 1966: 45). This distinction corresponds to Tanselle's insistence that the book is "its own competent witness," separate from the indirect testimony of the archive. But can the distinction hold, and does it always mean what Coleridge (and Erdman) wants it to mean? In forgery, it clearly cannot, for the forged document passes itself off as containing authentic internal evidence while being at best an incompetent external witness to something else. What can be known about the documentary profile of Latin culture when, as Anthony Grafton estimates, "some 10,576 of the 144,044 inscriptions in the great *Corpus* of Latin inscriptions are faked or suspect[,] many of them ... the work of imaginative Renaissance antiquaries" (1990: 28)?

Distinguishing between the authentic and the forged document from internal evidence of character, initially paleography, was the basis of the linear arrangement of cultural phenomena known as historical criticism, established as an evidentiary paradigm by Lorenzo Valla and other Renaissance scholars. Valla invoked the historical principle that the fake descends from the authentic, not vice versa, and used linguistic and historical evidence to determine that, for example, the Donation of Constantine, purportedly written in the fourth century by the first

Christian Roman emperor to cede all temporal power to the papacy, was a fake because its character was eighth or ninth century. A. R. Braunmuller (1993) suggests that Valla's "destruction of the Donation of Constantine was a moment when criticism turned a text from document into work" and that Valla's denial of the documentary authority of the Donation and affirmation of an "ulterior purpose" (that is, a forged authorial intention) are comparable to early Stuart parliaments' changing the Magna Carta from a "transparent legal document (like a judicial decision in the year-books) into a source of endless constitutional debate and, consequently, interpretation."[14] Braunmuller regards Valla's bibliographical skepticism as "the founding act of the modern editorial tradition" (1993: 224). This tradition reaches its apotheosis in Tanselle's distinction between the texts of "works," created by authors, and historical "documents" (1989, 1990c).

The principles of Valla's interrogation, which adduced the inauthenticity of internal evidence from external evidence, are central to textual study. It is not clear, however, that these principles can hold for all cases that rely on Coleridge's conceptual division between internal and external witnesses. Lee Patterson accepts the premises of the Coleridge-Erdman formula as a working distinction: "external evidence has to do with manuscripts in which a reading occurs and the frequency of its attestations[,] . . . internal evidence [with] the quality of a reading in relation to its variants." He recognizes that external evidence so defined is usually considered "documentary," existing "to be dated, counted, and assessed," whereas internal evidence is "judgmental," and the distinction "must be drawn by the skill of the editor" (1985: 55). But unlike Coleridge and Erdman, Patterson rejects any assumptions about a qualitative or critical difference between external and internal evidence:

> At heart, external evidence is nothing other than the fact that a particular reading occurs in one or more manuscripts, that is, attestation; internal evidence is nothing other than the fact that there are on many occasions more than one reading, that is, variation. Both internal and external evidence are evidence of originality; both are, in themselves, equally factual, equally

---

14. Similarly, the U.S. Constitution has been transformed from an authorless document into an authored work through being read hermeneutically by strict constructionists and historical relativists.

objective, equally historical. Both are used for the same purpose, which is to discover the history of transmission, on the presumption that once this history is known, the editor will be able to revise it, to run the process backward until the original comes into view. (1985: 57)

Patterson's strategy is to demolish the presumption that the external has inherent authority as unambiguous historical evidence and that the internal, in contrast, is a conjectural or temporary critical construct. This strategy brings a hermeneutic dimension to the classification of documents into external and internal, just as Davison brings hermeneutics into the finding and creating of evidence.

Moreover, external evidence may not be as neutral as it seems, and it may work only for those who are already convinced of its probity. Gary Taylor (1987) playfully posits an external document that might provide "reliable early testimony to Shakespeare's habits of composition. An autograph letter, for instance. 'Dear Anne, I'll be home next week, as soon as I finish revising that old play of mine, *King Lear*. Your loving Willy. London. 1 April 1610.'" But Taylor undercuts the probity of even this evidence by suggesting that "[a]rtists, after all, do, often enough, lie about their work. For all we know, 'revising *King Lear*' might have been Shakespeare's alibi, to cover an adulterous weekend" (1987: 296–97). Indeed, how can "external" evidence be considered purely external, since it may establish its authority largely by being a reliable witness to itself? The apparent neutrality of the external document seems transparent witness to the evidence for the text to which it refers. Before accepting the theory of Shakespeare's adulterous weekend, the critic/historian would demand a second level of external evidence (say, an innkeeper's register), which should be confirmed by another external witness, down the *mise-en-abyme*. The question is whether testamentary transparency can ever exist and, if so, how it can be recognized.

Transparency of testimony depends on a witness to the witness and on the establishment of genre (among other things). External demonstration that Melville was responsible for the cutting of the criticisms of Christian missionaries in the second edition of *Typee* is not enough evidence to convince Tanselle and his co-editors, because the cuts "represent not so much his intention as his acquiescence." Seeking a hermeneutics of external evidence, Tanselle declares that "one cannot automatically accept such statements at face value; as in any historical research, statements can only be interpreted" (1976: 193–94). Similarly, the arguments over whether D. H. Lawrence approved of the cuts to his early work by the editor Edward Garnett depend on which parts of the Lawrence correspondence are given authority as transparent external evidence—those that praise Garnett's intervention or those that castigate it. And Yamashita is confident that he can ignore Akutagawa Ryunosuke's explicit preference for the version of "Rashomon" in the second, *Hana* edition of the complete works because the letter expressing this authorial instruction was "probably meant only to remind him to take note of the revisions found in this edition" (100). In such cases, both the authorizing of external evidence and the use of it become critical acts.

Citing the external as a potential class of evidence assumes that the editing of a text has some relation to an external reality. In an essay on this topic (1979), Tanselle shifts from disjunctions between internal and external (such as Keats's historically inaccurate "stout Cortez" surveying the Pacific in the sonnet "On First Looking into Chapman's Homer") to more problematic cases (for the most part, in the Melville texts) of an evidentiary conflict between truth derived from external, historical, and cultural research and accuracy, and fidelity to a document or an intention whether or not it is truthful. Confronting the same conflict, Fredson Bowers (in Davison 1992) states that an editor would be fully justified in emending Fitzgerald's geography of New York City so that, in walking from West 158th Street to Central Park, one proceeds southward not eastward (Bowers 1992: 249). Following a similar principle, an editor preparing the first book publication of Natsume Soseki's novel *I Am a Cat* reduced the number of kittens from eight, in the original serial publication, to four, on the authority of "a zoological garden" (Yamashita 1995), and Matthew J. Bruccoli's edition of *The Great Gatsby* (1991) changed the age of Daisy's little girl, Pammy, from three to two, because otherwise Daisy would be nine months' pregnant at her marriage. John Worthen dismisses Bruccoli's argument (that "[t]he editor of a critical edition is not compelled to retain a factual error because it derives from an authoritative document" [quoted in Worthen 1994: 12]) and defends the right of an author of imaginative fiction to be wrong about external fact.

These adjustments exemplify the general problem of the truth claims of literature, at issue since Plato's *Ion* and *Republic*, book 10, and Aristotle's resuscitation of poetry as more philosophical or general than history. As Mario Valdes notes, the sort of "fit" between external and internal demanded by Bowers and Bruccoli would be incomprehensible to analytical philosophy, which argues "that the imaginative experience is non-falsifiable and also non-verifiable; therefore, it is not a truth-claim, for verifiability requires the possibility of confirmation, and thus, since any claim to truth on my own terms must be simultaneously a rejection of falsehood, the imaginative construct is neither true nor false" (Valdes 1992: 16–17). For Valdes, the literary "truth-claim is always a relationship between the text and the reader," and truth in literature is "primarily a matter of the action of appropriation, which at all times calls for judgement" (19). Bowers and Bruccoli, in contrast, attempt to adjudicate the action of appropriation while adhering to a "correspondence" theory of literature, in which "[w]hat is expressed must in some sense conform to what is actually the case" (T. M. Greene, *The Arts and Art Criticism* [1940]; quoted in Valdes 1992: 18). To appropriate the evidence of external phenomena, such as the location of Central Park, is proper to "realist" textual critics and invalid to Worthen and Valdes.

The choice of what to appropriate and why is fairly clear in such circumstances, but only if the external evidence does not contradict the rival internal truth claims of the literary work being edited. External evidence suggesting that Keats wanted to correct his historical error by substituting "Balboa" for "Cortez" would contradict internal evidence—Sherbo's symptoms of style—since the emended line would barely scan. David C. Fowler responds to the same kind of contradiction in the Kane-Donaldson *Piers* when he rejects the edition's metrical regularity, which the editors impose even when there is no documentary evidence for it. Fowler asserts that the author's comment on the issue would have been, "It may not alliterate, but it's true!" (Fowler 1977: 32).

The problems with which textual critics grapple—truth, accuracy, and the fit between textual testimony and a constative reality—are central to current epistemological and ontological concerns. Researchers in scientific, social, and humanistic areas of contemporary study ask the same type and range of questions as practicing textuists, bibliographers, and editors. What kind of thing is this concept or episteme called "text," and how can its properties and its history be known? Can there be any universal standards of testamentary authority, from within or without the text, to which all researchers can appeal—an abstract, general, and replicable Galilean description and formulation of the laws of textuality? How is internal evidence to be distinguished from external evidence, direct from indirect, conclusive from circumstantial, primary from secondary, as the probity, authority, and reliability of a text are explored? Is the construction of a narrative of cause and effect (or motive and action) necessary for the disparate elements of evidence to be established and connected, and would the presence of gaps in this narrative vitiate its evidentiary status? Would such a narrative inevitably be the product of the narrator's technical characteristics, idiosyncrasies, and resources, and could procedural constraints account for these influences? Does the observation and examination of one type of evidence affect or predetermine the results obtained from measuring other types? Does the body of evidence have to be of a certain size—or be "complete"—to be susceptible to a single evaluation? In a quantum universe, is Newton's fourth rule of reasoning, on the counterexample, still valid? Or are human subjects in the twenty-first century left only with Morelli's flourish: the datum or act without meaning or made without volition—inscrutable, as it always was and always may be?

These are real, substantive questions, not rhetorical ones. The relations between substance and accident, whole and part, truth and accuracy, cause and effect have been called into question with renewed urgency by the postmodernist dispersal of form, authority, and essentialism. If Jameson's "blank parody," or pastiche, in which all such relations are indeterminate, is the presiding figure for the postmodern ethic, then the attitudes in textual study toward evidence may enact and display this ethic with particular resonance.

FIVE

Facts, Truefacts, Factoids; or, Why Are They Still Saying Those Things about Epistemology?[1]

Epistemology still looks classy to weak textualists.

RICHARD RORTY

Vulgar pragmatism [is] an unedifying prospect. . . . There could be no honest intellectual work in Rorty's post-epistemological utopia.

SUSAN HAACK

Those are pretty nasty things to say. On the one hand, who would want to be thought of as a "weak" textualist and therefore be accused of thinking good things about epistemology because of failing to be a "strong" textualist?[2] On the other, who would want to be a "vulgar" pragmatist advocat-

---

1. This essay is complementary to my earlier study "Textual Forensics" (Greetham 1996e), which was presented in a revised form in the previous chapter of this book. In that study, I argue that textual scholarship, having no definable *Fach*, or subject matter, is an exemplary postmodernist anti-discipline and can serve as a site for testing the epistemological assumptions and protocols of the debate over the status of evidence and the nature of proof. Since text is authority and original and yet also network and tissue, and since forensics encompasses both hard physical facts and the rhetorical formulation that gives such data interpretive meaning, a textual forensics will codify and test the interaction of the phenomenological world and the hermeneutic analysis of its evidence. With procedural and conceptual links both to scientific empiricism and to rhetorical strategies for persuasion, textual scholarship becomes a vehicle for anatomizing the postmodernist breakdown of the master narratives, including that of evidence and proof.

2. According to Rorty's prescription, contemporary textualists of both stripes have in common with nineteenth-century idealists "an opposition to the claim of science to be a

ing a cynical and hypocritical post-epistemology in which there was only "dishonest" work to be done?[3] The battle lines between pragmatists and epistemologists are polemically if not substantively well defined: Rorty

---

paradigm of human activity" (1982: 141). The difference between idealism and textualism is that the former is "a philosophical doctrine" and the latter "an expression of suspicion about philosophy" (ibid.). Within the textualist camp, the weak variety, represented by conservative critics like M. H. Abrams (especially in his opposition to what he calls "Newreaders"), "thinks that there really is a secret code [to literature] and that once it's discovered we shall have gotten the text right. [The weak textualist] believes that criticism is discovery rather than creation" (152); the strong textualist, however, represented by postmodernist and poststructuralist critics, "doesn't care about the distinction between discovery and creation, finding and making" (ibid.). The humanistic critic of the Abrams type puts faith in a "large, overarching, communal vocabulary" through which literary texts can be given a grounded, definitive, and permanent signification, whereas the "strong misreader" of poststructuralism is a full pragmatist "with his own vocabulary" that is contingent and idiosyncratic. The strong textualists are full pragmatists because they reject universalist decoding and the privilege accorded literary expression, arguing that "there is no interesting difference between tables and texts, between protons and poems" (153), whereas the weak textualist is a "victim of realism," of the "metaphysics of presence," so that, despite an avowed humanistic resistance to science, the weak textualist is imitating science, or at least the empirical science of positivism and probity—in other words, the science of hard evidence and direct demonstrability.

3. As part of her general brief to promote "foundherentism," Haack rejects both Rorty's argument for an "edifying" rather than an "epistemological" philosophy and "the fashionable thesis that different cultures or communities have widely divergent standards of evidence" (1993: 6). Her conflated concept of "foundherentism" (foundationalism + coherentism) is "neither purely causal nor purely logical in content, but a double aspect theory, partly causal and partly evaluative; and essentially gradational" (2). But while Haack obviously wants to bestow a "sweet reasonableness" upon foundherentism, rather than throwing out the whole epistemological package as Rorty does, her adoption of the crossword puzzle rather than the mathematical proof is nonetheless put in service of "the true structure of relations of evidential support" (ibid.), thereby begging several questions about truth, structure, evidence, and support. Thus, her apparently moderate argument for the gradational ("there may be no intuitively satisfactory analysis of knowledge to be had, no sharp line to be drawn between cases where a subject does, and cases where he doesn't, know" [7]) sounds somewhat like Rorty's mandate for "replacing *confrontation* with *conversation*" (see Haack 1993: 183). Finally, the concessive tone is a rhetorical gesture which falls before her insistence that "the foundherentist criteria *are* truth-indicative" and that "the poverty of . . . post-epistemological utopias indicates just how indispensable epistemology really is" (6). Even after distancing herself from such foundationalist positions as "epistemic objectivism" (190)—that form of epistemology most common among analytical and descriptive bibliographers—Haack is passionate (and polemical) in her defense of "the legitimacy of epistemology" (189) against the "relativist and cynical" (193) and "incoherent" (194) conversationalism of Rorty. Dismissing Rorty's thesis of the "contingency" of language and the "conventional" nature of evidentiary justification (see Rorty 1989), Haack finds that Rorty's new definition of the "ironist" as one who denies any objective choice between philosophical vocabularies is "thoroughly misleading; Rorty's ironist is no fallibilist, he is a cynic hiding behind a euphemism" (Haack 1993: 194).

looks disdainfully on those who "think that by viewing a poet as having an epistemology they are paying him a compliment" and is scornful of the "tendency to think that literature can take the place of philosophy by *mimicking* philosophy—by being, of all things, *epistemological*" (Rorty 1982: 156). Giving no quarter, Haack describes Rorty's "dichotomy" between the "irrealist" and the "grandly transcendental" options as "grossly false,"[4] and sternly advises that her own epistemological typology will "enable us to struggle free of the wool Rorty is trying to pull over our eyes" (Haack 1993: 189). Noting that, although a couple of chapters in Rorty's *Philosophy and the Mirror of Nature* (1979) have "truth" in their titles but "*there is no entry under 'truth' in the index!*" (italics and exclamation mark in original), Haack tartly observes, "Rorty is, I take it, letting us know the importance he attaches to the concept" (188).

Apart from the obvious conclusion that an intellectual disagreement often seems to take on the attributes of a moral crusade against unbelievers (a condition documentable in the trade of textual criticism and editing from St. Jerome down to John Kidd and the continued battle between G. Thomas Tanselle and Jerome J. McGann [see, for example, Tanselle's 2001 attack on McGann 1997]),[5] what can these exchanges between the pragmatists and epistemologists tell us about the state of text as a pragmatic or epistemological object, and what can the battle between the philosophers tell us about such concepts as textual "truth," "fact," "proof," and "evidence"? This is a wide-ranging charge for an essay on evidence and

---

4. Haack claims that Rorty distorts the "gradational" range of epistemology by reducing it to simple "FOUNDATIONALISM" (1993: 188; scare caps in original). By endorsing the "irrealist" conception of truth as purely rhetorical and contingent ("what you can defend against all comers"), Rorty has, according to Haack, omitted at least three intermediate states of epistemology: the "pragmatist," the "redundancy" and "semantic" varieties of "minimally realist" epistemology," and the "strongly minimalist." The specific definitions of these intermediates are less significant than Haack's charge that Rorty has misrepresented the choices: "[d]eclining the irrealist option does not oblige us to go grandly transcendental" (1993: 189).

5. Jerome was as passionate in his textual ideology as he was in his theology, and the tradition of holy war continued in such major confrontations as John Kidd's polemics against the edition of Joyce's *Ulysses* by Hans Walter Gabler (see, for example, Kidd 1985, 1988a, 1988b; and Gabler's responses 1985, 1991, 1993; and see my coverage of these "Joyce wars" and the similar "Lawrence wars" in Greetham 2010). Tanselle's rhetorical style against McGann is typified by such language as "[a]fter this unfortunate beginning, McGann weakens his essay further with another fallacious piece of theorizing" (2001: 38), on McGann's "Rationale" (1997).

contamination, and will necessitate my moving from legal terminology to particle physics to mathematics to biblical hermeneutics and, eventually, to *Monty Python and the Holy Grail;* but the narrative and the journey will, I hope, be illuminating for the reader encountering the other specific examples of contamination in the rest of this volume.

To begin, take my ex-wife, who unwittingly provided the first part of my title, or more properly, take her dialectics as a very successful litigation lawyer in a high-powered mergers and acquisitions firm. Trained in, or at least familiar with, the Abelardian dialectic of *sic et non*,[6] I was quite prepared for the adversarial rhetoric of litigation when she became a lawyer ("them" and "us"), but not for the specific, and subtle, vocabulary in which its polarities of "truth" and "error" were represented. If memory serves, my ex informed me that there were degrees of truth (and thus of the "facts" whereby truth could be accommodated): (1) raw *facts* were the common ground of the dialectic, the *données* of evidentiary materials, and could thus be appropriated by both sides in a lawsuit; (2) on one side of this common ground were the *truefacts* of one's own case, those facts that had been appropriated by only one party in the dialectic and had thereby not lost some of their probity by no longer being "common knowledge," but on the contrary, had acquired a new level of revealed truth by being frankly partisan, and thus *more* true than mere facts; (3) and on the other side were the lowly *factoids* of the opposing team, those evidentiary fragments and pieces of rhetoric that would have had the potential to become facts or even truefacts if accepted by one's side, but, lacking such espousal, were only latent and incipient rather than manifest and fulfilled. *Facts, truefacts,* and *factoids* thus cumulatively spanned the range of forensic epistemology, and, like signifiers in a structuralist linguistic analysis, had no constative or determinative link to a fixed external reality but depended on their relative *position* in the rhetorical arrangement to achieve their meaning. As we shall see, the dialectic of jurisprudence, particularly as it relates to probity, guilt, and witnessing to the truth, is one of the most powerful imported discourses in the conduct of textual theory and practice, and it is thus quite appropriate that the shifting designation of *fact* in the courtroom should be similarly slippery.

---

6. For a consideration of medieval dialectic, and specifically *sic et non* as it relates to textual theory, see "The Philosophical Discourse of [Textuality]?" in this volume.

Or take the hopes once placed on the eighty-six-kilometer supercon-ducting super collider (SSC) to have been built in Waxahachie, Texas, at a cost of $11 billion, before it was canceled by Congress in a budget cut. The cancellation provoked something of a crisis among particle physicists, and it remains to be seen whether the construction and operation of the even larger CERN supercollider under the Alps will mitigate that crisis (or provoke another one by destroying all matter). In a survey of the original crisis in 1993, John Horgan (1994) describes two conflicting current views among physicists on the value, and practical plausibility, of empirical evidence in the formulation of scientific theory. On the one hand, there are those like Leon M. Lederman of the Illinois Institute of Technology, who claim that without the evidence provided by the Waxahachie SSC, the field of particle physics—and with it cosmology—"may come to an end" (quoted in Horgan 1994: 98). Lederman is supported by Sidney R. Coleman of Harvard (a respected theoretician of such concepts as parallel universes and wormholes), who, despite his theoretical leanings, nonethe-less believes that "[e]xperiment is the source of scientific imagination. All the philosophers in the world thinking for thousands of years couldn't come up with quantum mechanics" (quoted in Horgan 1994: 105). On the other hand, Howard Georgi of Harvard contends that *no* possible experi-ment could prove or disprove a grand unified field theory, providing only "circumstantial evidence" at best: "We've been spoiled over the past few decades, because you get not just one [datum confirming a theory] but many, so you really know you're right. Now I'm afraid we're going to have to be satisfied with data that convince only those who were already con-vinced" (quoted in Horgan 1994: 106). Georgi does have a practical point: an SSC capable of proving a unified field theory of quantum gravity would have to be 1,000 light-years in circumference (in other words, very much larger than the entire solar system, with its circumference of a mere light-day, making even Texas look puny). And so John Ellis of CERN concedes, "I think we will be looking at only indirect evidence" (quoted in Horgan 1994: 98) of unification with or without the Texas SSC and its progeny.

Or take the pursuit of π. Irrational, because it cannot be represented in a single fraction ($22/7$ is merely an approximation), and transcenden-tal, because it cannot be represented in a finite algebraic form. Given these metaphysical properties, π should long ago have ceased to be of much meaningful significance to empirical investigation. That is, we know quite enough about the useful properties of π without having to tame it by describing it in full. But this cognitive compromise shows no signs of occurring, as supercomputers have enabled us to push the empirical envelope ever further, with the record as of August 2009 standing at 2,576,980,377,524 decimal places, established on a T2K Open Supercomputer. Why? What can we possibly need to know about π that is not already usefully available to us? Or, as Alexander Masters (1997: 28) put it in reviewing David Blatner's *The Joy of Pi* (1997):

> [T]he race to find the exact value of π has got out of hand. . . . [W]hat is it one is looking for among the billions? Even in the most pernickety areas of quantum physics, fifteen digits is more than enough accuracy, and thirty places is sufficient to calculate the circumference of the universe to within a microscopic fraction of an inch. Are the computer scientists simply chasing after size, or are they, like modern-day ancients, still hoping that π will suddenly give up its universal mystery and become an ordinary number?

Granting Masters's pointing out the ironies, the answer to his question is contained in Blatner's history of π (and in Masters's own review): the goal of squaring the circle, for which π is an essential element, was to the ancients the formal challenge of conflating the universal and natural (the perfect circle) with the contingent and human (the square): in other words, the most comprehensive form of contamination at the base of human knowledge. So of course π began to achieve both metaphysical and empirical properties, properties that reinforced each other as the process of extending the empirical reach of π along the line of decimal places confirmed its irrationality and transcendence. The answer to Masters's question is thus not the usual empiricist Everest trope of "because it is there"; rather, it is the deconstructive aporia or Schrödinger's cat trope of "because it is there *and* because it is not there": there in theory (*and* in mundane, workaday practice) but not there in perfected demonstration. And what is even more challenging, or galling, to the empiricist exercise is that, unlike the paradox of Zeno's arrow, we can never even tell how close we are to arriving at that final point of completion and rest.[7]

---

7. This problem of the law of diminishing returns, or more correctly, the law of not *knowing* whether returns are diminishing, has become a staple even among conservative bibliographers and textuists. In the roundtable discussion opening the special issue of *PMLA* on the status of evidence, David Vander Meulen, editor of *Studies in Bibliography* and an analytical and descriptive bibliographer of impeccable positivist and empirical credentials, notes:

Or take the hermeneutic intertextuality of biblical commentary, and the shifting definitions of textual (and bibliographical) "proof," "evidence," and "probity." The manipulation or construction of evidence in sacred texts has a long and necessarily tortuous and contradictory history: the evidence is massaged to suit the requirements of the current ideological or theological context. Thus, the range of attributes that God assumes in Exodus 34:6–7 becomes a rich trove from which later biblical authors will draw differing evidence. On Mount Sinai, God provides Moses not only with the commandments of the covenant but also with a perplexing self-portrait: "The Lord, the Lord God, merciful and gracious, long-suffering, and abundant in goodness and truth, keeping mercy for thousands, forgiving iniquity and transgressions and sin, and that will by no means clear the guilty; visiting the iniquity of the fathers upon the children, and upon the children's children, unto the third and fourth generation." We do not have to wait for later patristic commentary or even for the fulfillment of the Old Testament text in the New to expose the aporia; it is already there in the Hebrew Bible itself, for Nahum's celebratory polemic against Nineveh cites the passage from Exodus, but only those parts emphasizing God's wrath and jealousy ("God is jealous, and the Lord revengeth," etc.; Nahum 1:2–3), whereas Joel, in a call for repentance, similarly selects from the Exodus attributes but this time *omits* all reference to the wrath of God in favor of his mercy ("for he is gracious

---

The question . . . is whether we have enough evidence. I think of it especially—though not exclusively—from the point of view of analytical bibliography, which is chiefly inductive. First of all, the answer would seem to be that the amount of evidence required depends on the goal we have. But if we proceed inductively, we probably never will have access to all the particulars that constitute the full range of evidence, and we will always fall short of fully substantiating our generalizations. . . . we can never fully demonstrate a hypothesis; we simply make better and better attempts as we go along. (1996: 31)

Similarly, G. Thomas Tanselle, bearing even more impressive empiricist authority, confronts the Aristotelian concretion of the vehicles of text in relation to the putative Platonic forms behind them, and nostalgically affirms:

Verbal works, being immaterial, cannot be damaged as a painting or sculpture can; but we shall never know with certainty what their undamaged forms consist of. . . . Textual criticism cannot enable us to construct final answers to textual questions, but it can teach us how to ask the questions in a way that does justice to the capabilities of the mind. (1989: 93)

I discuss the concept of "complete" evidence in the chapter on "Textual Forensics."

and merciful," etc.; Joel 2:13), and even adds a phrase, "repenteth him of the evil." Were Nahum and Joel committing conscious misprisions (to different ends) on the text of Exodus? Or was the misprision already there in the Exodus text, which in its rich and logically inconsistent imbalances demonstrates "the indeterminacy of language, the fallacy of objectivity, the propensity for multiple meanings and the desire to negotiate meanings," as Phyllis Trible (1997: 8) put it in reviewing this and other passages of textual (re)construction and co-option covered in James L. Kugel's *The Bible as It Was* (1997)? Trible quite properly draws an analogy between the misprisions recorded in Kugel's book and the activities of deconstructive textualism, but just as properly notes that, despite such evident contradictions, the Bible could still be regarded in premodern criticism as "perfect and harmonious," while also being "cryptic" (8). Kugel's charge is rather to show how the apparent discontinuities are part of a coherent, or at least comprehensive, attempt to bestow meaning on the ellipses and textual enharmonics or discordancies of the Bible, even to the point of rescripting the syntax when a received reading jarred against the necessary meaning of a passage for a later cultural context, as in the textual revision that managed to argue that Jacob did not actually *lie* to Isaac about Esau; he was misquoted![8]

But a more active bibliographical misprision was surely at work in some of the evidentiary protocols with which Erasmus was faced in his edition of the New Testament. Thus, when he went to the (Latin) Vulgate to provide the basis for a Greek translation for the missing last leaf of Revelation for his Greek New Testament text, he reversed the evidentiary (primary/secondary) status of the two languages. As Bruce Metzger aptly noted in his evaluation of this reversal of evidence: "As would be expected from such a procedure, here and there in Erasmus' self-made Greek text are readings which have never been found in any known Greek manuscript—but which are still perpetuated today in printings of the so-called Textus Receptus of the Greek New Testament" (1992: 100). The most

---

8. Kugel shows how the image of Jacob as a liar and cheat became unacceptable for the founder of Israel, and how, to secure a more appropriate reading of the famous birthright scene, the commentators repunctuated the text to produce a different syntax. According to this repointing, Isaac did not say, "Who are you, my son?" but "Who are you? My son?" so that Jacob could correctly respond, "I am. [But] Esau is your first born" rather than "I am Esau, your first born" (see Trible 1997: 7).

notorious of Erasmus's Greek inventions is undoubtedly the Comma Jo-
hanneum, the Trinitarian statement in 1 John 7–8 (King James Version),
which was lacking in all Greek manuscripts. This evidentiary omission,
which Erasmus had promised to rectify if a Greek attestation could be
found, was "corrected" by a Greek manuscript (probably written to order,
about 1520) by a Franciscan friar, who, like Erasmus in Revelation, supplied the missing Greek phrase—with all its ideological freight—from
Jerome's Latin Vulgate. Erasmus dutifully honored his promise and in-
serted the spurious passage into his third edition of 1522, albeit with an
editorial note recording his suspicion that the Greek manuscript had been
specially manufactured to supply this very reading (Metzger 1992: 101).

All of these cautionary tales, from the jargon of mergers and acquisitions litigation to particle physics to experimental versus practical mathematics to the gaps and miraculous inventions of biblical commentary, are
based on a conflict between the empirical and the evidentiary, or rather,
on a contamination of the interests of the two. They all involve problems
in the status and role of evidence, in the relation of evidence to probity,
and in the cultural requirements of demonstration. Whether Rorty ap-
proves or not, they are all problems in the perceived role of contemporary
epistemology, the examination of the process whereby we *know* things.

Various aspects of these concerns with documentary, historical, technical, and scientific evidence—and its translation into proof—will appear
in this chapter, but the issue with the greatest ramifications for textual
study is probably that which is the most contentious element in Horgan's
survey of the crisis of confidence: the suspicion by some physicists (and
bibliographers and logicians cum epistemologists)[9] that a certain type of

---

9. Thus, Haack (1996: 230) argues that because "truth does not come in degrees," such
an eminently practical, but classically untenable, concept as *fuzzy logic* "is not properly
describable as a 'logic'" at all, for it is not "an attempt to represent truth-preserving inferences" (231). Resisting the claims of its apologists that "we should prefer to change our logic
to cope with vagueness rather than to regiment informal discourse and continue to rely on
formal logic" (237), Haack very deliberately consigns fuzzy logic to an extradisciplinary
position, just as Fredson Bowers has argued that the sort of bibliographical work done by Jerome McGann is not "real" bibliography (or textual criticism): confronting the sort of "documentary evidence" (of book production and reception) that McGann typically includes in
his purview of bibliography, Bowers asserts that "this is the language of literary criticism . . .
not of strict textual criticism, and certainly not of that applied form of textual criticism that
we may call editorial theory" (1988: 7–8).

research, especially that extending or interrogating the former boundaries of the discipline of physics (or logic or bibliography), is "not even physics, because it is so divorced from any experimentally accessible phenomena" (Horgan 1994: 103). For example, both black holes (which by their very nature should destroy the evidence of their own existence—with a "permanent loss of information" [102]) and superstring theory (whereby "different observers can have different pictures" [103] of the physical past) would, to such critics, seem to flirt dangerously with subjectivism and personal relativism. The work cannot be proven on the pulses (or at least, not in the laboratory)—just as some new forms of logic (fuzzy logic, deviant logic) do not comport with the requirements of classical logic and just as some new varieties of textual study do not seem susceptible to the sort of empirical demonstration traditionally associated with Anglo-American bibliography.[10]

Because the terminology of textual scholarship is derivative and co-optive (from such fields as science and philosophy), and because it inherits its evidentiary status not just from the scientific model of the natural sciences, but from other arenas of evidence and proof, particularly jurisprudence and criminology, it participates in, even emblematizes, the postmodernist crisis of demonstrability and probity characterizing

---

10. For example, John Sutherland (1988) finds that the anecdotal (i.e., New Historicist) bibliographical evidence typically cited by Robert Darnton to support large theses about book history in the Enlightenment is too narrow and too speculative: "a single example is made to bear an inordinate load of general significance" (578). Sutherland is disturbed by the lack of "intellectual controls" in this anecdotal method, for it is not clear that "Darnton's single 'cas' is 'typique' or whether it is as eccentric as single cases are prone to be," and he finds that there is therefore a "surprising disparity between the titles of Darnton's works and their actual content." Thus, "*The Business of the Enlightenment: A History of the Encyclopédie, 1775–1800* turns out to be a history of one reprint edition of Diderot's work. 'Readers Respond to Rousseau: The Fabrication of Romantic Sensitivity' turns out to be (essentially) one reader's response" (ibid.). Sutherland's unease over the necessary range and completeness of a body of evidence (and its putative foundation on independently verifiable data) can prove to be a major issue in the forensic codes of contemporary textual criticism, just as it can in particle physics. The quality of evidence may be (as we have seen in David Vander Meulen's concerns, see n. 7 above) directly related to the goal of a specific enterprise; thus, for Darnton's New Historicist, anecdotal method, the individual "cas" may not have to be "typique"—indeed, its very idiosyncrasy may be its main value. Haack considers this issue in terms of the variable questions the researcher may ask of the evidence, and argues that "the question: what counts as better or worse evidence for believing something? seems both deeper and more important than the question: supposing that what one believes is true, how good does one's evidence have to be before one can count as knowing?" (1993: 7).

so many areas of current epistemological activity. Thus, in sharing the rhetoric of jurisprudence and criminalistics, textual study turns documents into "witnesses" ("sincere" or "untrustworthy") that might offer "testimony" to the "probity" of a text's transmission. In the genealogical or stemmatic method still commonly used in both classical and vernacular traditions to determine the relative authority of such witnesses—their position on a family tree of descent—a witness that relies entirely on the evidence of another which was closer to the scene of the action (the crime or the composition) is dismissed as having no independent authority (see the chapter on witness, proof, and genealogy: "Phylum-Tree-Rhizome"). Witnesses and testimony in both law and textual criticism are to be "weighed, not counted"; they may be seen to establish or refute the probity of the testimony they present; and other formulaic analogies are common between the two disciplines.[11] Indeed, the current crises in both juridical/criminological and textual forensics[12] respond to similar interrogations of the disputable value of evidence as it bears directly and unambiguously on a desired conclusion: innocence or guilt, authenticity or corruption. In both disciplines, presumptive evidence formerly had self-evident credentials, as long as it could be shown to reflect the formula of "scientifically accepted knowledge." Under current evidentiary rules, the admissibility of forensic evidence will, in both fields, depend on a demonstrable *interpretive* strategy, a rhetorical or hermeneutic connection between the apparently free-standing empirical data and the very

---

11. In his study of the editing of *Piers Plowman*, Robert Adams (1992) continually makes correlations between textual criticism and jurisprudence, for example, "in editing as in law it seems essential that we decide in which direction we will err—either by convicting some of the innocent or by letting some of the guilty go free" (63); editors "treat these witnesses . . . as guilty until proved innocent" (34); "to have done otherwise would have been to tamper with the jury of his own mind by introducing inadmissable [*sic*] evidence" (48). And this analogy is sustained in Adams's account by a constant allusion to evidence, attestation, motive, and the "burden of proof" (35, 47n24).

12. See, for example, Deforest (1983), Roberts (1989), Saferstein (1997). The general shift noted in all three of these basic textbooks is that criminalistics has moved from a reliance on the hard facts of the forensic laboratory to an incorporation of this evidence into the general rhetorical structure and tenor of the presentation (thereby reverting to the original, argumentational meaning of *forensic*, from which the specialized meaning of scientific and objective evidence was a derivative). I am grateful to my colleague James P. Levine, of the doctoral program in criminal justice, for having drawn this shift, and these particular texts, to my attention.

characterization of authenticity. As Stephen Orgel puts it in the *PMLA* roundtable discussion on the status of evidence: "evidence isn't evidence unless it's a part of an argument. Evidence isn't any different from what it is evidence of; that is to say, both of them have to be read and interpreted. . . . You see, even facts have the same kinds of problematic status" (see 1996: 22n7).

At the roundtable, there was some unease about Orgel's incorporation of fact (via the protocols of evidence) into the hermeneutics of rhetoric (Heather Dubrow cautioned that Orgel was "implying no truth value at all to the notion of evidence" [22]), for such a formulation as Orgel's would seem to limit severely any claims to a *grounded* demonstrability of textual reality that did not depend upon the forensic context in which it was presented and received. In other words, Orgel's formulation is, for bibliographical and textual evidence, the same acknowledgment of the "interpretive community" endorsed by Rorty for (defective) epistemology, and rejected by the more conservative, or nostalgic, Haack.[13]

The interpretive and evidentiary problems pointed to in Orgel's (and my ex-wife's) redefinition of *fact* are well illustrated in the famous case of the supposedly displaced chapter in James's *The Ambassadors*. As I noted in "Textual Forensics" (1996e and in this volume), Jerome McGann (1992) has argued that it is very much a question of the receptional moment in which the evidence is perceived and interpreted that the epistemological (and therefore the critical) meaning of the problem of *order* must be confronted. The metahistorical "facts" are more or less as follows: the current received reading of the fact that the first English and the first

---

13. Unlike Rorty's view of the contingent nature of truth and logic, Haack articulates the classical concept of logic as "the most basic, the most general, of theories" (1996: 91). "[M]athematics is to be reduced to logic, and the epistemological value of the programme lies in the presumed *fundamental* nature of the latter" (ibid.). Clearly, if classical logic is somehow to be grounded in universal truth relations independent of their context or usage, then such "deviant" logics as fuzzy logic are unacceptable. Denying L. A. Zadeh's claim that "true" and "false" are vague determinants and lack such firm epistemological value, Haack finds that the "second stage of fuzzification . . . a family of systems in which the indenumerably many values of the base logic are superseded by denumerably many fuzzy truth values, *true, false, very true, fairly true, not very true*, etc.," is inadequate to formal logic because it is "not well-motivated" (i.e., if truth does not come in degrees, then "fuzzy truth values" must arise out of semantic and "illogical" error; Haack 1996: xi).

American editions (1904) had two chapters in different orders is (a) that the two orderings were not even noticed until 1949 (i.e., the "phenomena" did not yet exist as usable bibliographical "evidence"); and (b) that the order in the American edition was a printer's error. McGann argues that this current received bibliographical reading is itself an error: using both external evidence (James's correspondence with Mrs. Humphry Ward concerning a "fearful though much patched over fault or weakness . . . which no one has noticed") and internal evidence ("the novel's internal problems, its fictional chronology" [1992: 103]), McGann demonstrates not only that the rule of *durior* (or *difficilior*) *lectio* would sanction the "more difficult" and therefore the more authorial reading—the supposedly faulty American edition—but McGann also claims that the sudden awareness of apparent error in Robert Young's 1949 "detection" of error "arose because he read the order of the fictional events as symmetrical with the order of textual presentation" (104). That is, Young noticed what seemed to be a disjunct between the evidence derivable from the constative referential reality *outside* the fiction and the depiction of that reality within the fiction. Reversing the chapter orders (or rather, accepting the English order as correct and the American as erroneous) made an *easy* rather than a *difficult* fit between internal and external (just as the famous Bradshaw shift in *The Canterbury Tales* moved six of the tales—group B2—to a position earlier in the pilgrimage because of a difficult, or constatively inconsistent, reference to place names on the journey). Like most modern editors of Chaucer, who reject the shift, McGann prefers to read the order of *The Ambassadors* as difficult.

In placing this sort of historical evidence (and the criticism, even the awareness, of the evidence) under the purview of receptional rhetoric, McGann uses the "rhetorical event" as the distinguishing mark of historical criticism, as opposed to hermeneutics (which he defines as "a method for elucidating symbolic forms" [1992: 167]). While I agree that textual historicism is indeed rhetorical and dialogical (as does Gary Taylor [1988: 53]: "the fact did not change; we just saw it differently. Or rather, the problem did not change; but we phrased it differently" and "[t]extual criticism is about rhetoric, rhetoric is about persuasion, persuasion is about audiences" [47]), I am not completely convinced that McGann's dialectic of historical criticism/rhetoric versus hermeneutics/symbolic form will hold. His prime example of the object of historical criticism and rhetoric is "an act of language [which] . . . we could also call a word" (1992: 167); but surely, by such variant models as Saussure's, Peirce's, or Chomsky's, "language" is the very emblem of symbolic form, as well as a focus for rhetorical analysis. Moreover, I would contend that the "bibliographical channels of communication" that McGann quite properly regards as "part of the message of the texts we study" can (and do) "impinge upon [the work's] symbolic form" (167), but that if they do, then the "bibliographical codes" are just as hermeneutic—and symbolic—as are the words of texts in the task of providing evidence for meaning. When Ben Jonson was upbraided for publishing his *Works* (i.e., plays) in the magisterial format of folio formerly reserved for philosophy, theology, or "serious" (i.e., classical) literature—instead of in the vernacular, more ephemeral medium of quarto—and when he simultaneously rewrote those "plays" to turn them into "literature," he was consciously playing on the symbolic form of the "mode of production" (McGann 1992: 167) and on the bibliographical codes, to construct simultaneously and through the same evidentiary device a different hermeneutics (i.e., "elucidation of symbolic forms") *and* a different rhetoric. I see the two concepts as reinforcing rather than contradicting each other, not only in Jonson but in each (and that means *every*) case where, as McGann insists, "reading must cover the entirety of the literary work, its bibliographical as well as its linguistic codes" (168). Going yet further than Orgel, I would suggest that the hard physical "facts" from which evidence may be drawn will very likely already have rhetoric embedded in them, a rhetoric of forensics, and that this is particularly the case where these facts are bibliographical, and therefore betray various levels of human motivation, intervention, and contamination.

Moving through the medieval trivium, if rhetoric is a sine qua non for the study of evidence, what of the logic that is supposed to present it in its constative relations? And what particularly of that form of logic that Rorty sees as a modernist, Romantic elevation of epistemology to a grounded evidentiary and procedural status *outside* the sublunary objects of its contemplation? Can we, as Haack would have it, still take faith in logic as a secure, timeless, ineffable, and unchangeable modality unaffected by communities, interpretive or otherwise? (see Haack 1993: n. 14). Or, as Rorty argues, is logic in the "classical" (i.e., "modern") sense just another pragmatic construct that depends on its manipulators and receivers for its efficacy?[14] The witch trial scene from *Monty Python and the Holy Grail* will offer as "final" a statement on this problem as we can hope for, but for the moment, let us turn to that form of forensic logic that treats texts as structural arrangements to be decoded through a trained awareness of the logical necessities of *form*. What textual evidence may confirm or disrupt the logical analysis that the Holmesian semiotician (see "Textual Forensics") is supposed to bring to the critique of narrative? This sounds like an Aristotelian question, and it is, if we regard structuralist and formal logic as a means (via such devices as the syllogism) to confer order on disorder and to give us a firm sense of the true shape of those rhetorical events called texts as they cohere into a totalized utterance: for Aristotle, or at least that part of Aristotle's *Poetics* that survives, this rhetorical event is, of course, the genre of tragedy.

And again, let us approach this question via the modern versus the medieval. Was Peter Ramus right when, in his famous oration of 1546, he declared that not only had contemporary learning overcome the Scholastics' dependence on Aristotle, but that all the major classical authors were now being read in good editions instead of in the inherently corrupt medieval compilations? Leaving aside the fundamental aporia of Ramus's claim for textuality (early modern critical editing was in many ways an exemplification of Aristotelian formalism, though admittedly often operating under the transcendental dictates of Platonic idealism), the documentary evidence on which these new reliable editions were based was, of course, the "corrupt," "fragmentary," "unreliable" medieval manuscript tradition. There were no Homer or Virgil autographs, and the documentary *remaniements* of classical culture dating from *before* the Carolingian and the twelfth-century Renaissances are, well, corrupt, fragmentary, and unreliable. So Ramus, as a good modernist, does not recognize the hermeneutic and procedural double bind in which he has placed "modernist" textuality. It is still "medieval" in the sense that it still plays by the rules of the detective novel: given enough information,

---

14. The apparent paradox is that, while classical logic does indeed derive from Aristotle, the positivist epistemology that Rorty sees as untenable is a distinctly modern (i.e., Enlightenment) view, fulfilling the empiricist credo of seventeenth-century experimental science. See the chapter "The Philosophical Discourse of [Textuality]?" for a further analysis of the textual significance of this modern dispensation.

we should be able to construct a "meaning-ful" relation between *signum* and *res* in that totalizing experiential mode that is the natural, physical universe: the *text* as textile, or as woven figure in the carpet. But unlike the dialectic of Abelard's *sic et non* (yes *and* no, not yes *or* no), modernist textuality from Ramus and Bacon and the Royal Society to the "Age of Reason," the Enlightenment, and the modernism of the early and mid-twentieth century, has in general not been able to accept that textual *revelation*, the detective novel scene in the drawing room of the country house, the clarifying and totally satisfactory tying up of the strands of the woven narrative, is forever deferred, delayed, and, well, again, corrupt, fragmentary, and unreliable, because raw empiricism based on human faculties can never know whether it has reached the real end of the story. We may think we are at the end, but we may be really still in the middle, or maybe even at the beginning. Just as Oedipus thinks he has understanding of the text of his own life when Jocasta assures him that her own son was killed or, more pointedly, when Hercule Poirot's enthusiastic assistant confidently asserts, "He [or she] did it!" at the end of each and every interview with the suspects in *Murder on the Orient Express,* a player in the game of textuality—and like it or not, all textual scholars and detectives are players—will never see that reassuring, though annoying, message on the video game screen: "GAME OVER."

The reason that we turn to the detective, the private eye, and to the novelist and/or to God or the forensics laboratory or the textual editor for reassurance is that we feel that they ought to be somehow above and beyond the game, and will therefore really know when it's OVER. The technical device of dramatic irony can even give us, as observers of the game, this excruciatingly painful assurance of authority outside the internal logic of any of the apparent players *because* we already know the story—or think we do. For just as authors like John Fowles (in *The French Lieutenant's Woman,* 1969) can disturb novelistic teleology by giving us at least two, and possible three, mutually exclusive endings, so can a poet like Wilfred Owen seem to be playing on the audience's guilty knowledge of dramatic irony in recounting the slaughter of the First World War in terms of the Abraham and Isaac story of God's testing of the faithful, only to cynically repudiate the narrative typology by closing, not with Isaac's release ("Lay not thy hand upon the child"), but with Abraham's rejection of God's favor: "But the old man would not so, but slew his son,— / And half the seed of Europe, one by one, . . . half the seed of Europe one by one" ("The Parable of the Old Man and the Young" 1918).

By the rules of the textual commentator or detective, such events must not be predictable, even by the most informed of private eyes, and the reliance we have placed on our licensed textual detectives (critics and editors) to see more than we can see, to make all cohere into a consistent narrative, is itself sacrificed, as is the cathartic release from the tensions of contradictory or apparently irreconcilable evidence upon which the whodunnit is founded. If creators do not play fair, by either Aristotelian formalist protocols or by Platonist transcendental ones, what hope for the textual detective? Some examples: (1) Fowles introduces a spaceship (or something that *might* be a spaceship) into the otherwise linguistically, typographically, and culturally constrained simulacrum of eighteenth-century discourse at the end of *A Maggot* (1985). (2) John Gardner similarly introduces the logically impossible extraterrestrial into the dry realism of one of the alternating narratives of *October Light* (1976). (3) The author(s) of Genesis give(s) us two completely different accounts of the creation of Eve—one out of Adam's rib and the other simultaneously with Adam. (4) Alfred Hitchcock plays against the rules of the medium by showing us what turns out to be a *falsified* "flashback" at the beginning of *Stage Fright*. (5) Alain Robbe-Grillet seemingly allows us into the omniscient mind of the killer/detective in *The Voyeur* (1958), and yet we still cannot be sure, beyond a reasonable doubt, that any murder has in fact occurred. (6) Faulkner's "factual" appendix to *Absalom, Absalom!* (1986) is irreconcilable with the events of the novel as we have just experienced them.[15] (7) Mozart suddenly breaks out of the structural rules of tonality at the end of *Ein musikalischer Spass* to produce what we hear as perhaps mid-period Schoenberg. (8) Philip Johnson plays on the modernist, essentialist geometry of his own past in the stark purity of the central portion of his AT&T Building, only to undermine that self-referential, enclosed, spatial harmonics by sticking a Romanesque cathedral at one end and a Chippendale grandfather clock at the other. When all these things hap-

---

15. For an account of the editorial principles involved in dealing with this epistemological gap, see Polk (1991).

pen deliberately in the texts before us, what advantage can be gained by the detective or textual critic from being *outside* the narrative and having a more than acute sense of semiosis, if the narrative itself won't lie still and if the signs are forever shifting? It's not fair.

Note that I am not speaking here of *error* (by the measure of a constative reality outside the work) or of internal incoherence that is a discernible gaffe in the text, as when Fitzgerald tells us in *Gatsby* that we would walk east rather than south to get from West 158th Street to Central Park, or when Robinson Crusoe can't get the sex of his goat straight; this issue of realism versus textuality has been effectively dealt with by G. Thomas Tanselle and others. And I concede that the distinction between the two classes of empirical and evidentiary swerve may sometimes be blurred (as in the modernist ironies of disruption in *The Ambassadors,* or the apparent inconsistency in *Beowulf* as to whether he did, or did not, have a misspent youth: such cases can be seen as a critical complexification rather than a structural flaw).

No, I am disturbed here, as a textual investigator, with those bibliographical, structural, narrative, and, if you will, *intentional,* instabilities that seem to be an inherent and necessary part of the text that is the pattern in the carpet. So even though Gardner soothingly? ironically? begrudgingly? appears to lay to rest the ghost of instability by taking up the "final" final chapter of *October Light* with an epigraph from the Marquis de Lafayette ("The play, Sir, is over"), those who have experienced either Simon Schama's revisionist history of the French Revolution, *Citizens;* or John Corigliano's rewriting of Beaumarchais' rewriting (*La mère culpable*) of his own "revolutionary" *Marriage of Figaro* in the opera *The Ghosts of Versailles* know that even that great survivor Lafayette had this time got it wrong. The play was by no means over; we were not at the end, not even in the middle, and there were narrative disjunctions yet to come. Let me put it as starkly, and as dangerously, as possible. Steven Mailloux's account (virtually just a transcription) of congressional hearings into the Reagan administration's attempt to authorize the Strategic Defense Initiative (Star Wars) program from the intentions, language, and social reception of the ABM Treaty shows, with a macabre sense of irony, just how unstable even a fully intended and rationalized text can be and how the evidence locatable in the text may change its signification (even to its author) over time:

CONGRESSMAN LEE HAMILTON (to Paul Nitze, who had negotiated the
original ABM Treaty): If I understand you correctly a moment ago, and
I may not have, you suggested that the agreement says something that
you didn't think it said at the time you participated in the crafting of the
treaty; is that correct?

PAUL NITZE: That is approximately correct. I think the facts of the matter are that it is hard to recollect exactly what one thought at the time 13
years ago. I know that some time thereafter I was asked a question about
the treaty which differs from what I now understand to be the negotiating
record.

CONGRESSMAN HAMILTON: Well, what then comes through to me is that
you . . . have given us all the impression that this treaty is to be interpreted
restrictively, but that you now say that the lawyers have persuaded you
that you reached an agreement that you didn't know you reached?
(Anti-Ballistic Missile Treaty 1986: 41, quoted in Mailloux 1990: 131)

If Ronald Reagan and Paul Nitze had both sat at the knee of Jacques
Derrida in the École Normale Supérieure, or if they had been devotees
of Lacan's thesis that the signifier is forever being displaced, or if they
had embraced a nonlinear, noncausal mode of historicity like Foucault's
epistemic disjunctions (where, for example, the homosexual is invented
as a "species" in the 1860s [1990]), then this exchange would not surprise
us, though it might make those of us who had voted for Reagan's hard-line
strict constructivism a little uneasy. But Reagan and Nitze were presumably not on the barricades in Paris in 1968, and if they had been, they
would have been on the *other* side, the side of positivist surety and clear
semiotic boundaries, not reconstructive difference and slippery signifiers.
The problem for this textual detective and interpreter, Lee Hamilton,
was not that the *text* was unstable in its linguistic formulations, or what
French medievalists now refer to as *mouvance,* a generalized intertextual,
intercodicological condition of crossing the membranes separating states.
No, the original treaty read quite clearly: "Each party undertakes not
to develop, test, or deploy ABM systems or components which are sea-
based, air-based, space-based, or mobile land based" (Article V.I). There
were no conditionals, quodlibets, or *sic et nons* in this formulation, so
Hamilton had to fall back on *agency,* and in this case both a reconstructive
and retroactive agency, on the one hand (Nitze's having recast his own
intentions to fit a desired result that had not been manifest at the time of
the signing), and an alienated, nonprivileged agency, on the other (those

"lawyers" of whom Hamilton speaks derisively, who have caused Nitze to change his mind).

All of this—the shift in agency and its relative privilege, the changing hermeneutic based on an unchanging text—is a problem only if the model of textuality (and thus of forensics and proof and rationality) is a modernist one, that is, one derived from the third century BC and the librarians of Alexandria. Yes, by my skewed historicity, the Alexandrians were more "modernist" than either medieval *sic et non* or postmodern fragmentalism, simulacrum, and deferral. And they were modernist in Habermas's sense of endorsing the search for the *grands reçits,* those "master narratives" the breakdown of which Lyotard sees as emblematic of the "postmodern condition" (1984; see also Ess 1994). For us, those *grands reçits* might be Marxism, Christianity, constitutionalism, nationality, empirical science, or whatever systemic pattern of text would be both comprehensive (that is, Linnaean in its capacity to account for all phenomena) and teleological, even eschatological, in its predictive competence to arrange these phenomena on a linear path of causality, constative reference, and completion. "Given enough evidence, we can . . . [name your desire, and the genie of modernism will fulfill it]." In the world of textual study, modernist avatars might include (1) the attempts of Mabillon and the Maurists to construct a linear and secure system of graphic forms and thus to make paleography into the first of the historical sciences; (2) the predictive claims of historical linguistics to be able to fill in the "missing" (that is, actually absent or grammatically unacceptable) forms that a comprehensive *grand reçit* of language demands—usually with the starry emblem of the asterisk; (3) the construction of "universal bibliographies" by such enumerative bibliographers as Konrad von Gesner and Johann Fabricius to "comprehend" all writing, a totalizing plan that Roger Chartier (1994) has seen adumbrated in the "libraries without walls" of electronic media; (4) the similarly universalist bibliographical *systems* from Gabriel Naudé's *Avis pour dresser une bibliothèque* to Dewey decimal to Library of Congress (LC), from which no book, including those "unimagined yet in prose or rime" could escape the theory of categories;[16] (5) the increasing

---

16. On the Aristotelian theory of categories as a bibliographical and textual issue, see Greetham 1998.

identification of analytical and descriptive bibliography (including the use of cyclotron analysis) with "hard" science and the history of technology; (6) the faith, under the modernist auspices of the "well-wrought urn," in the timelessness of the truly definitive edition, that which could stand outside the history of its own making and, conveniently for funding agencies like the National Endowment for the Humanities, could honestly claim "would never have to be done again."

As I have argued on various other occasions, such figures as Zenodotus of Ephesus and Aristophanes of Byzantium were prototypically modernist in their Platonizing desire to construct, through the collation of multiple corrupt witnesses, the authentic Homeric line, complete, unchanging, well wrought. Through the system of *analogy* (what McGann [1991b] has scornfully labeled as "critical editing" in its attempt to create an ideal, originary "text that never was"), the Alexandrians sought to overcome the corruptions of actual evidence and to see through the evidence to the truth that lay hidden behind it. And I have argued that Cartesian logic, Newtonian laws of motion and probability, French and American constitutionalism, and Victorian faith in technological progress were all mutually reinforcing aspects of that same positivism, a positivism founded on the absent presence of a creator, who was safely *dead* as far as his handiwork was concerned; or, as Joyce puts it, "[t]he artist, like the God of creation, remains within or behind or beyond or above his handiwork, invisible, refined out of existence, indifferent, paring his fingernails" (1964: 215).

But let me briefly play a textual St. Thomas Aquinas, and ask a disturbing quodlibet of the modernists. *What if* (as Derrida continually undermined John Searle [1977] in his logical critique of *Limited Inc.*) the text were "doing something else"? What if, in the terms of Bakhtin, the text was carnivalesque rather than serious, seditious rather than authoritative? What if the laws of logic (whatever they are) were deliberately ignored or countermanded? The apoplexies of such textual and critical fundamentalists as Brian Vickers (1994) against the monstrous regiment of feminists, poststructuralists, and postmodernists fail to convince (even by their own laws of rhetoric), not only because Vickers, in accusing his adversaries of "appropriating Shakespeare," cannot see that *his* construction of Shakespeare is as much an "appropriation" as anyone else's, but because, as a scholar of the early modern (or what we used to call the Renaissance), Vickers cannot seriously entertain the dialectic: he can do *sic* OR *non*, but his Boolean operators hesitate before *sic* AND *non*.

So where can we turn for an alternative textual modus operandi? Again, as I have argued in other contexts, the "uncanny" methods of Alexandria's great rival, Pergamon, can be set up against the canny school of Zenodotus and Aristophanes. Indeed, Harold Bloom has gone so far as to declare that it is in the anomalists of Pergamon, with their cultivation of a linguistic and textual "interplay of differences" (1979: 13), rather than in the "equality of ratios" sought by the Alexandrians that we should look for a true poetic. Texts are by nature anomalies and uncanny, and are therefore done a disservice by the modernist, positivist sciences of epistemology and empiricism. Because each utterance is anomalous to itself and not bound into a totalizing structure of linguistic or textual coherence, evidentiary norms, or protocols of forensics, it would presumably not surprise an uncanny anomalist from Pergamon to find that the two trials of O. J. Simpson (using basically the same evidence, except for the Bruno Magli shoes) had reached two entirely different verdicts. The interplay of difference in the Simpson cases was rhetorical (that is, the original sense of "forensic") not evidentiary: in the second trial, the defense was not allowed to play the "race card." Nor presumably would it surprise an uncanny anomalist to discover that Simon Schama's dialectically constructed *Dead Certainties/Unwarranted Speculations* (1992) is bestrewn with artifacts that *look like* evidence ("exhibit A, for the prosecution, your honor"), but are not specifically invoked as such in the text (fig. 5.1), just as Fowles plays the game of meaningless artifactual evidence in *A Maggot* by introducing facsimile pages of contemporary newspapers

---

FIGURE 5.1. *(facing)* A page from Simon Schama's *Dead Certainties*, with reported/invented dialogue, prose extract, and contemporary "evidence." Note that there is no caption specifically linking the illustration beyond that in the original document, and that the text also makes no reference to the illustration as evidence.

FIGURE 5.2(a–b). *(following pages)* An opening from John Fowles's *A Maggot*, with reported/invented dialogue facing a facsimile from a contemporary news journal. Despite the reader's expectations that these facsimiles will have some bearing on the content of the reported dialogue, none is pointed out in the text of the novel, and the events recorded in the newspapers have no connection with the narrative proper.

Facts, Truefacts, Factoids

Accounts Rendered

tion) and some blueness under the left axilla—leaving the skin soft, and easily broken. An opening slightly ragged, about one and a half inches in length under the left nipple.

When the inventory was done, the measurements of the separate pieces enumerated, he told George Bemis that nothing about them was dissimilar to what he might have expected to find in Dr. Parkman's body.

"But," asked Mr. Sohier with an extremely direct gaze at the witness, "had you not known he were missing, would you have said, right away, these are his mortal remains?"

"I would not."

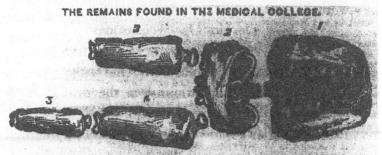

THE REMAINS FOUND IN THE MEDICAL COLLEGE.

No. —Represents the vertebræ and thoracic cavity which is charred, and contains the lungs.
No. 2 —Represents the pelvic cavity. covered by flesh in its lower part.
No. 3 —The right thigh disarticulated from the pelvis.
No. 4.—The left thigh disarticulated from the pelvis.
No. 5 —The left leg disarticulated from the thigh and foot.

A. Not that wise travellers take, nor cumbered as they were. Nor would they know them, sir, being strangers. Nor even if they did, take them if they were truly for Bideford.

Q. They were asked of there?

A. Yes, sir. But the scent was cold. For it is a busy town, and full enough of strange faces. Those Dr Pettigrew sent had no gain for their pains. 'Twas said as much at the second inquisition.

Q. That night they passed beneath this roof, heard you no quarrels? High words?

A. No, sir.

Q. None came to speak to them, apart from Mr Beckford? No messenger, no strange person?

A. No, sir.

Q. Mr Brown, may you describe his looks?

A. Why, sir, more fierce in face than manner.

Q. How, fierce?

A. Rather I would say grave. Such as a learned doctor, as us say here.

Q. Then unlike to his supposed occupation? Was he not said a merchant?

A. I cannot tell, sir. I know not London. But they be great men there, 'tis said.

Q. Was he fat or thin? How tall?

A. Why, middling in all, sir. A sound carriage.

Q. Of what age?

A. Near fifty, sir, I can say no more. Perhaps more.

Q. No other thing that bears upon my enquiry?

A. Not that I can think of at this present, sir. Naught of importance, ye may be sure.

Q. Very well, Master Puddicombe. I thank you. And at your pain to keep my commission secret, as I warned.

A. I have sworn, sir. My word is my bond, I assure ye. King and true church, I am no fanatick nor meeting man. Ask any here.

> Jurat tricesimo uno die Jul.
> anno Domini 1736 coram me
> Henry Ayscough

Hiſtorical Chronicle, 1736.

MAY.

Saturday, May 1.

General Court of the *Chari-table Corporation*, order'd the Proſecution againſt their late Directors to be carried on with A the utmoſt Vigour.

The Ld Mayor, and Court of Aldermen of *London*, were en-tertain'd at Dinner by Ld *Baltimore* in *Groſve-nor-Square*, on the Part of his R. Highneſs the Prince of *Wales*, who invited them when they preſented their Congratulations; which He received with ſuch Marks of Condeſcenſion B and Goodneſs as are peculiar to himſelf: A-mong other obliging Things, told them, That he was ſorry the Princeſs was not ſo well ver-ſed in the *Engliſh* Language, as to return an Anſwer to them in it; but that he would be anſwerable for her, that ſhe ſhould ſoon learn it; and enquir'd of Sir *John Bernard*, if he underſtood *French*, to ſpeak to her Royal High- C neſs in that Tongue. Sir *John* handſomely excuſing himſelf, referr'd to Alderman *God-ſchall* who, with Alderman *Lequeſne*, made ſhort and agreeable Compliments to the Prin-ceſs, and received gracious Anſwers from her.

At One this Morning, and at Noon the pre-ceeding Day, was a terrible Earthquake along the *Ockil-Hills* in *Scotland*, which rent ſeveral D Houſes, and put the People to flight, it was accompanied with a great Noiſe under Ground.

Monday, 3.

Notwithſtanding the Example made laſt Month, *(See p. 229. E.)* the People of *He-refordſhire* cut down the Turnpikes again

Tueſday, 4.

At a Court of Aldermen held at *Guildhall*, *Denn Hammond*, Eſq; an eminent Attorney in *Nicholas Lane*, was ſworn Comptroller of this City, purchaſing the Place for 3,600 *l.*

Wedneſday, 5.

His Majeſty went to the Houſe of Peers, and gave the Royal Aſſent to the Bill for Exhibit-ing a Bill for Naturalizing the Princeſs of F *Wales*.—To the Geneva Bill.—To a Bill for better enlightning the City of *London*.—To ſeveral Road Bills,—And other private Bills, to the Number of 41.

A Cauſe was try'd in the Maſhalſea-Court, *Southwark*, wherein *Wm. Berkins*, Joyner, was Plaintiff, and the noted *Julian Brown*,

alias *Gueliano Bruno*, an *Italian*, (on whoſe ſole Evidence, *Wreathock, Bird, Ruſſet, Camp-bell* and *Chamberlain*, were found guilty for robbing Dr. *Lancaſter*) was Defendant, for Joyner's Work in fitting up a Chandler's Shop, *&c.* for the ſaid *Brown* in *Bloomsbury*: The Work was admitted; but *Brown*, in order to prove Payment of it, ſet up a Receipt in full given to him by *Berkins* for Work done in 1731, having altered the Date to 1734; but the Fraud appear'd ſo plainly to the Court, that a Verdict was given for the Plaintiff; and the Receipt detained, in order to have the ſaid *Brown* proſecuted thereon, to the great Satis-faction of all Perſons then preſent.

Thurſday, 6.

His Majeſty in Council order'd, that at Morning and Evening Prayers, in the Litany, and all other Parts of the publick Service, as well in occaſional Offices, as in the Book of Common Prayer, where the Royal Family is particularly appointed to be pra ed for, that the following Form be obſerv'd, *viz.*

For his moſt Sacred Majeſty King *George*, our gracious Queen *Caroline*, their Royal High-neſſes *Frederick* Prince of *Wales*, the Prin-ceſs of *Wales*, the Duke, the Princeſſes, and all the Royal Family.

Friday, 7.

Several Merchants of *Dublin* met at the *Tholſel*, to conſider of Means to prevent any Alterations in the Coin, and afterwards went in a Body to wait on the D. of *Dorſet*, Lord Lieutenant. The Rev. Dean *Swift*, and their two Repreſentatives in Parliament, were with them, and the Dean ſet forth the ill Conſe-quence it would be to that Kingdom, if the Coin ſhould be reduced.——Notwithſtanding this Zeal of the *Iriſh* Merchants, a Writer in the *Daily Advertiſer*, *May* 10, charges it on them not only as an Error, their raiſing our Guinea to 23 *s.* Moidores to 30 *s.* and our Shilling to 13 *d.* but ſays, it is very obvious, that their Intent was to make it profitable to carry Money to *Ireland*, and a Loſs to bring it back to *Great Britain*; and as it was done without Authority, is unwarrantable, and has not had any good Effect. That they have raiſed the Gold Coin much too high, and thereby have been drained of almoſt all their Silver. Tho' he allows the Guinea ought to be raiſed (but by Authority, and in both King-

doms,

at various points in his narrative, but without demonstrating the specific relevance (if such there be) between these illustrative glosses and the text proper (fig. 5.2), with both authors using their epilogues to celebrate the ambiguities.[17] And I fancy that, conscious of the lurking Alexandrians and their idealist facticity, our uncanny Pergamene would perfectly well understand why such positivist historians as Lawrence Stone and Gertrude Himmelfarb[18] felt that Schama, as a professing historian with an impressive track record in straight empiricist narrative, had betrayed his profession not only by failing to establish (or even to claim) an evidentiary status for these exhibits but also by licentiously crossing the borders, at unmarked points, between documentary authority and, well, fiction, between real evidence and falsified.

We obviously live in confused times, and I will close this chapter by adding to the confusion with two exempla. In an ABC News broadcast (March 22, 1997) about the Oklahoma bombing trial that was then about to begin, the "news" (if that is the proper term) was that there was a fear that some of the "forensic" (i.e., pure, scientific, canny, laboratory analysis) had already been contaminated by interpretation, which would therefore render it less valuable, or even suspect, as forensic evidence. Leaving aside the historically curious inversion of the terms ("forensic" develops out of "forum" and refers to the "art and study of argumentation and debate" [see Greetham 1996e], and therefore a "forensic" act is precisely an interpretive and rhetorical one, not a contaminating of forensics by interpretation, as my earlier comments on criminalistics indicate), it is exactly in this so-called contaminated area of rhetoric that the most exciting developments are taking place in the discipline and in the training of forensic experts. So in which direction has the line been crossed?

---

17. Fowles, for example, claims that he knows "next to nothing of various . . . characters . . . who also come from real history" and that "[i]t may be that books and documents exist that might have told me more of them in historical terms than the little I know: I have consulted none, nor made any effort to find them" (1985: 449). Schama's disingenuous(?) note (327) that some of his book is based directly on documentary transcripts and some purely "fictional" sources similarly muddies the historical border between fact and fiction.

18. For an account of the criticisms of conservative documentary historians against Schama's *Dead Certainties,* and the significance of this quarrel for textual study, see the "History of the Text" chapter of Greetham 1999b.

Is rhetorical forensics less or more canny or uncanny than lab science in the development of the discipline's self-construction?[19]

But the last word must go to Monty Python. In the witch trial scene from *Monty Python and the Holy Grail*, there is a wonderful parody of evidentiary, rhetorical forensics in the demonstration that the accused must be a witch.

A crowd of villagers drags in a woman with a carrot on her nose and a crude black hat on her head; the villagers tell Sir Bedevere, "We have found a witch. May we burn her?" Bedevere replies, "How do you know she is a witch?" An easy one for the villagers: "she looks like one!" The problem, of course, is that the crowd has dressed her like a witch, doctoring the external evidence. Bedevere, playing Pontius Pilate, sends the question back to the crowd: "What makes you think she's a witch?" only to be told by a villager, "Well, she turned me into a newt." Since this witness to guilt is clearly *not* a newt, on interrogation by Bedevere he

---

19. The apparent "objective empiricist" forensics (as opposed to rhetorical forensics) of lab science has been most successfully interrogated by Bruno Latour (1987). Latour brings the same anthropological analysis to the scientific community as has long been practiced on primitive tribal cultures. Thus, in addressing the question of how scientific order is created out of disorder in the laboratory, Latour and Woolgar proceed from a "hunting and gathering" model to a rhetorical one: "Sorting, picking up and enclosing [i.e., sifting through empirical data to write a scientific paper] are costly operations, and they are rarely successful; any slackening can . . . drown a statement in confusion. This is more so because a statement exists, not by itself, but in the agonistic field (or market) made up of the laboratories striving to decrease their own noise" (247). Latour's argument on anthropological science and the accumulation of evidence thus parallels Rorty's on epistemology: an attempt to reduce "noise" so that a premise can be "defended against all comers." The supposed forensic opposition between rhetoric and science as regards the use of evidence is specifically denied by Latour:

> Galileo was quite mistaken when he purported to oppose rhetoric and science by putting big numbers on one side and one "average man" who happened to "hit upon truth" on the other. . . . My contention is that on the contrary we must eventually come to call scientific the rhetoric able to mobilise on one spot more resources [Latour calls these resources "external allies"] than older [rhetorics]. (1987: 61)

The implications of Latour's method are beginning to be appreciated by some textual theorists (for example, Tanselle 1995b notes, like Rorty and Latour, that a bibliographical truth "depends on whether it can stand up under criticism. . . . If a consensus forms in support of [a] position, the result will be another historical fact *produced by informed imagination* and validated by repeated reexamination of the argument supporting it" [284, 285; emphasis added]); but in general, textual critics and bibliographers have been slow to take up the discursive and anthropological challenge in the weighing of evidence and probity.

meekly admits, "I got better . . ." Turning the epistemological discussion to the general phenomena of nature rather than idiosyncratic anecdote, Bedevere asks the villagers what they might burn "apart from witches." "Wood" is the obvious and expected answer. "So . . . why do witches burn?" Clearly because "they're made of wood." To discover whether the accused is made of wood (and therefore a witch), the villagers smartly reject such patently illogical arguments that we should "build a bridge out of her," because "you can also make bridges of stone," and instead, focus on the physical *properties* of wood (e.g., that it floats). Again looking for logical analogy, "bread," "apples," "very small rocks," "cider," "great gravy," "cherries," "mud," "churches," and "lead" are all rejected as inadequate equivalents, in favor of Arthur's brilliant suggestion, "a duck." A villager slowly struggles with the logical inference: "So . . . logically . . . if she . . . weighs . . . the same as a duck . . . she's made of wood, and therefore . . . a witch."

An enormous pair of scales is brought on, a duck and the "witch" are placed on each end, and lo, they are seen to weigh the same! In the face of this overwhelming evidence plus the density of the forensic argument, the accused has to admit: "It's a fair cop." Justice and logic have been served by evidence and rhetoric.

The real irony of this clever parody of syllogistic logic, legal argument, and demonstrable proof lies not simply in the confused and fragmentary logic of the accusers, but in the *acceptance* of this illogical evidence by the accused: "a fair cop." Is it a "fair cop"? Well, only if you are taken in by the sequentiality of the apparent epistemology, without investing much in its substance. Only if, in other words, you accept the traditional, rhetorical meaning of *forensics* and not its current popular meaning of objective evidence. Only if *Holy Grail* is, in its formal logic, similar to what David Kolb observes (1994) of the philosophical paradoxes of hypertext representation of analytical, syllogistic logic, where the sequential fluidity and ambivalent narrative of electronic phenomenology may occlude, or actually misrepresent, logical paradigms, like the syllogism, that are based on linearity. In the parodic world of *Holy Grail,* these various categories can be collapsed for comic effect. But I think there are signs of their having collapsed in the world of textuality as well.

PART TWO

The Contamination of Text

The Contamination of Text

SIX

Who's In, Who's Out: The Cultural Poetics of Archival Exclusion

Use everything.

R. P. BLACKMUR

Trust nothing.

PYRRHO

Decide how well it works.

RICHARD RORTY

Only the exhaustive is interesting.

LUDWIG WITTGENSTEIN

A search . . . would yield an overwhelming mass of material, much
of it erroneous or loony, a great deal of it flatly contradictory,
and at the best, most of it endlessly, uselessly redundant.

RICHARD KNOWLES

Librarians and archivists know that a good collection, like a good book,
is made in the editing. . . . Too much information can numb the mind.

DEANNA B. MARCUM

[Fuck] ... Funk, Buck, Duck, Guck, Huck, Luck,
Muck, Puck, Ruck, Suck, Tuck.

WORDPERFECT 8.0, AUTOMATIC SPELL-CHECKER'S
SUGGESTED SUBSTITUTIONS

Fuck ... Çụṇṭ.

NISUS WRITER PRO

I think it would be safe to say that every poet and indeed every
writer is assailed by contradictory impulses, both to say and to leave
unsaid. "I am forbidden to speak and cannot be silent." ... And
both impulses validate annotation, the first directly by actually
annotating, the second by leaving a void that must be filled.

TRAUGOTT LAWLER

Extracts.

HERMAN MELVILLE

Every anthology is a political statement or a series of political statements.

JAMES SHAPIRO

Nothing is less reliable, nothing is less clear today than the word "archive."

JACQUES DERRIDA

Some like [the perfume from Spain].

COLE PORTER?

Here's my archive, or as Jacques Derrida would have it, my exergue that "plays with citation" (1996: 7), for to "cite before beginning is to give the tone through the resonance of a few words, the meaning or form of which ought to set the stage" (7). From the citation within the title (Pope? or was it Swift? or Dryden? Who knows?),[1] to Richard Knowles's fear of the "loony" in the variorum, to WordPerfect 8.0's refusal to "recognize" the word *fuck* (as opposed to the more recent Nisus Writer Pro "allowing" *fuck* but still flagging *cunt* as inadmissible), to my extracting "Extracts" from *Moby-Dick*, to the still-current mis-citation from Cole Porter, I am building an archive of exhibits, cultural artifacts that, like the Elgin Marbles, have been wrenched from their original context and placed together under a form of protective custody for the *collect* that is this present chapter. These are unabashed co-options (indeed, some of them are co-options of co-options, shifted two or three times out of context and now made to perform as epigraphs,[2] and they have thus crossed several membranes [*membranae,* or "leaves" of a book] to interrogate the integrity of the archives from which they have been drawn [and redrawn] and the one into which they are imported). I have constructed a "*typographical...* *exergue*" in that "the archive seems here to conform better to its concept. Because it is entrusted to the outside, to an *external* substrate and not, as the sign of covenant in circumcision, to an intimate mark, *right on* the so-called body proper" (Derrida 1996: 8). And they can be unabashed precisely because the cultural context in which I am now acting as the "editor" of my archive encourages, even demands, this rhetorical gesture: as Derrida notes, the exergue serves to "prearchive a lexicon... according to a proven convention" (7), for a scholarly essay without an epigraphic license (in the title or elsewhere) would be a provisionless and rudderless boat, a vehicle with no sign of where it was coming from or where it was

---

1. Of course, I could easily have found out, but the point of the "Who knows?" was to set the citation beyond recall from the immediate archive—of memory. The fact that it is a famous passage from a famous play, *King Lear,* and that I do really know the source, makes the disjunction between archive and enunciation even more telling.

2. For example, the citations from Blackmur, Pyrrho, Rorty, and Wittgenstein are now at three removes from their original archival sites, for they were initially co-opted by Richard Knowles in his essay on variorum editing (1994), then in my "Supplément" chapter of *Theories of the Text* (1999b), and now as apparently free-standing epigraphs for this chapter. My archive is thus archaeological—in its layers and misprisions—in both the conventional and the Foucauldian senses.

likely to end up and with no cargo of previously masticated obiter dicta to sanction its narrative and give sustenance for its journey. All of these epigraphs will be embedded yet again in the body of my chapter, all will be explicated, annotated, provided with an additional freight of commentary to add to my archive, although I will admit that the temptation to provide an archive consisting entirely of the texts of "other men's flowers," determinedly refusing gloss and *explicatio*, was difficult to resist. That is, I took Derrida's challenge ("But where does the outside [of the archive] commence?" [8]) very seriously, not just *typographically* but *substantively* as well: I might have constructed an *essai* (a "trial") of the archive that would have been forever an exergue, and thus eventually (as the reader began to realize that this trial was becoming a commonplace book) a bibliographical invagination of foldings of the membranes in which the anticipated outside of the exergue established itself as the substrate of the inside (see Greetham 1991b: 23). According to Derrida, this swerve would have been quite proper (though even in the depths of *mal d'archive,* he does not "essay" it himself) for "where does the outside commence?" is "the question of the archive. There are undoubtedly no others" (1996: 8). One might ask, if there are no others, why is it that Derrida does not take up his own challenge? It is surely not simply that, in discussing the repression and suppression and impression of the archive, he will admit that "in the end I have nothing new to say" (9), for the repressive act of archiving is always a determination and admission that there is "nothing new" here and that active internal memory has become hypostatic. No, the challenge of rendering my entire *essai* as an exergue was difficult not because it would demonstrate typographically that "in the end I have nothing new to say," but because my theme of archival exclusion, in both its political and rhetorical modes, is an activist and not a passive figure, and plays very much out of and seemingly against Knowles's presiding metaphor of *digestion* and *assimilation,* of the archivist "editing" the "book" that will become the collection, as when he claims that "no researcher will prefer hundreds or thousands of pages of undigested data to a syncretic statement—selected, assimilated, digested, organized, *when necessary evaluative* [my emphasis]—by a competent authority" (Knowles 1994: 47n7). The digestive metaphor is a comforting one for those who, like the infant penguin, would prefer to have their input previously chewed by another, but digestion is inevitably a form of exclusion, even if it is further supported by such additional metaphors as separating wheat from chaff or extracting the nutrients from the waste matter, and my placing Knowles's "evaluation" under emphasis clearly suggests my contention that all such digestion and assimilation on behalf of others is unavoidably evaluative. But I similarly recognize that even my giving in to the temptation to compose an archive entirely of text without gloss (or rather, gloss without, or masquerading as, text) would be as evaluative and discriminatory as overt commentary, though operating under the *cover* of the "nakid text."

No, the more pressing or more pertinent question, given that all archives are digestive in one form or another, is to ask *who* is Richard Knowles that he can do the masticating and digesting for us? Who are we to recognize (in Derrida's terms) as the archons, the "first of all the documents' guardians" (1994: 2), those who do not "only ensure the physical security of what is deposited and of the substrate" but "are also accorded the hermeneutic right and competence[,] . . . the power to interpret the archives" (ibid.). It is, as usual, a question of agency, and a question of the social formation of that agency. I speak therefore not just of an "interpretive" (i.e., receptional) community in the mode of Stanley Fish (whose formulation [1980], we should recall, came out of a study of that very genre—the variorum—in which Knowles is operating) but also of an "interpretive" (i.e., compositional) community, a clerisy that Derrida recognizes as having the "virtue of a privileged *topology*" for they "inhabit this uncommon place, this place of election where law and singularity intersect in *privilege*" (1996: 3), a clerisy whose social and cultural function and responsibility is to provide those archival, textual records through the exercise of a "*topo-nomology*" or "patriarchic function" (ibid.) in an accessional form that will allow the Stanley Fishes of this latter-day world to go about their interpretive business. As we shall see, this "archontic power, which also gathers the functions of unification, of identification, of classification, must be paired with what we will call the power of *consignation* . . . the act of assigning residence there [and] the act of *consigning* through gathering together signs" (ibid.). Residence, place, the gathering together of signs: yes, all of this Derridean play will be shown in action in this essay, in action as (despite Knowles's demurral) a highly empowered interpretive agency.

Let me then start with a truly masterful interpreter—Frank Sinatra. In a 1959 concert in Australia, Sinatra sang that line derived from Cole

Porter's lyrics for "I Get a Kick Out of You" as I have presented it in the final epigraph. Nothing surprising here, for the line as sung in 1959 had become a *textus receptus,* and Sinatra was simply working in an accepted tradition. But there's one moment in the performance that plays against this tradition, and it has all to do with perfume, booze, and drugs. Employing his famous skills in the voice control of legato and tempo rubato, Sinatra sings the line describing "perfume from Spain" ("even one *sniff* / would bore me ter*rif*ically too") by drawing out the first syllable of "ter-rifically" beyond its normal measure so as to put even more emphasis on the second syllable (teeeerrrrrrr*rif*ically). This is an astute and musically interesting maneuver, but by concentrating melodically and rhythmically on the half-line rhyme of *rif,* Sinatra (inadvertently?) draws attention to the weak content of the previous line: "perfume *from Spain*" is hardly the accurate designation one would expect from the sophisticated and knowledgeable Porter. It sounds like a desperate filler. And so it is. For the original 1934 lyric had expressed boredom not with Spanish(!) perfume but with *cocaine.* But by 1959, the textual archive had been adjusted to fit the measure of the times, for by the fifties, cocaine, having long since been banished from Coca-Cola, was no longer a permissible social peccadillo: booze ("champagne") could remain, but drugs, even fashionable drugs, were no longer allowable utterance.[3]

In performance media like songs, musicals, operas, plays, and dances, there is no textual surprise in charting the continual moral, aesthetic, or political recalibration of the contents of an archive as they are released into public text by the imposition of social and cultural constraints. Every theatre historian is presumably aware that, for over a century, the Tate "happy ending" version of *King Lear* (see Bate and Massai 1997) was the only one to be publicly presented on the English stage, for by neoclassical tastes, the original tragic ending was deemed insupportable. And I have

---

3. This was not the only concession to historical sensitivity. Even before the song was performed, the lines referring to the Lindberghs ("I shouldn't care for those nights in the air / That the fair Mrs. Lindbergh goes through") were canceled after the Lindbergh child's kidnapping and replaced by the less specific "Flying too high with some guy in the sky / Is my idea of nothing to do," which became the accepted performance and textual tradition, though the archive with Porter's typescript survives and clearly shows his original intentions. I know of no revival of *Anything Goes,* even those claiming rigorous historical authenticity (for example, the John McGlinn recording), that restores these intentions even now that the Lindbergh affair is no longer such a touchy subject.

elsewhere commented on the sexual significance of the separate performance history of the reconstituted third-act ending of Berg's opera *Lulu*, for which Patrice Chéreau, Pierre Boulez, and Friedrich Cerha, in the first performance of the complete work, ignored the sexually neutral "voiceless sigh" in Berg's score at the moment that Geschwitz, the lesbian lover of Lulu, is murdered by Jack the Ripper, and instead went back to Wedekind's original theatrical text to substitute the moral self-condemnation of Geschwitz singing *Verflucht* ("cursed"). Thus, lesbianism now earned its just rewards, whereas in Berg's version, a sigh was just a sigh.

The ontological peculiarity of performance history as a social archive is, of course, that while just about every living person who has heard Cole Porter has heard booze but not dope and that all those who have made it through to the final curtain of the three-act *Lulu* have heard Geschwitz condemn her lifestyle, the assiduous researcher could presumably still discover an alternative reading, one lacking a social imprimatur but nonetheless documentarily extant. Sometimes, however, that documentarity, the "original" archive from which performance may or may not proceed, may itself be compromised or constrained by social or personal pressure; it may cease to *live* culturally. As Derrida notes, "the archive has always been a *pledge*, and like every pledge [*gage*], a token of the future. To put it more trivially: what is no longer archived in the same way is no longer lived in the same way" (1996: 18). Thus, the late twentieth-century recording of the complete four-act version of Britten's *Billy Budd*, rather than the truncated three-act version, drastically changes our understanding of Britten's original intentions and the relationship of E. M. Forster and Eric Crozier's libretto to the text of Melville's novella, and provides new evidence of the power of Britten's tenor (and lover), Peter Pears, in reshaping archival and performance history—and therefore making the totalized archive of *Billy Budd* "live" in a different way. Briefly put, Pears "simply did not want to perform" (Miller 1998: 14) the stirring, patriotic, military exhortation that Britten had written for Captain Vere for the original ending of act I, an aria with full male chorus that "shows [Vere] as a man of action and an officer who could inspire men to die for him" (ibid.). Pears's discomfort led to excision and the reformulation of the structure of the opera, and it removed much of the psychological motivation for Billy's last words, "Starry Vere, God bless you!" It is doubtful that, given the resistance and conservatism that John Glavin reports of

major performance agencies,[4] the new "complete" *Billy Budd* will change
the stage history of the work, just as the decision by the Sibelius estate to
allow only one performance (and a recording) of the original version of
the Violin Concerto obviously cannot affect the cumulative performance
tradition of the concerto, at least until the "publication" of the original
version goes into the public domain. Thus, the archive of public memory
and the archive of documentary record often bear an uneasy, shifting
relation to each other: I once asked a friend to inquire directly of Evelyn
Lear, who had sung the Geschwitz role in the refurbished *Lulu* at the
Metropolitan Opera, whether she had indeed done the "wordless sigh"
or sung "Verflucht." The answer? She couldn't remember! And without
a formal recording, and with the complete absence of "Verflucht" from
any of the scored versions of *Lulu* (the "Suite," the two-act version with
just the orchestral parts for the third-act conclusion, the Cerha complete
three-act version), the textual archival evidence for "Verflucht" does indeed depend on memory—the performers', the audience's, the reviewers'
(though I do suspect that somewhere in the Met's private archives there
must be an unreleased audiotape record of that performance by Lear).

This sort of slippage has encouraged those textual critics interested
in establishing the ground rules for evidentiary witnessing of the "work"
to turn to F. W. Bateson's (1961) probing question—"If the *Mona Lisa* is
in the Louvre, where is *Hamlet*?"—as a demonstration of the ontological
distinction between spatial and linear texts (see Bateson 1961: 74). One
would have to destroy every copy of Shakespeare's original *Hamlet* (whatever that was) in order to effect the equivalent of burning the *Mona Lisa*—
or so the argument frequently runs. But even if we accept this ontological
distinction as a given,[5] the cultural and historical problem remains that
there have indeed been many instances when every copy of an "original"

---

4. Glavin (1988) charts not only the enormous liberties theatrical directors have taken in
their misrepresentations of dramatists' intentions but also the inherent conservatism (confirmed by the box office) of producers. In attempting to persuade the Arena Stage in Washington, D.C., to score a theatrical coup by producing the original four-act version of Wilde's
Importance of Being Earnest rather than the unauthorial, truncated, three-act version
patched together by George Alexander, the first producer of the play, Glavin was presented
with the unassailable indifference of "Frankly, it's hard to argue with success" (390).

5. See Nelson Goodman's history (1969) of the growing distinction between what he calls
the "autographic" and "allographic" arts. The distinction is also based on the presence/

absence dichotomy, for an autographic art is, to Goodman, one in which "the distinction between [the] original and [the] forgery of it is significant," and where "duplication . . . does not count as genuine" (1969: 113, quoted in McLaverty 1984b: 87). Thus, for Goodman, non-autographic (allographic) arts, such as music and literature, are susceptible to notation, which is a system of discrimination or refining—isolating those qualities of the work that are "constitutive properties" (1969: 116) from those that are only contingent. The notated score in the allographic art work is thus a set of instructions for iterability, whereas the autographic art work (e.g., painting, sculpture, and architecture) cannot be repeated without betraying its ontology. Goodman's distinction is similar to those posited by Wollheim (1972) and Urmson (1976), and its concentration on notation as the emblematic mark of difference can perhaps be perceived in the allographic reduction of sound to digital codes in a CD recording versus the attempted reconstruction (almost literally reshaping or forging) of that sound in an autographic analog recording—although it is doubtful whether most listeners of CDs and LPs are aesthetically aware of the distinction in these terms. The importance of Goodman's reliance on notation to the presence/absence debate is in his presumption that all arts were initially autographic, but while some survived in their physical properties (painting, sculpture, architecture), others required memory (that is, repetition or iterability) to survive and therefore developed a system of notation. And this notation is the physical trace of absence which to both intentionalist and deconstructor is the inherent quality of belated inscription—although to Goodman it functions as almost exactly the opposite, the constitutive rather than contingent properties, and is a mark not of belatedness but of essence.

The weakness in Goodman's argument can be illustrated by reference to Kendall L. Walton's essay "The Presentation and Portrayal of Sound Patterns" (1988), which points out that it would be theoretically possible for two entirely different notation systems to produce aurally the same performance of a musical work. Walton playfully suggests:

> [Martian scores might] not indicate what pitches a performer is to play, or for what durations. Instead they [might] give detailed instructions concerning dynamics, tempos, articulations, vibrato, nuances of accent and timbre, etc.—instructions which are much more detailed than those provided by (traditional) scores in our society. The performer of a Martian work is free to decide what pitches to play and for what durations, but s/he is expected to play them with the dynamics, articulations, timbres, etc., indicated by the composer. (1988: 4)

Walton acknowledges that performances deriving from our and the Martian system might conceivably be "acoustically indistinguishable," but this would be the result of coincidence and would not be dependent on the notation, which is purely conventional. If notation is thus convention and not constitutive, then a musical work—the paradigm for Goodman's distinction between the autographic and allographic media—shifts out of its secure position in Goodman's schema. This is demonstrated by Leo Treitler (1993) in an account of three differently notated versions of Chopin's *Nocturne Op. 62, No. 1*, sent off on the same day to three different publishers in France, Germany, and England (see Kallberg 1990: "Are Variants a Problem?"). Treitler claims:

> [A]ltogether the Chopin examples show . . . a fluidity from the processes of composing and inscribing right through to performing. They tend to loosen the image of a hierarchical order from work to score to performance, and they suggest the possibility of a shared ontological level for all three—the possibility that the work may be realized in the performance as well as in the writing down. (1993: 495)

And Treitler quickly dismisses the objection that all this means is that "one needs a performance or a score to make the work present or concrete." Rather, the "shared ontology"

text has been lost, and sometimes that loss has been not just by accidents of time, corruption, and worms, but by active book burning, or sometimes by an agency even more powerful because it is culturally insidious—the agency to be responsible for, and to have the prerogative over, the transmission of archival texts from one medium to another, from one cultural moment to another. Without even considering the numerous stories of the intransigence of archive owners in making their textual riches available to scholarly perusal—an active and often dog-in-the-manger exclusion as a mark of the prerogative of property,[6] we can see that even such apparently blameless and seemingly neutral roles as the agency of

---

requires that to have an edition of a musical work like the Chopin "that identifies the work, not just exemplifies it, you must include all the versions" (ibid.). If the autographic/allographic distinction becomes difficult to sustain in music, so do the other textual theories of essentialism and contingency using the same opposition. While Goodman holds to this basic taxonomy, in his later writings he acknowledges that the reservations expressed by Monroe Beardsley (1978), Donald Davidson (1978), Jens Kulenkampff (1981), Jenefer Robinson (1978), Søren Kjørup (1978), Richard Martin (1981), and Richard Rudner (1978) require some further clarification of his theory of representation and notation, and he devotes substantial parts of the study of "reference" in his *Of Mind and Other Matters* (1984) to modifying or enlarging upon his fundamental binaries, without fully recognizing the textual ambiguities that his theory is incapable of mapping consistently or coherently. Nonetheless, Goodman's account—together with the commentaries thereon—remains a valuable source for textuists confronting representational ontology, as McLaverty's reliance on it (1984b) demonstrates. See the "Pictures and Paragraphs" section of W. J. T. Mitchell's *Iconology: Image, Text, Ideology* (1986) for further discussion.

6. Such famous cases as the proprietorship (and the petulance) of "owners" of the J. S. Mill *Autobiography* manuscript, the Tennyson archive, and, perhaps most notoriously, the Dead Sea Scrolls are testimony to the ubiquitousness not just of the Lockean concept of private property but of the perhaps inherent conflict between conservators (even those whose motives may be less than honorable) and researchers: the first group wants to restrict access (even to prevent it entirely) and the second to encourage access. Clearly, the British Library is only carrying out its archival responsibilities by displaying a single opening of the *Beowulf* manuscript to the public at large, while occasionally recognizing that the research projects of scholars like Kevin Kiernan (1996 and *Electronic Beowulf*) need more open access. It is this balancing act that renders the archive "troubling," as Derrida would have it (1996: 90), for the archive may "inhibit sight and knowledge" and will encourage the "trouble of secrets, of plots, of clandestineness, of half-private, half-public conjurations, always at the unstable limit between public and private" (ibid.).

The third act of Berg's *Lulu* is a notorious example of such inhibitions and "half-private, half-public conjurations" for, as recorded by Friedrich Cerha, who was ultimately to be responsible for completing the scoring of the third act, Berg's widow, Helene, after having initially turned to Schoenberg, Webern, and Zemlinsky to "complete" her husband's work, then decided that "the torso was stageworthy and that there was therefore no need at all to make a performance version of the third act" (Cerha 1979: 9). The widow Berg, believing she

description, of mere listing and cataloging (or, more pointedly, deciding not to list or catalog or to omit from the list or catalog), can obviously have enormous potential for exclusion, even when an item or artifact has survived in earlier listings. And this is especially true at moments of great documentary shift in the methods of production and preservation: from orality to literacy, from epigraphic inscription to papyrus rolls, from papyrus to parchment, from rolls to codex, from manuscript to print, from print to digitization. We are at one of those critical moments right now, and an awareness of the cultural force of such transitions simply reinforces the theoretical, ontological issue with an empirical practicality beyond dispute. Crudely put, if the acid-paper publications of (say) nineteenth-century documents are left to self-destruct, as they surely will, given enough time and enough acid, where will we look for the records of that culture?

We will not be able to look in garbage heaps, the way that papyrologists have been able to uncover such astounding finds as the texts of the Gnostic Gospels at Nag Hammadi, discarded for millennia as eminently disposable cultural detritus but therefore, ironically, preserved *as garbage* in the hot, dry climate of Egypt.[7] We will not be able to look through the upper texts of palimpsests, the way that codicologists have been able to discover what earlier cultural treasures have been (almost) scraped off the parchment and treated as, again, eminently *disposable*. For the acidic bibliographical wrecks of the nineteenth century, there will be no equivalents to the finding of the only witness to Cicero's *De Republica*

---

was in direct communion with the spirit of her deceased spouse, then "made the material inaccessible and determined finally in her will that the third act should not be looked into by anyone" (ibid.). The conjuration of her husband's posthumous intentions notwithstanding, Helene was finally unable to prevent the Berg archive from being exhumed and resuscitated. See Donald Reiman's *Study of Modern Manuscripts* (1993) for further discussion of the private/public dichotomy in documentary ontology.

7. The bibliographical (in addition to the textual) preservation is particularly remarkable, for the Nag Hammadi gospels document a codicological system very different from that of later periods. The Gnostic Gospels are the earliest fully bound extant codices, in the sense that the bindings are still an integral unit with the contents: of the thirteen volumes, eleven are in the original covers, and all are in single-quire codices, of up to seventy-six leaves, rather than in the quaternions (four-leaf bindings) that later became the norm. This "Coptic" method of binding is basically similar to the modern single-quire pamphlet with staples. See Needham 1979 for further discussion on this binding, and see Greetham 2004a for the implications of garbage for textual study and archiving.

as the almost obliterated lower text beneath a codex of Augustine's *In Psalmos*.[8] No, without a full cultural program of archival reconstitution, perhaps into the new medium of digitization, much of the documentary evidence testifying to the nineteenth century will become not merely garbage but dust.

That the Nag Hammadi garbage dumps were the conserving repository for the Gnostic Gospels clearly brings into question the cultural forces by which garbage is to be defined, with (one hopes) the awareness that one cultural moment's garbage may be another's treasure trove. The well-rehearsed accounts of the eminent disposability of the manuscript witnesses from which the first printed editions by humanist scholars were created remains (for us, at our moment) a sad story of what to us would have been primary documentary sources being destroyed because they had now been rendered obsolete (even documentary embarrassments) by the supersession of the new medium of print. The manuscripts simply had no function any more. Even the most scholarly of humanist printer/ publishers, like Aldus Manutius of Venice, who was famous for having invited the most learned textuists of his day (including Erasmus) to stay with him in his *neakademia* while preparing the new editions, did not attach much independent testamentary or archival status to the superseded manuscripts, the great bulk of which have simply vanished. It is rare indeed to come across what seem to be a printer's markups on a manuscript, as in the partial use by Wynkyn de Worde of the Plimpton manuscript of Trevisa's Middle English version of the *De Proprietatibus Rerum* of Bartholomaeus Anglicus, the most "popular" (in various senses) encyclopedia of its day (see Gaumer 1971; Mitchener 1951). It may even be that the survival of the Plimpton manuscript with its printer's marks is a result of de Worde's having decided to change the copy-text to another (now lost)

---

8. As I have observed elsewhere (1992c: 54), this displacement of a lower (classical, pagan) text by an upper (Christian) one may not be just a matter of a previous culture's *remaniements* becoming the garbage of a successive one, but may be compounded by practical considerations as well. In this case, for example, the Cicero text is copied in an expansive and codicologically wasteful uncial (inch-high) script, while the Augustine is in a version of the more efficient Carolingian minuscule, in which a typical page might accommodate ten times as much text as in uncial. Like the miniaturization of data storage accomplished through the digitization of print materials (the whole of the *OED* [1933, 1989, 1994–] or the *Encyclopaedia Britannica* [1998–] on a single CD-ROM disk or DVD or online), cost efficiency was also a consideration in the bureaucracy of Charlemagne's chancellery.

manuscript when, for some reason, the Plimpton was deemed unsuitable. It is possibly the Plimpton's *unreliability* or *inadequacy* that has ensured its survival: had it been a better witness, it might have been destroyed, as garbage. The archive thus always bears an uneasy function between past and future: "the word and the notion of the archive seem at first, admittedly, to point toward the past, to refer to the signs of consigned memory" (Derrida 1996: 33). But if this were all that the poetics of the archive were concerned with, then the consignment would indeed be of "everything," for the artifacts of the present would naturally slip into the category of memory. The problem, for Aldus and those others bestriding this potential moment of slippage, is that "the archive should *call into question* the coming of the future" (ibid.: 33–34). Yes, Aldus was calling the future into question by destroying, repressing, or returning to oblivion those *former* "signs of consigned memory" called manuscript witnesses, creating the archive of the future by effacing the archive of the past.

Thus, the tales told by Nicholson Baker in "Discards" (1997) of the wholesale "deaccessioning" of library catalog cards, once the digitization of the collections they represent is complete, should come as no surprise to the cultural historian of bibliographical garbage, past or future. Baker's claim that the library cards have independent bibliographical and archival status and are not mere "representations" of a collection has, from his accounts, been discounted by most librarians, and especially those librarians who ought to know better: the custodians of the major research collections on which cultural history depends. To these custodians, the sort of individual commentaries and markups that Baker illustrates—part of the cultural history of that very custodial prerogative that now wants to destroy them—have become *garbage* by being superseded. Baker's charting of the very moment of bibliographical repression thus aptly embodies Derrida's psychoanalytic formula: one can "recall and archive the very thing one represses, archive it while repressing it (because repression is an archivization), that is to say, to archive *otherwise*, to repress the archive while archiving the repression; *otherwise*, of course, and that is the whole problem, than according to the current, conscious, patent modes of archivization" (1996: 64). The "otherwise" in Baker's account is precisely that being removed from the formal archive of the original libraries of which they were the accessional mode; the re-archived card catalogs are simultaneously repressed and archived through this repression. Like the mountains of rusting cars or the sunken nuclear waste pits that so emblematize the U.S. culture of landfills and waste products, the library card catalog has moved from an active and productive role (those cars were once new and shiny, the plutonium core of the nuclear reactor was once the source of energy) to not just the passive role of irrelevance but to the more embarrassing position of a dangerous excrescence. It is quite fitting that Don DeLillo should have written his fifty-year traversal of America in *Underworld* through the theme of "dangerous" garbage, garbage continually produced by our all-consuming culture. The apocalyptic threat of global garbage obviously hit a popular and critical nerve with the 2008 Pixar movie *WALL-E* (in which the entire earth is a vast dump and humans have abandoned the planet to a lovable garbage-sorting robot), which grossed $536 million and earned nominations for six Academy Awards. And it is similarly fitting that the presiding figure in Derrida's *Archive Fever: A Freudian Impression* should be the archive as personal, cultural, and social *repression,* a *mal d'archive* that thrives on potential garbage, on the "possibility of a forgetfulness which does not limit itself to repression," for the fever is empowered by the "threat of this death drive" (1996: 19).

The problem of garbage, bibliographical or otherwise, is thus compounded by time and function. Even if we accept that "we can't save everything" (the title of Deanna B. Marcum's op-ed piece in the *New York Times*); even if we accede to the practical dictum that "the paradox in all this abundance is that the easier it is to create and store information, the harder that information is to manage" (Marcum 1998: A15); even if we endorse the seeming counsel of despair that "too much information is as bad as none at all" (ibid.); even if we respect the necessity of selection that now means that "only 5 percent of all Government records are selected for permanent retention" (ibid.), the practical, taxonomic, and ontological question remains: what is the *everything* from which those select few shards will be saved, and how do we identify the documentary limits of a body of material which is then to be winnowed? And, yet more challenging, what cultural protocols can we use to demonstrate and check that the current principles of bibliographical conservation are not themselves so constrained and determined that, just as the neglected or actively destroyed documents have been superseded, so our very principles of selection may themselves be superseded by a later culture's very different standards? For example, what was reported to me as the British Library's (recent?) decision to invoke a commercial or distributional principle in continuing to conserve (or ignore) the national bibliographical patrimony might seem to subvert the library's role as a required depository: my colleague W. Speed Hill claimed that his edition of Hooker's *Works* had not been acquired by the BL because of the policy that only books with sales in excess of fifty copies need to be deposited—a claim disputed by BL staff and, as of this writing, still unresolved. This apparent capitulation to commercialism as a determinate of the division between treasury and garbage would be a viable bibliographical principle only within a very specific cultural moment: Hill's *Hooker* might not be a national treasure now (because it has demonstrably not reached the fifty-copy threshold), but that may be all the more reason why it ought to be conserved by a national depository rather than relegated to garbage, if Hill is right about the British Library's policy. The popular or consistently canonical works and editions do not need the protection of bibliographical deposit to be conserved: they will take care of themselves. But it may be those items that have fallen below the commercial threshold that the BL ought to be most concerned about as it constructs its patrimony for future generations. We are always in danger of looking like conservational idiots, saving the chaff and throwing out the wheat. In fact, one ironic rule of thumb might very well be that the more culturally valuable or commercially popular an item might appear to be here and now, the *less* eligible it ought to become for conservation.

The problem of conservation and the former "signs of consigned memory" has been put into high relief by the Google Books Library Project, especially as the project positions itself culturally in a similar moment as that occupied by Manutius. By scanning print archives from research libraries into digital form, the project will "make it easier for people to find relevant books—specifically, books they wouldn't find in any other way such as those that are out of print" (http://books.google.com/googlebooks/library.html), and thereby act as a conservator for the sort of "orphan" witnesses that, as in the days of Manutius, might otherwise slip below our archival horizon, as one medium takes over from another. With the initial involvement of such prestigious archives as those at Columbia University, Cornell University Library, Harvard University, the New York Public Library, Princeton University, Stanford University, the University of California, the University of Texas, the University of Virginia, plus such overseas repositories as the Bodleian, the Bayerische Staatsbibliothek, and libraries in Ghent, Keiko, Lyon, Catalonia, Madrid, Lausanne (see http://books.google.com/googlebooks/partners.html), the Google project is the single largest attempt to acknowledge a shift in medium in the history of the transmission of texts.

Inevitably, the project has stirred up both commendation and re-sistance, particularly from those who have an "interest" (legal, social, or financial) in the restrictions imposed by current archival access and those who have concern that in concentrating on *text* the Google proj-ect privileges the "linguistic codes" over the "bibliographic codes"—the physicality of the containers of texts. In 2005, the Authors Guild and five representative publishers (McGraw-Hill, Pearson, Penguin, Simon and Schuster, and John Wiley) sued Google, prompting the inclusion of an opt-out provision, which may or may not determine how comprehensive and flexible the project will become (see Band 2006; Jeweler 2005). No matter how the legalities are addressed, the function of the Google project is an attempt to re-archive what might otherwise be lost in the transfer and to recognize the paradox of the distinction between wheat and chaff in which chaff may very well have its own independent cultural function.

This paradox is one familiar to most historians of editing, for while it is clear that we do not really *need* another edition of Shakespeare, we can be pretty sure that, even after *Arden,* 3rd series (1996–), the *New Folger* (1992–), and the *New Cambridge* (1984–) are completed, there will be other "new" editions to supersede them. One of the main reasons Gary Taylor embarked on his multivolume edition of Middleton (2007)—after having co-edited the one-volume Oxford Shakespeare (1986)—was to effect an act of cultural displacement: to turn what had been regarded as chaff, and thus disposable, into wheat. The prestige attached to an Oxford monumental edition presided over by a well-established editor of an al-ready preserved text may or may not result in Taylor's aim of enfranchise-ment, but the cultural politics driving his Middleton edition (see Taylor and Lavagnino 2007) is quite overt: to put our documentary and scholarly resources in the service of a "garbage" author rather than a "treasure" author, in an act of cultural displacement.

Thus, when several responding letter writers to the *New York Times,* in challenging Marcum's nostrums on the realities of *not* "saving every-thing," could declare that, to a future culture, it may be more likely that the bibliographical ephemera—the ticket stubs and laundry lists, the jottings on the backs of envelopes—will appear more valuable as evidence than the self-evident monuments we have chosen to represent us, they were provocatively challenging the current garbage-treasure distinction and arguing . . . what? That we can never know; all conservational decisions are contingent, temporary, and culturally self-referential, even self-laudatory: we want to preserve the *best* of ourselves for those who follow. When the space probe bearing "universal" signs of our culture was sent off, like a bottle with a message onto the high seas of deep space, it did not preserve for those distant cultures images of Auschwitz or Passchendaele or Hiroshima or My Lai or Abu Ghraib, but rather showed the "ideal" male and female and our achievements in science and the arts: a sort of Arnoldian "best that was ever thought and known in the world."[9] That is, the "everything" from which this mini-archive was selected was already a selective archive: everything had already become only some things, just as even Foucault's apparently liberal definition of "everything" in capturing Nietzsche documentarily is, as I have shown elsewhere, already (ironically?) constrained by a capitulation to the intentionalism of the traditional, rather than the poststructuralist, concept of *author*.[10] There are other, equally selective and often equally paradoxical ways in which the mini-archive can be constructed from everything. One of the major cultural bibliographical ironies has always been the peculiar evidentiary status of the Roman Catholic *Index* of "prohibited books." Even leaving aside the obvious psychological titillation of creating an inherent prurient interest by placing a book in the *Index*, the very existence of the *Index*

---

9. See O'Connell's "Time in a Bottle" (1999) for further discussion of the changing cultural roles and contents of such time capsules.

10. Foucault's prescription is as follows:

> Even when an individual has been accepted as an Author, we must still ask whether everything he wrote, said, or left behind is part of his work. The problem is both theoretical and technical. When undertaking the publication of Nietzsche's works, for example, where should one stop? Surely everything must be published, but what is "everything"? Everything that Nietzsche himself published, certainly. And what about rough drafts of his work? Obviously. The plans for his aphorisms? Yes. The deleted passages and the notes at the bottom of the page? Yes. What if, within a workbook filled with aphorisms, one finds a reference, the notation of a meeting or of an address, or a laundry list: Is it a work, or not? Why not? And so on, ad infinitum. How can one define a work amid the millions of traces left by someone after his death? (1984: 103–104)

as a bibliographical and cognitive construct (a pointing *to* something) has always meant the Catholic Church was trying to construct exactly the opposite of the contents of that space probe: not the best but the worst, not the artifacts that ought to represent our culture but those that ought not to. How can you point *to*, how can you direct a culture's gaze toward those very things that you do not want people to see, toward those things that you would wish to be destroyed? Well, the easy answer to all such questions of access and prohibition is again the issue of agency, for the entablature of the *Index* bears, in its inscription, the same negational authority of the Decalogue ("Thou shalt not . . ."), what Derrida refers to as the "nomological principle of the *arkhē*, the principle of the command-ment" (1996: 1), given prerogative by a version of that earlier question I posed: "Who is Richard Knowles?" and provided with a further exemplar by the orders of the Vatican Congregation for the Doctrine of the Faith (the successor to the Inquisition, presided over by Cardinal Ratzinger, now elevated to pope) to destroy all copies of a book on women and the priesthood written by a British nun and published by a reputable scholarly press. The order to the Liturgical Press in Collegeville, Minnesota, to "in-cinerate or pulp" (Chambers 1998: 9) all copies of Sister Lavinia Byrne's *Woman at the Altar* (1999) was issued not because of anything substantive in the book (indeed, there is no evidence that anybody in the Vatican had actually read the work), but because the mere *discussion* of women and ordination had been forbidden by Pope John Paul II's apostolic letter *On Reserving Priestly Ordination to Men Alone* (which was included in By-rne's book): not only the text, but the topic itself was to be "indexed" and thus, by being included in one sort of (forbidden) archive, removed from

---

As I point out (1992c: 362), Foucault's documentary agenda for "everything" is not even as extensive as the guidelines for the MLA's Center for Scholarly Editions, which raise the question of the status of "second-party" textual materials (such as letters to as well as by the author, or textual changes made by persons other than the author: copyeditors, composi-tors, proofreaders, literary executors, and so on). Moreover, Foucault's hierarchy (from published works down to laundry lists) shows just how documentarily time-bound (i.e., "modern") is his evaluation of the status of documents. For a premodernist, a document like Thomas Hoccleve's personal notation, with his admonition to remember to "buy clean linen" (i.e., a laundry list) is culturally much more significant, because much rarer for its pe-riod, than would be yet another scribal copy of *The Regement of Princes*. To the modern ar-chivist, the Hocclevean laundry list might indeed seem excludable from the textual archive, but to the medievalist, such a document is invaluable.

Catholic discourse in general.[11] For just as the rood screen deliberately kept the enactments of the mass *hidden* from the populace at large and available only to the clergy actually performing the enactment, and just as, to this day, the Eucharist in the Roman Catholic Church is, despite the efforts of Vatican II, often taken in both kinds (bread and wine) only by this same clergy,[12] with the people taking only the wafer of bread, so the contents of the archive paradoxically called the *Index* (normally, of course, a device for accessing material, not for forbidding such access)[13] could be directly experienced, directly accessed only by those whose responsibility it was to decide what works were to be admitted to the *Index*. While one may sometimes suspect that not all the books in the *Index* have

---

11. The book was, almost immediately after its "publication" in 1998, listed as "out of print" at www.amazon.com, and the only reader's review then posted commented on the absence of any substantive material: "This book does not cover theological issues behind the ordination/non-ordination of women in the Catholic Church in depth. However, since the Vatican has demanded its withdrawal by the publisher, it must either have content that is seen as threatening by the Vatican or else the Vatican is just using a minor incident to show others how it can flex its muscles." A later review read:

> [T]he book was originally published by a "Catholic" publishing house owned by an order of Catholic monks. When the topic became a no-no for discussion according to the Vatican, the monks destroyed their 1300 remaining copies. The method of destruction however may (deniably, of course) have been a subtle answer to the Vatican clamp down on discussion. The monks burned the books in their furnace system, generating thereby for themselves "light and warmth." Painful as the experience was for author Sister Lavinia Byrne, she also could appreciate the humor. (www.amazon.com/review/R1HK3XRA6DJ7NA/ ref=cm_cr_pr_viewpnt#R1HK3XRA6DJ7NA)

Sister Lavinia has published many books on devotional matters, specifically on women mystics, but this one will doubtless achieve rare book status. In fact, the Amazon site specifically noted, "This item is only available from third-party sellers" (i.e., there are no "publisher's" copies available), although subsequent to the burning by the Liturgical Press, the book was picked up by Continuum and reissued with the added inducement: "Banned by the Vatican." See also Power 2000. Sister Lavinia has since left her order.

12. "The realism of belief in the presence is associated with the Roman Catholic practice of distributing only the bread to the laity, a serious modification in the sacramental sign. Not yet universally restored, Holy Communion under both species has become much more common since the second Vatican Council" ("Eucharist," *Encyclopaedia Britannica* CD-ROM [1998]).

13. That the accessional expectations of the formal index are taken for granted can be illustrated by two tales. In the first, William F. Buckley is reputed to have sent a copy of one of his books to Norman Mailer, since Mailer was one of the literary/political figures discussed

actually been read by the censors, it is clear that it is the delegated agency of these censors that has the theoretical prerogative to read and reject.

In a supremely hierarchical organization like the Roman Catholic Church, it should hardly be surprising that the specific quality and attributes of agency should indeed be the standard invoked (after all, the debate over the ordination of women has been conducted very much in the same terms of the "proper" agency, just as the Donatist heresy led eventually to Luther's declaration of the fallibility of agency). But such archival and documentary agencies are familiar throughout our culture, and they are often, perhaps usually, associated with some form of "editing."

Thus, while Marcum could put a fairly positive spin on her claim that a "good collection, like a good book, is made in the editing" (i.e., editing in the archive is a form of "critical judgment to select items that would be of value"), the usage range for the word *edit* demonstrates not only the neutral or even culturally commendable aspects of editing but the more insidious, repressive, and restrictive ones as well. The etymology from *edere* ("to put forth") sounds productive and promising, especially when this productive role is applied to the *remaniements* of earlier cultures, as in *OED* sense 1: "to publish, give to the world (a literary work by an earlier author, previously existing in MS)." And this positive value bestowed on editing is confirmed in the application to what we would normally call "*scholarly* editing" (*OED* sense 2a: "to prepare an edition

---

in the text. In the index to the book, Buckley had merrily written the salutation "Hi, Norman!" next to the entry for "Mailer," fully expecting that Mailer's egotism would ensure that his position in the text and index would be the first place he would look: for Mailer, the book as archive was useful primarily insofar as it gave access to himself. In the other example, Hillel Schwartz's immensely erudite and copiously documented and indexed *The Culture of the Copy: Striking Likenesses, Unreasonable Facsimiles* quite properly provides a subject and name index to the huge archive that is very detailed and very helpful to the researcher: the entry on "copyright," for example, includes subheadings for "algorithms," "boxing matches," "Marxism," and so on, and the entry for "repetition" has subheads for "compulsion," "disorders," "enabling and disabling myth," "Platonic," "war," and many others. But there's a catch, or a game: any reader familiar with poststructuralist theories of iterability, supplementarity, and the rest would assume that the talismanic name of "Derrida, Jacques" would have a major entry in such an index. But when we turn to the D's, we find the following: "Derrida, Jacques, nary an appearance in the text." Now this is not terribly helpful, of course, but with a different spin from Buckley's reprimand to Mailer, the refusal of this entry to behave in the conventional way, its deliberate *withholding* of information at a place we would expect to find it (given the protocols of documentation established elsewhere in the archive), is a repression of indexical function at the same time as it is an admission that Derrida is, of course, everywhere (and thus nowhere) in the text. He cannot be "indexed."

of a literary work or works by an earlier author; so with the name of the author as obj., e.g. 'to edit Horace, Shakespeare', etc." and 2b: "to prepare, set in order for publication [literary material which is wholly or in part the work of others]"). Indeed, the role of cultural facilitator or servant is emphasized by the precedent standing of "the work of others." But then things begin to get less morally clear, even within sense 2b, which, according to the editors of the *OED*, can "sometimes" also allow the word to be used "euphemistically for: to garble, 'cook' (e.g. a war-correspondent's dispatch, etc.)." One might question whether such a semantic swerve does not really merit a separate meaning, for "cooking" the "books" one "edits" inevitably suggests some sort of mendacity or fraud, particularly when the *OED* gives as its example the (deliberate?) interference with the firsthand, primary *truth* of a "war-correspondent's dispatch." This semantic confusion is compounded when the *OED* does not provide any documentary citations for this negative extension of sense 2b (this in a "historical" dictionary supposedly founded on direct documentary evidence), and instead buries the opprobrious usage in one of the citations provided for the more neutral sense 2c: "to be or act as the editor of (a newspaper or other periodical)," which, in addition to this neutral tone (cited as "1835 Dickens *Lett.* [1880] I.3 'To write and edit a new publication'") also cites "1885 *Harper's Mag.* Mar. 647/2": "It has not been guilty of the ... folly of attempting to 'edit' the news." By putting the word in quotes, *Harper's* obviously wanted to draw attention to the moral *mis*use of the editorial prerogative, while having to admit that such editing practices did exist. And when we come down to sense 2d, this moral ambiguity is more fully articulated: "to prepare a film for the cinema or recordings for broadcasting, etc. (by eliminating unwanted material, etc.); = CUT." Well, yes, "cut" in both the production and reception (i.e., censorship) stages of filmmaking and distribution is such a familiar part of the jargon of the craft that we have probably lost much of the concrete (actual, physical cutting of film stock) in favor of the figurative act of licensed editing: the "cutting-room floor" has become a metaphor for those unwanted, rejected readings that may later be prized by film archivists but have dropped out of the production. Several of the citations for film editing in the *OED* demonstrate both the act of rejection and its uneasy position between the concrete and the figurative: "1961 *Encounter* XVI.49": "Her [*sc.* Ada Leverson's] frequent use of film scenario devices ... 'editing in' scenes and themes apparently unrelated to the one that, in realistic terms, she is just then evoking." "1962

A. Nisbett *Technique Sound Studio* 265": "*Pot-cut,* editing a short segment of unwanted material out of a programme . . . by quickly fading out and fading in again." "1969 J. Elliot *Duel* iii.v.312": "Keep running. . . . We can edit this out."

In charting the restrictive, exclusionary senses of *edit,* I am assuming that no reader of a scholarly article in a learned journal or a university press publication is likely to quibble about my citing the *Oxford English Dictionary* as an authoritative archive of historically demonstrable meanings. Real people said (actually, usually *wrote*) these things, so they surely have documentary probity just by their very existence. The OED is widely acknowledged as the most freighted and lexically abundant historical archive of a language yet produced, and it is often assumed that, unlike such ideologically motivated archives as *Webster's Second* or the (infamous) *Third,* the *OED* is relatively free of, well, "editing." To be sure, somebody had to arrange the myriad slips sent in by the thousands of amateur researchers into some semblance of order, but since the really substantive part of the dictionary—its documentary citations—are arranged primarily by date, mere chronology could hardly provide much of the "editing" prerogative documented in the *OED* entry for *editing:* the concept of "unrelated . . . themes" or "unwanted material" is clearly not to be recognized as an agency of selection as powerful as in, say, fiction, or even in most other scholarly research, where the summa or compendium is not the primary motivation. Indeed, the professed neutrality of the *OED* archivists, their inability to exclude if they are to be true to their mission, occasionally has got them into trouble, even in the more liberal context of the second edition. The well-known lawsuit over the verb "to jew" illustrates this potentially exclusionary force, whereby Oxford University Press was sued to prevent the inclusion of the entry for the verb (meaning "to cheat or overreach, in the way attributed to Jewish traders or usurers. Also, to drive a hard bargain, and intr., to haggle. Phr. to jew down, to beat down in price"), even though the editors included the disclaimer, "these uses are now considered to be offensive," and even though the citations attempted some sort of ethnic balance by including a quotation from Leo Rosten's *Joys of Yiddish* (1968: 142): "Just as some Gentiles use 'Jew' as a contemptuous synonym for too-shrewd, sly bargaining ('He tried to Jew the price down,' is about as unappetizing an idiom as I know), so some Jews use goy in a pejorative sense." The lawsuit failed.

And while, like the programmers of the WordPerfect spell-check system, the editors of the first edition of the *OED* had been unable to overcome the cultural prejudice against such common words as *fuck* and *cunt* (that is, both WordPerfect and *OED*1 do not "recognize" the existence of such terms),[14] the second edition was able to proclaim its historical credentials by finding documentable citations for *fuck* from the sixteenth century on.[15] As with the "jew" verb entry, after the expected learned discussion of etymology (all current theories rejected, and etymology thus "unknown"), the *OED* editors issued the minatory "for centuries, and still by the great majority, regarded as a taboo-word; until recent times not often recorded in print but frequent in coarse speech," even *before* hazarding a meaning: "1. *intr.* To copulate. trans. (Rarely used with female subject.) To copulate with; to have sexual connection with."

The easy historico-cultural explanation for the *volte face* in *OED*2 is that we were now in a post–*Lady Chatterley* age, where the distinction between the written and spoken language was no longer as secure as it had been under the Victorian auspices of the first *OED*. When Ann Thompson chastises a series of male editors for their pusillanimous attitude toward the sexual puns in the "Franglish" scenes of *Henry V*[16] in standard "schol-

---

14. Of course, I was continually reminded graphically of the non-existence of *fuck, cunt*, and so on in the composition of this essay by WordPerfect's placing the words, not exactly *sous rature*, but emblazoned as "error," with a red wavy line (yes, red) to alert me to my "mistake." Since WordPerfect also assured me that *supplementarity, iterability*, and *poststructuralist* were also improper formations not included in the spell-check archive, one might argue that the suppression of *fuck* and *cunt* is not prudery but a necessarily limited lexical vision. The problem with this argument is that the four-letter words are inadmissible because they are well known for their inadmissibility, whereas the poststructuralist vocabulary is omitted for exactly the opposite reason: those words belong to a clerisy that guards their utterance and has not released the vocabulary into general circulation.

15. The only citations in the sixteenth century are from Scottish sources: "1503 Dunbar *Poems* lxxv.13": "Be his feiris he wald haue fukkit"; "1535 Lyndesay *Satyre* 1363": "Bischops . . . may fuck thair fill and be vnmaryit"; "1535–1536 *Answer to Kingis Flyting* 49": "Ay fukkand lyke ane furious Fornicatour"; "1598 Florio *Worlde of Wordes* 137/1": "Fottere, to iape, to sard, to fucke, to swive, to occupy." Perhaps English writers were more cautious in setting down the word than were their northerly neighbors.

16. Thompson's comment on male equivocation is worth quoting in full:

> Frequently, editors use coy phrases such as "bawdy quibble," "double entendre," or the even more quaint "sexual equivoque" without spelling out what precisely is going on. They go to extraordinary lengths to avoid using "rude" words themselves,

arly" editions of Shakespeare[17] and claims that a modern feminist editor would not blanch at spelling out the obscenities, she is in part making a historical statement (that was then, this is now) and in part declaring that if the female can not only acknowledge but actually *use* such terms as *fuck* and *cunt,* then the argument for their being acceptable colloquially by one gender but offensive (or even unknown) to the other no longer holds. But while it is doubtless true that a woman writer/editor's empowerment and ability to resurrect such forbidden vocabulary from the repressed archive is now acceptable in academic discourse, the popular (especially the self-consciously "quality") press may still pussyfoot (pun intended) around the issue of "all the news that's fit to print," the peculiarly coy disclaimer on the *New York Times* masthead. Thus, a reporter's piece on Chris Rock's having uttered a "vulgarism" three times on the early morning *Today* show (see Barron 1988) alluded to this "vulgarism" several times without ever mentioning what it was. So the reader was left pondering a blank, to be filled in by his or her own vulgar vocabulary. The point of the reception of the piece was that the reader must already have a sufficiently wide lexicon of obscenities in order to process the withheld information, but the *Times*'s own "fit to print" rule forbade any confirmation of the reader's speculations. Rather like the famous story of a taped

---

as can be illustrated from the English lesson scene in *Henry V* (3.4). One 1965 editor informed his readers that *le foot* and *le count* are "similar in sound to the French equivalent of English 'four-letter' words." A 1968 editor volunteered the information that *foutre* means "coition" and that *con* means "female organ." The year 1976 saw a regression from this brave outspokenness with an editor who remarked that the scene in general exhibits "some gentle humour in a number of mispronunciations" and that *foot* and *count* are "close approximations to obscene words." A modern feminist editor would surely make less fuss about printing *fuck* and *cunt* and commenting on the kind of humor that is being generated in this scene between two women. (1997: 95)

17. And lest we should think that the bowdlerization noted by Thompson is restricted to Shakespeare, it is only fair to acknowledge that one of the more absurd examples of editorial repression occurs in the standard scholarly edition of Chaucer, even for those works in which "four-letter words" might be expected. Thus, for the line "caughte hire by the queynte" (A.3276) in "The Miller's Tale," the editorial glossary provides "**queynte**: elegant, pleasing (thing), i.e., pudendum" (Benson 1987: 69), which manages both to accept the sexual reference and at the same time to distance it from English by using a Latin word. Victorian editing *redidivus.* The *OED* is very direct, citing not just the Chaucer line but Florio (1598), *Becchina,* "a womans quaint or priuities" as corroboration, with a cross-reference to *quaint* under the main entry for *cunt* (from 1230 on).

interview on television in which a speaker's "contemplating his navel" was "blipped" because of the "offensive" navel (to become "contemplating his [blip]"), the editing out of the "obscenity" actually makes the undisclosed utterance even more likely to stimulate a prurient interest than would the disclosure itself. The matter of exclusion was then brought up in a series of responses to the *Times*'s "Public Editor," where the consensus (among readers, but not yet in *Times* editorial policy) was that "[r]eporting only that [a] remark was vulgar or substituting a euphemism deprives us of the opportunity to make our own assessment of the situation" (Hoyt 2008).

The social argument behind the *Times* piece on Rock was that it was not the medium or the gender that was significant but the timing and the access. Chris Rock mentioned his "unmentionable" on a daytime network show, whereas his usual format was a late night talk show on the premium cable channel HBO: Rock "discovered that there was at least one word that cannot be said on early morning network television" (Barron 1988: A24). Again, the difference in pressures between Derrida's "public" and semi-"private" archives is apparently what is at stake: "not in front of the children" (or the servants?).

But while conceding the significance of place and social context to archival access, Thompson's point about gender still holds, and perhaps especially in the history of textual studies. So while it has become a critical commonplace that pre-feminist literary analysis, even when conducted by female critics, was usually conducted as if from a male viewpoint (see Culler 1982: "Reading as a Woman"), the historical critique of linguistic, documentary, or cultural archives has resisted the charge of being colored by a prejudice dependent on gender, sexual orientation, class, ethnicity, or any of the other "personal" identifiers that might sully the objectivity of the "harmless drudges" who produce dictionaries or catalogs, or who influence the collecting of the documents or data from which such descriptions will be drawn. Even though Elisabeth Murray (1977) had already shown that the work of her grandfather James Murray in editing the earlier parts of the first *OED*, was by no means a series of a-critical acts, it took John Willinsky's analysis (1994) of the cultural practices of *OED* editing to demonstrate that gender, class, and a sense of an "imperial destiny" were present from the very beginnings of the project in the mid-nineteenth century. In fact, one of Willinsky's most persuasive discussions is of the dictionary's practices in the "representation" not just of woman as a gender but of the idea of woman in the actual citations under that term. Arguing that there is an almost inevitable "gap that can fall between citation and definition" (1994: 187), Willinsky ironically testifies that it is in the apparently objective historicity of the selected citations rather than in the "banality of definition" that an "unsettling sense of reference" can embody not just "misrepresentation" but a "record of jaundiced literary and theological viewpoints" together with a "filtering process" (editing?) for the "defining attributes" of a term. Where Elisabeth Murray (1977) concentrated on sorting and definition as the most editorially problematic stages in the production of the total cultural meaning of the OED, Willinsky claims that the "best lesson in reading the OED" (1994: 187) is in the cumulative values and endorsements of the citations included, as played against those excluded,[18] for it is through the citations that "we can see how the dictionary lends its weight to creating a natural history constituted by the inequity and exclusionary nature of the citations" (ibid.).

Inequity and exclusion: surely these are not the values or practices we would endorse for a historical, descriptive archive of any sort, particularly one aiming at the status of national monument. But national monuments are, of course, already constrained by the prevailing definition of the nation itself and of the qualities which a particular moment in the evolution of the nation might wish to have inscribed on its monument: we are back with the lesson of the space probe. We are back, in fact, with the very first attempts to render an account of the documentary or historical "everything" by which a culture can be memorialized: Kallimachos of Alexandria and his compilation, the Pinakes (see Blum 1991). Long before the Rerum Britannicorum medii aevi scriptores (1858–1891) began to define the documentary record that was Britain; and before the Rerum gallicarum et francicarum scriptores (1783–1904) did the same for France or the still ongoing Monumenta Germaniae historica (1840–) for Germany (currently under the Scriptores of MGH series); long before the halt-

---

18. Willinsky 1994 mentions the very different series of attributes for *woman* that the dictionary might have produced had it included citations from Mary Astell, Fanny Burney, Hester Chapone, Catherine Macaulay, Mary Wortley Montagu, Charlotte Smith, Hester Lynch Thrale, Phillis Wheatley, and Mary Wollstonecraft rather than Fielding, Congreve, Wordsworth, and Byron.

ing attempts of antiquarians such as John Bale and his *Illustrium majoris britanniae scriptorum summarium* (1548) or John Pits's *Relationum historicarum de rebus anglicis* (1619), or Thomas Tanner's *Bibliotheca britannicohibernica* (1748) to define the "British" documentary heritage, Kallimachos had used the enormous riches of the Alexandrian library to define and describe a meaningful cultural everything for his moment and place. Kallimachos was thus in a Derridean "privileged" position of "archontic power" and could aspire, indeed, to become the "*arch*-example ... [the] historian who wants in sum to be the first archivist, the first to discover the archive, the archaeologist and perhaps the *archon* of the archive. The first archivist institutes the archive as it should be, that is to say, not only in exhibiting the document but in *establishing* it. He reads it, interprets it, classes it" (Derrida 1996: 55). But while the comprehensive agenda of the *Pinakes* was based on the largest archive ever assembled at the time, and did give Kallimachos the role of bibliographical first mover, there was still an ideological blindness in operation, an attempt to "institute" the archive *as it should be.* For Kallimachos, the (literary, philosophical, theological, historical, scientific) world meant the *Greek* world, and everything therein; thus the *Pinakes* could, in its attempt at documentary universality, include the menus and other delights prepared by a retiring courtesan for the instruction of her daughter in the world's oldest profession: the menus and other desiderata were, after all, in Greek. No prude, Kallimachos. But no multiculturalist either. Of the Torah, there is no mention in the *Pinakes,* and there is no mention because Kallimachos's compilation was made *before* the Hebrew Bible had been translated into Greek as the Septuagint and deposited in the Alexandrian library. Thus, the Bible did not (yet) exist, although Kallimachos must surely have been aware that, at the time of his compilation of the *Pinakes,* there was already an expressed cultural need by Alexandrian Jews for a version of the sacred writings in their own language—Greek.[19] But there are further ironies. We know of the attempted scope, range, and cultural omissions of Kallimachos's work not from direct documentary access but largely through interme-

---

19. See Nicholas Ostler, *Ad Infinitum: A Biography of Latin* (New York: Walker, 2007), for an account of the cultural rivalry between Latin and Greek during this period, especially the status of Greek in Alexandria and the East versus the ultimate triumph of Latin in Jerome's Vulgate.

diaries. There are no extant copies of the *Pinakes,* but only citations of it and extracts from it by later writers in later compilations. Kallimachos's universal bibliography of everything is reduced to the state of those "Extracts" with which Melville chose to preface *Moby-Dick.* Few of even the most devoted of Melvillians are even aware of the works from which the "Extracts" are drawn, and fewer still have actually read them as Melville (presumably) must have done. Even the Northwestern/Newberry editors of *Moby-Dick* have had to wrestle with the sometimes tenuous relationship between the texts contained in Melville's "Extracts" and the putative originals from which they were excerpted.[20]

To the problems faced by the Melville editors in reconciling those gobbets with their originals, any scholar of the Byzantine compendia of Greek writings would only murmur, 'twas ever thus. The change in taste that brought about the shift toward anthologies and abridged versions of the Greek canon during the first century AD was compounded by the shift in medium from papyrus rolls to codex books, so that belated compilations like the ninth century *Bibliotheca* of Photius (a summary of 280 Greek prose works) or the tenth-century *Suda* were consciously retrospective attempts to hold on to the remains of a documentary culture that was fast disappearing. When we add to these records of documentary loss the even more destructive history of active book burning (like that of Sister Lavinia's book on the ordination of women) together with the loss of entire libraries (see Polastron 2008), it is all the more remarkable that anything even made it to these anthologies. Such ironies as the restorative work of Maximus Planudes (ca. 1255–1305) being better known in a Latin translation than in the original Greek and the reduction of Byzantium in 1204 during the Fourth Crusade having probably destroyed more manuscripts than the Turkish conquest in 1453 reinforce this general sense of loss, created by a combination of willful neglect, change of medium, shift in taste, and outright destruction. It should be no wonder to a documentary historian that much of Greek writing survives only as citations within other works or not at all. The work of Demetrius Triclinus (fl. 1305–1320) did manage to transmit the texts of 9 plays by Euripides

---

20. See Tanselle's analysis (1979) of the relation between the historical "facts" of the original citations and Melville's co-option in the "Extracts."

otherwise unknown in the West, but the more sobering statistic may be that of the approximately 330 plays reportedly written by Aeschylus, Sophocles, Euripides, and Aristophanes, only 43 survive today. Similarly, of the authors listed in the anthology made by Stobaeus in the fifth century, three-quarters have entirely vanished. The Byzantine custodians of classical culture were clearly aware that of the making of bibliographies and anthologies there can be no end, for each age will select not simply from what is available but from what is ideologically desirable: as James Shapiro put it in one of my opening archival epigraphs, "Every anthology is a political statement or a series of political statements" (quoted in Pogrebin 1998: A17). And if this could be true of a fairly staid volume like the *Columbia Anthology of British Poetry* (1995),[21] which Shapiro edited with Carl Woodring, it has been a fortiori true of such avowedly "political" anthologies as the *Heath Anthology of American Literature* (Lauter 1997; over which there was a very contentious ideological fallout) and the *Dictionary of Global Culture* (1997), edited by Kwame Anthony Appiah and Henry Louis Gates, which might be considered as a multicultural counterblast to E. D. Hirsch's *Cultural Literacy*.[22] All such compendia, *collectanea, florilegia,* and so on will inevitably consist of desirable scraps, gathered together to reinforce cumulatively each other's cultural status. When the Paleologi's collection of the revised *Greek Anthology* included material not to be found in the tenth-century *Palatine Anthology,* this was partly an accident of recovery but partly an activist intervention on the previous boundaries of the anthology, a redefinition of not only the "best that was ever thought and known in the world," but a redefinition

---

21. Shapiro notes that the "political" problem was often in the definition of "British," and that "there were Irish distributors who had the rights who did not want to part with those poems unless we changed the name of the anthology—they didn't like the idea of British" (quoted in Pogrebin 1998: A17). In other words, Kallimachos and the definition of "Greek" is still around to haunt us.

22. While Appiah deliberately undercut his and Gates's status in an interview over the selections (claiming that "[w]e've had the general democritization [*sic*] of culture in which there is a wider range of people who rightly feel entitled to declare their views"), as Pogrebin (1998) points out, the jacket copy nonetheless asserts empowerment for these two Harvard professors and their selection (and deselection): "What every American needs to know as we enter the next century." A marketing ploy, no doubt, but no different in the assertion of archival prerogative from Hirsch's subtitle: *What Every American Needs to Know.*

that was an external "consignment of signs" demonstrating that "there is no political power without control of the archive, if not of memory" (Derrida 1996: 4n1).

So we have cultural scraps, garbage, leftovers, selections, bits of memory, and even though some of these may indeed be Arnoldian "touchstones," we feel uncomfortable about this because we probably still retain a desire for a structuralist sense of comprehension, for a grid on which all perfected works could be plotted. While more bibliographically liberal documentalists like Marta Werner may have succeeded in convincing us that for some authors (notably Emily Dickinson) the scrap and the fragment may be the *preferred* mode of composition and transmission, we are generally dismayed by the gaps that fragments expose, and try to fill them. In historical linguistics, the function of the asterisk in admitting to documentary defeat while still retaining the desire for full grammatical tabulation is a perfect exemplar of this dissatisfaction: yes, the asterisked form is unattested, but damn it, this is what it *should* have been if the documentary caretakers had done their work properly. As early as Varro's *De lingua Latina*, this "analogist" form of linguistics—whereby a "full score" of nonhistorical (i.e., unattested) forms could be resuscitated by being placed in a plausible position on the structuralist grid—was already methodologically invoked, and is present even in the *OED* entry for the "forbidden" word *fuck*.[23] The linguists' asterisk, the desire for a totalized archive that reaches beyond the happenstance of actual documentary survival, is perhaps the most Linnaean of bibliographical/textual typologies, and I believe that it is no historical accident that this symbolic testimony to the absent presence which would complete the linguistic grid arose during the same period of philological positivism in which such monumental projects as the *OED* were conceived. The basic conceit of this positivist empiricism is that, given enough hard, solid evidence, we should be able to solve every bibliographical and textual problem with standards of probity derived from the physical sciences and mathemat-

---

23. In a part of the etymology I omitted in my earlier account, the early modern form (*fuck, fuk*) is described as probably "answering to" a Middle English "type *fuken" (with the appropriate asterisk), a "weak verb" that is unfortunately "not found." Even the "synonymous" German *ficken* "cannot be shown to be related."

ics (or more properly, from the application of scientific principle to the analysis of those cultural shards that would otherwise remain mute). This estimably optimistic view underwrote such methodological advances as Lachmann's pseudobiological genealogical arrangement of the data for textual dissemination (see discussion in Tarrant 1995; Kristeller 1984), in which the inferred witnesses gradually began to achieve the same authority as those that had happened to survive, culminating in the construction of the physical properties of the archetype for Lucretius's *De Rerum Natura* (down to such details as the number of lines per page, the foliation, gatherings, and so on)—a document which had no historical attestation but which was needed to fulfill the complete Linnaean structure of Lachmann's stemma. As I have pointed out (see "Phylum-Tree-Rhizome" in this volume), this asexual pseudoscience was in fact a subversion of the biological principles of sexual reproduction rather than a representation of it, and (like the *OED*) served to reinforce a patriarchal system of power relations and paternal descent whose effect was to efface the female from documentary history. In other words, far from being comprehensive and biologically complete, with a niche for every possible witness to transmission, Lachmannian stemmatics was as culturally selective as the *OED* in the citation of textual meaning, or even more so, for the admission of the female line into textual descent was very deliberately labeled "Kontamination" and thus inadmissible (again, see "Phylum" for further discussion of the "female" line in genealogical maps).

It is true that, at some stages in their institutional development, such organizations as the Modern Language Association's Center for Scholarly Editions did seem not just to make concessions to the full documentation (including the "contaminated" female) but to require it. From the founding of the progenitor Center for Editions of American Authors in 1972 to the radical revision of the guidelines for approved editions in the early 1990s, this insistence on the full tabulation of "rejected variants" and "historical collation" was supposed to ensure that documentary encyclopedism would provide the full range of evidence from which any state of the text could be eclectically (re)constructed. As I have noted, however, this *principle* of apparent inclusion was subverted by the *practice* of a Platonic idealism that not only motivated the artificial construction of the "text that never was" but also meant that the physical separation of the clear-text ideal from the literally "inferior"[24] collations made it virtually impossible to achieve this encyclopedic nirvana. The structuralist poetics of Franco-German genetic editions, in which all variants are theoretically ascribed an equal documentary status (and there is an ideological resistance to the teleological idealism of Anglo-American eclectic Platonism), might seem to embrace the concept of documentary "everything," except that (a) in practice—as in the Gabler synoptic edition of Joyce's *Ulysses*—the use of authorial intention and of the concept of "error" (*Textfehler*) as constraining editorial procedures may limit the range of the apparent encyclopedism; and (b) the general reliance on the historical accident of preserved documentary features, and a concomitant rejection of Lachmannian *inferred* lections, for the most part make these genetic editions into structuralist-inspired arrangements of data that lack the bravura of a fully Linnaean systemics (see Bornstein, Gabler, and Pierce 1996).

In this documentary limitation, genetic editing does not aspire to the archival hubris of either historical linguistics or universal library cataloging. Such universal systems as Library of Congress or Dewey decimal or UDC (Universal Decimal Classification) are descendants of earlier attempts by Naudé, Leibniz, Fabricius, Gesner, and others to leap beyond the more modest (though chauvinist) aims of Kallimachos and to achieve an anatomy of the archive that will somehow derive from an empirical analysis of the full body of extant writings and yet try to stand outside the time and place of its making. Like such other structuralist totalizations as Propp's fairytale "transformations" or Frye's "anatomy" of criticism, Library of Congress (LC) and Dewey rely on the formal generic attributes of a current (global) archive and then attempt to play futuristics, by constructing a fully articulated Linnaean system within which "things unattempted yet in prose or rime" will be safely accommodated. Inevitably, such a globalization can produce some paradoxical (even amusing) results, as I demonstrated in an earlier analysis of the CIP (the LC's cata-

---

24. In the fully achieved clear-text editions (almost all of those given seals of approval by CEAA and CSE), the rejected collations did not even make it onto the textual page at all (as "inferior" readings). More commonly, they were placed in the back of the book, in smaller type of course, or even in separate volumes, a practice that continues to be almost the norm in the rigidly documentary editions produced by the Early English Text Society.

loging-in-publication number) of Jonathan Goldberg's *Writing Matter*,[25] and the artificiality, the constructed quality, of these totalized systems may be initially masked by the seeming neutrality of the categorical designations: but "PR" (the LC designation for English literature) as a pure sign (or even as a Peircean index) is no more *natural* a representation of British literature than is the Cotton Library's sign of Nero a.x for *Sir Gawain and the Green Knight* and *Pearl* or Vitellius a.xv for *Beowulf*. If anything, the medieval logistical arrangement of the archive, both in practice and in theory, was eminently more "natural" or at least phenomenological than LC or Dewey. Books in monastic collections were often assigned physically to those locations in which they would be immediately used: service books in the chapel, school books in the school, lectionaries in the refectory, and so on. Even today, most households adopt a similar practical system: we do not keep our cookbooks in the bathroom. And, as demonstrated by Mary Carruthers and others, the medieval system of memory and the compartmentalization of mnemonic structures were often based on architectural models, with certain types of knowledge to be mentally "stored" in predesignated parts of an artificial building.[26]

And so we have tried to find ways to navigate among the cultural remains that simultaneously repress and constitute our archives of memory. And to this moment of simultaneity, I bring Derrida's psychoanalytically motivated point that "the archive ... will never be either memory or anamnesis as spontaneous, alive and internal experience. On the contrary: the archive takes place at the place of originary and structural breakdown of the said memory" (1996: 11). But I part company with Derrida's too-rigid formulation of memory precisely because it fails to achieve that premodern and postmodern distinction between volatile and stored memory,

---

25. See my account of the peculiarly constraining (and even misleading) LC subject categories for Goldberg's amazingly wide-ranging book (Greetham 1996a).

26. A similar logistic/architectural storage system is often used in electronic virtual reality data retrieval. The method occurs, for example, when the Michael Douglas character in *Disclosure* dons his VR headset and tries to open the secret files stored in virtual file cabinets: he enters a Gothic library and has to negotiate its alcoves before getting access to the data. See my 1999 STS Presidential Address, "Against Millennialism" (Greetham 2004a), for further discussion of this phenomenological issue of the "procession of simulacra" in archival storage systems.

between RAM and ROM. The "death drive" that "threatens every principality, every archontic primacy, every archival desire" (12) may be the outward show of the *mal d'archive*, the archive fever, but that is because of its volatility, its RAM-like recursive and, yes, spontaneous experience. What medieval memory archives and the methodology behind them tried to achieve was a ROM-like stasis of organization, repressed perhaps, but nonetheless accessible through an architecture of re-collection. We have tried to find principles not just of order and classification but also of acceptance and rejection, inclusion and exclusion. This cultural poetics is heavily dependent not only on the historical accidents of transmission but on various types of agency that receive cultural prerogatives at particular times. And while the prerogatives bestowed by culture may often have been taken seriously by the standards of the time, attempts either to predict the archival needs of the future or to find universalist systems of classification are inherently doomed by the force of local prejudice. Hoccleve would have doubtless been amazed to discover that his shopping list could have been prized by later centuries, just as those who piled more garbage on top of the Gnostic Gospels at Nag Hammadi probably had no idea of the cultural significance of the rubbish and would (ironically), by attempting to save it, probably have condemned it to destruction. So the poetics of exclusion works, like the mind of God, in mysterious ways, ways in which it is impossible to establish either permanent principles of exclusion or methods of ensuring that what we deem to be excluded will remain so. Yes, the overt cultural acts of exclusion—the book burnings, the placing of works in an index of forbidden literature, the removal of offensive books from school libraries, or the suppression of certain words from comprehensive dictionaries—all may seem to contribute to the formulation of such a poetics, except for the irony that the more overt (and the more successful) the cultural exclusion, the higher the prurient and intrinsic value of the excluded.

I close with a sad personal tale. While in college, I found summertime work in the warehouse of Penguin Books in my small hometown of Harmondsworth, Middlesex. Penguin had decided to challenge the ban on the publication of D. H. Lawrence's *Lady Chatterley's Lover* in the United Kingdom and had publicly announced that it was printing hundreds of thousands of copies for potential distribution. The expected trial followed, even though none of these copies intended for mass distribution had yet left the warehouse over which I presided as a grunt worker. So what did I do? Obviously, I secreted a copy of *Lady Chatterley* in my underwear as I left the warehouse, hoping that the trial would go against Penguin and that I would thus possess the only copy of an "illegal" printing of a still-excluded work. Unfortunately for me and my bibliographical prurience, Penguin won the trial and my copy became just one of thousands. I still have it, a little battered forty-odd years after the event, and eventually it may actually become a rare book. But the poetics of exclusion worked against my self-interest in this case. May they continue to do so, despite the *Index,* despite the garbage heaps, despite worms, fire, and flood, and despite the exclusionary stratagems of catalogers, descriptive bibliographers, lexicographers, and book burners.

SEVEN

Phylum-Tree-Rhizome

I have yet to see any problem, however complicated, which, when you
look at it the right way, did not become still more complicated.

POUL ANDERSON

My great-aunt Florence Ada Greetham had always looked like a dead
end. There she sat in the records of the family Bible and on the family
genealogy: fruitless, without issue, "given away to be looked after by Aunt
Eliza in Sefton Park." And then, a few years ago, there came a letter from
someone claiming to be her great-granddaughter. With the letter was an
elaborate and detailed *Stammbaum,* a family tree bearing several recent
branches of whose existence I had known nothing. The mysterious Florence Ada had apparently married one William Whittle Barton and, far
from being without issue, had provided me with more than fifty newly
discovered blood relations. Since then, my newfound Barton "cousin"
and I have been corresponding with news of one another's research into
our different parts of this tree. I will probably never meet most of these
new relations (we are, after all, separated by an ocean as well as three
generations of ignorance), but their massive presence on my personal map
of who I am is disturbing: it changes the balance, disorients my sense of
place and filiation, even though none of the relationships of which I had
previously been aware has been changed by the discovery. My patrilinear
descent is still intact.

For a (quondam) medievalist and a student of the genealogical descent of witnesses, this cautionary tale of that which was lost being found
is cautionary precisely because there was no loss involved. The fact that

my patrilinear descent remained unmoved was exemplary of our still-patriarchal culture: my new female cousin had found the link to my great-aunt and thus to me only as an offshoot of her research into her own patrilinear inheritance. She is a Barton for whom Greethams are just a parallel but unauthoritative set of witnesses. To me as a Greetham, the Bartons have the same function.

If G. Thomas Tanselle (1983, esp. 23–24) is right that "ancient" editors (biblicists, classicists, and medievalists) have been obsessed by classification, taxonomy, stemmatics, genealogy, call it what you will, then my familial fable should strike an immediate chord for editors of Middle English. The heroic failures of J. M. Manly and Edith Rickert (1940) in pursuit of the grail of the archetype are emblems of our history of class consciousness. While recension has taken some knocks subsequently, particularly from George Kane and E. Talbot Donaldson in their editions of *Piers Plowman* (1960, 1975), I think it is still accurate to say that one of the first tasks that an editor of a multiple-witness medieval work will undertake is to distinguish (say) the Bartons from the Greethams and to reduce the Florence Adas to collateral but inherently contaminated witnesses to the patriarchal name: to classify the witnesses according to their putative position on a patrilinear *Stammbaum*.[1] After all, it was only the failure of recension and stemmatics to plot adequately and consistently the shape of the descent of the A manuscripts of *Piers* that led Kane to endorse "deep editing"—the individual scrutiny of every lection as it bore witness to the poetic of Langland—as the only proper method for adjudicating among the witnesses.[2] As Paul Maas readily admitted in his ideological and pro-

---

1. In both of my editorial projects, on Trevisa in the late sixties and early seventies and on Hoccleve a decade later, this was the first editorial problem to be confronted; and both manuals of textual criticism and the textual introductions to medieval works usually mandate a discussion of descent and filiation. See, for example, Foulet and Speer (1979), Blecua (1983), Moorman (1975), and Lixačev (1983).

2. See, for example, Kane's conviction that the "descent of hypothetical genetic groups from their respective exclusive common ancestors thus bears no relation to the various shapes of the manuscripts" (1960: 20); his discussion of the "effects of manipulation of an A copy by a scribe imperfectly familiar with the poem and ignorant of the purposes behind the revisions which he was conflating with their unrevised originals" (32); and his decision to sacrifice genetics to shape in the cause of "authenticity" (40). See Anne Hudson (1977) on what she calls "authoritative conflation" in the transmission of the Wycliffite Bible. Hudson cites Kane and Donaldson's attack on the circular logic of genealogical editing: "to employ

cedural brief for stemmatics, there is no "cure" for "contamination," since contamination[3] (or what W. W. Greg [1927: 11ff.] more delicately refers to as "cross-fertilisation")[4] is the equivalent of introducing females into family trees. Stemmatics assumes a nonsexual, parthenogenetic biology of descent, for its two-dimensional space cannot adequately map a sexual system that combines features from different parents. Rather, it turns the conventional biological schema on its head, with single parents having multiple offspring. It was in this sense of downward divergence and patrilinear origins that my cousin and I did not need one another's set of female-derived witnesses to establish the basic topography of our life lines. The witnesses added by the female (that is, sexual) interposition on the stemma might have given each of us a greater sense of placement, of belonging to an enlarged tribe, but they were not necessary to that basic, monogenous tribal identity. To the stemmaticist, such female witnesses are evidence of the breakdown of the system.[5]

[recension] the editor must have a stemma; to draw the stemma he must first edit his texts by other methods. If he has not done this efficiently his stemma will be inaccurate or obscure, and his results correspondingly deficient; if he has been a successful editor he does not need a stemma, or recension, for his editing" (Kane and Donaldson 1975: n. 10). But she then argues that the *Piers* editors have allowed their enthusiasm for deep editing and the editorial empowerment it promotes to run away with their critical judgment: "Emendation is carried beyond that warranted by manuscript collation or the necessity of sense, to include alterations based on the editors' view of the total textual history of the poem in all its versions, and on their conception of Langland's poetic habits" (1977: 42). Quite so, and it is precisely this freedom—and responsibility—to adjudicate the poetic of an author that is the major rationale in deep editing for sacrificing the genetics of recension. For a lucid and convincing account of these conflicts, see Adams 1992. For further references in this discussion of recension versus deep editing, see Edwards 1995; Pearsall 1994.

3. Maas 1958, esp. 49 ("No specific has yet been discovered against contamination"). As R. J. Tarrant (1995: 108–109) notes, this "despairing final sentence" in Maas's handbook on stemmatics is "even starker in the original: 'Gegen die Kontamination ist noch kein Kraut gewachsen.'" See the "Stemmatics Past and Present" section of Tarrant's essay (103–115) for a concise and illuminating account of the theory of genealogical editing; and see Weitzman (1985) for a sophisticated typology of stemmatic (or at least spatial) models in contaminated or conflated transmission, using such tools as lattice algebra, cluster analysis, and enchainment to map out the trees and tangles of filiation.

4. In Greg's largely algebraic mapping of the relations among witnesses, he uses the term "cross-fertilisation" to refer to the influence, or "contamination," of one branch of a family tree on another, collateral rather than disseminated, branch.

5. See, for example, James Willis's attack on both stemmatics and scribal transmission: "to impute rationality to scribes is dangerous" (1972: 22); "a stemma can sometimes tell us

My discovery was different in kind, therefore, from the sudden appearance of *Symbion pandora,* that wonderful creature that inhabits the mouthparts of a lobster, eating its table spills ("A Whole New Animal," *New York Times,* 17 Dec. 1995: 4.2). My newfound witnesses enriched and confirmed the biological plan without changing its fundamental shape, but *Symbion pandora* dislocated it. Unable to place the new creature on any of the current grids of classification, its discoverers were forced to construct a new phylum, *Cycliophora,* for the lobster's guest, of which it is the only exemplar. That is, the differences of *Symbion pandora* from any other inhabitant of the Linnaean system at the level of species, genus, family, or class were greater than its possible similarities. It had therefore to be moved up into the level of phylum (of which there are only thirty-five or so in biological classification) and just missed making it to the top level of all, kingdom (plants, animals). Whether the phylum of *Cycliophora* will survive further research into its differences, or whether *Symbion pandora* will continue to be its sole witness, the importance of the rhetorical and taxonomic move made by its discoverers can hardly be overstated, nor can the epistemological implications of the rhetoric for other systems of classification, like the filiation of manuscripts.

The status of a textual witness as phylum, genus, and so on within a map of difference is an indication of its level of authority. Under the dictum "Witnesses must be weighed, not counted," a single exemplar of one branch of a family tree of descent has the authority of a hundred or even a thousand witnesses to a collateral branch. But this is so only if the purpose of the weighing and evaluation is a quest for origins rather than a demonstration of dissemination.[6] If medieval textual editing is still

---

which is the reading best attested, never which is the best" (32). Finding that the "breakdown" of the monogenous system is virtually the norm in the (medieval) transmission of classical texts, Willis polemically argues that "in defending all readings that cannot be proved wrong, the conservative critic must necessarily defend many that are in fact wrong, but cannot be proved so" and that "the professedly conservative critic is a professed patron of error" (11). These are more or less the terms under which Kane and Donaldson reject stemmatics in favor of deep editing.

6. The metaphor of dissemination is of course a particularly charged one, given the gendered discriminations that stemmatics and manuscript genealogy endorse. That seminal engendering should be the operative figure for the tree organization confirms the parthenogenic, nonsexual model we have intuitively privileged in the mechanics of textual devolution.

primarily driven by a desire to reconstitute the singularity of authorial intention (admittedly a very fraught issue these days),[7] then the status of a newly discovered witness on the level of phylum is inevitably greater than one designated a new genus, and so on down the levels of the tree. If, with respect to all other parts of the classificatory system, the differences are greater than the similarities, we have a new and unique insight into the quest for origins. Adding another few *codices descriptes* to an already blooming branch of a tree is not going to set the textual world of intentionality on fire. Discovering a hyparchetype or an undreamed-of parallel text with a new and independent access to the big bang of authorial composition may merit a textual Nobel.[8]

But if the grail of intention and origins is not the focus of our editorial ministrations, then, ironically, it may well be that the lower, better-attested, even more "corrupt" witnesses (as measured in terms of the putative distance from the archetype or fair copy or in terms of the adaptability and cross-fertilized state of the text) could become more culturally significant than the single, lone exemplar with no relatives and no descendants. That is, ants, spiders, and cockroaches, because they are virtually ubiquitous and adaptable to so many different contexts, become more interesting than *Symbion pandora*, precisely because of their "contaminated" or "corrupt" condition, their ability to change their features in order to survive. Under such a socialized view of descent and survival and authority, the more a document may show signs of its adaptation to new contexts—the more it departs from a putative originary form—the lower on the *Stammbaum* it is to be placed and the more iconic it becomes of the biological condition: adapt or die.[9]

---

7. See the general coverage of this complex issue in the "Intention in the Text" chapter of Greetham 1999b. The basic document remains Tanselle 1976.

8. Consider, for example, the cultural significance given to such discoveries as the Winchester manuscript of Malory, the "lost" first part of the manuscript of Twain's *Huckleberry Finn,* and the Leningrad Codex of the Bible. Compared to such phylum-like discoveries, an article on a "new" manuscript deriving from an already well-attested descent, published in a bibliographical or codicological journal, will usually be of interest only to specialists.

9. The iconic cultural status of filiation informs continued contention over questions such as the genealogical position of the Neanderthals in the development of the European tree of human life. Did they simply die off in the face of competition from Cro-Magnon, or are most of the current European stock just adaptations of this foreparent? Were they like my great-aunt Florence Ada *before* I heard from the collateral Bartons (a dead end) or like

The issues confronting the taxonomist of any living and therefore corruptible tradition of transmission (biological, racial, documentary, or linguistic) will include: How close and mappable do the similarities of classification need to be for a plausible genetics to be constructed? How different do the exemplars, live or without issue, have to be before a new phylum must be postulated? What sort of divergent and convergent evidence do we need to place an empirical witness to historical development (a fruit fly, a dialect, a script, a manuscript) securely within a specific niche of a perfect phylogeny?

The ongoing struggle over the descent of the Germanic languages from Proto-Indo-European offers a particularly rich analogical model for observing these questions and their relation to theories of manuscript classification. *Perfect phylogeny* is a biological term, but one with economic ramifications. Just as Archibald Hill (1950–1951, esp. 87–90) argued for the "simplification" model in stemmatic analysis (the tree with the fewest branches possible to explain the bibliographical data), and just as Vinton Dearing demonstrated the similar "parsimony rule" in breaking an apparent "ring" of manuscript filiations,[10] so biologists need an algorithm that will produce a taxonomic chart that reduces the likelihood of mistaking "convergent evolution" (we textuists would call it "convergent variation") for linear descent. As George Johnson (1996) noted in an account of the descent of the Germanic languages from Proto-Indo-European, it might be tempting to regard the common traits of birds, insects, and bats (e.g., that they all have wings) as demonstrating a common descent, but this would be mistaking the empirical datum—the specific trait—of convergent evolution for linear development, and if plotted on a taxonomic chart this would produce "a tangle instead of a tree." This is exactly the problem

---

the enormously expanded tribal map that the unexpected letter from my unknown cousin created? That the question can still be debated, and regarded as an important element in a European's sense of self and place, is clearly an indication of the cultural value endowed on filiation. If the Neanderthals prove, like Florence Ada, to be not the dead ends we have thought them but an essential part of the breeding stock of Europe, then their status will undoubtedly rise on the biological roster. But if they remain as a collateral fruitless branch, then we can afford to continue our disdainful attitude, based on a teleological sense of progress, but progress by patrilinear rather than corrupted descent.

10. See 1974, esp. 95, where he defines a ring as "a closed sequence in which all elements are intermediary." See the analysis of Dearing's filiation method in Greetham (1992c: 328–29) and in the "Structure and Sign" chapter of my *Theories* (1999b).

that can be seen in the manuscripts of the A text of *Piers:* the "hypotheti-cal genetic groups" obscure the "shapes" of the manuscripts (Kane 1960: 20). And the algorithm that Kane came up with in these complex circum-stances of overlap and common trait was, of course, deep editing. Now, one can immediately see why, when faced with a tangle instead of a tree, there is a great temptation simply to cut the Gordian knot, or the manu-script kudzu, with the sword of a poetic of intention called deep editing. That is, one postulates the features of a common ancestor (the originary moment of composition) and then adjudicates the status of bastardized or legitimate readings by their genetic similarities to this postulated origi-nal: call it, as Joseph Grigely has done in a different context, "textual eugenics" (Grigely 1995b). As Jay Jasanoff has argued in criticizing the applicability of algorithmic analysis to linguistics, when constructing taxonomic charts there is always a danger that linguists (or biologists, or textuists) will unconsciously pick data that confirm their prejudices (discussed in Johnson 1996). Well, yes, the perfect phylogeny preferred by Kane was not the perfect phylogeny advocated by T. A. Knott and David C. Fowler (1952) in their stemmatic analysis of the *Piers* manuscripts. But given the exponential variability in complex traditions,[11] we can see the attractions of an algorithm that reduces the tangle and gives us a tree.

Indeed, the variations between the results of different algorithms (or the phylogenic variations produced during the implementation of a single algorithm) may be instructive. In this case, the algorithm result-ing from the deselection of all possible features of convergent evolution still produced two different trees, with the Germanic languages in two different positions. Once the data for Germanic were removed from the algorithm, the number of anomalies was drastically reduced, down to a number that could be accounted for by "undetected borrowings." In using an algorithm to keep the perfect phylogeny chartable in two dimensions, the linguistic research thus came up with two different genetic descents for Germanic. According to this schema, the Germanic languages were initially an offshoot of Balto-Slavic (the root of Lithuanian, Latvian, Rus-sian, Czech, and Polish), but then, migrating westward, the Germanic speakers came in the orbit of both Celtic (origin of Irish, Welsh, and

---

11. For example, it is estimated that there are 34 million possible ways to draw the genea-logical chart for the descent of the Germanic languages from Proto-Indo-European.

Breton) and Italic (origin of Latin, French, Spanish, Portuguese, Romanian, and Romansch). By the lights of an idealist like Kane, Germanic becomes a doubly bastardized group of languages, the result of at least two stages of evidentiary conflation and/or contamination.

For someone working back to that moment of originary speech, Germanic would therefore offer at best inferential and secondhand evidence for a prototypical reading, because its combination of convergent evolution/variation and linguistic migration from one language affiliation to another would demonstrate its highly socialized, acculturated status rather than its value as a channel to an originary poetic. Germanic is, in stemmatic terms, unmappable with any consistency, since different features would place it in different positions: it is the duck-billed platypus of languages.

But that is so only if we determinedly remain in two dimensions and use an algorithm to sort the linguistic/textual sheep from the goats. There is another type of model available, as Johnson noted: "Some linguists have used Germanic's ambiguous position in the Indo-European family to argue that, in their early stages, these languages were more like a network than a tree; instead of neatly cleaving one from the other and developing in isolation, they hovered nearby, trading innovations back and forth" (1996: B15). The Barthesian overtones of the "network" rather than the "tree" hardly need to be spelled out here. I have elsewhere dealt with the direct textual (that is, textile) function of both the etymology of *text* and Barthes's endorsement of the network, tissue, and weave over the solidity, fixedness, and determinedness of work.[12] In this study of phylogeny, I am more concerned with the taxonomic significance of the shift from tree to network, and with its implications for the possible production of editions (especially of Middle English) in the future. If the classical taxonomies of phylum and tree have tried to produce unambiguous maps on which authority could be directly related to position and level, what sort of edition can come out of the tangle that is the alternative to the tree? Is there still a viable protocol of taxonomics in the biological realm of the rhizome and the network?

---

12. See, for example, Greetham 1991b and the "Ontology" chapter of Greetham 1999b. Note that G. Thomas Tanselle, in such writings as 1989 and 1990a, uses the text/work dichotomy with a significance exactly the opposite of that laid out in Barthes's famous essay (1977).

Referring back to the epigraph for this chapter, I could provide a quick answer to these questions: that is, no editions (at least in the conventional sense of critical and lexically stable editions) are possible under the figure of the tangle, and there are no stable taxonomics under the figure of the rhizome. But such an answer would be the equivalent of Michael Warren's co-opting of Beckett's *rien à faire* as the motto for an anti-editing textuality in the face of what he has called the "theatricalization of text" (1990);[13] of Randall McLeod's declaration that "photography has killed editing. Period. (*Someone* has to tell the editors)" (1990: 72);[14] of Derek Pearsall's rhetorical campaign against "critical editing" (1985);[15] of Lee Patterson's having offered the counsel of despair that all editing is circular reasoning (1985);[16] and finally, of Gary Taylor's messianic view of the "end of editing" for Renaissance texts (1993). I have argued that such contemporary rejections of taxonomically and lexically "strict and pure" textuality are the quite proper and predictable bibliographical conceits in the age of poststructuralism and postmodernism, but that they mistake the vehicle for the tenor. Editorial thinking can still go on in a fragmented, dissociative, and unstable cultural environment, but such thinking will not manifest its operations in critical, documentary, eclectic, ideal-text editions. In other words, we are all now inhabiting the universe of threads, networks, and nonlinear, nonhierarchical relationships laid out in Deleuze and Guattari,[17] whose rhizome model lies behind much of what is discussed in this essay (see also McCauley 1994; Moulthrop 1994).

One might argue that because the rhizome figure—grass rather than tree—denies a hierarchy of form and function, then editing under rhizome auspices might be not only much easier (because of the lack of "critical" decisions) but also a perfect exemplar of John L. Casti's program for the properties of the "simply complex" formal system. Casti's definition

---

13. See my demurrals against Warren's prescription in Greetham 1992b, esp. 10–12.

14. See my co-option of McLeod's anti-editing argument, especially as it relates to the evaluation of textual evidence, in 1996e, esp. 37–38.

15. See my critique of Pearsall's case in Greetham 1988.

16. See my response to Patterson's argument in Greetham 1997f.

17. See the discussion in my "Editorial" (Greetham 1993a) and the "Forms of the Text" and "Deconstruction" chapters of Greetham 1999b.

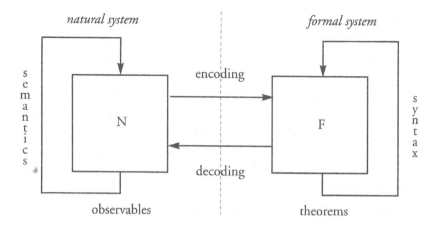

FIGURE 7.1. The modeling relation.

of such a system as having "[p]redictable behavior . . . [f]ew interactions and feedback/feedforward loops . . . [and] centralized decision-making . . . [and being] decomposable" (1995: 271–72) might seem to comport very well with McLeod's notion of the photograph (and singular reproduction) or Warren's "nothing to be done." But ironically, the very singularity of the rhizome and such simple systems may prevent our getting a firm and permanent grasp on their structure—despite attributes like centralization and predictability. Stephen Jay Gould (1996) has noted our cultural resistance to considering "root" or "rhizome" biological structures as anything but primitive, headless precursors of our more hierarchical notion of system. If the symbolic representation or theorem (F) for the structure of a rhizome (in Casti's diagram of the relations between a "natural system" and a "formal system"; see fig. 7.1) cannot take advantage of, and indeed does not need, the encoding of a semantics into a syntax, then F ceases to function as the "formalization of the idea of complexity . . . to mirror our informal ideas about what it is that makes a system complex" (Casti 1995: 275). There is a sort of self-reflexive essentialism about the natural system (N) that appears to be irreducible according to conventional fractalization.[18] But appearance is exactly the problem:

18. See, for example, Casti's demonstration (via Kenneth Hsu) of the fractal "compression" of Bach's Invention 5 to a Bachian "essence" (1995: 248–49), a mathematical confirmation of Schencker's analyses of tonality to produce a refined basic structure for each composition.

the breakdown of fractal compression in the case of the rhizome occurs because we can never find a ground from which to perceive the structure at large (because it is incomprehensible, cannot be grasped). In the epistemological darkness created by the rhizome, all cats are indeed the same.

Now this lack of a ground is obviously disturbing to textuists (they do like to know where great-aunt Florence Ada is to be found), and it might make us fall back on photography and "nothing to be done" because there's nothing to be seen. But that is because complexification is inherently counterintuitive, and is not a property of the system itself but of those "surprise-generating mechanisms."[19]

And if complexification is counterintuitive, then, as Casti reports, there is an inevitable "problematic" in trying to

> translate some of these informal notions about the complex and the commonplace into a more formal, stylized language, one in which intuition and meaning can be more or less faithfully captured in symbols and syntax. The problem is that an integral part of transforming complexity (or anything else) into a science involves making that which is fuzzy precise, not the other way around, an exercise we might more compactly express as "formalizing the informal." (1995: 270)

Within the tangle of the network, it is only to be expected that everything will look fuzzy, especially if the network's nonrelating components appear to be headless rhizomes (which way is up?). The challenge for the student of complexification—that is, the observer of the textile that is text—is to find a formal system (F) that can represent both the fractal and the semantic coding of the phenomena. For more than a century, this particular F has been the tree or *Stammbaum* of Lachmannian stemmatics. Now that we have seen the rhizome close up, what will the new F be for the dislocated, fragmentalized textuality of our postmodernist moment?

---

19. The mechanisms are, according to Casti: "logical tangles" (producing the "surprise effect" of "paradoxical conclusions"), "catastrophes" (producing "discontinuity from smoothness"), "chaos" (producing "deterministic randomness"), "uncomputability" (producing an "output [that] transcends rules"), "irreducibility" (producing "behavior [that] cannot be decomposed into parts"), and "emergence" (producing "self-organized patterns"). Textual study tends to reverse the causality, with a phenomenological observation of, say, discontinuity from smoothness leading us to postulate catastrophe in the transmission of the text, but Casti's main point that it is the interposition of the observer between these two classes of epistemic phyla that produces the relationship remains valid for any phenomenological and epistemological enterprise, including textual study.

While I recognize the justice of Casti's citation of the old adage "When you don't know what to do, apply what you do know" as a warning to taxonomists (the motto when put into practice may "translate into an attempt to decompose the hard problem into a collection of simpler subproblems that we understand" [1995: 273]), I am still enough of an empiricist to argue that we don't really have any other choice but to decompose down to a scale that is comprehensible to our limited faculties. Yes, the rhetorical and procedural holes in extrapolating local comprehensibility onto a map of the total structure may be exposed by later, more sophisticated systems of analysis, as when Robert Adams can discover pre-computer logical inconsistencies in some of Kane and Donaldson's arguments for a *Piers* poetic and for the specific exemplification of this poetic in individual lections.[20] But it is difficult to play the textual God or unmoved prime mover when one can never get outside the tangle one is analyzing. Recognizing the value of Poul Anderson's caveat on complexification in the eye of the beholder, I nonetheless retreat slightly from the god-like pretensions of my argument so far, and suggest some practical taxonomies for this critical moment in the epistemological evolution of our discipline.

All such attempts at a sort of anthropological "thick description"[21] of a cultural moment partake of both the liabilities and the advantages of any local systemic analysis.[22] The entropic condition toward which Lachmann's stemmatics aspired[23] would indeed remain constant, if described in perfect and complete detail. And it may be that during the period Don-

---

20. For example, Adams points out in "Editing *Piers Plowman B*" that the formula "me it + transitive verb" (in the phrase "for kynde wit me it tau3te") is rejected as stylistically improper at B iii.284 (just as Kane had rejected the analogous phrase in A); but that at B xviii.351 exactly the same phrase is allowed as authorial, as is the general formula at other places in B where an analogy from Kane's A "offers no reading and thus no potential embarrassment" (Adams 1992: 50).

21. For an account of the textual and editorial significance of the local knowledge derived from thick description, see the "Culture" chapter of Grootham 1999b.

22. As Murray Gell-Mann has noted (1994: 226), everything from "effective complexity" to the kind of "algorithmic information content" we have already seen in the reduction of the 34 million possibilities of the genealogical placement of the Germanic languages "depends on coarse graining—the level of detail at which the system is being described."

23. With every page of the non-extant archetype of Lucretius being reconstitutable by a deft relation of the formal system F successfully decoding the natural system N.

ald H. Reiman (1984, esp. 240–50) has described as the "brazen age" of textual editing, the empirical positivism derived from an association of textual study with science might have encouraged such entropic pretensions of stability and stasis. Murray Gell-Mann has argued that, despite the seductiveness of such mathematical entropies, "a system of very many parts is always described in terms of only some of its variables, and any order in those comparatively few variables tends to get dispersed, as time goes on, into other variables where it is no longer counted as order" (1994: 226). To this extent, Patterson is correct in suggesting that all editing is a form of circular reasoning (variant-order-variant-order) and, as Gell-Mann would have it, a demonstration of the "real significance of the second law of thermodynamics." But it is exactly this movement outward from the few variables to order and back again that Kane and Donaldson employed in their adjudication of lections.[24] For this present discussion of phyla, trees, rhizomes, and cross-fertilization, the apter figure for the dispersal of (textual) authority is that suggested by Gell-Mann in terms of the entropic relation between macrostates and microstates:

> A system that is initially described as being in one or a few macrostates
> will usually find itself later on in a mixture of many, as the macrostates will
> get mixed up with one another by the dynamical evolution of the system.
> Furthermore, those macrostates that consist of the largest number of mi-
> crostates will tend to predominate in the mixtures. For both these reasons,
> the later value of entropy will tend to be greater than the initial value. (1994:
> 226)[25]

---

24. Kane and Donaldson's "scientific" method was to establish unambiguous moments of a transmissional "norm" in the evaluation of authorial versus scribal practice, and then to extrapolate a poetics from this norm in order to formulate rules of order. I think it is important to note that Kane and Donaldson attempted to neutralize the qualities of the putative norms they discovered by shedding any immediate influence of environment and descent—perhaps an inevitable strategy, designed to reduce the evidence of cultural and bibliographical noise in order to observe the entropic features more clearly.

25. While I accept the usefulness of this formulation for the dispersed bibliographical macrostates of many medieval texts (especially anthology manuscripts, *florilegia*, compendia, and the like), I recognize that the entropic value given to the cumulative power of microstates in Gell-Mann's hypothesis is countermanded by the stemmatic dictum that witnesses must be weighed, not counted. On the level of socialized (i.e., evolutive) entropy and stasis, Gell-Mann's thesis works perfectly well: the more microstate copies of a macrostate exemplar that are in circulation, the greater the value of the later textual states. But in systems emphasizing big bang or intentionalist entropics, the later value—even of microstates reproducing in multiple macrostates—will always be less than that of the initial state.

Recognizing that my report from the front line of textual taxonomy will therefore be neither fully entropic (I do not aim to describe any system in its full detail) nor even a complete macrostate, I can nonetheless hazard a few speculations on the task confronting a (textual) discipline of classes.

As I perceive it, there are three basic challenges for biologists, historical linguists, and genealogical textuists: to differentiate among (a) linear, parentally derived features, (b) the effects of immediate environment, and (c) idiosyncratic aberrations, what we may call (after Pliny) *ingeniosa natura*, or the monstrous.[26]

Now let us turn to these three challenges and see how the phylum-tree-rhizome figure may illuminate the discussion.[27]

LINEARITY

Seeing the traits of the parent embodied in the child has been one of the main operative strategies for text editing for several centuries. Thus, when Eugène Vinaver cited his "F" as evidence for resolving variance between "C" (the Caxton print) and "W" (the Winchester manuscript), he was presumably confident that genetics would establish a link between the textual DNA of a parent and of its child. For the microstates of Vinaver's *Works of Sir Thomas Malory*, the problem was whether the two children maintained a consistent genetic relation with the parent or whether the relations might shift, from one macrostate to another or even within a macrostate. The ideal entropic stasis would have been one in which, as Gell-Mann suggests, every detail of the genetic system was mapped with mathematical security so that the system could not increase. Could Vinaver achieve this happy state? In the case of *Le Morte Darthur* v. *The Works of Sir Thomas Malory*, the shape and teleology of the total system were, of course, further complexified by the transdiscursive interfer-

---

26. On *ingeniosa natura* and the monstrous, see Greetham 1981. On the transmissional ramifications of these arguments on the aberrant and the norm, see Greetham 1904.

27. The fraught and contentious history and taxonomy of the Germanic languages have already shown some of the ideological and cultural ramifications of these features (one need only imagine what the response to the "double bastardy" thesis for Germanic would have been under the Third Reich to see how cultural conditions may be less or more hospitable to certain textualized concepts). See especially the chapters on "History" and "Culture" in Greetham 1999b, for an examination of this contingency theory of textuality—even of textual contingency itself.

ence of "translation" (whatever that meant to Vinaver, to Malory, and to Caxton) from one language system to another and by the differing bibliographical formats (manuscript or printed book). But Vinaver's basic genealogical rationale of kind was essentially the same as that motivating *Altertumswissenschaft* (the reconstruction of the historical past through a positivist "science" of empirical observation) as a whole: that phenomenological features could be placed on a linear path from sameness to difference according to the principles of divergent variation. That is, phenomena become less "kind"—less singular and more multiple, complex, and different—as history progresses. According to Gell-Mann's map of complexification,[28] such "frozen accidents" as a fossil or a coin of Henry VIII (or a medieval manuscript reading) can be interpreted under not only the second law of thermodynamics but also "the initial condition of the universe." He maintains that "we can then utilize the tree of branching histories and argue, starting from the initial condition and the resulting causality, that the existence of the found coin or fossil means that a set of events occurred in the past that produced it, and those events are likely to have produced other such coins or fossils" (1994: 228).

The problem (or one of the problems) of this model is that it assumes a relation of causality behind the dynamics, whereas (as we have already seen) convergent variation can produce the effects of causal relations without the substance (those winged bats and birds and insects). While the research of Valla into forgeries might successfully expose the bibliographical inauthenticity of the Donation of Constantine, and while the work of Mabillon and the Maurists might equally successfully place specific scripts on a map of orthographic development according to the dictates of evolutive development, this pre-Foucauldian concept of "archaeology" is always layered. It involves further digging further back, and it assumes causative and gradually evolutive parental relations, without

---

28. A complexification I have tried to formalize in my essay "Textual Transmission" (1984), using my work on Trevisa's translation of Bartholomaeus Anglicus's *De Proprietatibus Rerum* as a trove of examples from which to generate ideal stemmatic models. See the critique of this attempt in Mary Hamel's essay "Sources" in Moffat and McCarren (1997). My subsequent demurrals against my own practice appear in the "Interweave" to the reprint of the Trevisa essay in *Textual Transgressions* (1998) and in "Uncoupled" (2008). For Vinaver's theory and practice, see the textual introduction to his *Works of Sir Thomas Malory* (1967, esp. c–cviii).

epistemic disjuncts and without convergent variations. Contamination can no more be represented in Valla's distinction between the forgery and the original than in Maas's stemmatic model for textual transmission.[29] I suggest not that Valla's early formulation of a linear *Altertumswissenschaft* is improper or inaccurate, but that it is a conceptual and methodological mistake to regard it as the only transmissional game in town.[30]

Recension (especially as it is regarded as conceptually and methodologically distinct from *emendatio* and *divinatio* with the attendant problems of circular reasoning already touched on) is therefore based in a post-Edenic biology: it assumes an ideal state of deathless, invariant, nonproductive textual *quidditas* from which the bibliographical expulsion into the corrupt world of transmission is a falling off, and by no means a *felix culpa*.[31]

In my own work, such a predilection in favor of the uncirculated and unworldly was seen in the disdain of the editorial team for manuscript C (Cambridge University Library, MS Ii.v.41) in the transmission of the text of Trevisa's late fourteenth-century translation of Bartholomaeus Anglicus's thirteenth-century *De Proprietatibus Rerum*.[32] This paper manu-

---

29. For an account of Foucauldian archaeology and its implications for textual study, see the "History" chapter of Greetham 1999b.

30. Causality was so regarded in my neophyte work on the (translated) text of Trevisa's *De Proprietatibus Rerum*. The editors were instructed that they should always attempt to find a paleographic explanation for why an original (correct) lection x in the Latin might have produced the deformed and corrupt translating text's y, using the evidence of causal paleography. A. E. Housman, of course, was notoriously impatient with such conservative historicity: "The practice is, if you have persuaded yourself that a text is corrupt, to alter a letter or two and see what happens. If what happens is anything which the warmest good-will can mistake for sense and grammar, you call it an emendation; and you call this silly game the palaeographical method" (1921, as reprinted in 1961: 142).

31. It is with this Edenic, Romantic view of composition and transmission that the so-called social textual critics (and specifically McGann 1983, 1992) take issue.

32. My editorial/textual narrative has traversed the critical and methodological topography of our cultural moment, beginning with a recensional editing of Trevisa's encyclopedia *De Proprietatibus Rerum* (*On the Properties of Things*) in the late 1960s to early 1970s (see Trevisa 1975), moving to a still-linear ethic but often rhizome-like method in setting up the editing protocols for the normalization of Hoccleve's *De Regimine Principum* (*The Regement of Princes*) in the late 1970s to early 1980s (see Greetham 1985, 1987a); from there to a concern with the network of citation that is so endemic to medieval texts; and then to a full

script showed all too many signs of socialization and worldly accommodation: it was clearly not a memorial presentation copy; it was undecorated, sloppily written, full of erasures and interlineations and changes of mind. And, most pertinently for our editorial philosophy, it was less "kind" than the other manuscripts, for its variants contained many more *hapax legomena* than any other witness, more divergencies from the common stock as its text was adapted to a new social environment. These days, I might look at such a manuscript as the most interesting of witnesses, for it shows a scribe actively participating in the construction of a text. In those days (the early 1970s), such scribal meddling created an inevitable reduction in the authority of the witness, for it placed the document either further down the genealogy than a more faithful witness or off in a Neanderthal-like collateral and unproductive branch.[33]

I doubt that even the peculiarities of C would have led us to declare it a new and aberrant textual phylum (that is, too unlike any other witnesses to be mappable at the same level of classification). The *Cycliophoras* of this world, the new phyla, are potential embarrassments to the classificatory system itself, which loses its claims to entropy every time an unrecorded phylum has to be plotted on its axes. That is, a perfect Linnaean system of ecological niches should be able to account for, even predict, the proper biological disposition of any witness, documentary or inferred.[34]

---

espousal of a postmodernist hypertextual and hypermedia environment of constantly shifting links in my work *Copy/Right©* and in the various challenges posed by contamination in this present book. See Greetham 2008.

33. This narrative is illustrated and analyzed in *Textual Transgressions* (1998). As I remark in "Reading in and around *Piers Plowman*" (1997f), there are traces of traditional print genealogical approaches even in the initial methodology and aims of the electronic Piers Archive, for the eight manuscripts originally selected for digitization were those "necessary to establish the B archetype" (Duggan 1993: n. 15); and it was only at a later stage of the project that full transcriptions of all witnesses were to be included, extending to the two "spurious" and "unauthoritative" manuscripts (Huntington Library, MS HM 114, and Tokyo, Toshiyuki Takamiya, MS 23) that had previously been rejected by Kane and Donaldson (more or less on the same grounds that we Trevisa editors regarded the evidence of C as untrustworthy). Fidelity in the Piers Archive was thus partly inherited from print culture, until it was recognized that even the less than "faithful" witnesses might "represent two kinds of reader response to the poem" (ibid.: n. 10).

34. An ideal entropic system should thus account not only for the extant niches—those biological and bibliographical phenomena that happen to have survived, as living, usable entities or as fragmentary or fossilized *remaniements*—but also for every intermediate non-

Indeed, the historical linguistics that was one of the most productive results of the linearity of *Altertumswissenschaft* placed a predictive premium on the construction of forms that happened to have no exemplars in extant documents. Just as according to Grimm's or Verner's laws, one could predict the phonological mutations from a parent language to its descendants and collateral branches, so a textual scholar could (re)construct the grammatical form that ought to be found in a specific linguistic ecological niche even though there was no such form empirically available either in the document being edited or in any other witness to the text (or language). The innocuous-looking * that conventionally marks such reconstructions is testimony to the residual force of the historical linearity of philology, a linearity that can therefore look both backward and forward on the putative line of development. Varro did no less in filling in the blanks in Latin documentary testimony for the complete (that is, entropic) mapping of his *De lingua Latina;*[35] and the analogists of Alexandria used the same systemics in both the construction of the perfect Homeric line and the rejection of "spurious" lections by a code of marginal sigla.

So, a transmissional version of Wordsworth's apothegm that "the child is father of the man" has motivated much of the history of Western editing, from the third century BC to the positivist and idealist editions of nineteenth- and twentieth-century fiction produced under the auspices of the MLA's Center for Editions of American Authors and its successor, the Center for/Committee on Scholarly Editions. The basic challenge is one of perspective: find out where one is standing in the developmental phylogeny of the text; look both backward and forward along the branches and trunk of the stemmatic tree; fill in the blanks caused

---

extant stage in the evolutive history. That is, by convention the stemma should include both the Latin sigla for actual documents (ABCD and so on) and the Greek sigla for inferred witnesses (αβγδ, etc.). It is when the system has failed to account for these "missing links" or, worse yet, has not even allowed for their existence, that the level of embarrassment rises when the new phylum is discovered. An inferred hyparchetype is therefore just as systemically necessary to a stemma as is an archetype, and bibliographically the existence of the Winchester manuscript was just as necessary to complexifying the meaning and status of the text as was the Caxton print, or as necessary as any other putative copy-text or collateral manuscript of a printed book.

35. See Fantham 1989, esp. 241–43, for an account of Varro's methods of analogical grammatical/textual formation.

by scribal incompetence or the effects of time; discover which way is up (in the upside-down tree) or down (in the archaeology of the transmission); and resuscitate either a lost physical archetype (as per Lachmann's Lucretius) or a text that never was (as per Greg-Bowers Platonism).[36] Throughout this perspectival analysis, the textuist will be charged with separating the legitimate from the bastardized, the patrilinear descent from the collateral, in a biological typology that is Darwinian, evolutive, and both originary and teleological. So much for lines.

ENVIRONMENT

If the philology and predictiveness of *Altertumswissenschaft* is truly Darwinian, then it must also recognize the impact of environment on the survival and mutation of species. The Lamarckian biological heresy is heretical only because it conflates the two processes of genetics and environment (giraffes get long necks, which are then passed on to their offspring, as a result of straining upward to reach for the leaves at the tops of trees) not because of its invocation of environmental stress. Such stress is what informs the twin disciplines of textual bibliography and codicology.[37] The bibliographer and codicologist look for signs of environmental pressure not only at the level of the macrostate (affecting the likelihood of production or obliteration of texts) but also at the level of the microstate (the dubious lection or print variant that can be more plausibly produced in one bibliographical environment than another). The first level can obviously have enormous ramifications for the construction of trees, and every major technical shift in production (from oral to written media, from roll to codex, from script to print, and now from print to electronic storage) has its casualty list of those species that did not adapt and therefore did not survive into the next age of transmission. The existence of palimpsests, the discovery of putative scroll exemplars for codices, the corrected proof

---

36. See the "Ontology" and "Formalism" chapters of Greetham 1999b for an account of the Platonism of Greg-Bowers editorial theory.

37. Philip Gaskell (1972: 337) defines *textual bibliography* as "Textual Criticism adapted to the . . . problems of editing printed texts." In the "Textual Bibliography" chapter of *Textual Scholarship* (1992c), I extend this definition to cover manuscript study, particularly with regard to the environmental stress that Gaskell records for the transmission of texts.

or marked-up manuscript fair copy for the printer—all of these intermediate stages (especially in their comparative rarity) are testimony to
the devastating effects of the shifts in production environment and their
effects on linear transmission. The second level is such a staple of textual editing that we have perhaps taken its cognitive and epistemological
principles for granted. For while some systems of linear analysis (Greg's
algebraic calculus, Dearing's rings, Quentin's collational tables) have attempted to separate the lexical from the physical transmission, the effect
of environment on the production of specific textual variants is usually
an unconsidered or unarticulated modus operandi for textual scholars of
both manuscript and print. But while we may know that, say, the letters c
and t are more likely to be confused in a textura script than in a humanist, and that problems in casting off copy in folios in sixes may cause
verse to become prose and vice versa, it is still rare for students of such
transmissional aberrations to try to map out the procedures and results of
textual slippage within a specific environment. Vinaver's attempt (1930)
to construct an entropic template for all transmissional errors between
exemplar and scribal copy[38] is, to my knowledge, still the only systemic
model for the most fundamental unit in textual reproduction in a manuscript environment. I have elsewhere remarked on the absence of similar
studies of, say, QWERTY keyboard errors.[39] Moreover, a systemics of
electronic transmissional variance is still at a clumsy and disorganized
stage. While I have tentatively suggested some models for variance that
could occur only within electronic environments (Greetham 1992c, 1994:
289–91), other scholars, notably Tanselle, have emphasized the cognitive
and procedural continuities in the production of error from one medium
to another, claiming that electronic text production merely exacerbates
or modifies the transmissional and presentational functions of text.[40]

---

38. See the analysis of Vinaver's methodological template as an important aspect of textual
bibliography in Greetham 1992c, 1994: 279–80.

39. See the "Psychoanalysis" chapter of Greetham 1999b; and see also Goldberg 1990, esp.
281–91, for an analysis of Barthes's position on typewriter keyboarding errors.

40. This argument—that there are fundamental principles that remain constant throughout shifts in medium and genre—is one of the basic themes (with some carefully calibrated
distinctions) of Tanselle's *Rationale* (1989).

A major question still to be fully addressed is thus whether the move from the *Stammbaum* of fixed print stemmatics to the rhizome of structural tags and hypertextual links changes not just the technical medium of recovery but also the very epistemology of text. While we may recognize that some of the earlier environmental shifts acted as cognitive as well as material filters,[41] responses to hypertext as a transmissional environment range from Tanselle's insistence on continuity to McGann's messianic enthusiasm[42] to Duggan's similarly optimistic claims for the Piers Plowman Archive and Peter Robinson's for the Canterbury Tales Project,[43] with Arnold Sanders (1996) occupying a middle ground in an attempt to link the manipulation of electronic text to cognitive and even mechanical paradigms drawn from manuscript culture. David Kolb (1994) has argued that some of the most basic of our cognitive processes (as, for example, the tripartite and sequential structure of the syllogism) cannot operate in an electronic medium of headless rhizome structures.[44] While it is clearly too early to predict how this cognitive battle will play out, I think we can already recognize that in an electronic environment it is difficult to see how the secure parental genetic features necessary to the project of recension could not become irrecoverably blurred and, yes, contaminated in the shifting multilevel and idiosyncratic traversal of a hypertextual coding of relationships. All parent-child affiliations would

---

41. For example, patristic discourse was dependent on a citational complex of authority very difficult to accomplish in the roll format as opposed to codex; the inter-referentiality of the codex therefore encouraged or perhaps even created the dialectic, the *sic et non,* and Scholasticism.

42. See, for example, McGann 1994, a descriptive analysis of the cognitive and structural shifts involved in constructing and navigating his archive of Rossetti; and his "Rationale" (1997).

43. See Duggan 1993 and "Creating" (1994). See, too, Peter Robinson (1994, 2006); McGillivray (1994b); and Mosser (1994). See also the SEENET site: www.iath.virgina.edu/seenet; the *Middle English Compendium,* at www.hti.umich.edu/mec; the Beowulf Project at www.uky.edu/~kiernan/eBeowulf/guide.htm; Murray McGillivray's electronic *Book of the Duchess* at www.ucalgary.ca/ucpress/online/pubs/duchess/Websample/mainmenu.htm; and the Harvard Chaucer pages at www.courses.fas.harvard.edu/~chaucer/index.html.

44. See chapter 8 for an examination of the cognitive effects of multiple, even infinite, states of intertextuality generated by digital morphs from one identity/image to another by minute calibrations between the "beginning" and "ending" states.

become contingent and temporary, the product of an individual and non-replicable linearity that would be no more than the on-screen history of a series of visits to certain sites, at least before the introduction of "Track Changes" and other storage records (see Kirschenbaum 2008). So while it is true that computer analysis can be parsimonious and reductionist—using algorithms to render the infinite visible and comprehensible—so too can hypertext exponentially explode the number of models available, with all visitors to the archive/museum of interwoven texts constructing a nonce taxonomy peculiar to themselves.

By the standards of phylogenic biology, historical linguistics, and recensionist editing, such conditions will produce an existential anxiety. Will it be different from the sort of anxiety D. F. McKenzie has inferred from the production shifts during the seventeenth century from speech to script to print?[45] Will our children find the click of a mouse such a natural way of entering, traversing, decoding, and encoding a text that the very idea of the secure fixity of the codex will be as foreign to them as the bibliographical impenetrability of the roll or the unreliable authority of oral transmission is to us?[46]

IDIOSYNCRASY

However our descendants construct and react to text and its transmission, their negotiations with textuality will be the result of an interplay between cultural determinacy and personal production: in biological terms, the reconciliation of environment and genetic makeup. Medievalists have often found the character analysis (even psychoanalysis) of textual transmitters to be a puzzle and a challenge (see Donaldson 1970 and the "Psychoanalysis" chapter of Greetham 1999b), just as textuists in later periods

---

45. McKenzie, "Speech—Manuscript—Print" (1990). But see the examples of a similar cultural anxiety in earlier (i.e., medieval and Renaissance) text production in my critique of McKenzie in "Enlarging the Text" (Greetham 1992a, esp. 16–18).

46. This has been borne out in my familial history: my eighteen-year-old son, Alex, has been brought up as a digital native connected to one form or other of digital media. And the disparity between these natives and the digital immigrants of an older generation was illustrated in a joint presentation (Greetham and Greetham 2008) he and I gave at the Boston Editorial Institute conference of the Society for Textual Scholarship, for which he worked entirely online, using such sites as YouTube with a familiarity I could not match.

have done studies of the personal idiosyncrasies of compositors. In fact, even the most technically severe attributes of analytical bibliography as a component of the history of technology (cyclotron analysis, collation formulas) are usually in the service of some level of intentionality—authorial, compositorial—and are therefore aimed at some sort of reconstitution of the personal, even the idiosyncratic. There has been a wide spectrum of critical responses to such characterological studies, from James Willis's dismissive diatribes against scribal follies (1972)[47] to Derek Pearsall's acknowledgment of scribes as the[48] first authoritative editors of Chaucer, with a creative engagement in the construction of the text. In general, originalists and idealists will regard any scribal interposition as inherently corrupt (things can only get worse in this worst of all possible worlds), and social textual critics will see the continued involvement of scribes as testimony to the living organism of the work.[49] For the idealist, the more species that diverge from genera, genera from families, families from classes, and classes from phyla, the less Edenic the textual situation becomes. It is therefore the task of the idealist to use the interactions among environment, transmission, and (putative) originary intention in order to reconstruct a psychoanalytic case profile of the author. For the socialist, the more species and the more cross-species fertilization, the more resilient the organism will become to changing environments,

---

47. Willis is particularly hard on their "pernicious desire to do good" (1972: 3).

48. See his arguments in "Editing Medieval Texts" for the "activity of intelligence" (Pearsall 1985: 95) and "wealth of insight" (103) to be found in the fifteenth-century "editors" (i.e., scribes) of Chaucer.

49. One caveat here. By "involvement," I do not necessarily mean the mere replication of text, a sort of unthinking cloning of an organism, but rather the critical intervention that we see in the transmission of such texts as Piers. In the terms of Barthes's distinction, the Piers scribes were confronting a scriptible or "writerly" text, one that invited construction and misconstruction, whereas virtually the same number of scribes who participated in the transmission of Hoccleve's De Regimine Principum obviously regarded that text as lisible, or "closed," and rarely offered the sort of speculative or interrogative co-authorship that Piers seems to have encouraged. Again, it is a matter of witnesses being weighed not counted, and it is not simply the raw number of descendants that a parent witness may have but the degree of evolutive distance from that parent and adaptation to changing bibliographical, cultural, and ideological circumstances that are the real challenges to the textual biologist and geneticist. I confess that there were times during the dreary collation of the forty-odd manuscripts of the Hoccleve when I fondly wished for a scribe with a bit of the Piers spirit.

as a mark of its distance from the biological big bang. The psyche of the author is thus only one among many possible psychological profiles that can inform our continued rehabilitation of the work.[50]

Just as feminist critics have recalled us to a personalist criticism that celebrates rather than hides the narrative of the storyteller;[51] just as folkloristic and anthropological studies have placed the participant/observer back into the critical matrix from which textual meaning is generated;[52] just as the New Historicist analysis of Renaissance texts has emphasized the history of the anecdote as the fictional medium for the telling of history (see Fineman 1989), so bibliographical work now recognizes the function of the idiosyncratic in the formation of a textual narrative and a textual discipline[53] (ibid.). When Seth Lerer (1991) offers a critique of Malcolm Godden's "Wordsworthian" account of William Langland's rewritings of Piers Plowman, he challenges not only the applicability of the Romantic model of the life work to medieval texts but the authority of literary documents in our constructions of authorial biography.

Such personalist intervention can therefore have enormous ramifications in the adjudication of textual authority,[54] especially when the per-

---

50. See, for example, McGann (1983): "In each case, so-called . . . author's intentions is one of the factors to be weighed and studied" (114–15).

51. Miller 1991. I co-opt Miller's personalist method in the autobiographical "Interweaves" of my Textual Transgressions (1998).

52. See the account in Foley (1995), esp. "The Performance Approach," 611–14; and see Geertz (1973, 1983). I demonstrate the textual significance of these maneuvers in the "Culture" chapter of Theories of the Text (Greetham 1999b).

53. See Reiman's call for a "personalist bibliography" (1993, esp. xii); and see my writing (1995a) of Reiman's method into the recent history of textual scholarship.

54. See, for example, James L. W. West III's argument (1995) that editing is essentially a form of biography. West claims that, working from exactly the same documentary evidence, an editor may construct two totally divergent biographical explanations for the evidence (he cites the "censorship" of William Styron's first novel, Lie Down in Darkness, as his primary exhibit). He concludes that editors will "sometimes find themselves working in reverse order—deciding first what texts they want to bring to life and then creating authors who will approve of what they wish to do" (302). See my analysis of West's argument in "If That Was Then, Is This Now?" in the same issue of Studies in the Novel (427–50, esp. 436–37), and see my "Editing" in The Blackwell Encyclopaedia of the Novel (2010) for an account of the biographical/censorship issue in the editing of novels.

sonal is reinforced by the apparent neutrality of history or nationhood. I have dealt elsewhere with the textual symptoms of this sort of prejudicial reading of evidence: Lachmann's use of the term *itali* as synonymous with a Mediterranean (that is, humanist) disrespect for the lineage of medieval manuscripts, or Alberto Blecua's disdain for the failures of "Anglo-Saxon" textual critics to recognize the virtues of the genealogical analysis of medieval Spanish texts.[55] A. E. Housman's English commonsensical disdain for the benighted German stemmaticists having mistaken textual criticism for mathematics (1921, as reprinted in 1961: 132) and Bédier's famous repudiation of Germanic genealogy in favor of French best-text theory (1928) are just further symptoms of the setting of a personal perspective within a national prejudice that has come down to us in the culture wars of Anglo-American analytical bibliography and French *bibliologie* and *l'histoire du livre*. For our purposes, the best exemplum might again be George Kane, but this time the Anglo-Americanist (modernist, intentionalist, originalist; see Patterson 1985, esp. 80–89) sets himself against the Gallic structuralist, for whom the post-authorial complexes of textuality are not an embarrassment but a source of pride. Thus Kane, having already committed apostasy against the stemmatics of Knott and Fowler and having constructed a hermetically sealed A text obeying a specific theory of transmissional corruption, then remakes the B text in the light of his previously constructed A, as he must do if his earlier editorial credentials are not to be vitiated. It can be no other way unless, like McGann in the case of his evolving attitude toward his Byron edition, an editor forswears his misspent textual youth and declares that, if he had it to do over again, it would be very different (see McGann 1991b).

And so, it is time for me to do the same thing. In brief: as an older man surveying earlier and current involvements in textual production (especially as they exemplify the basic phylum-tree-rhizome figure of this chapter), what do I understand myself to have done in the matter of textual transmission, and how might it have been different? The story is all too easily told: brought up in a patriarchal culture, I did not question the linear assumptions about transmission made during the editing of

---

55. On Lachmann, see Tarrant (1995), esp. 110; on Blecua versus the Anglo-Saxons, see "Medieval Castilian Texts and Their Editions" (Blecua 1995), esp. 468. On nationalist prejudices in textual editing, see "Textual Imperialism and Post-Colonial Bibliography" (Greetham 1997c).

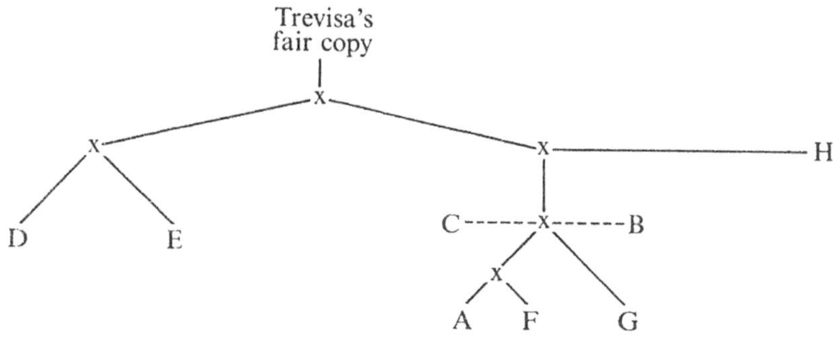

Trevisa in the sixties and seventies. Our aim was obviously to cut through that scribal kudzu, work our way back up the tree, and, via such other linear postulates as paleographic error from exemplar to copy, reconstruct an authorial voice in its Edenic, uncorrupted space (fig. 7.2). And all of this was so, even though the external "correctives" applied to the linear descent of the Middle English text (references to Latin texts of Bartholomaeus, one a print later than Trevisa's own translation) disturbed the logic of this linearity. I have since recanted (see Greetham 2008), or at least re-rationalized the affair. My work on Hoccleve initially inherited a stemmatic, patriarchal system but had to account for contamination. Therefore, while a fairly conventional stemmatic model of transmission (fig. 7.3) was constructed by Marcia Smith Marzec (complete with the displaced and thus unmappable manuscripts that showed evidence of contamination and bastardy), we also relied in the actual normalization of the text on an editorial flowchart that was part linear, part cyclical (fig. 7.4). This flowchart thus modified the tree model of strict recension, but could still be read as a reinforcement of Marzec's *Stammbaum*. My work on, for example, a hypermedia archive of citation presupposes some degree of linearity (cited and citing texts must ideally be differentiated as belonging to different phyla, and an individual user's following the path of citation, while nonteleological, is still a system of links), but a model of embedding rather than descent forbids any resolution of citationality.

FIGURE 7.2. (*above*) A stemma for Trevisa's *De Proprietatibus Rerum*.

FIGURE 7.3. (*following page, left*) The genealogy of *The Regement of Princes* manuscripts.

FIGURE 7.4. (*following page, right*) An editorial flowchart for normalization.

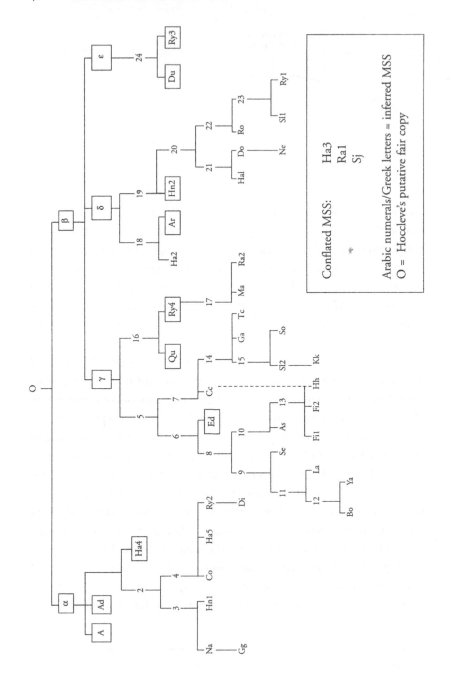

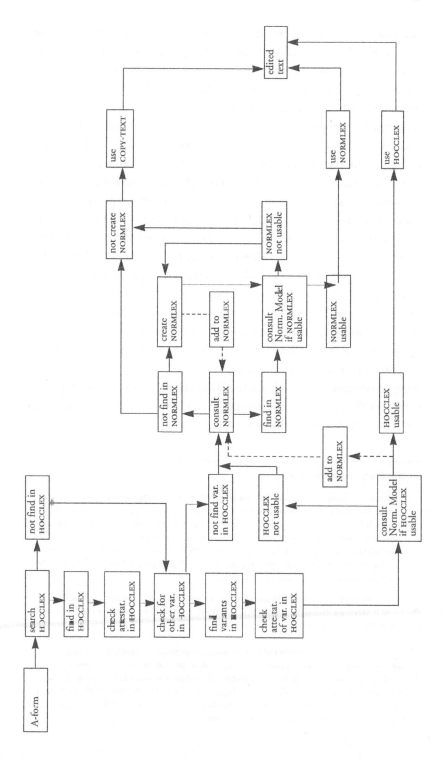

Each traversal of a hypermedia archive is by definition idiosyncratic, even when replicable by accident or by following the history of visits: such a history of sites visited is not history in the *Altertumswissenschaft* sense of linear evolution but a Foucauldian archaeology of couches or epistemic disjuncts.[56] I like to think that there is an intellectual as well as a procedural development in this series of models: one supersedes another because it better describes the documentary circumstances. But I retain enough cultural modesty to recognize that changing intellectual environments have made each model more or less plausible, and I am by no means the sole, idiosyncratic constructor of these entropic representations of data. I also like to think that a hypertextual model of free-floating links is a better simulacrum of medieval textuality than the fixed critical text of the codex ever was—or, at least, of some types of medieval textuality, the *scriptible* rather than the *lisible*. If Bernard Cerquiglini is correct that *mouvance* is not merely a form of medieval textuality but that very textuality itself,[57] then a hypertext (and ideally a hypermedia) representation of textual relations is surely a more accurate and more honest reflection of these conditions. And yet I still keep thinking of those new editors and new projects: what is the first thing to which they address themselves? Is it the construction of the rhizomes of hypertext? Probably not. My guess is that it's the possibility of finding the right tree on which to hang their witnesses. Phylum-tree-rhizome . . . tree.

---

56. See Michel Foucault 1972a:

> History has long since abandoned its attempts to understand events in terms of cause and effect in the formless unity of some great evolutionary process, whether vaguely homogeneous or rigidly hierarchized. It did not do this in order to seek out structures anterior to, alien or hostile to the event. It was rather in order to establish those diverse converging, and sometimes divergent, but never autonomous series that enable us to circumscribe the "locus" of an event, the limits to its fluidity and the conditions of its emergence. (230)

For an analysis of the textual and bibliographical significance of Foucault's noncausal theory of history, particularly as it illuminates theories of transmission, see the "History" chapter of Greetham 1999b.

57. Bernard Cerquiglini: "Medieval writing does not produce variants, it is variance. . . . Variance is its foremost characteristic: fluidity of discourse in its concrete alterity, the figure of a premodern writing, to which editing should give primary recognition" (1989: 111–12), cited in translation by Fleischman (1990: 27); re-cited by Stephen Nichols (1990: 1); re-cited by Pearsall (1985: 124n41). See also the Wing translation (1999), for example: "Variance is the main characteristic of a work in the medieval vernacular" (37).

EIGHT

Iſ It Morpþin Time?

Whenever the Mighty Morphin Power Rangers get into real trouble (surrounded by slimy, amorphous, self-replicating creatures), like Byrhtnoth at Maldon or Henry V at Harfleur, they have a battle cry that strengthens them in adversity: "It's morphin time!" Once the ritual phrase has been uttered, the teenagers become—like Clark Kent changing into Superman in his telephone booth—a different order of being; they transcend their crudely human physical limitations to become—what else?—superheroes. The incantation is thus a form of wish fulfillment: wouldn't it be convenient if we could fly and beam ourselves biomorphically from one location to another, overcoming the merely temporal, logistic, and single-state to become demigods and shape-shifters? It's morphing the self as an exemplum of the law of the preservation of energy. Tricksters' transmogrifications in the folklore of Native Americans; Wagner's *Tarnhelm* (the wearing of which can turn a dwarf into a dragon or a toad, and give the weak and timorous Gunther at least the appearance of being the heroic Siegfried); Zeus as swan or cloud or bull to advance his amorous predilections—all of these are part of the powerful cultural testimony to the omnipresence of morphing wish fulfillment. If only we were like the gods, if only we had some technical device (like the *Tarnhelm*) to make morphing the normal and ordinary state of nature rather than only a consummation devoutly to be wished. The question for this chapter on morphing—perhaps the most emblematic in a collection on contamination—is thus whether we might be close to achieving that new norm, whether the brave new world of biomorphs and cybernetics has begun to change the temporal and logistic contours of identity so that, just as the agency of the human subject may be called into question as a biographical, biological, and coherently historical figure under postmodernism, so may the textual productions of a newly digitized sensibility. To put it bluntly: is digitized morphing different in kind, in phenomenology, in ontology, from previous forms of textual morph? What does digitization do to the sensibilities of the morph producer and the morph consumer? Are we now Victor Frankenstein without the technical (or moral) limitations of his time, or have we just donned this year's new fashion in *Tarnhelms*?

For some messianic enthusiasts, there can be no doubt that morphing is now. In awe at the "technodazzle" of *Terminator 2* (and 3) and of Michael Jackson's $4 million, eleven-minute "music film," *Black or White* (especially in its closing sequence of multiracial, cross-gendered faces), Mark Dery can pronounce: "I have seen the future and it is morphed" (1992: 501).[1] But morphing is not just immortality, it is change itself, including the mutability and corruption that ordains the death of the self. In other words, morphing as a general biological phenomenon is already a condition of nature, according to the law of the preservation of energy. Publius Ovidius Naso knew this, as the opening lines of his *Metamorphoses* show:

> Now I shall tell of things that change, new being
> Out of old: since you, O Gods, created
> Mutable arts and gifts, give me the voice
> To tell the shifting story of the world
> From its beginning to the present hour. (Horace Gregory's translation, 2001)

Ovid's "present hour" might not have entertained digitization, but since his story is that of creation and mutability, not just as a metaphor but as the very nature of things, it is fitting that this contamination collection seek a benediction from a divine or at least technological guidance on the nature of the morph in this, our present hour: perhaps a *deus ex pentium*.

Ovid's family name, it has been supposed, arose from a morph, that bending out of the flatness of the norm that produces the warp of caricature. For Ovid, the warp was nasal: Naso→nose→Nixon and the former president's ski-sloped, familiar but barely recognizable, characteristic feature, as in the well-known series of Scarfe cartoons of that ever-extending proboscis. Now, through digitization and a deft recalibration of

---

1. I am grateful to my colleague Gerhard Joseph for having brought this article to my attention.

the characteristic features of the subject we wish to emphasize, we can all become caricaturists electronically, and thus set in motion "new being out of old." Ovid as precursor is thus more creative for us, more hopeful, than the warping melancholy of his own precursor, Lucretius, whose *De Rerum Natura* emphasizes not the startling anecdote and the miraculous morph of the *Metamorphoses* but rather the mutability of things under the law of the indestructibility of matter as grimly manifested in the mortality of form: "For whenever a thing changes and quits its proper limits, at once this change of state is the death of that which was before." Spenser's Platonist attempt in the Mutabilitie Cantos to find the necessary reciprocity between mutability and permanence, between recycling of form and the continuity of matter as *energeia,* is perhaps an epistemological halfway house between Lucretius and $e = mc^2$, and the Ovidian style of morphing on which I am going to play in this essay (the Derridean *jeu,* encompassing our cultural universe from Velazquez cum Francis Bacon to 2 Live Crew, and from the Jewish journal *Forward* to Simon and Garfunkel) will always be only a partial escape, a flight of fancy from the memento mori that is the presiding deity of all morphing: the skull beneath the skin.[2]

We may discover that the current digitization of the morph, while technically and conceptually a fulfillment of much of what Ovid, Lucretius, and even Spenser were reaching for, gives us only the illusion of suppressing the linearity of time. The digitized morph can give the morphist enormous power to adjust and calibrate the interstitial states within (and beyond) the opening and closing frames of a morph storyboard; and digital morphing is, moreover, the most culturally ubiquitous (in movies, popular music and music videos, graphic arts, print and television advertisements) electronic textuality familiar to, and accessible by, the general public. Even people who have never operated a computer—and for whom the mysteries of SGML and HTML, the World Wide Web and the internet are still terra incognita—are comfortable with the phenomenology of digital morphing, for the artifacts of our contemporary life surround them with its results in popular culture. Does this general cultural acceptance of the digital morph reflect the general postmodernist

---

2. This morph (*Mona Lisa*–skull–*Mona Lisa*) was played throughout the original conference presentation of the first version of this paper. Apparently, it disturbed several members of the audience—as it was intended to.

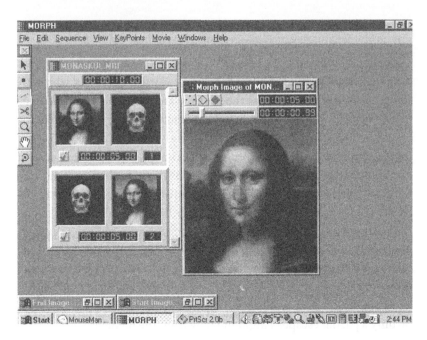

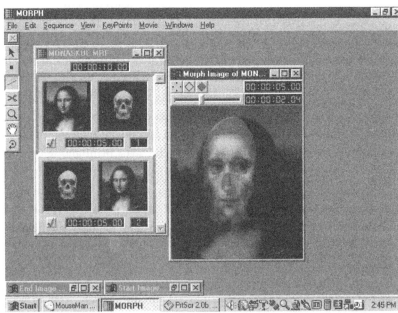

FIGURE 8.1(a–c). Digital morph of *Mona Lisa*–skull–*Mona Lisa*, with the opening and closing frames of the storyboard and intermediate states.

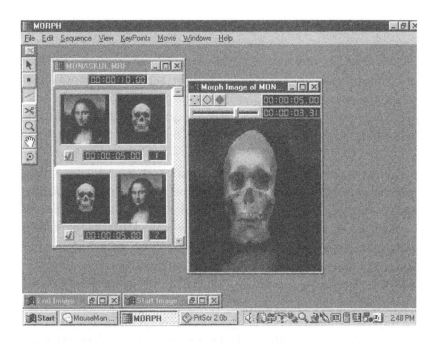

anxieties over identity, boundaries, and teleology? Is it different in kind as well as complexity from the morphing described and practiced by Ovid, Lucretius, and Spenser? How do the technical requirements and specific construction of the digital morph interact with the apparent formlessness and liminal freedom that digitization appears to confer? These are very large questions, and they cannot be fully resolved in a short exploratory chapter; but they are questions fundamental to our cultural as well as technical understanding of the morphing phenomenon as an ultimate form of contamination, and I hope to illustrate at least some of the ways in which the questions can be posed—in various media and in various disciplines.

These are clearly serious matters, and they respond to my central thesis that the current digitized morph cannot be considered in isolation from its nondigital predecessors, for digitization is only one stage in the evolution and signification of (meta)morphing. And these concerns are, in any case, mother's milk to most textual theorists, from Zenodotus of Ephesus and the Alexandrian librarians to Jerome McGann, his Rossetti Archive, and his essay "The Rationale of Hypertext." As McGann's title suggests, his deployment of electronic textuality is to redefine and develop both W. W. Greg's (1950–1951) and G. Thomas Tanselle's (1989) precursor rationales ("The Rationale of Copy-Text" and *A Rationale of Textual Criticism,* respectively). Where Greg offered a temporary resting place in the relentless morphing of texts by suggesting that we might strive for a sort of pragmatic ideality of form based on a cross-referential conflation of the substance and accidence of a text; and where Tanselle held out the lure of stasis, of the "inhuman tranquility" that would overcome "the hazards of the physical" (1989: 93); McGann celebrates the instability and nonlinearity of the electronic text, its inevitable calling into question of our positivist expectations for proof, demonstrability, and closure, as a "means to secure freedom from the analytic limits of hard-copy text" (1997: 23). I have elsewhere argued that the breakdown of the great modernist narrative of textual teleology, which had been formulated under the auspices of the "principle of thrift" that Foucault (1984: 118) delineated as the classic author, is but one instance of the general postmodernist failure and fracture of the *grands reçits:* a fragmentation (or, if you will, a pixelation) that Jean-François Lyotard (1984, esp. xxiii, 31–37) has declared to be the resident genius of the postmodern. Marxism, Whiggism, Christianity, nationality, textuality—none of these centers will hold, and it is in the margins of discourse, in the interstitial and the interlinear and the digressive, that our cultural conversations now take place. I have also argued that the pattern in the carpet that is text as textile (the two words are etymologically parallel) makes citationality—the presence of one text within another and the intertextual viral invasions of what Hillis Miller (1979: 217–53) has playfully described as *guest* and *host* (etymologically identical forms, morphed into opposites)—the *De Rerum Natura* of textuality, electronic or otherwise.

I have thus seen the history of textual debate (1991b; "Ontology" in 1999b) largely in terms of a struggle between text as *textile* (woven, indeterminate, cross-referential) and text as *textus,* text as the scriptures, that authority for which Platonists like Tanselle yearn as an escape from the morphing corruptions of the secular. Hypertext, and digitized textuality as a whole, I would contend, must therefore be seen as part of an epistemic history of 2,000 years and more, in which the morph has been feared as the sign of our corruptible nature and/or embraced as the energy driving the citational ethic of the (inter)text. Similarly, my play in the fields of morphing—through the algorithmic typology of the spatial, the linear, the recursive, and the receptional—is just one aspect of my fascination with the recursive power of the embedded citation in the body of the text.

The viral metaphor may be quite appropriate, but the appropriateness and aptitude of morphing to represent the *Zeitgeist* can lead to some heady claims, as when Mark Dery's enthusiasm for the morph as cultural icon (see above) is just a part of his history of the morphology of morphing, from the cyborgs of the research space scientist Manfred Clynes (see Channell 1991: 129; Dery 1992: 502–503), in which advances in biological engineering have "dramatized the permeability of the membrane separating organism and mechanism," through Coca-Cola's spots on the theme of "I'd Like to Buy the World a Coke" and Benetton's "faux-multicultural 'United Colors of Benetton,'" with side glances at the so-called cloaca concept of the movie *Aliens* (in which "the mensche machine's pathological fear of the glutinous feminine goo that will gum up its gears . . . is given ironic spin by the fact that the masculinist protagonist is a woman" [Dery 1992: 505; cf. Miller 1989: 306–307]). And there is Klaus Theweleit's *Male Fantasies* (1987), the anthology of Nazi *Freikorps* writings in which the hardened male body "becomes a mechanism for eluding the dreaded liquid and 'feminine' emotions associated with it" (quoted in Dery 1992: 504–505); and Donna Haraway, author of *Simians, Cyborgs and Women: The Reinvention of Nature,* declaring, "We are all cyborgs" ("A Manifesto for Cyborgs," 1985, quoted in Dery 1992: 504), and advocating a subversive use of cybernetic technology to overcome the "traditions of 'Western' science and politics" (Haraway 1991: 150); and most pertinently for this essay, there is Sherry Turkle, in her website at MIT (http://www.mit.edu:8001/afs/athena.mit.edu/user/s/t/sturkle/www/PowerRanger.html) endorsing the morph of Foucault's prognosis for identity under postmodernism by opening her site with Foucault morphing into a Power Ranger.

Whether or not the teenagers of the Mighty Morphin Power Rangers realize they are but emblems of Foucault's claim that power is a "multiplicity of force relations" (as quoted in the Turkle site), each gaining support from the other, Turkle's morph of Foucault (which I emulate electronically but do not "quote") is part of a polemical, and in her case, feminist resituation of computer aesthetic and power relations. Opposing what she calls "scientific," masculinist, early "hard" computing (for example, in the

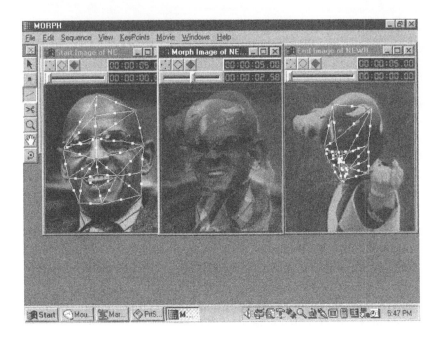

FIGURE 8.2. Morph of an intermediate state between Foucault and a Power Ranger, based on, but not replicating, the opening morph at the Turkle website.

rigidity of DOS-based command structures) by a flexible, transitional, and liberating feminist aesthetic of the continuous postmodernist morph, Turkle has turned the internet, and specifically the graphics-based web, into a cultural site for celebrating a "non-hierarchical," fluid composition, cognition, and reception (Turkle 1984, 1995).

While I recognize incursive fluidity as a useful, indeed powerful trope for a feminist sensibility (and have celebrated this fluidity in some of my theoretical writings on textuality and editing; see "Gender" in 1999b; and see also Silver 1991, 1997), I share Edward Rothstein's suspicion (1996) that Turkle's political and epistemological agenda for the morph of Foucault into a Power Ranger may be yet another "romance" of "pomo," and I will argue that such technoculture critics as Dery, Miller, Haraway, and Turkle have been too parochial in both their synchronic and diachronic contemplation of the morph. I am not going to act as techno-Luddite, but part of the function of this chapter is to show, *per exempla,* how the pixelation of the morph is just one stage in its own history of transformations (or what Randall McLeod playfully respells as "tranceformations"; 1990) in textual morphology; and as a technophile, I will demonstrate that the ontology of the morph is just as determined, linear, programmatic, and, well, "masculinist" as earlier forms of production, even though its phenomenology—the way we experience those tranceformations—may seem fluid, flexible, and "feminist."

I have promised a Derridean *jeu* and an Ovidian series of startling examples, so I will now cast off the philosophical/political *moralitas* and turn to the *exempla*. Like Chaucer's Pardoner (via a textual morph— what textual critics would usually regard as a variant or a corruption), "my theme is oon and alway ever was/*radix textorum est morbiditas*."[3] My own morphed texts in this essay will move from the spatial representation of the morph in textual history to the linear (and therefore usually chronological) to the loop of the recursive text, the basic tripartite tabulation of algorithmic logic—with an extension into the receptional morph. The exhibits will take us from the development of Gothic script out of Carolingian to the changing Chicago skyline to the ontological and legal function of parody as a powerful token of morphing and the simulacrum (or *fac-simile*; see Grigely 1991, 1995a; Greetham, "Ontology," in 1999b) in rap music to the morphing profile of the textual receptor: reader, auditor, observer, conceived individually and collectively as a data bank of variant responses to a singular text. All the morphs—spatial, linear, recursive, and receptional—are built on a narrative storyboard of beginning and ending images, sometimes with a storyboard loop that completes the cycle and begins it over again. Sometimes, the two ends, and even the intermediate states, of the storyboard may be experienced at a single glance (this is so in the spatial morphs), even when they represent diachronic evolution; but in all cases, the digitized version of morphing is no longer just an act of nature: it is a result of textual intervention by the morphist, a co-equal prime mover (literally), and of a laying out of strictly determined synchronic or diachronic collaterals, as the MRP file of a fairly straightforward morph shows (see fig. 8.4).

---

3. The "tranceformation" of the quotation is, of course, from "My theme is alway oon, and ever was/*Radix malorum est cupiditas*" (Chaucer, *Canterbury Tales*, VI (C).333–35).

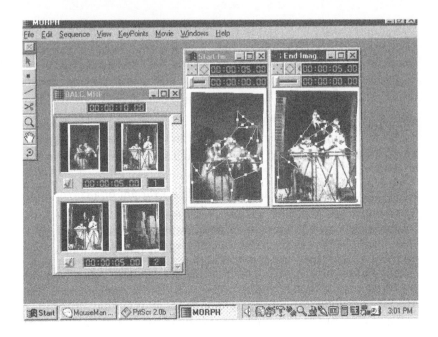

FIGURE 8.3(a–b). *(above and facing top)* Complex Morph storyboard, showing the selection of keypoints and keylines in a two-sequence morph on three states. Note that once a keypoint has been selected in the opening frame of each level of a storyboard, the morphist must then make a subjective decision on what will be the appropriate analogous keypoint on the closing frame of that level (i.e., the initial digital pairing of the two keypoints is based purely on the positions of individual pixels in the graphic frame, and it is the morphist who must then drag the corresponding keypoint to the pixel that best represents the formal or ontological equivalence in the morph narrative being constructed). Other technical and critical decisions made by the morphist that will have direct effects on every frame of the total morph movie include the setting of time codes, image resolution (in dpi), image resizing, chroma-keying (adjustment of color wheel), zoom ratio, setting of interpolation points (transformation control points along each keyline), degrees of rotation, the selection of cross-fade protocols, compression ratio, the relation between the quality of the animation image and the animation motion (in inverse proportion), frames per second (8 is standard low-end for computer animations, 30 for NTSC [U.S.] video, and 25 for PAL [European] video), and pixel depth (i.e., the number of colors in the transition image, which will depend on the technical capacities of the playback device, e.g., 8-bit, 24-bit). All of this demonstrates that, while the resulting morph may look like "free play" or "feminist fluidity," it is the construct of a complex series of technical and critical decisions made by the morphist.

FIGURE 8.4. *(facing bottom)* Spatial (synchronic) morph displaying linear (diachronic) formal changes in paleography between Carolingian and Gothic. Note that each of these actual documentary states could be digitized as the opening and/or closing frames of a morph storyboard, to produce intermediate states that do not reflect actual documents or actual scripts.

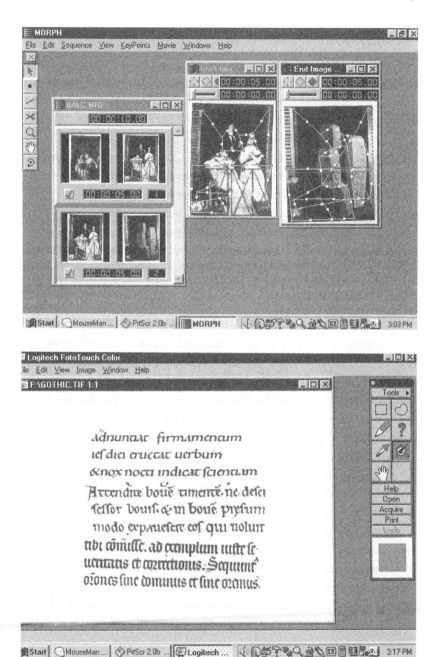

1

I begin with spatial morphs, some digitized and some begging for digitization, and take paleography as a first exhibit: the morph, conceived as a device of historical mensuration, lay at the heart of the positivist project of *Altertumswissenschaft*, the "science of ancient times" that was largely sponsored as a body of research by the historicism of Valla and his discrimination between the "authentic" and the "fake," and by the attempts of Mabillon and the Maurists to arrange orthographic morphs into a predictive morphology that would eventually result in the "laws" for change in historical linguistics.[4] This desire for order, a literal (i.e., letter by letter) ordinal configuration of the morph, was a sine qua non for positivist history, as the neat entablature of the development of Gothic out of Carolingian all too tidily demonstrates (see fig. 8.4). As we shall see later when we confront the less predictable (and more dangerous) recursive forms of the morph, this desire for neatness has no space for the successful simulacrum, or what I have referred to as the "recycling of scripts" ("Palaeography" chapter of 1994, and 1999b: 64–67)—Carolingian, for example, as a supposed reconstitution of roman, humanist as a refurbishing of Carolingian, twentieth-century italic as a return of humanist, and so on—but the basic model will serve. It gives direction and momentum to the morph in a spatial representation, just as the gradual morphing from Hebrew to Latin alphabets for the Jewish journal *Forward* (as the journal changed from Yiddish to English) incorporates the chronological progression within a singular spatial layout. In a God-like purview over the interlaced stages of change and corruption, we see the morph and its history writ large and whole both in paleography and in, say, the symptomatic cubist flattening of perspective and motion, where multiple viewpoints and diachronic actions are rendered simultaneously in two-dimensional space. Such variance in both synchronic and diachronic modes does not have to be produced digitally, of course, but the fine calibration through multiple states can be more exactly achieved in a digital format, as in Donald Knuth's Metafont program, where the gradual stylis-

---

4. On the textual problem of the fake and forgery, see Grigely 1991, 1995a: n. 19; Jones 1990, esp. Barker's "Textual Forgery" (22–27); and the "Ontology" chapter of Greetham 1999b. On the role of the paleographical work of Mabillon and the Maurists as it relates to a theory of historical linearity, see the "History" chapter of Greetham 1999b, esp. 69–71.

FIGURE 8.5. *(above) Forward* magazine's spatial morphing of a
chronological process, from Hebrew characters in the original Yiddish
version to the Latin alphabet in the English-language version.

FIGURE 8.6. *(following page)* Spatial morph displaying linear formal changes. Knuth's
Metafont, showing the digital calibration between old-style and modern typography.

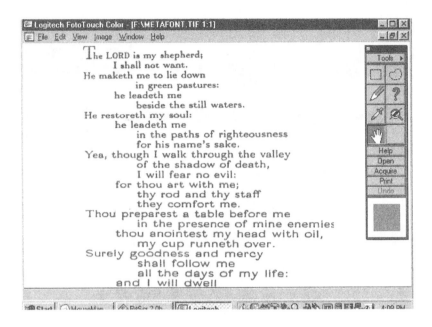

tic changes between old-style typography and modern can be calibrated through minute adjustments on the interstitial stages between the two ends of the morphing storyboard. This digitized series of reformulated images is, of course, ahistorical, in that we should not suppose that every letter-form on the storyboard actually existed; but it is the nonhistorical, undocumentable artifice of the morph storyboard that gives it its unique phenomenological function: apparent seamlessness constructed out of infinitesimally small calibrations.

2

From spatial morphs, or the diachronic observed as synchronic, I turn to linear morphs, usually on a chronological continuum. In these examples, the morphist first determines the opening and closing images (and multiple interstitial positions) in complex, multistage morphs, then decides which elements of those images are to be the graphic (or auditory) anchors around which the morphing will be mapped, then plots out such parameters as speed, compression, pixelation, and graphic radiation, before producing the morph movie and modifying its direction, looping, and size. Such movies as *Willow, Terminator 2, Indiana Jones and the Last Crusade,* and *Sleepwalkers* have used digitized morphing along the storyboard as a basic narrative ingredient. But long before formal digitization, the movies were quick to realize the potential for the frame-by-frame reconstitution of shape, form, and thus identity. The 1932 Fredric March version of *Dr. Jekyll and Mr. Hyde,* for example, while technically rather clumsy, seized on the morph as the perfect visual embodiment of the shifting identity between the two parts of the protagonist's personality. Similarly, pre-digital, stop-frame, live-action children's movies—where each movement of a figure was photographed separately and then strung together in a complete storyboard to form the total action—have been a major influence on the phenomenology of fully digitized animation and have not been entirely superseded by the digitized equivalents of the same stop-action technique, as in the Wallace and Gromit shorts or *Chicken Run.* Indeed, the digitized construction of intermediate states in such genres as parody (of which digitized morphing is a primary example) may even occlude or subvert the conceptual gap upon which the parodist is relying between the target image and the parodic extension, as in the mixed-state digitized frame between Manet's *Le Dejeuner sur l'herbe* and a contemporary (updated) parody, with the intimacy of the woods and nudity in Manet replaced by screaming traffic and a beleaguered group of urban picnickers. Digitization, while instructive in showing the gradual morphing achieved by the parodist, may ironically reduce the conceptual value of the parody by removing the necessary disjunctive gap between target and parody. Similarly, a digitization between two actual historical states, as in the storyboard and interstitial frame of the changes in the Chicago skyline over several decades (see fig. 8.9), may be both amusing and graphically instructive as a seamless morph movie, but because the actual architectural changes of form took place in major disjunctive leaps (tearing down one building and putting up another), the interstitial frames will not only be ahistorical—texts that never were—but will also literally distort the shape-shifting phenomenology of the total architectural changes. On the other hand, constructing a digitized morph movie of a painting used as a graphic target and its later version (again, an essentially parodic exercise, since it results in caricatured states that were never actually produced by either artist) may clarify and illuminate the formal liberties that the belated artist may have taken, as in the intermediate frame representing a non-extant state between Velazquez's original *Portrait of Pope Innocent X* and Bacon's later deconstruction of it in his

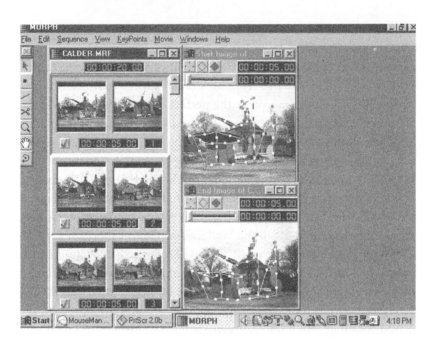

Study after Velazquez's Portrait of Pope Innocent X—a digitally produced state that is not the property of either Velazquez or Bacon but a hybrid "in the style of" some completely fictitious intermediate artist sharing and combining formal attributes of the two artists. As we will see later, such linear extensions of an original are ultimately to be seen within the generally recursive or looping effect of Bacon's oeuvre.

While it is easy to see the basic ontological permutations in the visual mode of the linear morph—within the conventions of "text" conceived as any object of study that embodies a textile, cross-referential function— these relations along a linear morph have, to my mind, been most convincingly and eloquently set out for all media in Justice David Souter's opinion in the U.S. Supreme Court's decision in the famous parody case concerning the Roy Orbison song "Pretty Woman" and the 2 Live Crew rap parody. Souter noted that the relations between the "target" (the opening of the storyboard) and the "parodic" stretching in the closing image of the storyboard must have a measurable "critical element" (but note, not an element that is susceptible to "evaluating its quality"). As Souter acknowledged:

FIGURE 8.7. *(facing, top)* Complex multilevel storyboards, in adding sequences that may then be looped back to the original frame of the first-level storyboard, create a recursive morph. Note that all the technical and critical decisions have to be made for *each level* of the multisequenced morph. In this case, since there are four states to be recursively morphed (so that the final image of level 4 can be linked back to the opening image of level 1 in the continuous playing of the morph movie), there are five levels of storyboard, and opening and closing frames for each one. Only the first three levels and the opening and closing frames of the first level are shown here. The other two levels of the storyboard can be scrolled up as needed. There is no theoretical limit to the number of levels, only the practical limits of RAM and the storage capacity of the equipment (and the patience of the morphist).

FIGURE 8.8. *(facing, bottom)* Intermediate digitized state in parody, reducing the parodic disjunction but displaying a graphic overlap, or "see-through," of the specific frame. Note that varying states of the formal distance between "target" and "parody" can be produced by moving the time-scale slide to different positions within the total morph movie and then morphing to that point in the sequence.

FIGURE 8.9. *(following page, top)* Chicago skyline storyboard and an ahistorical intermediate state, showing the formal distortion produced by morphing to a non-extant interstitial slide point on the time scale.

FIGURE 8.10. *(following page, bottom)* Non-extant, parodic, digitized state between Velazquez and Bacon, "in the style" of an artist who is formally an amalgam of the two.

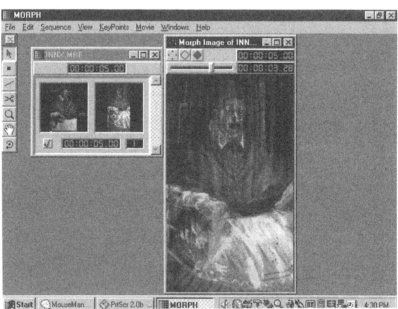

Parody's humor, or in any event its comment, necessarily springs from recognizable allusion to its object through *distorted* imitation. Its art lies in the tension between a known original and its parodic twin. When parody takes aim at a particular work, the parody must be able to conjure up at least enough of that original to make the object of its critical wit recognizable [through] quotation of the original's most distinctive or memorable features, which the parodist can be sure the audience will know. . . . the heart is what most readily conjures up the song for parody, and it is the heart at which the parody takes aim. (Souter 1994: n.p.; emphasis added)

In reversing the decision of the circuit court and in finding for 2 Live Crew's parodic version of Roy Orbison's song,[5] Souter made an important conceptual distinction between what he called the "duplicative" and the "transformative" natures of the copy, that is, between the facsimile or simulacrum and the morph (see Baudrillard 1995, esp. "The Precession of Simulacra" and "Simulacra and Science Fiction"). "This distinction between the potentially remediable displacement and unremediable disparagement is reflected in the rule that there is no protectable derivative market for criticism" (Souter 1994: n.p.). This sophisticated argument— especially as it emphasizes the parodic formal and cultural distancing ("unremediable disparagement")—is a perfect rationale for the digitized morph, conceived as a series of "disparagements" based on a "critical" element that re-forms the "characteristic . . . heart" of the opening storyboard frame. Moreover, the argument that parody, as exemplified technically by the fine calibrations of the digitized morph, is not an infringement of copyright under U.S. law, frees the parodist/morphist from any claims of

---

5. The first couple of lines of the lyrics of the 2 Live Crew version of Orbison and William Dees's "Pretty Woman" are virtually identical to the target of the parody. And even when the rap version then substitutes "Big Hairy Woman you need to shave that stuff" for Orbison's "Pretty Woman, won't you pardon me," and then morphs still further into "Bald headed woman," "Two timin' woman," etc. (with a significant recursive return to "pretty woman" in the last line), there is a notable absence of the pornographic, violent, "gangsta rap" qualities that had previously brought notoriety to the group. The specific morphing parody (including the musical riffs) thus falls squarely within Souter's requirements of "recognizability" and the "transformative." There is a canonical joke being played here as well, for the album on which the 2 Live Crew parody appears (*As Clean as They Wanna Be*) is itself a parody, by diminution and acceptable acculturation, of their earlier *As Bad as They Wanna Be*, which was full of the violence and sexual aggression that is absent from the parodic "Pretty Woman." The main quality connecting the two albums is the misogyny and anti-Romanticism that is, as Souter observes, a cultural antidote to the squeaky-clean, sentimentalized vision of sexuality promoted in the original Orbison version.

proprietorship that might otherwise be made by the target of the morph/ parody. And Souter's insistence that the "germ of parody lies in the definition of the Greek, *parodeia* . . . a song sung alongside another" and that the audience must be able to gauge the distance between the original and the parody will, as we shall see, be a perfect link with the concluding, "reception" part of this chapter.

Perhaps the most pervasive form of the linear morph is in the musical variation, where, after laying down an opening frame for the aural storyboard, the composer proceeds to push against the perceptible limits of this frame by a series of narrative warps away from it. The challenge for the composer is to play with enough variability to give a sense of development and thus narrative line, while at the same time always keeping enough of the template that has been established in the opening frame (the theme) phenomenologically and conceptually active in the auditor's consciousness. This formal requirement is most severely challenged in, for example, digital sampling (Sanjek 1992) and jazz improvisation, which are both virtually impossible to map in a non aural medium like this essay (at least, without embedded MIDI files). But we can see a simplified, and at the same time, a culturally conditioned version of the problem in the opening and closing processionals of Britten's church opera *Curlew River,* where the plainchant "Te lucis ante terminum," cited more or less straight in the opening processional, is morphed into a Balinesque, "orientalized," melismatic, gamelan version *of the same musical line* in the closing processional.[6] It is comparatively easy to trace the intermediate narrative frames of the *Curlew River* morph, for we can establish that Britten was heavily influenced by his visit to Japan and Bali as he was composing the opera. The morph is both intentional and culturally definable, two of the qualities that Souter claimed should be present in the successful playing of one "song sung alongside another." Similarly, the permutations, inversions,

---

6. Britten's morph from direct quotation of the tradition of the spare, masculinist, linear form of Gregorian chant illustrates the nineteenth-century reformation of the history of Western chant as a rejection of the perceived "oriental," "feminine" origins of old Roman and Ambrosian chant and the codification of a "masculinist," linear, nonrecursive tonal Gregorian form that more conveniently historicized the position of German post-Beethoven music as a fulfillment of the Western tradition. Thus, Britten's subsequent "orientalization" of "Te lucis" is itself a recursive morph (perhaps unconsciously) into the pre-Gregorian tradition. See Treitler 1992 for a brilliantly argued critique of this putative (but historically and formally inaccurate) morph from the feminist Oriental to the masculinist Western.

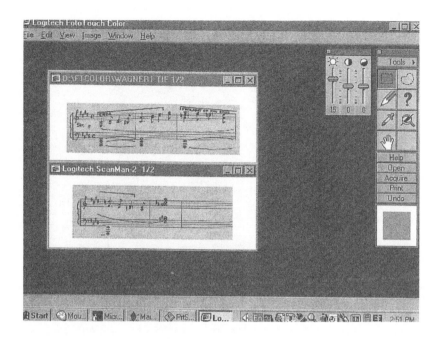

FIGURE 8.11. Wagner's *Nature/Erda* and *Götterdämmerung* motifs as paired morphs of each other: spatial (in score) and linear (in aural medium). Note that in other, more complex parts of the score, Wagner not only morphs these two motifs together but also morphs one motif into others through intermediate slide points on the aural scale. For example, Deryck Cooke (1968: 8, 13) demonstrates the "embryonic," "intermediate," and "definitive" states of the *Ring* motif as well as the relations between the "harmonic basis" and "outline" states of the same motif to produce, for instance, the "scheming" motif (from the "outline") and the "resentment" motif out of the "diminished triad" version of the harmonic basis of the *Ring* motif. As in the spatial morph of figure 8.4, all of these extant aural morphs could, of course, be digitized to produce non-extant yet more intermediate and extended states.

and paired linear morphings that are the fundamental formulations of both identity and meaning in the Wagnerian leitmotif system can graphically as well as aurally illustrate the ironic distance that Souter saw as perceptually necessary in the successful functioning of the *parodeia*: witness the mirror-like ironic pairing of the *Nature/Erda* (rising, positive) and *Götterdämmerung* (falling, negative) motifs from *Der Ring des Nibelungen*.

3

From the linear, I turn to the recursive, those lines of "disparagement" and ironic distance that eventually fold back up to the original frame of

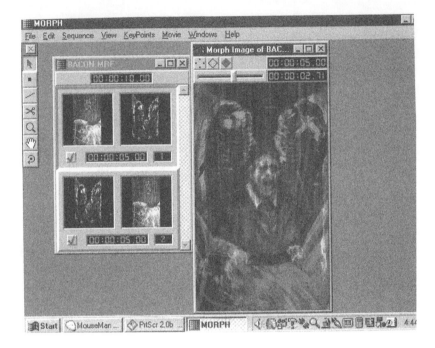

the storyboard. Here, Justice Souter's distinction between disparagement and displacement will no longer serve as an epistemological or even a procedural model for the recursive morph's invaginations.[7] Its turning inside out to become a doppelgänger of its original re-forms the linear into a circle, one that questions the boundaries of identity even more problematically than Foucault becoming a Power Ranger. *Terminator 2* provides the most chilling examples of the recursive morph, when the Terminator morphs from its base, "Romantic" identity into a replication (and therefore simultaneous duplication) of another identity: in one scene, the Terminator rises out of a linoleum floor and takes on the shape of a prison guard; the "authentic" guard gazes uncomprehendingly on his own simulacrum and is then killed by the Terminator. In formal terms, the guard thus murders "himself." In a later scene, the Terminator takes on both the voice and shape of the mother figure, so that her son is confronted by two apparently identical "mothers" and has to decide, in a critical moment

---

7. On the concept of Derridean invagination and its textual/bibliographical function, see Derrida 1979 and Greetham 1991b.

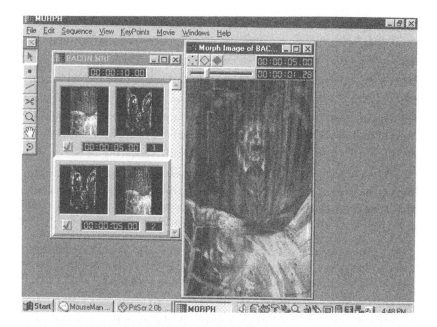

which must rely more on intuition than sensory perception, which is the authentic and which the morphed simulacrum—as stark and disturbing and threatening a playing out of the anxieties of the "Are you my mother?" theme as we are ever likely to encounter. The morphing Terminator abandons the Romantic precepts of his sense of self and invades and replicates the self of another, while that other is simultaneously present.

But we can observe the recursive morph even in spatial media, when seen as a sequence in, say, the intertextual relations within an artist's oeuvre, or through digitization, in the parodic disparagement of the actual compositions of an artist into the production of morphed extensions of the style, which do not represent any work actually created by the artist.

As I suggested earlier, the digitized, non-extant, and non-proprietary intermediate state between Velazquez's *Portrait* and Bacon's *Study* should be seen as not only a straightforward linear morph, but also within the

---

FIGURE 8.12(a–b). (*facing and above*) Digitized emblem of a recursive Baconian style. The morph emulates the artist's recursive mode in his oeuvre by producing a state that is paradoxically both an electronic *distillation* and an *extension* of the stylistic manner of Bacon; that is, this slide point on the morph does not exist and is not the "property" of the artist, even though it displays, in caricature form, the "properties" of the artist's style.

recursive reformations of Bacon's oeuvre. This similarly non-extant digi-tized state, reflecting certain stylistic formulations that may cumulatively distill a Baconian vision without ever representing an actual painting—especially if played as a looping morph movie—illustrates this recur-sive tendency and overlapping of formal and ontological boundaries in Bacon's work, and any one of these non-extant frames could be digitally morphed to other similarly recursive aspects of Bacon's production. In so doing, we would be constructing a parodic rendering of Bacon, but not necessarily of a specific work: the individual paintings would cumu-latively become a complex of recursive form, in which digitization would further obscure the boundaries of a work even more than is already done in Bacon's actual canon.

4

The spatial, linear, and recursive morphs have all assumed a fairly stable reception history, as did Justice Souter's declaration that the audience must recognize the original. But one of the major problems confront-ing the textual scholar is that the audience for a work is not stable: it morphs both in space and in time. In fact, some textuists (Hanna 1991, 1993; and Small 1991 come to mind) have argued that the editorial desire for "plenitude" in annotating the perceived allusions in "difficult" texts should be resisted, and that an editor should take care not to provide for a modern audience more information than the originating author might have intended. I have major problems with such appeals to a deliber-ately obfuscating or opaque intentionalism, but I do find the calibration of differing levels of referential awareness in different audiences to be a particularly valuable tool in the analysis of morphs. To put it as directly as I can: if a later or other audience than that envisaged by the morphist does not recognize the gap between the morphed conclusion and the original in a visual or aural storyboard, can we still say that a morph has in fact taken place? Berg's reported claim that, in writing the last part of his Violin Concerto, he did not know the Bach chorale "Es ist genug" from Cantata No. 60, *O Ewigkeit, du Donnerwort II* (see James 1994), despite the universal critical assumption that the last part of the concerto quotes directly and then produces variations on the Bach theme, obviously calls into question the transparency of authorial intention in morphing (or, of course, in a mendacious or faulty or misreported recollection).

At the conference on digital resources in the humanities at which the first version of this essay was presented, I conducted an experiment in receptional morphing by giving the audience a copy of the lyrics of Simon and Garfunkel's 1960s song "A Simple Desultory Philippic (or How I Was Robert McNamara'd into Submission)," which consist almost entirely of specific cultural references (Norman Mailer, Maxwell Taylor, Ayn Rand, Phil Spector, Lou Adler, Barry Sadler, Lenny Bruce, etc., mostly in verbal formations), and then asking the audience to check off those references for which they might now need a gloss. This information was then calibrated against the personal and demographic information that the respondents chose to provide as "potentially significant" in graphing the morphed responses (age, gender, nationality, native language, political leaning, education, field, etc.). I was thus able graphically to illustrate the gap that a morphed historical context and demography had created, especially in the light of the new meaning of the verb "to McNamara" (to be contrite for one's earlier actions) after the publication of Robert McNamara's Vietnam memoirs ("We were wrong, terribly wrong") and after the satirical extension of "Doing the McNamara" in the *New Yorker,* which attached a similar changed meaning to such figures as Idi Amin Dada and Jack the Ripper, all of whom, like McNamara, supposedly confessed to past sins and claimed that, if given the chance, they would do it all differently. Simon and Garfunkel's verb "to McNamara," associated specifically with "submission" and political control, had become a new verb—albeit only temporarily—in a different chronological and political climate.[8]

Inevitably, this survey of spatial, linear, recursive, and receptional morphing has fallen into the trap of seeing morphs under every bush. But the morph has become so ubiquitous, in advertising, in movies, in video games, that it has become a particularly apt figure for a period in which the boundaries of identity are so challenged. And this is because the morph is both figure and ground, tenor and vehicle, metaphor and substance. As I hope I have demonstrated, my brief for the morph is greater and yet more modest than the utopian or dystopian romances of some other commentators. For example, Turkle's claim for the feminist fluidity of the

---

8. I have continued to test the widening morphing of information since the original song, by assigning the text as an exercise in annotation in my graduate classes. Inevitably, as the years pass, the amount of additional editorial information required for a current audience to appreciate all the references has increased.

morph concentrates primarily on the phenomenology of the morphed result and its seeming instability; it ignores (or at least prefers to pass over) the fact that this apparent instability is based on a careful, in fact extremely tedious, plotting of storyboards, correspondent pixelation, intermediate points, compression ratios, frames per second, video transfers, and so on. As Don McKenzie remarked to me in e-mail correspondence (1996) while I was composing the first version of this essay, recalling his experiences in observing and participating in the Michael Jackson *Black or White* music video, "I was struck by the technical processes and found greater interest in the continuity so many of them showed with traditional skills required in the more traditional media (e.g., the supreme importance of register in printing, especially colour printing, and in plotting the detailed stages of morphing)." Quite so. The morphist operator is confronted with a battery of critical and technical choices that will collectively determine the characteristics of the apparently seamless morph observed and/or manipulated by the viewer. The finer the register and the more detailed the investment of pixelation control, the more seamless will be the transformation from Foucault to Power Ranger or from Velazquez to Bacon and Baconism. And there may be times (for example, if one concentrates primarily on the opening and closing images of the morph storyboard) when it is the very shock of the disjunction between the two rather than the transparency and fluidity of change that needs to be emphasized. Ironically, caricature and parody may become less, not more, cognitively effective as a result of the intervening frames of the complete morph movie.

So, my sense of the morph is both much more and much less than some of those utopian romances of digitization I cited earlier: the morph is not just our future but our past and present too, and it inhabits phenomenologically not just the diachronic but also the synchronic axis—space as well as time. The morph is thus not something added to our human condition by technology, and specifically by digitization, but is already deeply embedded in both our hopes (our progressional, ameliorative mode) and our fears (our acknowledgment of mutability and "nature corrumpable"). As Hamlet expostulates to the skull of Yorick, "Now get you to my lady's table, and tell her, let her paint an inch thick, to this favour she must come. Make her laugh at that" (v.i), just as the digitized human face and skull that was my presiding deity at the conference presentation

FIGURE 8.13. Digital morph from video games showing a midpoint between *Super Sonic* and *Super Saiyan Goku*. *Reproduced by permission of Alex Greetham.*

had already shown. But because the warp of the morph enables the continued recursive return of the living human from the skull, Hamlet is also right on target in his deft but cynical demonstration of how "the noble dust of Alexander [may] stop a bung-hole" (v.i) or how "a king may go a progress through the guts of a beggar" (iv.iii). E does indeed equal mc^2. Like Wordsworth's Lucy, "rolled round in earth's diurnal course, / With rocks, and stones, and trees," Alexander in the bung-hole and the king in the beggar interrogate the very boundaries of identity: where does Lucy stop and the rocks and stones begin?

Spenser's figure of Nature in the Mutabilitie Cantos tries to answer this question by recalibrating the balance of Foucauldian "power relations" between change and stasis. Replying to Mutability, Nature declares:

> I well consider all that ye haue sayd,
> And find that all things stedfastnes doe hate
> And changed be: yet being rightly wayd
> They are not changed from their first estate;
> But by their change their being doe dilate:
> And turning to themselves at length againe,
> Doe worke their own perfection so by fate:
> Then ouer them Change doth not rule and raigne;
> But they raigne ouer change, and doe their states maintaine.
> (Mutabilitie Cantos, vii.58)

This formulation may adequately describe the recursive morph (dilating, via Change, to its "perfect" or "maintained" state), but it is hardly much comfort in contemplating the spatial, linear, or receptional morph. Indeed, Spenser the narrator recognizes this inadequacy, for after Nature's disappearance, he "bethinks . . . on that speech whyleare" and, in the appropriately "vnperfite" Canto vii, longs for that Platonic "stedfast rest of all things firmely stayd," in fact the same stasis that Tanselle had wished for texts.

But no matter how the matter is resolved morally, philosophically, or ontologically, morphing is recognized by Lucretius, Ovid, Spenser, and Tanselle, in their different ways, as an inevitable condition of nature. Given this long human experience of, and wrestling with, the condition of the morph, then it is surely not surprising to discover that the power of modern technological morphing, by digital pixelation and audio mixing, to emblematize this condition—in both its ontology and its phenomenology—is a special pertinent resource for the humanities and a particularly valuable epistemological tool in exploring the multiform states of the electronic text in various media, and perhaps a perfect descriptor of our postmodernist anxieties over boundaries and identities, and the contamination thereof. But it is only that: a "re-source" for digitization of the morph and a tool for testing the limits of electronic textuality. Like the electron microscope or the ultrasound scanner or the radio telescope, morphing may allow us entry into a field of micro- and macroscopic observation that was technically impossible in earlier times. But just as Douglas Hofstadter (1995) has reminded us that ultrasound scanning does not provide "reality" but only a morphed medium of perception that we take for reality (sound waves converted into the visible spectrum),[9] so our apparent mastery of pixelation is as much a function of our will and our desire as it is of our empiricism. The thing that allows Hamlet to morph Alexander is, what else, Coleridgean "Imagination";[10] and good,

---

9. As elaborated more fully in chapter 12, "The Telephone Directory and Dr. Seuss," Hofstadter uses ultrasound scanning to exemplify the distinction between "observation" and "inference."

10. "The poet, described in *ideal* perfection, brings the whole soul of man into activity. . . . He diffuses a tone and spirit of unity, that blends, and (as it were) *fuses* each into each, by that synthetic and magical power, to which I would exclusively appropriate the name of Imagination" (Coleridge 1983: ch. 14).

stolid Horatio predictably feels that "'twere to consider too curiously, to consider so" (v.i). Have I considered "too curiously" in finding, creating, and showing the digitized morphs of painting, film, architecture, fiction, advertising, music, and so on? I hope so. Digital morphing is a stretch, sometimes quite literally so, but in stretching it provides a renewed sense of the intertwined warp and weft of a text, and how it may be done and undone. I cannot yet fully endorse the Mighty Morphin Power Rangers' confidence in their battle cry for transmutation, but I can at least ask: "Is it morphin time?"*

---

*I am grateful for the cooperation of Gryphon Software in allowing storyboards and individual frames generated by the program Morph to be used throughout this chapter. Unfortunately, Gryphon's Morph software is no longer supported, but similar programs do exist.

PART THREE

The Contamination of Voice

The Contamination of Voice

""""What Does It Matter Who Is Speaking,' Someone Said, 'What Does It Matter Who Is Speaking'?"""" (Greetham Version), or "'What Does It Matter Who Is Speaking?': Editorial Recuperation of the Estranged Author" (Eggert Version)

This chapter would not have taken its present form without Paul Eggert. And I do not just mean that I was pleased to be invited to speak on this topic at a conference Paul convened but also that, through his active intervention as conference convener and editor, I became temporarily an estranged author of my own paper, needing active recuperation, as the two versions of the title of my essay attest: the one I submitted (""""What Does It Matter Who Is Speaking,' Someone Said, 'What Does It Matter Who Is Speaking'?""") and the one Paul printed in the conference program ("'What does it matter who is speaking?': Editorial Recuperation of the Estranged Author"). It has become a commonplace of the conference circuit that a speaker must begin with a rhetorical *planctus*—either, "I have changed my mind about the topic I had promised to address," or "my title has been changed, damaged, corrupted, and otherwise subjected to the ills of social transmission": in other words, "That is not it at all. That is not what I meant, at all." Indeed, the speakers at that particular conference were alerted to the latter likelihood, when Paul told us in correspondence that he had "taken liberties with the titles ... in order to have them reflect in some way the conference's subtitle." That is, the social pressure on a collective meaning for the sum total of our utterances at the conference had determined the degree of editorial intervention necessary to make the expressed authorial intentions correspond to their desired reception. No need to ask where Paul's sympathies lie in the great debate between originary intentionalists and socialized textuists, except (and it's a very big except) that, in the same correspondence, he gave speakers the "opportunity to censor or amend" his intervention in our abstracts or on the day of presentation.

I am making so much of this exchange on authorial utterance and editorial intervention not just because it is an expected rhetorical trope at conferences but because Paul's specific emendations are emblematic of my subject. He removed my speaker—the "someone" who is the au-thorial "voice" behind the originally two, now one, question(s)—and he also removed the two outer sets of my parallel quotation marks, so that the utterance "What Does It Matter Who Is Speaking?" now appeared to be cited from only one source instead of the three embedded citations of my original formulation. Those three are Foucault's (1984: 101) citing of Beckett's (1967: 85) citing[1] of "Someone" having said "What Does It Mat-ter?" surrounded by Greetham's citing of the entire package. And by sup-pressing the second question as well as the voice that would have spoken it, Paul acted as if the second were merely dittographic, an unintended (scribal) repetition which needed cleaning up; or, he perhaps accepted Freud's interpretation that textual repetition (or perseveration) indicates that the author is unable to let go of the utterance, that "if a writer repeats a word he has already written, this is probably an indication that it was not easy for him to get away from it" (Freud 1965: 129). Finally, by glossing my now-truncated question with a statement ("editorial recuperation," etc.), Paul turned my open, "writerly" (*scriptible*) text into a closed, "readerly" (*lisible*) one. And his Barthesian *lexia*—his cutting up of my title and pasting it back in a different form from the authorial (just as Barthes [1974] cuts up Balzac's *lisible* novel *Sarrasine* into a *scriptible* "network" of "texts")—rhetorically curtailed the possibilities of a Foucauldian "prolif-eration of meaning" (Foucault 1984: 118) by literally inscribing the inter-rogative within a declarative that is, or ought to be, its social context. All

---

1. In this context, it is quite appropriate that Foucault should not cite a specific authorial source in Beckett for his quotation of Beckett's "Someone." I am grateful to my colleague David Gordon for having allowed me to make good Foucault's omission.

of these devices are part of my subject, and I'm obviously very grateful for Paul's having articulated them so well in his edited and socialized version of my title.

What follows is a whirlwind tour of some of the places where it *does* matter who is speaking—from the Bible to Barbie dolls to gay pornography—or rather, of textual situations where the reader and editor are confronted with the question of whether it matters whether it matters. Does voice—attributed, concealed, distorted, disseminated, glossed— function as a sign of meaning, even if very indirectly, and how would a change in the attribution, glossing, etc., of voice change an editorial understanding, and perhaps closing off, of the proliferation of meaning? To continue my allusion to Foucault, but with wider textual ramifications than the famous essay "What Is an Author?" suggests, does the "principle of thrift" (1984: 118), an "economy" of understanding, operate for that "someone" who speaks within an author's text, as well as for the author himself speaking outside the text?

Let's turn to Barbie for a very clear example. What did those children who were recipients of a socially motivated practical joke think and how did they respond when they opened their Christmas "Teen Talk" Barbie dolls to find the voice box in the still unrealistically curvaceous blonde yelling, "Attack!" "Vengeance is mine!" and "Eat lead, Cobra!"? And how did those other children opening up their "Talking Dukes" G.I. Joes deal with the dulcet tones of "Let's go shopping," "Will we ever have enough clothes?" and "Let's plan our dream wedding!"? (Firestone 1993: A12). Whether the response was tears or laughter, it presumably registered at a very coarse (and sexist) level the fact that the "corrective surgery" done by the so-called Barbie Liberation Movement (in substituting the voice boxes of the two dolls) depended for its effect on the canonical status of sexual stereotyping that generations of such dolls had reinforced and on the assumption that there was an attributable voice for both Barbie and G.I. Joe that could be recognized, just as the authorial voices of Homer, Virgil, Chaucer, Shakespeare, and others of the Western canon have become similarly recognizable as a result of many generations of social accommodation and refinements to the acceptable canonical texts—as I will show later. In other words, the surgically altered dolls were offending against the principles of E. D. Hirsch's theory (1967: 86) of utterance (and the correct interpretation of utterance) as a series of generic limitations

placed on the possibilities of authorial proliferation,[2] and against the various stylometric studies in attribution which have argued for a "signature
of style" (Erdman 1966) based (ideally) on a fusion of internal evidence,
the marks of an idiolect within the document, and external evidence, the
testable material circumstances of production. In this case, the external
(the dolls themselves) and the internal (the textual idiolects) were in
wonderful collision.

The Barbie/G.I. Joe collision is also a form of ventriloquism, with
the "authentic" voice repressed by an incursive one, which is immediately
identifiable by its disjunctive rhetoric. A subtler form of ventriloquism
can, however, occur without such overt signs, as when it was discovered
that the group Milli Vanilli merely lip-synched their concert performances. Their fans inevitably felt some betrayal when they found that
the group's "real" voice was not present at "live" performances, but had
been replaced by another. Since then, in some circles, the verb "to Milli
Vanilli" has been adopted to describe any such repression and supersession. It would be tempting to think that such manipulation is limited only
to "popular" music, where authentic voice might not be as highly valued
as in more "serious" performances. Then came the discovery shortly after
the 2008 Beijing Olympics that the august Sydney Symphony Orchestra had "mimed its entire performance" at the opening ceremony (Julie
Bloom 2008: A20). But there was worse to come: the managing director
of the Sydney orchestra also admitted that "some of the music was not
even recorded by it, but by the [uncredited] rival Melbourne Symphony
Orchestra." This substitution will doubtless exacerbate the long-standing
feud between the two Australian cities for cultural supremacy, and the
excuse that the Olympics organizers "wanted to leave nothing to chance"
is hardly sufficient to justify the substitution of voice, especially on top
of the earlier revelation that nine-year-old Lin Miaoke had lip-synched
her song at the opening ceremonies. And in the world of video games, a
similar problem of substitute voices (and avatars) occurred when Gwen
Stefani of the band No Doubt sued the makers of Guitar Hero for having

---

2. Hirsch (1967: 86) suggests a series of contextual formulas toward the critical elucidation
of the meaning content of a text and cruces in a text, beginning with "the words that surround the crux" and ending with "the entire physical, psychological, social, and historical
milieu in which the utterance occurs"—as in the case of Barbie and G.I. Joe.

represented her electronic simulation as performing songs that No Doubt never recorded, including "Honky Tonk Women" by the Rolling Stones. The lawsuit claimed that such a misrepresentation of voice "results in an unauthorized performance by the Gwen Stefani avatar in a male voice boasting about having sex with prostitutes" (Itzkoff 2009b: C5).

Such collisions (once they are discovered) are examples of textual disharmony (a sort of bibliographical disjunction) that draws attention to its atonality: the contamination of each voice by the other. But its opposite—harmonization—is (as has long been recognized by biblical and classical textual scholars) an equally disturbing phenomenon and can affect what is reported to have been said by that most authoritative of authorial voices: God himself. Thus, Bruce Metzger (1992: 197) asserts that the passage at Acts 9:4–6 describing St. Paul's conversion is in some manuscripts harmonized to the fuller form in Acts 26:14–17,[3] and that the short form of the Lord's Prayer at Luke 9:2–4 is sometimes harmonized with the more familiar long form at Matthew 6:9–13. What Metzger does not note, however, is that the expanded account in Acts 26 is, in narrative terms, told after the event by Paul, whereas the first, shorter version passes itself off as a third-person, "objective" account. In these circumstances, it is surely telling that the harmonizing scribes selected the subjective, recollected voice of Paul—in which God is just a reported voice (moreover giving Paul a much greater mandate than does the earlier voice)—as the norm against which to harmonize the direct-speech

---

3. Acts 9:4–6:

> And he fell to the earth, and heard a voice saying unto him, Saul, Saul, why persecutest thou me? And he said, Who art thou, Lord? And the Lord said, I am Jesus whom thou persecutest; it is hard for thee to kick against the pricks. And he trembling and astonished said, Lord, what wilt thou have me to do? And the Lord said unto him, Arise, and go into the city, and it shall be told thee what thou must do.

Acts 26:14–17:

> And when we were all fallen to the earth, I heard a voice speaking unto me, and saying in the Hebrew tongue, Saul, Saul, why persecutest thou me? It is hard for thee to kick against the pricks. And I said, Who art thou, Lord? And he said, I am Jesus whom thou persecutest. But rise, and stand upon thy feet: for I have appeared to thee for this purpose, to make thee *a minister and a witness* both of these things which thou hast seen, and of those things in which I will appear unto thee. Delivering thee from the people, and from the *Gentiles, unto whom now I send thee.* (my italics; King James Version)

account in the earlier version. As in the emendation by Paul (the other Paul, Eggert, not Saint) of my title, the socially contextualized function of voice is used as a standard of meaning to reformulate the precedent utterance. To put it as bluntly as I can: St. Paul needed to justify himself as the creator of a new religion, distinct from Judaism, and so the longer reported mandate given by God (in which Paul becomes a "minister and a witness" to be sent out to "the Gentiles"), rather than the shorter, more limited injunction, is vital to his position as textual disseminator and proselytizer.

In a similarly contested ideological arena—gay studies—we can see the same conflict over mandate and authorial voice in the struggle over the attribution of the homoerotic novel *Teleny* to Oscar Wilde. As one of my former graduate students, Jason Tougaw, puts it, the "'evidence' for the publication history, textual transmission, reception, and especially authorship of *Teleny* is at present located almost entirely between multiple sets of quotation marks. It is third-hand gossip—frustrating for a contemporary editor, or liberating, depending upon his/her stance" (Tougaw 1993: n.p.). Tougaw notes, for example, that the lost manuscript for the 1893 edition (in which the novel is just "attributed to Oscar Wilde") probably underwent various distortions of authorial voice at the hands of the editor and publisher, Leonard Smithers, specifically to preserve the anonymity of its author.[4] Two twentieth-century editions illustrate how this problem of distortion can be used in two very different types of authorial recuperation: the Gay Sunshine Press edition (1984), based on the French translation of 1934 now retranslated back into English, is a serious attempt at recuperating Wilde as a queer author; but the BadBoy edition of 1992, only partly trading on Wilde's significance as a canonical author, uses (or abuses) the Olympia Press edition of 1958—based on the Smithers text of 1893—to produce an erotic vehicle for yet another sort of socialization, the "contemporary gay audience expecting certain things of pornography—mainly the facilitation of orgasm without too many interruptions" (Tougaw 1993: n.p.). To the editors at BadBoy press, the status of the originary (Wildean) voice possibly mutilated by Smithers

---

4. The distortions can, according to Tougaw 1993, be measured from the French edition of 1934, which claims to be a translation of the original manuscript.

"doesn't matter that much because we made a lot of changes" (quoted in Tougaw 1993: n.p.), just as to St. Paul, the status of the originary voice of God didn't matter all that much because he made a lot of changes when he recollected the events on the road to Damascus in tranquility. But for the Gay Sunshine edition, without the pornographic purple passages, the recuperated text of *Teleny* is an attempt to question the boundaries of the Wilde canon and to reinstate a homoerotic voice at its center, rather than ambivalently on its margins. To Gay Sunshine, it *does* matter who is speaking, but to BadBoy it matters not at all.

This problem of the edges of the voice, as it slurs off into another idiolect, is, of course, the fundamental issue in attribution studies. But, as J. C. C. Mays has remarked of Coleridge, there may be authors for whom the very concept of oeuvre and of singular utterance (what Mays calls "outerance") is problematic. "Coleridge does not even have an oeuvre in the same sense as a modern poet like Yeats or Stevens: the body of his writings blurs at the edges.... Coleridge fed off what he could borrow or steal, and it is frequently uncertain where his own writing begins and ends" (Mays 1995: 217–37). And, as Tim Machan (1995) has demonstrated, the changing shape of the Chaucerian canon, generally growing by accretion until the Tyrwhitt edition of 1775, is reflective not just of the usual principle of a great author's presence in literary history attracting minor works by association, but also of the changing acculturated reconstructions of that author—his recuperation, if you will. Thus, for the early sixteenth century, Chaucer was the courtier poet and thus attracted such works as *The Flower of Courtesy, The Assembly of Ladies, The Complaint of the Black Knight,* and *The Remedy of Love* in William Thynne's edition of 1532; and, only a short time later, Chaucer was (like his contemporary Langland, whose *Piers Plowman* was first printed in 1550 as an anti-Catholic tract) also regarded as a precursor of the Reformation and thus "attracted" such antipapist works as *The Plowman's Tale* in Thynne's 1542 edition and *Jack Upland* in Thomas Speght's 1598 edition. As Machan remarks, it really is a question of cultural reconstruction:

> It may well be nearly impossible for modern readers ... to imagine that anyone could conceive that works as didactic and uninspired as the *Plowman's Tale* or *Jack Upland* could be by the same individual who wrote the *Troilus* or the *Canterbury Tales.* But to an imagination determined to validate both the historicity of Protestant beliefs and the preeminence of Chaucer, the

attributions are completely comprehensible and emerge, arguably, as much
from a cultural project as does Walter Skeat's Victorian attempt to reduce
the Chaucerian canon through empirical means. (Machan 1995: 151)

But after Tyrwhitt and Skeat and the gradually slimmed-down Chaucer corpus, it is surely peculiar that such editions as the authoritative
Riverside, while rejecting the various spurious poems I have listed, demonstrates such an ambivalent, not to say contradictory, attitude toward
authorial voice when the idiolect parts within a poem. So, while (as Larry
Benson admits, 1987: 686) it is by no means even clear whether the surviving Middle English translation of *The Romaunt of the Rose* is the one
alluded to by Chaucer in the prologue to *The Legend of Good Women*, it
is this version (for there is no other) that is included in Riverside. Moreover, although the B fragment of the *Legend* was composed in a northern
dialect and is definitely not by Chaucer, and although the C fragment is
"Chaucerian in language and manner but has been rejected by most scholars" (Benson 1987: 686), both of these fragments are nonetheless present
in the Riverside, along with the more authoritative fragment A. Clearly,
sometimes it does matter who is speaking, and sometimes it doesn't, for
the claim of completeness (the poem would not *read* if the middle fragment and/or the last were omitted) cannot be invoked in a contemporary
editorial tradition that celebrates incompletion and fragmentation. Thus,
the Riverside was not tempted to include the "continuation" of the otherwise truncated *Cook's Tale* (*The Tale of Gamelyn*, which became the source
for the Orlando part of *As You Like It*), nor even to include the marginal
scribal note in Hengwrt "of this Cokes tale maked Chaucer na moore,"[5]
nor, of course, to finish the interrupted *Squire's Tale* with Spenser's continuation in book IV of *The Faerie Queene*.

There is clearly a separation anxiety each time a formerly attributed
work is removed from its originating authorial voice, just as there is continued anxiety in the art world as the Rembrandt holdings of major muse-

---

5. The fascicle boundaries of both Ellesmere and Hengwrt suggest that space has been left
for a possible conclusion to the tale. Twenty-five manuscripts include *Gamelyn*, and Bodley
686 interpolates thirty extra lines in the body of the *Cook's Tale*, together with a closing
moral passage about the "myschefe" that "cometh of mysgovernance." Lansdowne 851 actually uses the incompletion itself for moral purposes, having the teller break off "for schame
of the harlotrie."

ums and galleries are removed from Rembrandt himself to his workshop or imitators, under the auspices of the Rembrandt Project (Sonnenberg et al. 1995). It may be that, loss of authorizing voice aside, we are not yet fully able to unread what has been written into our cultural consciousness, in the same way that (from the opposite perspective) we are probably not fully ready to experience, say, *Two Noble Kinsmen* as partly Shakespeare's (especially in the performance tradition), or such plays as *Henry VIII*, *1 Henry VI*, *Timon of Athens*, *Macbeth*, or even *Pericles* as collaborations,[6] so strong is our desire for the Shakespearean voice to remain the most idiosyncratic of idiolects. Thus, while a 2008 production of *Macbeth* (with Patrick Stewart in the main role) made no mention in the program of Middleton's revisions to the original Shakespeare, the publication of Gary Taylor's *Thomas Middleton* in 2007, with editions of *Macbeth*, *Timon*, and *Measure for Measure* as joint Shakespeare-Middleton plays, may begin to challenge the cultural reliance on the solitary voice, a movement that is promoted by such popular studies as Stanley Wells's *Shakespeare & Co.* (2006). Shakespeare is gradually being contaminated by Middleton, Fletcher, and others. It remains to be seen whether *The Reign of King Edward III*, as part of this "collaboratively voiced" Shakespeare, will become accepted into the performance canon, even though the usually conservative Brian Vickers was willing to endorse the findings of the software program *Pl@giarism* that the anonymously published play had hundreds

---

6. Of this group, *Two Noble Kinsmen*, a collaboration with Fletcher, is still not universally included in collected editions of Shakespeare (although it does appear in the Penguin; Arden, 3rd series; and Oxford editions). While a few editions (e.g., Oxford) do give co-authorship credit for some of the arguably collaborative canonical Shakespeare plays (First Folio plus *Pericles*), typically those plays (*Henry VIII* [collaboration with Fletcher], *1 Henry VI* [with Greene, Nashe, and/or Marlowe], *Pericles* [with Wilkins and Day], *Timon* [with Middleton], and *Macbeth* [with Middleton]) are more commonly listed as single-author works, especially in performance. For example, the New York Shakespeare Festival, which produced a so-called complete Shakespeare in the mid- to late 1990s had mixed feelings about including *Two Noble Kinsmen* in its roster (and this was dependent on whether the festival could find a qualified director and actors who were interested in mounting the play, not on whether the play was now canonical), and consistently advertised the collaborative plays as being by the single author William Shakespeare. Indeed, the publicity office was surprised to learn that most Shakespeareans regard only part of, say, *Pericles*, as being by Shakespeare. The 1993 production of *Timon* by the National Actors' Theatre on Broadway unambiguously announced the play as being wholly Shakespeare's, although there was some discussion in reviews of the problems of authorship. I am grateful to the New York Shakespeare Festival for this information.

of matched phrases with other accepted plays by Shakespeare. It is surely ironic that a program developed by the University of Maastricht to "keep its students honest" (i.e., to detect authoritative "voice") was used to authenticate the play, which is included in the Riverside and Oxford Shakespeares (see Itzkoff 2009a).

It is this desire to preserve idiosyncrasy that has led, for example, to various editors and translators (notably Ezra Pound) rejecting the last section of *The Seafarer* on ideological as well as attributional grounds.[7] It ought not to have been possible for the same voice which produced the bitter laments of the first part of the poem to have also uttered the religious sentiments of the last sixteen (or more) lines. But on these grounds—of ideological and intellectual consistency—could we not reject the religious apotheosis at the end of Chaucer's *Troilus,* undermining the values of *fin'amour* in the body of the poem? And, as Hershel Parker (1984) has displayed in a series of close textual readings of various classics of American fiction—from Twain's *Pudd'nhead Wilson* to Mailer's *An American Dream*—if we were to demand the resolution of all narrative and perceptual inconsistencies before admitting a singular authorial presence to the multiform acts of composition, we would be left with a very small canonical list indeed. Sometimes, authors may not notice, or may not even care, that they are speaking in more than one voice, that they are contaminated. Does this matter?

Well, yes, it does matter if you're a strict constructionist like Brian Vickers, demanding that the idiolectal evidence of *Hamlet* Q1, because it is a potential embarrassment to the different idiolectal evidence of Q2 and F1, be de-canonized, removed from the authorial voice. To Vickers

---

7. Such editors/translators as Malone, Gordon, Raffel, Kennedy, Wain, and Bradley believe that the poem is an integral utterance as found in ff81b–83a of the Exeter Book. Others, like Pound and Alexander, delete the last twenty-two lines, finding this section either repetitious or too homiletic for the secular character of the rest of the poem and seeking codicological support in the fact that f82b ends with 1.102, after which the material becomes unclear. Still others, like Spaeth and Faust, maintain that all the Christian material is additional and end the poem around 1.64. And others, like Whitelock, Hamer, and Crossley-Holland, end the poem around 1.108, at the stage in the manuscript where they believe the meaning is unclear. The point is that all these editors and translators have used their concept of a singular authorial voice to delimit the actual extent of the poem. This view was expressed in an edition by a graduate student of mine, Eric Wilson, who ended his edition and translation at l.108 because "the poem seems to find its ending there." I am grateful to Mr. Wilson for having provided some of the data on which this analysis is based.

(1994), and to other scholars claiming Q1 as a debased memorial reconstruction of an "authentic" text that was to lead to Q2, the evidence of my colleague Steven Urkowitz (1986) on multiple Shakespearean voices is inadmissible, as is the evidence of the compositors of Q2 itself, who, as Greg demonstrated long ago, and as is now generally accepted (e.g., in Wells and Taylor 1986), turned to Q1 as an authoritative source in their setting of the early sections of the play. Similarly inadmissible are

  · Wells and Taylor's claim (while still supporting the bibliographical independence of F1 and Q1 and the memorial reconstruction of Q1) that "the best evidence that F[1] represents a more theatrical text than Q2 is its repeated agreement with Q1 against Q2, in matters of verbal and theatrical substance" (1986: 400);
  · the testimony of those who have staged Q1 and found it eminently theatrical; and
  · the arguments of Evert Sprinchorn (1994) that the very differences between the text of Q1 and the putative source of Q2 are evidence *against* rather than *for* memorial reconstruction, since actors would slavishly reproduce a performance text rather than mutilate it as the memorialists would contend.

My point is not that Vickers is wrong and those arguing for Shakespeare's direct voice in Q1 are right, or vice versa, but that, to return to Foucault for a moment, the "author-function" and the authorial voice (and name) are mutually interdependent:

[T]he fact that several texts have been placed under the same name indicates that there has been established among them a relationship of homogeneity, filiation, authentication of some texts by the use of others, reciprocal explication, or concomitant utilization. The author's name serves to characterize a certain mode of discourse.... it is a speech that must be received in a certain mode and that, in a given culture, must receive a certain status. (1984: 107)

For Shakespeare to occupy the author function that he holds in *Hamlet* Q2 and F1, it is imperative to Vickers that the name and voice of Q1 not "characterize" the same "mode of discourse." As Mays was concerned about the blurring of edges, so Foucault acknowledges that authors (in the traditional sense of that term) generally function to prevent such blurring after the event: "the name seems always to be present, marking off the edges of the text, revealing, or at least characterizing, its mode of being. The author's name manifests the appearance of a certain discursive set and indicates the status of this discourse within a society and culture" (1984: 107).

Thus, for both Vickers and Foucault, the recognition of discursive sets of speech and their being linked to an author is as much an ethical as a procedural problem. Predicting Vickers's moral apoplexy at the newfangled "ideology" which drives textual studies to reject the very idea of an "authentic text,"[8] Foucault acknowledges that the "indifference" of contemporary writing (*écriture*) to the speaker of the question "What does it matter?" is an "immanent rule . . . not designating writing as something completed, but dominating it as a practice" (1984: 101). For Vickers, however, the discursive set must have been completed, for he insists on recognizing a firm and permanent distinction between "coherent order," fixed "conceptions of character and motive," and the "authentic," on the one hand, and "dross," "fustian verse," and "rubbish," on the other. But what really provokes Vickers's moral outrage is this new "immanent rule" whereby the ethical security of the very term "bad quarto" is undermined in the Holderness and Loughrey edition of Q1 by what Vickers calls "a new type of euphemism: instead of calling Q1 a 'Bad Quarto,' [the editors] let it be known as a text which has by-passed the crucial relationship to an authorial manuscript" (1993: 6). To Foucault, this is exactly the ethical point: all *écriture* bypasses such a relationship, for it "creates a space in which the writing subject constantly disappears" (1984: 102). And so, where the writer's death is to Vickers and all traditional attributional scholars a sign of a completion in which the characteristics of an oeuvre can be established, for Foucault death is simply a sign that "writing has become linked to sacrifice," a sacrifice in which "the relationship between writing and death is . . . manifested in the effacement of the writing subject's individual characteristics" (ibid.). As I have noted

---

8. Vickers 1993: 5. See also Vickers's attack on contemporary theory in general in *Appropriating Shakespeare* (1994), esp. chapter 4, "New Historicism: Disaffected Subjects," where Vickers bemoans the presence of "a by now familiar litany of Foucauldian jargon" among Renaissance scholars (particularly Stephen Greenblatt and Louis Montrose) and the baneful influence of Foucault's formula for discourse as an "anonymous, depersonalised system, deprived of a subject or author, circulating through 'sites' of power, appropriation and contestation" (Vickers 1994: 217), without recognizing that his own project for reconstructing the "traditional" Shakespeare is itself a "contestation" and "appropriation," as well as an academic power struggle for control over the literary remains of our most culturally potent author.

elsewhere, Foucault's concern with the way that, in *écriture*, "the writing subject cancels out the signs of his particular individuality" is translated into bibliographical terms in Roger Chartier's *annaliste* history of books, whereby the textual historian treats not of the creator himself but the "negotiations between the creator and the institutions of society," with Foucault's archaeology of the "human sciences" now employed in an archaeology of bibliographical history, perceived as the cultural history of bookishness (not textuality or authoriality) and the ordering of various qualities of bookishness into archaeological layers of cultural experience.[9]

And it is precisely this conflict over the cultural and moral status of a discursive set and its relation to bookishness or authoriality that can be charted, for example, in the arguments over who is speaking in the so-called Z version of *Piers Plowman*, about whose actual internal (idiolectal) and external (codicological) features there is comparatively little disagreement. To Charlotte Brewer and A. G. Rigg (1983), the Z version can be regarded as the most originary voice of all—Langland's *ur*-text for the poem, in which he speaks unmediated by social transmission—but to George Kane (1985), it is exactly the opposite: a late scribal garbling of Langland's voice beyond recuperation by the most practiced of editor/surgeons (see also Greetham 1997f).

---

9. See Greetham 1999b, esp. 99–101. I note, for example, that while it is true that Chartier has usually denied that he fully endorses a cultural history which displaces (Anglo-American, New Critical) *text* by (French, New Historicist) *book*, his insistence that the logic of textuality is not identical with the logic of socialization and his concentration on "authorless" or "author-functional" bibliographical modes, such as the commonplace book, the book-wheel (a device whereby many books can be read virtually simultaneously at one sitting), the *bibliothèques bleues*, and models for letter writers, serve to promote anonymity and the book over authoriality and the text.

Even where the author does reappear in Chartier's bibliographical history, it is not the author as Romantic originator but the author as constructed by, for example, London booksellers as a proprietary figure, by which ownership of the work was conferred by the fruits of labor, and the protectable work was defined by its form, not by its ideas, which were not copyrightable. Thus, while Chartier does distance himself from certain aspects of Foucault's account of the author function (for example, he rejects Foucault's assumption [1984: 109] that in the Middle Ages only scientific texts required authorial sanction), there can be little doubt that in general Chartier has teased Foucault's writing on the historical construction of authorship into a full cultural history of bibliography. In this way, Chartier as a proponent of *l'histoire du livre* has become the chief bibliographical witness to a postmodernist dispersal of the subject as a historical figure and its replacement by citation, pastiche, and materiality. See Chartier 1994, esp. "Communities of Readers."

But attribution of voice and its place in an archaeology of discourse conceived either as utterance or as cultural accommodation (too large a subject to be more than touched on here) is in any case only one part of the problem of why it matters who is speaking. The other aspect of the question—why does it matter?—can be seen in the evaluation and explication of speakers within the text, whether or not we have taken a position on the speaker outside the text. And lest we be tempted to shrug off this relationship between internal and external voices as a problem only for drama, or only for literary and textual criticism, we should not forget that the fatwa against Salman Rushdie was evoked by a misreading (by our Western standards of textual interpretation) of the function of speech markers and internal attribution: the dream in which the offenses to Islam occurred in the novel was attributed by the mullahs not to a character speaking according to the speech-act protocols of the genre, but directly to the author, as originary (and therefore unmediated) utterer. To the Ayatollah Khomeini, it *did* matter who was speaking, but it did not matter that an acknowledgment of a shift in genre would have resulted in a different speaker. The only possible speaker was always the author, who could never be estranged from his work. In this case, the historical author was contaminated by one of his own characters in a fiction.

In a short survey of this sort, I can provide only a prolegomenon to the problems of internal voice and of the contamination by external voices, confident that many other scholars have already dealt with the matter for specific authors and texts. What follows is thus a quick guided tour of some trouble spots, which together can be read as examples of the sort of evidence I have been examining in my research.[10] There will be many questions, but only a few answers.

For example, what measure of estrangement between speech and speaker did Laurence Olivier record when, in an anticipation of what Tom Stoppard was to do twenty years later, he cut the characters Rosencrantz and Guildenstern from his film version of *Hamlet* (1948) and assigned their lines to other speakers? As Guildenstern says in Stoppard's play (1968: 92), "And why us?—anybody would have done." In Olivier's ver-

---

10. These presentations, usually under the title ™*Copy/Right*©, have been given in Liverpool, Canberra, and New York, and are being worked into a book-length study.

sion, they are taken at their words—or lack of them: anybody will do to speak their lines![11] And Stoppard has had troubles of his own: his various attempts to cut Cecily's political lecture in act II of *Travesties* have generally not been observed, either in the reading text or in performance (Gaskell 1978: 260), and his cut of the phrase "except for my height, which can't be far off" in Carr's opening monologue is similarly not usually observed. Even editors can be cowed by the resilience of the text, as when Dover Wilson, after having argued on hard bibliographical grounds that a section of dialogue in *Love's Labour's Lost* was canceled by Shakespeare, nonetheless retains the dialogue in his *New Cambridge* edition, timorously marking it with tiny square brackets (Wilson 1962: 116–24). This timidity, however, was not displayed in J. Massyngberde Ford's edition of Revelation (Ford 1975: 69) where, arguing that the speaker of Revelation is John the Baptist and that the first three chapters are thus a later Christian interpolation in another voice, the editor is faced with having to begin the trimmed-down text with the fragmentary (and illogical) "After these things, I looked . . ."

Another related question is the effect of secondary, external voices on our textual perceptions of internal voices and citations. We all know the story (now doubtless to be deemed sexist and ageist) of the little old lady who went to a performance of *Hamlet* and complained that, while she thought the story was fine, she was disappointed that the text was so full of quotations. Leaving aside for the moment the possibility that she was a crypto-poststructuralist noting that everything is "always already written," what would she (and what do we) make of, say, Henry Chadwick's claim (1993: 13) that "To be or not to be" derives not indirectly from Cicero's *Tusculan Disputations* or Plato's *Apology* but directly, verbatim,

---

11. And note the irony that Stoppard's very title, *Rosencrantz and Guildenstern Are Dead*, is itself a quotation from *Hamlet* (Ambassador: "The ears are senseless that should give us hearing, / To tell him his commandment is fulfilled, / That Rosencrantz and Guildenstern are dead. / Where should we have our thanks?" [5.2.363–66]). That is, Stoppard's work is already contained within, and authorized by, the text of *Hamlet,* a relationship that was played upon in a Classic Stage Company production in the early 1970s, in which the intermediate or linking passages from *Hamlet* (which are happening *offstage* in Stoppard's play) were given in full, thus tilting the balance of textual power even further toward Shakespeare's play and characters than toward Stoppard's, and emphasizing Rosencrantz and Guildenstern's helplessness as minor figures in someone else's speech.

from a "standard school introduction to elementary logic," as testified by Richard Hooker?[12] And is James McLaverty's distinction between *intention* and *motivation* (1984a) sufficient for us to bracket (and thus ignore) the secondary voice of Bulwer Lytton registering dissatisfaction with the original ending of *Great Expectations*—pretty much on the grounds that it was not "Dickensian" enough—and thus precipitating a six-stage rewriting that gave us the more resolved, more "Dickensian" ending (Rosenberg 1981)? Was Dickens contaminated by Bulwer Lytton, without whom we have to assume that the original ending would have been the one published? And how do we process (culturally) the information that the specific form of the title *Catch-22*—and thus the colloquial use of the phrase to describe almost any illogical or self-contradictory statement or condition—was again the product of a secondary voice, Joseph Heller's editor at Knopf, Robert Gottlieb (Lyall 1994)?[13]

But what if the authorial voice is similarly splintered or fractured? Eugene Goodheart suggests[14] that D. H. Lawrence had "internalized much of . . . puritan morality" so that the "metaphorical displacements"—and actual cuts—which the Cambridge editors typically take for an external censorship imposed on an unwilling authorial intention are in fact Lawrence's psychological co-option of constraint so that sexuality might become a "transgressive force" (Goodheart 1991: 231). In other words, where the Cambridge editors of, say, *Women in Love* or *The Rainbow* see a single self struggling with external voices of social constraint, Goodheart sees two authorial selves struggling with each other. And what different model of authorial constraint is produced when Brenda R. Silver takes issue with the conventionally feminist view (of, for example, Radin 1977, 1981; Froula

---

12. Chadwick quotes Hooker, "To be or not to be are terms of contradiction which never fall together into one and the same thing, but where the one of them taketh place, the other utterly is excluded" (1993).

13. Gottlieb reports that Heller's novel was originally called *Catch-18*, but that the name (and presumably all references to it in the text of the novel) was "arbitrarily changed" because Leon Uris was publishing a book called *Mila 18* at the same time, and Knopf wanted to avoid confusion.

14. Goodheart: "Censorship may have been Lawrence's enemy, but in a sense it was a necessary and empowering enemy." Goodheart believes that the present "absence of censorship results in a lack of tension, an evaporation of the passional [*sic*] side of erotic writing" (1991: 230–31).

1986; Heine 1979; and DeSalvo 1979, 1982) that Woolf's revisions from manuscript to print—even in a print over which she had direct control as publisher—move "in one direction only" and manifest a "failure of courage" (Silver 1991: 213) from outspoken feminist candor to effete and muted modernist blandness, a "pargeting" or "whitewashing" of "explicitly sexual and angry" passages in earlier versions? In Silver's account, like Goodheart's for Lawrence, it is a reciprocal, not unidirectional, relationship between two aspects of an authorial voice, with a resulting "unstable and multiple" (ibid.: 214) text owing much to Hans Zeller's structuralist formulation (1975) of variance. For Silver's multivariant approach, it is not simply a matter of a male-dominated means of production suppressing the authentic female voice, as it clearly is to Elaine Crane (1988), for example, who documents the omission in earlier editions of the diary of Elizabeth Drinker (1889) of entries considered "unfeminine" by the male editors, or as it is to Ann Thompson in her call for a feminist sensibility in annotation, which might notice that the supposedly "universal" range that the variorum *As You Like It* (1977) finds in Jacques's "All the world's a stage" is in fact limited entirely to male voices, from whining schoolboy to whistling old man (Thompson 1997: 94)? No, to Silver, the suppression of voice or, rather, the contamination of one authorial voice by another is a sign of a complex psychological and textual instability, not of a simple ideological correction.

Signs of such instability, particularly as it affects internal voice, can occur in various modes. A famous example is the voice of Keats's urn, which speaks something, but what exactly? The phrase "Beauty is truth, truth beauty" (as in Stillinger's edition, 1978: 372–73; *Annals* 1820: 653–54)? Or the whole of the last couplet? Does the absence of quotation marks in both Brown's transcript (the only one derived from a holograph) and in the first printing in the *Annals* of 1820 support or disprove Stillinger's limited quotation? And what difference of meaning results from the longer or shorter record of the voice of the urn? Can one have it both ways, as Helen Vendler suggests,[15] in arguing that the limited quotes speak for

---

15. See also Stillinger 1967: 113–14, cited by Vendler to support her position. Other editions adopting the limited quotation "Beauty is truth, truth beauty" (without necessarily endorsing Vendler's ambivalent reading) are Allott 1970: 537 and Cook 1990: 289. However, Barnard (1988: 346) and Bush (1959: 208) place the whole closing couplet within the quota-

3

Ah, happy, happy boughs! that cannot shed
  Your leaves, nor ever bid the spring adieu;
And, happy melodist, unwearied,
  For ever piping songs for ever new;
25   More happy love! more happy, happy love!
    For ever warm and still to be enjoy'd,
      For ever panting, and for ever young;
All breathing human passion far above,
    That leaves a heart high-sorrowful and cloy'd,
30   A burning forehead, and a parching tongue.

4

Who are these coming to the sacrifice?
  To what green altar, O mysterious priest,
Lead'st thou that heifer lowing at the skies,
  And all her silken flanks with garlands drest?
35   What little town by river or sea shore,
    Or mountain-built with peaceful citadel,
      Is emptied of this folk, this pious morn?
And, little town, thy streets for evermore
    Will silent be; and not a soul to tell
40   Why thou art desolate, can e'er return.

5

O Attic shape! Fair attitude! with brede
  Of marble men and maidens overwrought,
With forest branches and the trodden weed;
  Thou, silent form, dost tease us out of thought
45   As doth eternity: Cold Pastoral!
    When old age shall this generation waste,
      Thou shalt remain, in midst of other woe
Than ours, a friend to man, to whom thou say'st,
    "Beauty is truth, truth beauty,"—that is all
50   Ye know on earth, and all ye need to know.

22 ever] never *Annals*   34 flanks] sides *CB*   40 e'er] ne'er *altered to* e'er *CB*   42
maidens∧ overwrought,] ∼ , ∼∧ *CB*   47 shalt] wilt *CB, Annals*   48 a] as *CB*   49
"Beauty . . . that] ∧Beauty is Truth,—Truth Beauty,—that *CB*; ∧Beauty is Truth, Truth
Beauty.—That *Annals*

the urn as "epigrammatist," not "historian" (1983: 132), but that the whole of the last two lines are nonetheless spoken by the urn as a "comment on its unique worth" (134)?

The problem in the voice of Keats's urn is that recorded speech (in documents) hovers between unmediated orality and third-person report: there is always an inferred "he said/she said" speech head. Using Joyce's (or rather Stephen Dedalus's) arguments in *Portrait of the Artist* as a model for the gradual opening up of an estranging generic space between speaker and speech, we might note that Keats's *Ode* is only partly in the pure lyric mode of the first person, in which speech is direct, not reported, and that it also partakes of features of the second-person epical mode (that of fiction) and the third-person dramatic mode, in which the artist—according to Stephen—like the God of the mechanistic universe, retires from his creation completely, "paring his fingernails" (Joyce 1964: 215). That so much of chapter 5 of *Portrait*, in which this theory of opening alienation occurs, is cast as dialogue—in the third-person dramatic mode (as compared with the lyric and epical modes of earlier sections of the book)—is doubtless indicative of Joyce's own opening of a Foucauldian gap between the writing subject and the text. And the shift into that gap can be seen whenever unmediated orality becomes potentially legible, as in the recording of speech in folk songs. An especially telling example is *The Three Ravens*, which must itself be charted on a declining ironic narrative and discursive path from the mystical *The Corpus Christi Carol*, which precedes it, to the macabre *Twa Corbies* and the vulgarized *Three Crows*, which derive from it.[16] In Friedman's edition (1956: 23–

---

tion marks of the urn's dialogue. Murry (1949: 366) avoids the issue by not using quotation marks at all—like the authoritative transcripts. Allott summarizes the arguments on quotation as follows: "(1) that the two lines are addressed by the urn to man, (2) that the passage outside the inverted commas [in her edition] is addressed [by Keats] to the reader, (3) that this passage is addressed [by Keats] to the urn" (1970: 537).

FIGURE 9.1. *(facing)* Keats, "Ode on a Grecian Urn" (Stillinger edition). How much of the last couplet is in the voice of the urn, and what differences in meaning are generated by different editorial placements of the quotation marks?

16. The shape-shifting spiritual mysteries of *The Corpus Christi Carol* (with a "fawcon" bearing away "my mak" to a series of dream-like scenes—an orchard, a hall, a bed, a stone with the legend "corpus Christi"—and with a wounded knight being wept over by a "may") are partially retained in *The Three Ravens* (with the anthropomorphized "fallow doe" sub-

24)[17] of the poem, the editor resolves the problem of the apparent incompatibility of the concluding motto ("God send every gentleman," etc.) and the dialogue of the carrion birds ("Where shall we our breakfast take?") by ending the dialogue at the fifth stanza. But there is no textual or narrative reason why this closure (which has the result of returning the following descriptive stanzas about the fallow doe, etc., to the voice of the external narrator, who overhears the dialogue)[18] should be any more authoritative or plausible than closing the birds' dialogue at other points in stanzas six through nine (or even after stanza ten, with no return to the external narrator, and the final couplet therefore an ironic self-reflection on the birds' own nature).[19] In the language of Foucault, the avian dialogue is indeed not "completed" but is only a "process," with any number of edges, each one representing a different narrative and a different meaning.

In another famous case, we might ask what is the meaning of the scribal (and editorial) uncertainty over the identity of the speaker of

---

stituting for the "fawcon" and/or the "may"); but the carrion theme of the poem is taken up with a cynical vengeance in *Twa Corbies*, in which the hawk, hound, and lady fair are no longer faithful to the dead knight. There is no longer any protection for his corpse from the ravages of scavengers. By the time of the American *Three Crows*, all of the spiritual qualities of the earlier versions are lost, and virtually all that remains of the narrative elements is "an old horse in yonder lane, / Whose body has been lately slain." Even the carrion theme of *Ravens* and *Corbies* is made ironic, for the expected assault on earthly remains ("We'll sit upon his old dry bones, / And pick his eyes out one by one") is itself satirized: "O maybe you think there's another verse, / But there isn't." Peculiarly, the rhetorical structure of the poem(s), that is, the dialogue form with spectator, which is barely hinted at in *Corpus Christi*, becomes the most resilient component of the folk song in its transmission. Thus, voice triumphs over substance or narrative.

17. Other editions using the same closure to dialogue include Eastman et al. 1970: 38; Donaldson 1962: 1 et seq.; and Danziger and Johnson 1968: 75. The edition by Trapp (1973: 439) avoids any quotation marks.

18. The role of this external strolling narrator is clearer in *Twa Corbies*, which begins in the voice of the observer ("As I was walking all alane, / I heard twa corbies making a mane"), but the dialogue of the corbies quickly takes over, and there is no (problematic) return to the voice of the narrator and the moral that he—if it is he—finds in the story of the *Ravens*.

19. I recognize that the dialogue closure adopted by Friedman and other editors is at least plausible, for it does mark what seems to be a shift from declarative to descriptive language, but the problem is not in plausibility but in the fact that *any* quotation marks in a print edition of ambiguous dialogue will permanently foreclose ambiguity.

1   There were three ravens sat on a tree,
     Downe a downe, hay down, hay downe
There were three ravens sat on a tree,
     With a downe
There were three ravens sat on a tree,
They were as blacke as they might be,
     With a downe derrie, derrie, derrie, downe, downe.

2   The one of them said to his mate,
"Where shall we our breakfast take?"

3   "Down in yonder greene field,
There lies a knight slain under his shield.

4   "His hounds they lie downe at his feete,
So well they can their master keepe.

5   "His haukes they flie so eagerly,
There's no fowle dare him come nie."

6   Downe there comes a fallow doe,
As great with yong as she might goe.

7   She lift up his bloudy hed,
And kist his wounds that were so red.

8   She got him up upon her backe,
And carried him to earthen lake.

9   She buried him before the prime,
She was dead herselfe ere even-song time.

10   God send every gentleman
Such haukes, such hounds, and such a leman.

FIGURE 9.2. *The Three Ravens.* The editorial problem is to decide when the birds' dialogue ends (if at all) and when we are returned to the voice of the external narrator.

the line "Nay, by my fader soule, that schal he nat!" in Chaucer's *Man of Law's* epilogue (Fragment II.1178)—should it be the Shipman, Squire, or Summoner, as various scribes have suggested in different witnesses?—and how is this uncertainty exacerbated by the speaker's reference to his (or more likely her) "joly body" later in the epilogue? These tokens are generally taken as further signs of the original *Wife of Bath's Tale* having been later assigned to the Shipman as Chaucer's vision of the Wife changed, with an imperfect revision in the current *Shipman's Tale* which retained the original speaker's references to an obviously female "we" and "us,"[20] just as the originally clerical speaker of what is now *The Merchant's Tale* still bears traces of his original ecclesiastical voice.[21] One voice, or one teller, is contaminated by another. And within *The Merchant's Tale*, there is a major problem of attributable voice in the long passage (IV.1267–1392) beginning "And certeinly, as sooth as God is kyng, / To take a wyf it is a glorious thyng," for if the passage in praise of marriage is not punctuated as the speech of the "olde knyght," January—and usually it is not[22]—then it must be in the voice of the narrator, the Merchant, who, however, has already informed us of his *negative* views on marriage in his prologue,[23] so that the speech would have to be seen as extended, and perhaps rather labored, irony.

There is a similar problem in the attribution to Miranda of the angry speech beginning "Abhorred slave, / Which any print of goodness will not take," in the folio *Tempest* (1.2.354–64), our only primary witness to the

---

20. As in such lines as "The sely husbonde, algate he moot paye, / He moot us clothe, and he moot us arraye, / Al for his owene worshipe richely, / In which array we daunce jolily" (*Shipman's Tale*, fragment VII.11–14).

21. For example, "As doon thise fooles that ben seculer" (IV.1251); "I speke of folk in seculer estaat" (IV.1322).

22. In the Riverside edition; Fisher 1977; Heiatt and Heiatt 1964; Hussey 1966; Pratt 1974; and Baugh 1963, it is punctuated as if in the voice of the Merchant/narrator. To my knowledge, no current edition of Chaucer recognizes the levels of irony by suggesting an alternative punctuation of the speech (or no punctuation at all, which is, of course, what the manuscripts present).

23. "I have ywedded bee / Thise monthes two, and moore nat, pardee / And yet, I trowe, he that al his lyve / Wyflees hath been, though that men wolde him ryve / Unto the herte, ne koude in no manere / Tellen so muche sorwe as I now heere / Koude tellen of my wyves cursednesse!" (IV.1233–38).

play. For such critics or editors as Dryden and Theobald, this is logically, philosophically, and logistically improper in Miranda's voice (it is out of character and diction, and speaks of events that Miranda would not have known about, given her tender years), and the speech must be reassigned to Prospero.[24] Most modern editors, however, retain F1's attribution to Miranda. Of course, where multiple witnesses exist for such versioned plays as *Romeo and Juliet* and *Lear*, the unstable speech attributions—or even the manner in which speech attributions are made—have been used to destabilize the plays themselves. Thus, Urkowitz (1980) and other versionist critics employ the shifting attribution of certain speeches in the quarto and folio *Lear* as evidence not of textual dissolution but of authorial reconstruction, demonstrating that, for example, the two assignments of the variant line "Who stockt my Servant" to Lear in the folio (referring to Kent) or "Who struck my servant" to Goneril in the quarto (referring to Oswald) both work dramatically, but work in different ways, and in different voices (Urkowitz 1980: 36–37). To Urkowitz, such variance in speech is not evidence of authenticity giving way to error but of multiple authenticities, a position interrogated in Ann R. Meyer's claim (1994) that problems in casting off copy in the L gathering of Q could equally well have caused such variants as Q's attributing "Breake hart, I prethe breake" to Lear in a compositorial error for Kent (as in the folio). Meyer's argument is significant in that, according to her, the Q attribution to Lear gives him a speech *after* his death, for the pressure on space caused by faulty casting off copy has forced the compositor to omit the stage direction for the death in its logical position (at Edgar's "He faints"), a direc-

---

24. Theobald's case (1740) for Prospero over Miranda is:

> In the first place, 'tis probable Prospero taught Caliban to speak, rather than left this office to his daughter. In the next place, as Prospero was here rating Caliban, it would be a great impropriety for her to take the discipline out of his hands; and, indeed, in some sort an indecency in her to reply to what Caliban was last speaking of. (quoted in Furness 1966: 73)

Theobald, noting that Dryden had given the speech to Prospero, attributes the error to "the players, who, not loving that any character should stand too long silent on the stage, to obviate that inconvenience with regard to Miranda, clap'd this speech to her part." Capell shared Theobald's view, as did Sharswood and Allen, who argued that the speech is "discrepant, in tone, from everything else Miranda says" while "identical in character with the speeches of Prospero." Furness 1966: 73, from whom these citations are taken, argues in favor of Miranda, as do most modern editors.

tion which Wells and Taylor now place two speeches *later* because of the faulty attribution of "Breake hart." Where the revisionists see two voices for Shakespeare, and for several for his players, Meyer sees one authorial voice, but competing compositorial ones.[25] And in *Romeo*, as Michael Basile (1994) demonstrates, Lady Capulet becomes more aggressive to both Juliet and her husband from the putative source (Arthur Brooke's poem *The Tragicall History of Romeo and Juliet*) to Q1 to Q2, culminating in the Zeffirelli film version (1968), in which Capulet's speeches threatening Tybalt at 1.5 in the banquet scene are assigned to Lady Capulet, even though neither Q1 nor Q2 show her as even being present during the contretemps (see Basile 1994: 48–55). And in *Romeo* Q1 and Q2, the typographic peculiarity—the mark of difference—of the Nurse's speeches in 1.3 (in italics) were at one time taken by Pollard and Wilson (1919) to indicate a *common* manuscript source which presumably included parts of a (previous?) text written in italics, but by Hjort (and most others) to demonstrate quite the opposite—that Q2 was based directly on Q1 plus (as Hjort argues) marginal notes or added "slips of paper" (Hjort 1926: 140–46). The very typographic peculiarity of the speeches is taken as a token of two different textual histories. In other words, the presentation of internal speech and speaker, even when marked by signs of difference, is still open to dispute over what that difference means in terms of the outside voice of the author. And, to my knowledge, the cultural difference of

---

25. Meyer's article makes the general claim that while "[r]ecent scholarship has frequently resolved the difficulty [of variance between Q and F] by emphasizing authorial revision . . . physical evidence does exist which suggests that he was not responsible for the variations" (1994: 144–45); and, of this specific scene, she says that, in ignoring the evidence of compositorial error in casting off copy, "[t]he Oxford editors' reconstruction of this scene in their edition of Q and their claim that it is authorial is incompatible with the physical evidence present in the extant text" (144). Other examples of shifting speech heads in *Lear* dealt with by Urkowitz and others include "Heere's France and Burgundy, my Noble Lord" (folio Cor[delia] or Cor[nwall]; quarto Glost[er]: Urkowitz 1980: 38–40); "Aske me not what I know" (quarto Gon[eril]; folio Bast[ard]: Urkowitz 1980: 112–13); and "Let the Drum strike, and prove my title good" (quarto Bast[ard]; folio Reg[an]: Urkowitz 1980: 131). Note also that, in the final scene, the concluding voice in the play is attributed to Albany in the quarto and Edgar in the folio.

FIGURE 9.3. *(facing) The Tempest:* Miranda's speech "Abhorred slave" in the First Folio (1.2.354–64). Is the rhetorical tenor of the speech consistent with Miranda's character, and is the "I" in the speech compatible with her experiences and actions? Would not the speech more logically belong to Prospero?

The Tempest.

Pro. Thou moſt lying ſlaue,
Whom ſtripes may moue, not kindnes: I haue vs'd thee
(Filth as thou art) with humane care, and lodg'd thee
In mine owne Cell, till thou didſt ſeeke to violate
The honor of my childe.

Cal. Oh ho, oh ho, would't had bene done:
Thou didſt preuent me, I had peopel'd elſe
This Iſle with *Calibans*.

Mira. Abhorred Slaue,
Which any print of goodneſſe wilt not take,
Being capable of all ill : I pittied thee,
Took pains to make thee ſpeak, taught thee each houre
One thing or other : when thou didſt not (Sauage)
Know thine owne meaning; but wouldſt gabble, like
A thing moſt brutiſh, I endow'd thy purpoſes
With words that made them knowne: But thy vild race
(Tho thou didſt learn) had that in't, which good natures
Could not abide to be with; therefore waſt thou
Deſeruedly confin'd into this Rocke, who hadſt
Deſeru'd more then a priſon.

Cal. You taught me Language, and my profit on't
Is, I know how to curſe : the red-plague rid you
For learning me your language.

Proſ. Hag-ſeed, hence :
Fetch vs in Fewell, and be quicke thou'rt beſt
To anſwer other buſineſſe : ſhrug'ſt thou (Malice)
If thou neglectſt, or doſt vnwillingly
What I command, Ile racke thee with old Crampes,
Fill all thy bones with Aches, make thee rore,
That beaſts ſhall tremble at thy dyn.

Cal. No, 'pray thee.
I muſt obey, his Art is of ſuch pow'r,
It would controll my Dams god *Setebos*,
And make a vaſſaile of him.

Pro. So ſlaue, hence.   *Exit Cal.*

Enter Ferdinand & Ariel, inuiſible playing & ſinging.

Ariel Song. *Come vnto theſe yellow ſands,*
       and then take hands :
       Curtſied when you haue, and kiſt
       the milde waues whiſt :

That the e
Pro. T
And ſay w
Mira.
Lord, hov
It carries a
Pro. N
As we hau
Was in th
With gree
A goodly
And ſtraye
Mir. I
A thing di
I euer ſaw
Pro. It
As my ſoul
Within tw
Fer. M
On whom
May know
And that y
How I may
(Which I
If you be N
Mir. N
But certair
Fer. My
I am the be
Were I bu
Pro. Hc
What wer'
Fer. A
To heare th
And that h
Who, with
The King r
Mir.
Fer. Ye
And his br

The Historie of King Lear.

Kent. That from your life of difference and decay,
Haue followed your sad steps.   *Lear.* You'r welcome hither.
  Kent. Nor no man else, als chearles, darke and deadly,
Your eldest daughters haue foredoome themselues,
And desperatly are dead.   *Lear.* So thinke I to.
  Duke. He knowes not what he sees, and vaine it is,
That we present vs to him.   *Edg.* Very bootlesse.   *Enter*
  Capt. Edmund is dead my Lord.   *Captaine.*
  Duke. Thats but a trifle heere, you Lords and noble friends,
Know our intent, what comfort to this decay may come, shall be
applied: for vs we wil resigne during the life of this old maiesty,
to him our absolute power, you to your rights with boote, and
such addition as your honor haue more then merited, all friends
shall tast the wages of their vertue, and al foes the cup of their de-
seruings, O see, see.
  Lear. And my poore foole is hangd, no, no life, why should a
dog, a horse, a rat of life and thou no breath at all, O thou wilt
come no more, neuer, neuer, neuer, pray you vndo this button,
thanke you sir, O, 0,0,0.   *Edg.* He faints my Lord, my Lord.
  Lear. Breake hart, I prethe breake.   *Edgar.* Look vp my Lord.
  Kent. Vex not his ghost, O let him passe,
He hates him that would vpon the wracke,
Of this tough world stretch him out longer.
  Edg. O he is gone indeed.
  Kent. The wonder is, he hath endured so long,
He but vsurpt his life.
  Duke. Beare them from hence, our present busines
Is to generall woe, friends of my soule, you twaine
Rule in this kingdome, and the goard state sustaine.
  Kent. I haue a iourney sir, shortly to go,
My maister cals, and I must not say no.
  Duke. The waight of this sad time we must obey,
Speake what we feele, not what we ought to say,
The oldest haue borne most, we that are yong,
Shall neuer see so much, nor liue so long.

FINIS.

The Tragedie of King Lear. 309

taine the ftone,	That we prefent vs to him,
:nd?	*Enter a Meffenger.*
or.	*Edg.* Very bootleffe.
	Meff. Edmund is dead my Lord.
liues:if it be fo,	*Alb.* That's but a trifle heere :
me all forrowes	You Lords and Noble Friends,know our intent,
	What comfort to this great decay may come,
	Shall be appli'd. For vs we will refigne,
	During the life of this old Maiefty.
Friend.	To him our abfolute power, youto your rights,
Murderors,Traitors all,	With boote,and fuch addition as your Honours
e's gone for euer :	Haue more then merited. All Friends fhall
Ha :	Tafte the wages of their vertue,and all Foes
e was euer foft,	The cup of their deferuings : O fee,fee.
hing in woman.	*Lear.* And my poore Foole is hang'd: no,no,no life?
nging thee.	Why fhould a Dog,a Horfe,a Rat haue life,
jne did.	And thou no breath at all ? Thou'lt come no more,
	Neuer,neuer,neuer,neuer,neuer.
good biting Faulchion	Pray you vndo this Button. Thanke you Sir,
I am old now,	Do you fee this? Looke on her? Looke her lips,
ne. Who are you ?	Looke there,looke there. *He dies.*
: tell you ftraight.	*Edg.* He faints,my Lord,my Lord.
vo,fhe lou'd and hated,	*Kent.* Breake heart,I prythee breake.
	Edg. Looke vp my Lord.
re you not *Kent* ?	*Kent.* Vex not his ghoft,O let him paffe,he hates him,
iant *Kent,*	That would vpon the wracke of this tough world
?	Stretch him out longer.
I can tell you that,	*Edg.* He is gon indeed.
e's dead and rotten.	*Kent.* The wonder is,he hath endur'd fo long,
am the very man.	He but vfurpt his life.
	Alb. Beare them from hence,our prefent bufineffe
of difference and decay,	Is generall woe : Friends of my foule, you twaine,
	Rule in this Realme,and the gor'd ftate fuftaine.
ither.	*Kent.* I haue a iourney Sir,fhortly to go,
	My Mafter calls me,I muft not fay no.
dly,	*Edg.* The waight of this fad time we muft obey,
re-done themfelues,	Speake what we feele,not what we ought to fay :
	The oldeft hath borne moft,we that are yong,
	Shall neuer fee fo much, nor liue fo long.
he faies,and vaine is it	*Exeunt with a dead March.*
	Ff 3

FIGURE 9.4. *(facing)* Lear's death scene in the quarto.

FIGURE 9.5. *(above)* Lear's death scene in the folio.

THE HISTORIE OF KING LEAR   Scene 24

biting Fauchon
m old now,
'to Kent) who are

you straight.

- hated,

Kent?

is your seruant

lat,
:ad and rotten.

in.

d decay,

welcome hither.

and deadly,
ie themselues,

co.

line it is,

lesse.

a trifle heere,
our intent,
:ay come,
ne

To him our absolute power, (*to Edgar and Kent*) you to
   your rights
With boote, and such addition as your honors
Haue more then merited, all friends shall tast   3080
The wages of their vertue, and al foes
The cup of their deseruings, O see, see.

LEAR
And my poore foole is hangd, no, no life,
Why should a dog, a horse, a rat haue life
And thou no breath at all, O thou wilt come no more,
Neuer, neuer, neuer, pray you vndo
This button, thanke you sir, O, o, o, o.

EDGAR He faints (*to Lear*) my Lord, my Lord.

LEAR Breake hart, I prethe breake.

EDGAR Look vp my Lord.   3090

KENT
Vex not his ghost, O let him passe, he hates him
That would vpon the wracke of this tough world
Stretch him out longer.
    ⌈*Lear dies*⌉

EDGAR   O he is gone indeed.

KENT
The wonder is, he hath endured so long,
He but vsurpt his life.

ALBANY (*to attendants*)
Beare them from hence, our present busines
Is to generall woe, (*to Kent and Edgar*) friends of my
   soule, you twaine
Rule in this kingdome, and the goard state sustaine.

KENT
I haue a iourney sir, shortly to go,
My maister cals, and I must not say no.   3100

ALBANY
The waight of this sad time we must obey,
Speake what we feele, not what we ought to say,
The oldest haue borne most, we that are yong,
Shall neuer see so much, nor liue so long.
            Exeunt, carrying the bodies

FIGURE 9.6. (*above*) Lear's death scene in the Wells-Taylor *Oxford Shakespeare*.

FIGURE 9.7. (*facing*) What is the bibliographical and dramatic significance of the
italics in the Nurse's speeches in the quarto versions of *Romeo and Juliet* 1.3?

of Romeo and Iuliet.

But to reioyce in splendor of mine owne.

         Enter Capulets Wife and Nurse.

Wife. Nurse wher's my daughter? call her forth to me.

    Nurse: *Now by my maidenhead, at twelue yeares old I bad her come, what Lamb, what Ladie-bird, God forbid, Wheres this Girle? what* Iuliet.

         Enter Iuliet.

Iuliet. How now who calls?

Nur. *Your mother.*

Iuli. Madam I am here, what is your will?

Wife, This is the matter: Nurse giue leaue a while, we must talk in secret. Nurse come backe againe, I haue remembred mee, thou'se heare our counsel. Thou knowest my daughters of a pretie age.

    Nurse. *Faith I can tell her age vnto an*   *vre.*

Wife. Shee's not fourteene.

    Nurse. *Ile lay fourteene of my teeth , and yet to my teene be it spoken, I haue but foure, shees not fourteene. How long is it now to* Lammas tide?

Wife. A fortnight and odde dayes.

    Nurse. Euen or odde, of all daies in the yeare come Lammas *Eue at night shal she be fourteene.* Susan *and she, God rest all Christian soules, were of an age. Well* Susan *is with God, she was too good for me : But as I said, on* Lammas *Eue at night shall she be fourteene , that shall shee marrie, I remember it well. Tis since the Earth-quake now eleuen yeares, and she was weand I neuer shall forget it, of all the daies of the yeare vpon that day: for I had then laide worme-wood to my dug , sitting in the sun vnder the Doue-house wall. My Lord and you were then at* Mantua, *nay I doo beare a braine . But as I said, when it did taste the worme-wood on the nipple of my dug , and felt it bitter, pretie foule, to see it teachie and fall out with the Dugge: Shake quoth the Doue-house , twas no need I trow to bid me trudge: and since that time it is a leuen yeares, for then she could stand by lone, nay byth roode she could haue run and wadled all about : for euen the day before she broke her brow, and then my husband, God be with his*

                            his

italic in itself (especially when postulated for the manuscript of an actor's part in a new Romantic tragedy) has not been critically confronted—an omission of graphical analysis which I find particularly striking for a period in which an educated person (like the queen) could opt for italic or secretary depending on the significance of the occasion of writing.[26]

A less ambiguous, but more typographically complex, case occurs in the multilayered (archaeological) signs of typographic and attributional difference displayed in John Whitgift's *The defense of the answere to the admonition against the reply by TC* (Thomas Cartwright), published in 1574. As Malcolm Parkes notes in his analysis of the levels of speech in this text, "the printer has exploited a hierarchy of type faces to distinguish different levels of interpolated discourse within the work, as well as citations" (Parkes 1993: 223). These levels include black letter for Whitgift's own voice, itself a commentary on a commentary on a commentary on a commentary, with emphasis marked in larger type and quotations from his adversary's voice in smaller; quotations in Latin from other voices represented in italic, with English translations in roman; roman type within black-letter passages for the names of authorities and sources; a marginal roman in large type for subheadings, referring back to the divisions in Cartwright under discussion; marginal italic for authorities quoted in the text proper; and a smaller marginal black letter for summaries of Whitgift's own argument. This dazzling display of an archaeology—in fact a "network" of "text"—of discourses embedded within discourses[27] is a wonderfully apt demonstration of why it can indeed matter *who* is speaking (and that the reader should know, at every level, who it is), in what must surely be acknowledged as an early experiment in the multilayering capacities of hypertext.

---

26. See Goldberg 1990 for a deconstructive/cultural-materialist analysis of the "domains of the hand" and the "practices of reinscription" (133, 134) that marked the English Renaissance as a site for a contentious, indeed "violent" conflict for control over "hands" (such as the distinction between secretary and italic).

27. See Hill 1997 for an account of the editorial problems of addressing such internal and external citations in Renaissance ecclesiastical debate.

FIGURE 9.8. *(facing)* Typographic layers of meaning and voice in John Whitgift's *The defense of the answere to the admonition against the reply by TC* [Thomas Cartwright].

Idolatrous
facrificers
and Maffe-
mongers.

150   The defenfe of the anfwere

haue fuffered punifhment for their finne, and haue receiued due rewarde for the wicked-
neffe which they committed : what reuengement fhall afterward hang ouer their foules, if
they haue committed no other fault,if there is no other finne,which may condemne them,
but onely haue committed this faĉt,and for the fame haue receiued the punifhment due by
the lawe ? The Lord will not punifhe one thing twife, for they haue receiued the rewarde
for their finne,and the paine for their offence is finifhed. And for this caufe is not this kind
of commaundement cruell(as the heretikes affirme, accufing the lawe of God,and denying
that there is any kinde of humanitie in it) but it is full of mercie : bycaufe hereby the people fhould rather be purged from their finnes, than condemned. But nowe there is no punifhment layd vpon the body,nor any purging of finne,through corporall punifhment, but
through repentance, which if a man doe worthily worke, fo that he may feme worthie to
haue the punifhment withdrawne, he maye finde forgiueneffe. But howfoeuer this anfwere of Cyrill,may in fome points minifter occafion of quarrelling to fuche as be dif-
pofed,yet this is euident,that the quantitie of finne ᵹ the heynoufneffe of it,is not to be
efteemed accoꝛding to the coꝛpoꝛall and externall punifhmente, but accoꝛding to the
commaundement of God,to the which it is repugnant, and accoꝛding to the thꝛeate-
nings of God in the fcriptures pꝛonoūced againſt the fame,foꝛ we fee that leffer faults
are by man punifhed with greater toꝛments,euen accoꝛding to the ſtate of euery cũ-
try. And this fmelleth not one whitte of the Manichees herefie, but the cleane contrarie.
Neither doe I make this difference betwixt the feueritie of the law, and le-
nitie of the Gofpell,in any other refpect, than of tempoꝛall punifhment appoyn-
ted in the lawe.

The true mea
ning of zacha-
rie.13.

The place of Zacharie doth not make foꝛ your purpofe,except you will giue to the
parents power of life and deathe ouer their fonnes and daughters, and giue libertie
foꝛ one pꝛiuate man to kill another. The pꝛophet in that place declareth what zeale
fhal be in the people againſt falfe pꝛophets, ᵹ how much they fhall pꝛeferre the true
Religion of God befoꝛe their owne naturall affection,and rather foꝛfake their childꝛe
yea hate them,and kill them,than by their meanes, they ſhould be withoꝛawne from
God : this is the true meaning of that place. If you will referre it to the time of the
Gofpell, But if you will apply it to the Ifraelites to whom this pꝛophet now pꝛea-
cheth ᵹ pꝛophecieth,then doth he declare vnto them what zeale and feruencie God re-
quireth in them, if they truely repent them of their foꝛmer Idolatrie : euen that they
fhall not fpare their owne childꝛen,but deale with them accoꝛding to the law Deu.13.

Luther.

ver.6.ᵹc. M.Luther expounding this place and referring it to the time of the Gofpell
faith thus:Et eſt hæc fententiæ fumma.ᵹc.The fume hereof is,that Chriſtians fhal reteine,&
defend true and pure doĉtrine,without refpeĉt of any perfop,whether it be his kinfman, or
friend, for it is neceffarie that there fhoulde be falfe doĉtrine, and herefies, that the truth
might be tryed,but yet they fhall not haue the vpper hande, or preuaile. And interpꝛeting
thefe woꝛdes) his father and his mother that begat him fhall thruſt him through when he
pꝛophefieth) he faith,id eſt,non ferreis aut æreis armis ᵹ gladijs ipfum conficient,fed verbo Dei,
erit enim fpirituale ᵹ fuaue certamen, quale eſt parentuin cum fuis liberis,ficut ᵹ diuus Paulus
Corinthios confodit,ᵹ ipforum errores verbo Dei reprehendit. That is to fay, they fhall deſtroy
hym not wyth Iron or brafen armour and weapons, but wyth the worde of God : for the
ſtrife fhall be fpirituall and pleafant, fuche as is betweene parentes and their Children,lyke
as Saynt Paule dothe pearce throughe the Corinthians, and reprehendeth their errors by
the word of God.

The bloudy
affertion of
T.C.

But would you in deede conclude of thys place, that thofe whyche haue taughte
falfe doĉtryne muſte of neceffitie be put to deathe, thoughe they repente ᵹ you that their
owne parentes and friendes muſte kill them, oꝛ caufe them to be kylled, and not rather receiue them willingly, if they will conuerte, and embꝛace them moſte ioyfull-
ly ᵹ vndoubtedly, the Pꝛophete hathe no fuche meaning : neyther haue you anye example of fuche extremitie committed by a true Chꝛiſtian towardes a repentant I-
dolater, from the natiuitie of Chꝛiſte vnto thys houre : neyther is there anye
thyng in the whole newe Teſtamente, whereby anye fuche faĉte can be warranted. And howefoeuer thys place maye make, foꝛ the feuere punifhyng of ſtub-
boꝛne

It is hardly surprising that politically motivated repression of the adversarial voice should be even more ubiquitous in our current (non-print) media, where not just repression but falsification of the adversary can be so easily accomplished. During the Russian invasion of Georgia in August 2008, there was no doubt that the overwhelming power of the Russian military would prevail; but, as noted by Levy (2008), while the Russians might have won the battle on the ground, the Georgians won in the battle for global opinion, with the Georgian president, Mikheil Saakashvili, using his "fluency in English [and his youthful good looks] to dominate coverage . . . in the world." To counter this public relations offensive, the Russians not only sent emissaries to CNN but also began to intervene electronically with the presentation of the voices involved. Thus, the version of a Fox News interview broadcast on Russian TV was "edited to make Fox News seem overtly hostile. The man who dubs [the interviewer] Mr. Smith's voice in Russian not only exaggerates the anchor's tone, but even coughs and groans loudly when [the interviewee] Ms. Tedeeva-Korewicki blames Mr. Saakashvili for causing the conflict—something that did not happen in the original" (Levy 2008: A9). This substitution of voice for political purposes came on top of the Russian dubbing of speeches by Saakashvili "in a shrill Russian intended to suggest a tin-pot despot who has maniacally plunged the region into chaos" (ibid.). Of course, none of the evidence for this manipulation of voice was made available in the tightly restricted Russian news media, but the repression can certainly be seen as another example of the recognition that voice is a significant part of the transmission of the message.

This brief catalog of competing, sometimes cacophonous, voices both inside and outside texts can only begin to suggest the various processes in which it does indeed matter *who* is speaking (and *how*), even if that speaker is only the neuter "someone" (Foucault's *on dit*). I end with a final caution: lest it should be thought that the multivocal, electronic post-Babel of hypertext editing should eradicate the problem of why it matters, I cite another voice. J. C. C. Mays notes that, just like the variant texts I have been discussing, hypertext "remains in suspension until it can be *spoken*" (my italics; Mays 1995)—in other words, until, in negotiating its windows on linked themes, phrases, collations, etc., we have done to the raw data what Whitgift's printer did to the embedded polemics of ecclesiastical debate. And, of course, it must be spoken by—who else?—

that maligned or marginalized or effaced "someone." The dream of an agent-free neutral environment (more or less corresponding to Talbot Donaldson's "editorial death-wish"; 1970: 105) is an illusion, for at each stage on the electronic highway there will be paths taken and not taken, and the cumulative mapping of these paths will delineate a presence, no less or more lacking in authenticity than all those other choices that editors and readers have had to make over the centuries.[28]

---

28. Note that, for example, Foley's (1984) hypertextual display of "object-text" in multi-variant oral epics emphasizes the active role of the reader (monitor viewer) in manipulating the variance so that the "transmission" of the text is not ended by electronic recording and editing, as it would be in print editions; and see Sanders (1996) on the "fossil hypertext" stack form of the traditional scholarly edition, with "horizontal reading leaps" unlike the linear reading of other print publications. Sanders finds other precursors of stacked hypertext in, for example, the multiple taxonomies of medieval libraries, chained books, and book-wheels.

TEN

Romancing the Text,
Medievalizing the Book[1]

Text has always been a problem. From its first appearance in Middle English in the fourteenth century, the word has carried a dual, indeed a contradictory signification. Inherited from the late Latin *textus* was the sense of authority, of *the* text, the scripture, the revealed truth and unmoved center of faith and transcendental reality; but parallel to, and competing with, this positivist acceptance of the singularity and invariability of text was another inherited strand of meaning, which comes down to us in the word *textile*.[2] From its earliest etymological stirrings in both Greek and Latin,[3] *text* has carried a less precise and more epistemologically challenging sense than "authority," a sense instead of a weave and pattern, a warp and weft, that threatens the stability of *quod scripsi scripsi* (John

---

1. This essay is a companion piece to the following essay, "The Philosophical Discourse of [Textuality]?" which examines the philosophical and cultural underpinnings of the modern as manifest in bibliographical and textual study, taking up the challenge of the arguments against postmodernism in Habermas's *Philosophical Discourse of Philosophy*. In that essay, I tentatively suggest that the theories of text espoused by the premodern (i.e., medieval) and the postmodern may have more in common with each other than they have with the intervening modernist view of text as authority and as definitive utterance. In the related chapter, "Facts, Truefacts, Factoids; or, Why Are They Still Saying Those Things about Epistemology?" I link this modernist conception of text with empirical science, technological positivism, and the faith in a transcendental logic that is universally applicable.

2. For an analysis of the complex etymology and meanings of *text*, see Greetham 1989, esp. n. 19, together with the "Ontology" chapter of Greetham 1999b. For a consideration of the confusion caused by postmodernist critics' generally being aware only of the *textile/network/weaving* strand of meaning, see "The Philosophical Discourse of [Textuality]?" in this collection.

3. See Scholes 1992 for an analysis of the developing meanings of *text* in Greek and Latin, and see Kimmelman 1996 for a critical account of the late Latin use of *text* in the sense of "authority."

19:22). Things can get unsaid by an interdiction (*interdit*); the fixed pattern can come unraveled and be rewoven as latter-day Penelopes continually remake the transmission.

For the most part, textual critics have not been unduly disturbed by this semantic and etymological aporia; in fact, they have pretty much ignored it. During the great period of positivist, definitive editing (especially that undertaken under the auspices of the Modern Language Association's Center for Editions of American Authors),[4] editors could take a proprietary responsibility for and delight in the "clear text," unsullied, newly pristine text pages of multivolume editions of the great canonical authors, while burying any possible evidence for unweaving discreetly and discretely in the back of the book.[5] The cognitive separation of what a medieval reader might have thought of as text and gloss was accomplished through the modernist technology of the printed codex book, that monument to stability and permanence. Thus, the modern agenda as exemplified in Ramus's famous oration, in which he declared that "modern" (i.e., sixteenth-century) scholarship had now overcome the corruptions of the Middle Ages, became not just a cultural trope but a hard, empirical, concrete exemplification, founded upon the twin altars of nationalism and positivism. Nationalism because of the need to fix the canonical status of the great white fathers[6] and positivism because these editions were perceived as the fulfillment of the nineteenth-

---

4. The CEAA was set up by the MLA as a means of promoting the production of scholarly editions of the major writers of the American literary canon, and soon extended its influence into related fields, such as philosophy, though not into the editing of American historical writers, whose editors generally follow the principles set down by the National Historical Publications and Records Commission (NHPRC). The theoretical conflict between the author-centered principles of CEAA and the annotational rationale of NHPRC is clearly set out in Cook 1981 and Robert Taylor 1981, both responses to Tanselle 1978.

5. A *clear text* is one in which all signs of editorial intervention have been removed, and the apparatus of variants and editorial emendations is available only in a separate tabulation. One of the arguments put forward by the CEAA editions, almost all of which were in clear-text form, was that having a pure text page unencumbered by editorial stigmata would promote the dissemination of such texts in other formats. Perhaps the most successful of these recyclings of CEAA critical editions has been the Library of America, now approaching its two-hundredth volume, of which the earlier publications in the series simply took their texts from established CEAA editions, but largely without the back matter of editorial textual apparatus.

6. The CEAA enlarged its scope by becoming the Center for (later Committee on) Scholarly Editions, though to the present the major focus of the CSE's attentions and its awarding

century investment in analytical and descriptive bibliography[7] as part of a progressional history of technology in which, given enough testing and enough evidence, all textual truths would be known.[8] In this historical and evidentiary paradox, the textile aspects of text (the fragmentary and the apparently reweavable) were to be put in service of the idealist view of text as scripture, idealist in that it represented a "text that never was" in this rude world of corruption and social negotiation.[9]

The further paradox, which is directly involved in the medievalizing movement of the last two centuries, is that the Enlightenment, rationalist view of perfectable utterance (what Habermas calls the "ideal speech situation")[10] finds its most potent distillation not in the neoclassical hopes for a grammar of textuality through a theory of more and more precisely

---

of "approved" editions has remained in editions of nineteenth-century American authors. While some medievalists have served on the CSE (myself and the distinguished scholar of Old French, Mary B. Speer), the CSE has not in general been successful in getting editors of medieval works to submit to either the principles or the jurisdiction of MLA.

7. *Descriptive* and *analytical* bibliography are closely linked and are at the heart of the Anglo-American bibliographical project. The former concentrates on the accurate, formulaic description of the physical features of the makeup of the printed book and the latter on the technological processes, from the compositorial setting of type to proofing, binding, and so on, that mark the printed book as an important exemplar of the history of technology. Descriptive and analytical bibliography have together emphasized the empirical, "scientific" nature of the history of the book, sometimes at the expense of its cultural and social history, which has been favored by French and other European bibliographers.

8. The technological bias of Anglo-American bibliography can be seen as an aspect of late nineteenth- and early twentieth-century confidence in the validity of impartial evidence in establishing historical "fact." For a critique of this faith in positivist and definitive appeals to evidence, see the chapters "Textual Forensics" and "Facts, Truefacts, Factoids" in this volume, together with Hellinga 1998.

9. "The text that never was" is a motto that emphasizes the Anglo-American (and specifically Greg's and Bowers's) aim to restore an ideal form of the text that has never seen actual documentary realization. This call for an overcoming of the corrupting state of nature toward the resuscitation of a formalism beyond the reach of social and historical decay has been seen by some critics as a (Neo)Platonic idealism, as against the Aristotelian descriptivist and concrete documentalism of other approaches to the reconstruction of the past. See the "Forms of the Text" chapter in Greetham 1999b for an analysis of the debate on textual Platonism.

10. See Habermas 1970, 1975; and, for the general Enlightenment and rationalist view of the possibilities of defining speech situations, see Habermas 1984. I take up the textual issues in Habermas's defense of Enlightenment modernity in the chapter "The Philosophical Discourse of [Textuality]?"

defined genres but, ironically, in that individualistic movement that supposedly put an end to genre theory and even textual taxonomy as a whole: Romanticism.[11] Where the Enlightenment (and even earlier periods) saw the medieval text as quaint and willfully illegible (indeed, requiring legibility to be imposed on it, through normalization and regularization),[12] Romantic theories of textuality and the "whole book" managed to combine an awe for the originary moment of inscription (in such cases as the supposed composition of Coleridge's *Kubla Khan* and Shelley's dictum about the "fading coal" of inspiration once pen had been put to paper)[13] with new commitment to the organicism of a totalized expression that could only be achieved under the impress of a powerful poetic imagination acting upon otherwise recalcitrant material.[14] Allied to the commodification of the text that had already begun to be asserted by John Locke, Daniel Defoe, and other promoters of literary proprietorship a

---

11. This ironic congruence of medievalism and Romanticism is most forcefully explored in Workman (see Utz 1998), where he demonstrates that the scholarly momentum for medievalism as a whole (and as an identifiable intellectual discipline) is dependent on the Romantic reconfiguration of both history and aesthetics. I obviously endorse much of what Workman argues in this piece, but would complement his perspective by suggesting that, at least in textual studies, it is in postmodernism that the medieval book (if not the medieval author) is fully resuscitated.

12. See, for example, Dryden's "modernization" of Chaucer (1700) and Thomas Percy's less overt but similarly motivated normalization of some of the texts of his *Reliques* (1765). On the cultural and political co-option of major medieval texts in later periods, see Machan 1995 and Thompson 1991.

13. See Stillinger 1994 for a documentary and critical demonstration that, at least in the case of Coleridge, the Romantic ideal of single and originary inspiration was contradicted by the multiple reworkings of the poetry, including *Kubla Khan*, which, according to Coleridge, had been composed in an opium dream and interrupted by the famous visitor from Porlock before the poet could get the full vision onto paper. On the concept of "fading coal," see Mendelson 1987. See also McGann 1983, 1992 for an account of the ironies implicit in this Romantic view of composition, especially as they have become institutionalized in the modern critical edition.

14. See Coleridge's famous definition of poetry as the product of creative imagination: "The poet, described in *ideal* perfection, brings the whole soul of man into activity. . . . He diffuses a tone and spirit of unity, that blends, and (as it were) *fuses* each into each, by that synthetic and magical power, to which we have exclusively appropriated the name of imagination" (1983: 14). See "The Telephone Directory and Dr. Seuss," in this volume, for an exploration of how Coleridge's Romantic formulation has had a major influence on the history and protectability of the modern literary work, especially in Anglo-American copyright theory and practice.

century earlier,[15] Romanticism added the economic and cultural element of the poet as "national treasure" to secure, through copyright, a legal as well as a philosophical protection of original and unitary utterance (see Vanden Bossche 1994).

As Jerome McGann and others have argued, it was this faith in Romantic individual expression (which was inherently sullied by the release of the text into society) that underwrote modernism's desire to re-achieve the originary moment and to fix it against such latter-day corruptions.[16] Romancing the text was a way to cordon off the incursions of bibliographical history and at the same time to situate the *author* as the prime, indeed the only, mover of literature. The modernist author thus took on the attributes of the medieval creator, an unworldly absence who nonetheless left traces of his presence (his "signatures") in the created universe of the text. Like the medieval Scholastic philosophers of the dialectic, it was accordingly the responsibility of textual critics as hermeneuts to make the connections between *signum* and *res*, to formulate anatomies or summas of text that could peer through what the New Bibliographers of the Anglo-American school termed a "veil of print" into the mind of the great *auctor*.[17] As I have noted, once this idealizing momentum, a reach for the true scriptures of text, could be attached to the manifest and incontestable epistemological truths of analytical and descriptive bibliography (a movement parallel to, or a part of, the charge of positivist science to discover the "laws" of nature through empirical observation and rigorous evidentiary protocols), then modernist textuality appeared secure on both transcendental and empiricist fronts.

But this neat scenario and this seemingly impregnable case for a re-medievalized ideal text on the model of God's relations with his uni-

---

15. See Rose 1993 for an account of the post-medieval growth of the concept of authorial intellectual property, deriving in part from Locke's economic theory of investment and profit in one's property. See also *Intellectual Property and the Construction of Authorship* (1992) for a wide range of important articles on the shift of attitudes to authorial control and responsibility in the post-medieval period. The seminal theoretical essay on the linking of authorial property with legal liability is, of course, Foucault 1984.

16. McGann has written widely on this topic, but the major statement remains his *Critique* (1983). Rajan (1988) questions McGann's thesis in a thoughtful essay proposing a different history of hermeneutics.

17. See Bowers 1959: 18; Rosenblum 2008: 30ff.; McLeod "Avail of Print."

verse contained within itself the seeds of its own undoing, the threads that would now begin to re-medievalize the book, and thus make the re-medievalized, Romanticized text give way before the later onslaught of that exemplary medieval bibliographical movement: postmodernism.

This was sometimes a paradox, but has of late become almost a truism. For bibliographical and textual history, it plays out as follows. On one front, the ideality of critical texts ran into a descriptive empiricism that increasingly concentrated on data without theory, the positive good of information. This movement is, for example, attested in the founding of the Early English Text Society by Frederick Furnivall as a specific linguistic database for the provision of evidence for the *new*. The dictionary was the raison d'être for EETS because Furnivall rightly assumed that a full historical taxonomy of usage, morphology, and syntax could not be constructed authoritatively without the prior accession and codification of the documentary record from which the descriptive catalog would be formulated.[18] Now, it is tempting to argue that historicity is itself a theory of knowledge, a confidence in the ability of the researcher to arrange data on a linear path of developmental change that would demonstrate the linguistic ethic of origins and teleology. After all, the same (sometimes mistaken) confidence had led Mabillon (1709) to codify the scripts of Europe into developmental histories and had provided the historical confirmation of, for example, the exposure of documentary forgeries by Valla (1440). Put simply, the faith was that all aspects of cultural progression, while sometimes apparently arbitrary, seemed so only because we did not yet have a large enough database to perceive the orderliness of natural law: Grimm's law, Verner's law, and the like are "laws" precisely because they are both predictive and descriptive; they can be used to fill in the blanks of the documentary record by demonstrating, through the minatory yet transcendental *,[19] what the missing part of the grid of evidence *would have been* if only it had had the good fortune not to

---

18. As is well known, the EETS was largely a result of the historical, documentary rationale for the *OED*. See Murray 1977.

19. By convention, an asterisk before a linguistic form acknowledges that no documentary record of the form has been discovered but that by the process of critical analogy, the asterisked form would morphologically and historically be expected. The inevitable evidentiary problem of such a synthetic complex is that it assumes a totalization of utterance within a specific linguistic moment and space. Would the asterisked form still be justified ("a text

have vanished (or, conceivably, never to have been used). So while the evidentiary protocols of EETS were indeed inductive and descriptive as they related to the larger agenda of the *OED*, the lurking desideratum of the linguistic organic whole was never fully banished from the supposedly raw empiricist, descriptive enterprise of both the editorial and the lexicographical projects. Besides, empiricism often seems to have a hard time among those looking to lexicography for a linguistic moral summa or for a code of social conduct: witness the cultural brouhaha over *Webster's Third* having abandoned the moral labels of "substandard" usage, etc., in favor of historical description[20] and that wonderful moment when James Murray was upbraided by a "prim, decisive" female visitor to his scriptorium for having included an entry in the *OED* for a "non-existent" word, that is, one she did not already know: "I am positive that I never saw that word before." Murray's only proper empiricist rejoinder was via shared ignorance and cultural complicity—that he himself had also not encountered the word (and many others besides) before he began work on the dictionary. As Elisabeth Murray recounts, this anecdote illustrated to Murray the fact that "not even one educated lady's English [or the English of the editor of the *OED*] is all English" (Murray 1977: 299–300).

The pretensions of the documentary record and the lexicographic coding of a culture toward completeness and toward the sort of organicist whole that Wordsworth and Coleridge claimed for the Romantic definition of poetic utterance could only ever be contingent, therefore, and inherently unstable in the real world of documentary representation. In this sense, the textual recovery of the medieval was forever similarly contingent and ephemeral. We do not even need to evoke studies of Klaeber's parochial "Germanic" editing of *Beowulf*[21] or Allen Frantzen's exposure (1991) of the similarly nationalist program for Anglo-Saxon studies or

---

that never was") if the conceptually implausible negative evidence could be assembled that the missing documentary evidence was missing not just because of the tenuous laws of survival of artifacts but because the putative form was, in fact, never used? It is a question of this type that the eclectic, idealist editors of modernism are continually confronting (except that the self-marking asterisk is often not present in their editions).

20. For the debate caused by this historicist and descriptive approach rather than the proscriptive and critical agendas of other American dictionaries, see Morton 1994.

21. See McGillivray 1994a; and Bloomfield 1994, who charges that Klaeber's patriarchal/paternalistic editing resulted in a "diminished" Wealtheow.

John Willinsky's account (1994) of the nineteenth-century imperialist agenda of the *OED* to acknowledge this contingency and partiality.

But the problem for organicist claims about text under Romanticism was compounded from within the bibliotextual establishment itself. Consider two very different cultural signifiers: Robert Proctor's incunabular descriptive bibliography (1898–1903) and William Morris's bibliophiliac achievements at the Kelmscott Press.[22] It hardly matters that the former was motivated by a nationalist bibliography that can be traced back to John Bale (1548) and John Leland (1549, 1774), whereas the latter was a Marxist-inspired attempt to overcome the alienation between the artisan and the artifact, to reinstate work as production rather than as hired labor. Both projects tended toward the same breakup of the Romantic hegemony of re-medievalized creation and authoriality, though both would presumably be horrified by the ultimate results. While Proctor's research into the bookishness of the book, its particularity and idiosyncrasy, was to be used in the service of the concept of *ideal copy* in descriptive bibliography,[23] the ideal espoused by this aspect of bibliography, while still Platonizing, was procedurally far removed from the "ideal text" of Platonic textual theory,[24] although there has been some cultural irony in the

---

22. On Morris's medievalizing aims for the Kelmscott, see his pamphlet *Note* (1898, 1969). For the production of the press, see Peterson 1984; for the political motivation behind the medievalization of the artisan, see Thompson 1955, 1977; and Faulkner 1980. Salmon 1996 provides a good survey of the ideological purposes behind Morris's various projects; and Dreyfus 1996 demonstrates Morris's reworking of a premodern aesthetic in the age of mechanical reproduction.

23. The concept of *ideal copy* is central to the research aims of descriptive and analytical bibliography. The term is defined by Philip Gaskell (1972, 1985) as "the most perfect state of a work as originally intended by its printer or publisher following completion of all intentional changes" (321); and in similarly intentionalist language by Tanselle, who notes that ideal copy excludes "alterations that occurred in individual copies after the time when those copies ceased to be under the control of printer or publisher" (1980: 46). Thus intentionality (printer's and publisher's) is as much a part of the rationale of the apparently technical or scientific aspects of strict and pure bibliography as it is in the recovery of unfulfilled authorial intention under the auspices of idealist, eclectic editing.

24. For an account of the Platonizing idealism of modern textual criticism, see the "Forms of the Text" chapter in Greetham 1999b. It has long been my contention that this modern Platonism is a cognitive inheritor of the principles of analogy used by the Alexandrian librarians and Homeric editors of the third century BC. See, for example, my textual elucidation (1991b) of Harold Bloom's argument (1979) on canny Alexandrianism versus uncanny Pergamanian "anomaly."

two procedures having often been practiced by the same bibliographers, notably W. W. Greg, Fredson Bowers, and G. Thomas Tanselle.[25]

In brief, by Proctor and his followers having placed the hard physicality of the *book* at the center of bibliographical identity, the transcendence of author (and therefore of authorial text) beyond the constricting confines of analytical bibliography made it increasingly difficult to sustain the author-focused centripetal ideology of the "great" and "unique" creator (the unmoved mover) in the face of the centrifugal ideology of bibliographical fragmentalism. For the medieval book, this undermining of Romantic authoriality was particularly stark, since the tendency of medieval codex production to be only rarely in the service of the singularity of the author (but instead to favor what Derek Pearsall [1985: 105] has referred to as a "history of taste," in other words, the receptional antithesis of individual composition) meant that the study of the artifactual history of books under the auspices of analytical bibliography and codicology would tend to reinforce the structuralist, non-intentionalist, culturally degressive assumptions of *l'histoire du livre,* itself a manifestation of the *annales* school of history versus the great-figure approach more favored by Anglo-American historians and bibliographers.[26]

Similarly, Morris's "liberation" bibliography, while obviously nostalgic in its imitations of medieval scripts and medieval book production in general, might have been motivated by a Marxist desire for the reintegration of artifact and artificer but itself became a particularly overt example of a growing concern for what Jerome McGann subsequently dubbed the "bibliographical codes" of textual meaning, those graphic signifiers that have little or no lexical variation but can determine major cognitive and receptional variance in the cultural signification of a work (see McGann 1991b). Words may remain consistent, but meaning changes according to the graphic phenomena in which the words are represented. The chal-

---

25. See "Materiality" in Greetham 1998 for an examination of these ironies and their cultural significance for the history of bibliography and textual criticism.

26. French *l'histoire du livre* has typically dealt with the phenomenon of the book as a cultural artifact and with the cognitive and social implications of its bookishness. A disdainfully acid response to this approach (as seen from an entrenched Anglo-American bibliographical disposition) occurs in Shaw 1992.

lenge that Kelmscott, Doves, Ashendene, and other "private" presses apparently resuscitating medieval bibliographic codes as offerings to authorial textual idealism was twofold. First, the private presses produced medievalized cultural simulacra, not the thing itself: they specialized in the manufacture of medieval*ism*, not in the constitution of an essentialist, Platonized, and historically plausible medieval bibliographic ethic. Second, they emphasized that a belated bibliographic control over the means of production could significantly open up an experiential gap between author and work, and thus make the claims for a transcendental authoriality yet more difficult to sustain. None of this was, I believe, observed at the time: Morris did not believe he was rendering Chaucer *less* medieval by drawing attention to the simulacra of bibliographical codes in the Kelmscott edition; but the effects of Kelmscott were to make Chaucer Victorian, not medieval, and were accomplished by Morris's very skill at creatively emulating his cultural paradigms to emphasize the constructed quality of the Chaucerian text. So much for textual transcendentalism.

But the situation was to become yet more fraught with bibliotextual ironies. It has (I hope) become a critical commonplace that textual criticism and bibliographical research are no more immune to the ideological and theoretical shifts that characterize the academy and society at large than is any other intellectual procedure. As I and various other historians of the book and the text have pointed out, the complex and evolving narrative of nineteenth- and twentieth-century critical theory, from (old) historicism through formalism to phenomenology, structuralism, poststructuralism, (new) historicism, feminism, and the rest, can be mapped in the changing dispositions, aims, and principles of bibliography, and even in the physical layout and appearance of the artifactual and scholarly products of the discipline. Thus, clear-text idealism may be seen as a manifestation of the "well-wrought urn" of the culturally isolated and artistically self-referential modes of Russian formalism and Anglo-American New Criticism (see "Forms of the Text" in Greetham 1991a, b), whereas genetic or inclusive-text editions owe more to structuralist principles of textual analysis (and it is therefore no great cultural surprise to discover that genetic editions are to this day more popular in France and Germany, where the philosophical roots of structuralism began, than in the Anglo-American textual community, which until the late twentieth century still overwhelmingly regarded the formalist principles of New Criticism as the talisman of textual production).[27] Admittedly, there has been some resistance among Anglo-American empiricists and positivists to this revelation that there really is a *theory* behind textual practice (indeed, several, often competing, theories), and the naively neutral motto of "doing what comes naturally" has not been easy to *de*naturalize (see Amory 1984). Nonetheless, when Lotte Hellinga (1998), a renowned scholar of the analytical bibliography of incunabula—and in a direct line of intellectual and procedural descent from Proctor (1898–1903), Burger (1892–1913), Duff (1886, 1970), Haebler (1905–1924), Holtrop (1857–1868), and other researchers in the medieval and early modern book—can argue that bibliographical "facts" are inherently unstable, for they will change their significance depending on the size (micro or macro) of the map or grid on which the data are observed,[28] then I think we can perceive that the most thoughtful and influential of contemporary bibliographers[29] have successfully *de*naturalized the study of the book and the text in their own work, and are now striving to persuade the last holdouts of recalcitrant positivist bibliography that "facts" are movable and constructable cultural phenomena, not transcendental (and Romantic) mystical entities.

---

27. See "Textual Imperialism and Post-Colonial Bibliography" (Greetham 1997c) for an account of such nationalist prejudices in editorial theory; and see the "History of the Text" chapter in Greetham 1999b for a coverage of the struggle for hegemony between Anglo-American and European schools. My general argument has been that such gestures as Tanselle 1981a have been imperialist maneuvers to co-opt or contain foreign (and specifically French) theories of the book within the big tent of Greg-Bowers eclecticism.

28. For example, Hellinga (1998), speaking out of not only her experience as a scholar of incunabula but also her role as coordinator of the European consortium on the records of early printing, demonstrates that a "fact'" like a simple list of publications from a particular town or press will change its significance when anachronistic modern national borders are imposed over a cultural landscape that was configured very differently. She notes, for example, that the obsession with "Costeriana" (print artifacts that have been used by Dutch book historians to suggest that the Netherlands has bragging rights for the invention of printing—rather than Germany, via Gutenberg) takes on an entirely different function as a "fact" when the artifacts are observed within a contemporary political landscape in which the national identities of "Germany" and "the Netherlands" were completely unlike those in the later period, when the international historical contention began.

29. See, for example, Tanselle's sophisticated analysis (1995b) of the problem of historical fact.

Nobody could accuse Dr. Hellinga of being a bibliographical post-modernist, but her deft demonstration of how the particulars of historical research may be reordered (at what Barthes 1972 would call secondary and tertiary systems of signification, in his analysis of the relations between orders of discourse) effectively challenges the earlier (modernist) bibliographical faith in essentialism and the "purity" of the various manifestations of knowledge and expression. To that extent, therefore, Hellinga's more flexible, more cautious, and more provocative use of those slippery pieces of information we call facts does demonstrate that her thinking is of its time and context. And that time and context, like it or not, is postmodernist.

And thereby hangs an inevitable conceptual and historical hermeneutic circle. Clearly, any of the various "post" disciplines and ideologies (poststructuralism, post-Marxism, postfeminism, postcolonialism) depends for its function and identity on the idea of supersession, and specifically a supersession of an earlier, more essentialist discipline. To come after and to celebrate that belatedness by the marker "post" is to claim that a former, self-referential, and enclosed critical method or social philosophy (enclosed because it did not denominate itself by reference to another, through such prefixes as post) has been superseded and is now a matter of historical curiosity but no longer a viable ethical, intellectual, or cultural force for the production of contemporary discourse. And now consider "post/modernism" under this template, especially with regard to the gap between the "modern" and the "post" as it affects our current concepts of, and work in, the book and the text, and specifically the book and text as medievalized (or even actually medieval) objects of study. In brief, what does a "postmodern" bibliography and textuality look like, and how do such views impinge upon our reconceptualization of the "medieval"?

One of the major ironies in the academic and scholarly renomination of the Renaissance as the "early modern" (even leaving aside the fact that "Renaissance" itself was not a Renaissance invention, but was back-constructed in the nineteenth century to justify and underwrite the Enlightenment and Romantic rehistoricizing of the past)[30] is that,

---

30. In the sense (1a) of the "great revival of art and letters, under the influence of classical models, which began in Italy in the 14th century and continued during the 15th and 16th; also, the period during which this movement was in progress." The OED's earliest citations

with pre- and post- now enclosing it, modernity is arrested in time, made an object of historical study, and demarcated against both its precursor and its successor.[31] Thus, the "premodern" (i.e., that which was formerly the "medieval") and the "postmodern" must now be seen as definable not only by what they are not ("modern") but by their structuralist affinities with each other by this bipolar opposition to the intermediary period and dispensation. At its crudest chronological remapping, modernity thus becomes merely a blip, an interruption, in the connectivity of the pre- and postmodern, between medieval and contemporary culture.

This effacement of modernity and reintegration of the medieval and postmodern has, of course, been one of the main features of that re-medievalizing associated with the work of Umberto Eco, especially in his influential essays on "rediscovering" the Middle Ages (1986)[32] and in his rereading, in *The Name of the Rose* (1983), of contemporary semiotic theory within or parallel to the medieval (specially Lombardian) hermeneutic interplay between *signum* and *res*, together with a re-playing of the nominalist/universalist battles of Abelard and William of Champeaux[33]in the context of a poststructuralist play on the infinite

---

are from the mid-nineteenth century. And, perhaps ironically, while this general sense was usually positive—the *OED* cites a first instance in Ford's *Handbook of Spain* (1842): "[a]t the bright period of the Renaissance, when fine art was a necessity and pervaded every relation of life"—the attributive senses associated with, say, architecture, were often quite pejorative, as in the T. A. Trollope first citation from *Summer in Brittany* (1840): "[t]hat heaviest and least graceful of all possible styles, the 'renaissance' as the French choose to term it"; or in Jephson and Reeve's *Brittany* (1859): "[t]he cathedral front is a huge mass of barbarous Renaissance." But for a period that oversaw not only the historical invention of the Renaissance but also the Romantic reinstitution of the Gothic (and pseudo-Gothic) as an architectural aesthetic, this irony is almost predictable.

31. The historical range of what is meant by the "modern" is itself a matter of dispute, and thus affects the values ascribed to the pre- and postmodern. For example, Habermas's version of *die Moderne* is coterminous with Enlightenment rationality at one end and the breakdown of this same rationality under the auspices of Foucault, Derrida, et al., whereas Stephen Toulmin (1990) pushes back the "modern" as a philosophical dialectic substituting (a) logic for rhetoric, (b) the universal for the particular, (c) the general for the local, and (d) the timeless for the timely—in other words, as Platonic rather than Aristotelian.

32. Eco, "The Return of the Middle Ages" and "Living in the Middle Ages," both in Eco 1986.

33. See the chapter "The Philosophical Discourse of [Textuality]?" for a further examination of the textual implications of nominalism and universalism.

deferral of *différance* as against the sureties of modernist, structuralist *différence*.[34]

Eco has, indeed, become perhaps the chief apologist for and scholiast on the text that declares a new Middle Ages in postmodernism,[35] rather

---

34. That is, the evidentiary protocols of the detective story genre of Eco's novel appear to play into the semiotics of structuralist *différence* (the detective observes a sign that can then be interpreted as a demonstration of inferable "fact" leading to the establishment of the bipolarities of "guilt" or "innocence"). Indeed, the usual structure of the detective novel is built on a series of "misreadings" of signs (by the reader and/or by other characters in the story), a structure that is necessary for the plot, in its most basic Aristotelian sense, to advance by a progression of such differences between, and misapprehensions of, truth and error, the prototype being, of course, *Oedipus Rex*. Structuralist *différence* is thus resolved into the full system of signification that typically concludes the detective novel, where the private eye explains how the complex of signs can all be fulfilled by the necessary narrative closure. However, as I argue in "The Philosophical Discourse of [Textuality]?" this apparent triumph of Enlightenment, modern rationality is an illusion common to all idealist philosophies, and the dialectical confrontation with the text that Habermas and other modernists strive after is an incomplete or weak dialectic, one in which the "negative" component of the dialectic is not negative enough. I contend that the implied simultaneity of the *et* in Abelard's *Sic et Non*, while it might appear to be in the service of structuralist resolution (like the detective story in Eco's novel), when read in its fuller postmodernist implications in the work of, say, Adorno and Horkheimer, becomes instead the precursor for the deeper cynicism of continually deferred resolution *différance, avant la lettre*) of Adorno's *Negative Dialectics* (1992). I claim that it may be plausible to regard Horkheimer and Adorno's *Dialectic of Enlightenment* (1944, 2002) as a modern equivalent of the systemics of Abelard's *Sic et Non* (in the suggestion that the pursuit of enlightened reason might produce new forms of irrationality), and that both pre- and postmodernism might move the irrational to another stage of development, resisting affirmative thought in any mode. Abelard's dialectic, because it gave prominence to the act of opposition, might thus look irrational to an early modern (or later modernist) but could at least point toward synthesis as an operational, if not a "real," resolution. By the time we reach Adorno's *Negative Dialectics*, however, the act of affirmation in both parts of the Abelardian contradictions (as well as the imputed synthesis) becomes untenable. For example, in his "Critique of Positive Negation," Adorno confronts the "mathematical" bias in Hegel's formulation of the dialectic ("to equate the negation of negation with positivity is the quintessence of identification"; [1992: 158]) as a "fetish" of "the positive-in-itself" (159). Like Abelard, who recognized the realist error of thinking of categories or classes as things ("It is monstrous to predicate the thing of a thing" [quoted in Leff 1958: 109]), Adorno addresses the issue of the *quidditas* ("whatness") of identity as fetishistic: "Against this [fetish], the seriousness of unswerving negation lies in its refusal to lend itself to sanctioning things as they are. To negate a negation does not bring about its reversal, it proves, rather, that the negation was not negative enough" (1992: 159–60). Because resolution, on the detective story model, can never be fully achieved in medieval theology or philosophy (we must await the revealed and singular truth of the next, transcendental world for that happy state), Adorno's refusal of modernist dialectic is, perhaps paradoxically, much more medieval (and thus postmodernist) than any structuralist closure could attain.

35. The qualities that Eco recognizes in this *nouvo medioevo* include "the collapse of the Great Pax" (1973: 75); a "new barbarianism" (76); the "insecurity . . . of chiliastic anxieties"

than yet another reconstitution of a medievalism (after the model of, say, Gothicism, Romanticism, Wagnerism, or Victorianism) that is simply a selective and ultimately distancing reconstitution of certain emotionally or politically attractive features of a retroactively invented "middle" age.[36]

Whether or not Eco will succeed in his agenda for re-periodization (and, ironically, to recast the period of Habermas's modernity as the next Middle Ages between the pre- and postmodern), there have been various signs that bibliographers and textual critics may be playing into Eco's model, by emphasizing the cognitive and even the physical or narrative codes of "medieval" and "postmodern" textualism, a sympathetic alignment that reflects the similar nostalgic or apocalyptic agenda of much twentieth- and twenty-first-century work in "new" medievalism as an academic discipline.[37] It is true that those supersessionist enthusiasts for electronic texts (what I like to call "pomo Romanticists") who are ignorant of the long history of bibliography still tend to lump the medieval manuscript "book" and its texts and readers together with the printed

---

(79); "politicized groups whose moralism has monastic roots" (80); the verbal elite's translation of an "alphabetic mentality . . . into images [of] the essential data or knowledge and the fundamental structure of the ruling ideology" (81); "the work of composition and collage that learned culture is carrying out on the flotsam of past culture" (82); and "an art not systematic but additive and compositive." As I note in the critique of Eco's formulation in "The Philosophical Discourse of [Textuality]?" for the textual historian, it is the formal shift from a "systematic" textuality to an "additive and compositive" one that best illustrates the conflation of pre- and postmodern aesthetics.

36. As is well known, Wagner added the paean to German art and to the unifying status of the specifically *German* Holy Roman Empire (together with warnings against the dangers of falling under the corrupting influence of a *falscher wälscher Majestät*) at the end of *Die Meistersinger von Nürnberg* partly at the promptings of the ultranationalist Cosima and partly as the fulfillment of his project to promote a new German identity founded upon the resuscitation of a Germanic Middle Ages, ultimately to find modern embodiment after 1871 in the new German empire. This project is just one aspect of the reformation of *Germanistik* under the protocols of *Modernismus* initiated by the philological and *volkisch* agenda of the Grimm brothers. (See Peck 1996 for an account of this identification among philology, *Altertumswissenschaft,* and the concept of a "new," i.e., "medieval," Germany.) It was, of course, no accident that the Nazis later chose Nuremberg as the contested site for the celebration of this newly "primitive" Germany.

37. See, for example, Bloch and Nichols's introductory account of this alignment, especially their emphasis on the late nineteenth-century's medievalists' "ambiguous relation to what they saw as the insidious modernism of the times as opposed to an earlier modernism of Newton and Descartes" (1996: 11). See further Nichols's essay in the same collection, "Modernism and the Politics of Medieval Studies."

book of the post-Gutenberg period, and in so doing betray their simplistic and unsophisticated (mis)understandings both of medieval bibliography and of the very hypertextualism they now wish to espouse. But a more careful reading of bibliographical history, one that does not simply attempt a "year zero" rejection of all that came before the new revealed truth of hypertextualism, can both clarify and illustrate the drawing together of the medieval and the postmodern, to form an arc (even perhaps a full circle) of bibliographical coding, whereby the conceptual principles of the textualism of the (old) Middle Ages can be fulfilled in the new episteme of the postmodern and the hypertextual. If this linking is plausible, then we may have progressed beyond the earlier romancing of the text as a form of re-medievalization to a medievalizing of the book at a moment of one of the major transmissional opportunities (or crises) of the last few millennia.[38]

Much has been made by pomo Romanticists of the forbidding, constrained finality and linearity of the printed codex book, especially as compared with the liberation technology of electronic text. Even leaving aside the political naiveté of these claims for an open inclusiveness and democratization as against protected and privileged access for a social elite, and even allowing the claims for electronic nonlinearity to stand unchallenged for the moment (though such preconceptions betray a remarkable ignorance of the cognitive psychology of reading),[39] let us concentrate primarily on the pomo Romantic ignorance of book history. To my knowledge, no hypertextual enthusiast has even acknowledged some of the basic formal distinctions in the format of the printed book (never mind the textual interplay of the medieval manuscript). The hypertextu-

---

38. If earlier moments in such cultural crises of transmission are any guide, the shift from print to electronic modes of production will act as a major epistemological, literary, and scholarly filter, through which only a small percentage of the documentary artifacts of the current medium will fully survive into the next. The precedent shifts from orality to literacy, from epigraphy to the roll, from roll to manuscript codex, and then from script to print, have all entailed critical (and sometimes quite accidental) losses. The example of the only documentary witness to Cicero's *De Republica* surviving as the lower text in a palimpsest of Augustine's *In Psalmos* is simply a useful token of the strategic significance of the cumulative decisions of all those participating in the cultural criticism that is embodied in these shifts.

39. For a further account of pomo Romanticism, see Greetham 2004b and "Is It Morphin Time?" in the current volume.

ists do not observe that broadsheet, codex, and roll (to take just three bibliographical examples) require entirely different acts of composition, layout, and reading. Instead, the pomo Romanticists take only the late (nineteenth- to twentieth-century) unannotated, narrative codex as their bête noir and extract their rules of linearity from this very limited model.

As Jerome McGann has noted (1990), there are several other protocols of reading that can inform even the printed codex, including what he calls "radial" as well as "linear" reading. Moreover, the pomo Romanticists seem entirely innocent of the complex intertextual relations of, for example, shoulder notes, footnotes, embedded notes, endnotes, marginal notes, and completely enclosing notes (or combinations of all these) in the bibliography of the printed book: to them and their supersessionist cause, where the "book" must be swept away as a cultural anachronism, even as a moral danger to society, all books are clear text: narratively encoded codices with entirely fixed Aristotelian beginnings, middles, and ends. Alexander Pope's play within, among, and across the supposedly fixed and separate entities of text and gloss[40] would be completely lost on those determined to find only linearity in the printed book. Now, if we extend our own bibliographical reach into the premodern, we will immediately find that the fixed linearity and enclosed and static narrative arrangement that hypertextuists ascribe to the "book" become the aberration rather than the norm. As scholars from Paul Needham (1979) on bindings to Barbara Shailor on makeup (1988) and Leonard Boyle (1988) on gatherings[41] have convincingly demonstrated, the medieval book, even in what looks like the severely constraining form of the codex, is, in both composition and reception, a fluid, unstable, and constantly shifting series of entities, rather than the solid edifice imagined by the hypertextuists. If anything, various features of the medieval book (perhaps more accurately designated as the medieval intertext), foreshadow the multiple links, the shifting levels of reading, the complex negotiations among different lex-

---

40. On the history and spatial, cognitive, and political function of various styles of marginalia and annotation, see Greetham 1997e and Barney 1991, with the references therein.

41. See also, for example, McLaverty 1984b and Cosgrove 1991. For additional references to the impact of codicology on textual analysis, see the bibliographies to the "Textual Bibliography" and "Making the Book: Manuscript Books" chapters of Greetham 1992c, 1994.

ias[42] of the text(s) characteristic of electronic hypertextuality. A typical university textbook of the twelfth century on Aristotle's works would only begin with the concept of a central text, on which the layout of the page would then encourage, in fact demand, that multiple layers of annotation and response be "downloaded" into the expanding text by multiple "end-users." The very form of the textual organization was predicated on the concept of texts upon texts upon texts, with the eye (and probably the finger) of the textual manipulator on the page and through the volume having no preordained or sequential linearity as a single paradigm in making the text(s) legible. Each end-user would construct a labyrinth or web of reading negotiations that might never be replicated exactly by another user. The major phenomenological difference between the mapping of a medieval (manuscript) and a postmodern (electronic) intertext of something like those Aristotle textbooks is that the electronic medium will usually record the progress of the reader through the links so that by hitting the "back" button or consulting the history of hypertext pages, one can give linear presence to a process that is, and always was, inaccessible to the medieval reader. It is not pushing the bibliographical features too far, I believe, to suggest that a medieval reading of Aristotle was quite as web-like, intertextual, and radial as a current encounter with such popular opaque metafictions as *Myst, Lost, Katamari Damacy, Halo,* or *Spore* (see Jones 2007).

Then, if we turn from the local unit of the textual page to the yet more complex and unstable phenomenology and cultural artifactuality of the book, we will see that the pomo Romantic view of codex linearity evaporates almost entirely. As is well known and well documented (by medievalist codicologists if not by hypertext enthusiasts), the medieval book is almost a complete misnomer if by that term we mean a stable, uniform, unchanging string (rather than web) of textual relations. When I first began editing the geographical sections of Bartholomaeus Angli-

---

42. The term *lexia* (for a "reading unit" of a text) is associated with Roland Barthes's (1974) having divided Balzac's novel *Sarrasine* into a series of nonlinear taxemes, which had the effect of breaking up the narrative of the novel according to a (post)structuralist ethic. George Landow 1992, 1993, 2006, then adopted Barthes's term to describe what he perceives to be the similar dismemberment of the linear, print book in the new electronic environment of hypertext.

cus's *De Proprietatibus Rerum,* one of the first (and, at that point, alarming) features of the Latin exemplars from which John Trevisa drew his Middle English text was that these geographical sections were, well, very mobile. Sometimes they were missing from the encyclopedia as a whole (presumably removed by interested armchair tourists), and sometimes they existed as independent pamphlets (possibly for the same reason). The text moved. I did not realize it then, but this continued mobility and interchangeability, both within a supposed work and within the codex collection in which that work was enshrined, were testimony to the permeability of the textual and bibliographic membranes (and I use the pun with all of its connotations and denotations) that typically went into the *ordinatio* and *compilatio* of the medieval intertext, which is best represented not by the word *book* but by the various contemporary terms used to suggest this fragmentation and permeability: *collectanea, florilegia, franciplegius, pecia,* and so on.

Yes, in the later Middle Ages, there were some attempts by vernacular authors to gather and control their texts into a sort of "collected works." The best example in English is probably Thomas Hoccleve, who did manage to collect various fugitive pieces and even to construct an interlocking (but highly ironic and perplexing) internarrative to bind some of these works together into the so-called Series poems.[43] But then Hoccleve was a professional scribe and thus in a privileged position to effect this ordering of parts (much like Pope's activities as a self-publisher 300 years later). And even Hoccleve failed to get his acknowledged magnum opus, *The Regement of Princes,* into the "collected works," and it thus exists only in corrupted, nonauthorial, scribal versions. There has been some argument that, a generation earlier, Chaucer might have been trying to construct a linear and enclosed collected works, but his control over this venture (if it ever really got off the ground) was limited at best, and his attitude toward textual transmission is probably more accurately displayed by his famous polemic against the depredations of scribes, in his poem "To Adam Scriveyn":

---

43. See Burrow 1982, 1984; and Greetham 1989, all of which consider the authorial and compositional ironies in Hoccleve's attempt to construct a collected works that would somehow reflect his complex and often unstable sense of self.

Adam scriveyn, if ever it thee bifalle
Boece or Troylus for to wryten newe,
Under thy long lokkes thou most have the scalle,
But after my makyng thow wryte more trewe;
So ofte adaye I mot thy werk renewe,
It to correcte and eke to rubbe and scrape,
And al is thorough thy negligence and rape. (Benson 1987: 650)

As virtually all responsible codicologists and most historians of the medieval book have long recognized, the proportion of medieval texts that remain in their original bindings[44] is tiny compared to the total book production, and the incidence of a specific text always having the same bibliographical disposition either internally or with other texts bound in the same volume is slight. Indeed, such a permanent (and linear) coherence may turn out to be non-existent.

So what conclusions may we draw from this bibliographical interface of the pre- and postmodern, and from the hypertextuists' typical conflation of all forms and representational systems of the codex book? Apart from the inevitable schadenfreude in the castigation of faulty history and unsophisticated thinking (always a critical pleasure to indulge in), one may observe that the terminological poles of the pre- and the postmodern might have peculiar validity in the realm of bibliography and book history, and it might behoove the self-nominated postmodernists of electronic text to be aware of this. If they are not, if they continue to ignore the medieval precursors for their "newfound" webs and hypertextualities, they will continue to be guilty of yet another Romanticism. After the authorial transcendentalists of the Enlightenment and the Romantic periods consummated the power, integrity, and ubiquity of the literary creator on the model of the godhead (even down to the principles of legal enshrinement and protection of that entity), the postmodern transcendentalists may have re-Romanticized the text, this time as the ineffable, indeterminate, and finally unknowable deity. And they may be doing this without realizing that in fact they are fulfilling an epistemological

---

44. See, for example, Needham 1979 for an account of the "migration" of bindings (the removal of treasure bindings from their original texts) as just one specific codicological exemplum of the apparently normative recirculation and recombination of medieval texts in relation to their bibliographical "carriers."

program, a way of textual knowing, that is in effect a re-medievalization of the book, but the book now conceived not under the modernist principles of control and closure, but under the pre- and postmodern principles of intertextuality.

I hope I am not misconstrued as an electronic Luddite, nostalgically preferring an earlier form of hypertext, for all of my current projects do have an electronic component, and I am particularly sensible of the enormous coding and recombinative textualities now available to us in the new medium. But I am disturbed by a supersessionist Romanticism that ignores the earlier hypertextuality entirely and imagines that "make it new" means "disdain the past." If only the electronic postmodernists were all appropriately sensitive to the ramifications of the prefix that defines their movement and their new textual ontology, and could see that a "post-" implies a "pre-," then an essay like this would not be necessary.

ELEVEN

The Philosophical Discourse
of [Textuality]?

Is there a philosophical discourse of textuality? I believe so, especially in the sense of that "discourse"—and the very title of this chapter—bearing the marks of contamination. My title is a co-option of Jürgen Habermas's *Philosophical Discourse of Modernity* (1987), a passionate defense of his faith in Enlightenment rationality and modernity.[1] But the title of this current essay is doubly variant. First, by substituting "textuality" for "modernity," I apparently reinforce the widely held assumption that textual criticism is a distinctly "modern" (i.e., post-medieval) enterprise, and I suggest that the great divide between modernity and *medievalismus* is firmly in place, as far as textual study is concerned.[2] Alterity

---

1. This collection of Habermas essays takes aim at the various prophets and exponents of the postmodern, from Nietzsche (seen as the entry into postmodernity) to Heidegger's "undermining of Western rationalism" to Derrida's "critique of phonocentrism" to Foucault's "critique of reason." Habermas finds all these postmodernist positions inadequate in different ways, and in his final essay, "The Normative Content of Modernity," he declares:

> The radical critique of reason exacts a high price for taking leave of modernity. In the first place, these discourses can and want to give no account of their own position. Negative dialectics, genealogy, and deconstruction alike avoid those categories in accord with which modern knowledge has been differentiated—by no means accidentally—and on the basis of which we today understand texts. (1987: 336)

This genre theory of discourse as increasingly fine taxonomic calibrations (textual predicates) from which the subject and thus intention can be drawn is similar to E. D. Hirsch's endorsement of Husserl's transcendental (rather than Heidegger's historicized) phenomenology and is explored more fully for its textual implications in the "Intention" and "Reading" chapters of Greetham 1999b.

2. See, for example, Machan 1994, the thesis of which is that the use of modern (i.e., humanist and Enlightenment) models of authoriality, intentionality, and textuality is inappropriate to the very different premodern protocols of medieval text production.

lives![3] But second, by posing Habermas's declarative statement (there is a philosophical discourse of modernity) as an interrogative (is there a philosophical discourse of textuality?), I question not only the congruence of modernity and textuality, but also the possibility of demarcating a single philosophy—especially in the modern sense of the proper purview of a rational philosophy—under which textual study can be examined. In this chapter, I adopt Stephen Toulmin's prescription (1990) for modern philosophy as the substitution of (a) logic for rhetoric, (b) the universal for the particular, (c) the general for the local, and (d) the timeless for the timely: in other words, it is Platonic rather than Aristotelian.

I will demonstrate, as Toulmin does for philosophy, that the conjugation or synonymy of "modernity" and "textuality" is itself deeply problematic; it has led to a grammar (or logic) of text rather than a rhetoric, a universalism rather than particularization, a generality rather than a locality, and a search for timelessness (what textuists have come to call the "definitive edition") in place of timeliness; and these characteristics have become a cultural liability for textual practitioners as the dominance of the modern has waned.[4] For example, under the auspices of grammaticality over rhetoric, we have been all too eager to construe a *subject* (authoriality, intention, the originary moment) from the *remaniements* of the *predicate* (documents, affects, or "[re]production"); see de Man's "Resistance" and "Return" (1986a, b) together with my "Resistance" in the present volume. Under the auspices of the Platonized ideality of the modern, we have devoted ourselves to the construction of such universal, general, and timeless conceits as "ideal copy," "ideal text," and the superhistorical, non-context-bound "text that never was."

---

3. For an examination of the differing national responses (by Paul Zumthor, Eugene Vance, Hans Robert Jauss, John Burrow, and others) to the "insuperable gulf" or *l'eloignement du moyen age* instantiated in the concept of alterity, see the special issue of *New Literary History* 10 (1979).

4. Habermas's original German title is *Der philosophische Diskurs der Moderne* (i.e., "the modern," as both a period and a particular disposition, emphasizing the Enlightenment virtues of reason, clarity, and transparency) rather than, say, *Modernismus* or *Modernität*. The English-language distinctions among "the modern," "modernity," and "modernism" do not quite parallel the German, and I will use "modernity" and "the modern" in this essay to denote both the post-medieval period as a whole and specific currents within that development, especially the modernism of the West in the early and mid-twentieth century.

This is a large agenda for a survey essay; in the main narrative, I can do no more than sketch the rough outlines of my argument, which should be understood as a heuristic experiment in postmodernist rhetoric, not as an evenhanded and comprehensive summa. I have deliberately selected the anecdotal, the particular, and the timely as provocative probes into modernity and textuality, fully conscious of the inevitable critique: "All this talk of a 'heuristic probe,' as if a probe could be anything but heuristic" (*Listener* 1967; see *OED2* "heuristic" A.a. on McLuhan's style).

For the purposes of my rhetoric at this moment, I can therefore claim that it is no accident that Habermas's declarative statement appeals to modernity as an enabling discourse, and it is no accident that, among conservative textual critics, Lawrence Rainey (1993; and see my response, "Textual Theory and the Territorial Metaphor," in Greetham 1999b) has invoked the fulfillment of the Enlightenment discourse observable in Habermas's conflicts with, say, Derrida and Lyotard, as the positivist, (old) historicist, and philological rock on which contemporary textuality should be refounded.[5]

Richard Rorty mocks the attempts of "weak textualists" to don the trappings of philosophy as an empowering discourse, "to think that literature can take the place of philosophy by *mimicking* philosophy—by being, of all things, *epistemological*. Epistemology still looks classy to weak textualists" (Rorty 1982: 156). In the same way, I will argue that the delimiting of textuality as the apotheosis of modernity in general, and of the rationalist project of the Enlightenment in particular, is not only a weak argument (and a cultural liability); it also misrepresents both the history of textuality as a multivocal discourse and the anti-epistemological, otherthan-rational modes of production and representation that textuality has always had available. Far from "mistakenly think[ing] to impress the populace by wrapping [our]selves in the shabby togas stripped from the local senators" (ibid.), I will contend that textuality, when viewed from the longer perspective that both the Renaissance and the Enlightenment sought to suppress, is already empowered with a multitude of discourses, of which modernity is only one, and a shabby one at that.

---

5. On Habermas versus Derrida, see n. 1 in this chapter. On Lyotard, particularly with regard to social enfranchisement or the constraint of electronic media, see Ess 1994 and the references therein.

I have dealt with some of the specific components—legal, taxonomic, biological, forensic, and annotational—of this thesis in various other writings and in other parts of this book. My intention here is to reimagine the production alternatives as well as the rival histories and agendas of textuality for our current cultural moment, with the caveat that, in order to see this moment as something other than just a fulfillment of the Renaissance/Enlightenment scriptures, it will be necessary to cast a wide chronological and discursive net, for which the *explicatio* and fuller *descriptio* can be found in the works just noted.

Quite properly, after all this invocation of the timely and the local, I begin with my own current moment, the moment of inscription (if that is still the right word for the electronic evanescence of composition on-screen) of this essay. I am using a Windows environment in which simulacra of *folders* and *disks* and *printers* and *scissors* and *text pages* and *paste* and *magnifying glasses* and even a humanoid *coach* infest the upper taskbar of my screen. These simulacra are *icons,* and their iconicity seems to depend on their textual transparency: they appear to dispense with (programmatic) language in order to provide an immediacy of comprehension and access. Of course, even the apparent immediacy and transparency have to be learned; scissors and magnifying glasses are familiar objects in some cultures and cultural moments, but less so in others. The icon does not do away with language as text; it simply transforms it into a different grammatical system. I confess that I came to Windows only grudgingly, after putting up a resistance based on my comfort and familiarity with the DOS-based language, which seemed to be more like "real" language, and thus more honest, more direct, more textual than those flying windows. As Sherry Turkle has documented (1995: 23), DOS users often liked to think of themselves as being in closer contact with the guts of the machine than they would have been in an iconic system. Having to enter long strings of alphanumeric commands on the keyboard seemed more "sincere," paradoxically more transparent, than clicking an icon with a mouse. I remember that when our technician installed an early version of Windows on my office computer, he waxed enthusiastic about the fact that he had not had to "touch the keyboard at all" to accomplish the tasks of installation. "So what?" I thought. "What's the big deal in *not* touching a keyboard? Isn't that where the real action is?" And so, when he left the office, I reassuringly shut down Windows, went back into my good old DOS system, and heard the comforting click of keys. I was still in command. As Turkle argues, and as I have since come to understand, such ontological comfort—a desire to be in direct communion with the vehicle of text production—was illusory. Yes, "Windows" is perhaps an unfortunate misnomer: far from providing textual transparency, far from enabling the textual producer to see through a piece of glass, Windows as a system and each individual window and the icon that calls it up render the textual glass even darker, less transparent: the alphanumeric codes that DOS would have used are hidden, obscured, elided by that click of the mouse. But even if Windows (and the Macintosh operating system that it emulates) is a textual con game, it is obviously one that our culture of text producers is eager to play: my word-processing system when I wrote the first draft of this essay (WordPerfect 7, now Office X4) was initially not even available in a DOS version. My then five-year-old son, brought up in a mouse-clicking textual universe in which he is completely at home phenomenologically (see Greetham and Greetham 2008), would doubtless react to DOS with the same astonishment that must have greeted Cardinal della Rovere's insistence that his print copy of Appian's *Civil Wars* be transcribed back into manuscript (a "real" text) before the book could be placed on his codicologically austere shelves.

Turkle's insistence that DOS aficionados were deluding themselves in thinking that punching a keyboard was a textually transparent and unmediated operation is part of her general concern with the reconfiguration of the textuality of identity in electronic environments. If the agent of text production misconstrues his or her prerogative and empowerment in operating the vehicle for text production, what hope is there that the interpreters of such text production (textual critics, scholarly editors, even "literary" critics) will comprehend that agency and its transparency, or lack thereof? What is the possibility that *text* as icon or as vehicle can be satisfactorily imagined, never mind *re*imagined, in a way that will prove semantically, practically, or epistemologically illuminating for our cultural moment, or any other?

An emblem: my friend and colleague Gerhard Joseph is one of the most percipient and sophisticated nonpractitioner textuists I know. (By "nonpractitioner" I mean only that he does not count himself as an editor or textual critic in his own text production, but he is as much a textuist in the sense of an interrogator of texts as any formal editor.) He has written a dense, provocative, and highly engaging book, *Tennyson and the Text*, taking his title from the weaving figure of text in "The Lady of Shalott" and artfully demonstrating how that figure can be used as a device for confronting Tennyson's textuality as a whole.[6] It looks like a strange match—the poststructuralist deconstructor of texts and the conservative, positivist, Victorian nationalist poet—but it is a match that has proved to be productive. Joseph's *Tennyson and the Text* (1992)[7] relies on, or at least takes off from, Roland Barthes's (1977) construal of text as "tissue" or "network," the weave or pattern of the textile, especially as that weave can be continually unwoven or rewoven and as it resists a formal, teleological, and definitive meaning. Barthes thus famously contrasts *text* ("a methodological field," "subversive," "paradoxical," "dilatory," "plural," "a weave of signifiers," a "network") with *work* (which "can be held in the hand," "the object of a literal science, of philology," "caught up in a process of filiation," and "an organism").[8] That dialectic is inverted (I would even say deconstructed) in G. Thomas Tanselle's redefinition (1990c) of the two terms in almost exactly the *opposite* configuration (see also Eggert 1994 and Grigely 1991). For Tanselle, it is *work* that is ineffable and beyond our grasp, and *text* that is concrete and specific and determined. *Tennyson and the Text* is on secure etymological ground in portraying text as tissue and network, for this strand of meaning (and its connection with the woven pattern of textile, etymologically coterminous) has been present in English since the very earliest occurrences of the word in Middle English.[9] Gerhard Joseph as a textuist is philologically sound.

But after the publication of his book, there came a chance encounter in a corridor at the City University of New York, when Joseph and I were discussing my textual brief for a guest appearance in his doctoral seminar "Alternative Worlds and the Technological Horizon." Yes, I would ad-

---

6. Joseph 1992.

7. Joseph artfully divides his book into "Victorian Warp: Perception" and "Victorian Woof: Representative Men and Mystified Women," with an "Interweave" on "My Lady('s) Shuttle: The Alienation of Work into Text."

8. Barthes 1977.

9. See *OED*2 headnote/etymology: "that which is woven, web, texture." See the examples cited in Greetham 1991a: 130.

dress the intertextuality of hypertext, and I might even show some of the digital morphs I had "written" for a presentation at a conference, "Digital Resources in the Humanities," at Oxford that summer. So "network" and "tissue" would indeed be one of the strands, but so would the other, alternative meaning of *text:* the text as *textus,* the authority, the original, the center, the revealed truth.[10] There was a pause. "What?" said my host, the reweaver of Tennyson. "You're saying there's *another* meaning to 'text' beside 'network' and 'tissue'?" It wasn't quite scales falling from his eyes, but I could see that this recognition of the unnamed, unthought-of other (especially if that "other" brought with it the very authority and determinability that the Barthesian network denied) had suddenly confronted him not just with a dialectic that had been culturally suppressed, but with a whole range of other models for (Tennysonian) textuality of which *Tennyson and the Text* had been innocent. Ever the critic quick on his feet (or the artful dodger), Joseph then gave "three sequential mini-texts or *lexias* for the price of a seamless one" at the annual meeting of the Modern Language Association within a few weeks of our conversation, addressing both aspects of transparency and objectivity, and tissue and network (published 2001). The revelation in the corridor opened up rather than closed off the text-critical options with which Joseph could now play.

But what did the encounter teach me as a textuist? First, it demonstrated just how culturally conditioned our textual choices might be: for the producer of *Tennyson and the Text,* "text" had to be Barthesian and tissue, whereas the *textus* as authority and revealed truth of scripture (and thus "scriptures" in general) was unthinkable for that moment. Second, it showed just how successful the Enlightenment and poststructuralism together (despite their very different ideological agendas) had been in cordoning off the critical, textile sense of *text* for a hermeneutic, nonphilological, intellectual medium (and thereby our having to assume, just

---

10. See *OED2* headnote text "the Scriptures, the Gospel"; 1b. "an original or authority"; 2b. "in the original form and order, as distinguished from a commentary, marginal or other, or from annotations . . . the authoritative or formal part"; 2c. "the original matter"; 3a. "the very words and sentences of Holy Scripture"; 4a. "a short passage from the Scriptures, esp. one quoted as authoritative"; 4b. "a short passage from some book or writer considered as authoritative; a received maxim or axiom." I would demonstrate this fixed, scriptural sense of text in a digital environment by showing the authority that the technical morphist has, while hidden by those Windows again, in controlling pixelation, compression ratio, and so on.

as de Man and strict and pure bibliographers alike had assumed, that philology was pre-hermeneutic, noncritical, and thus positivist).[11] Third, it provided an opportunity to reimagine textuality, an opportunity that I will run with in the rest of this essay.

There is one further irony, even paradox. The reimagination I will construe as our postmodernist discourse of textuality will indeed turn out to be a reaction against the rationalism, objectivity, and *grands reçits* of the Enlightenment and modernity; however, in one of those cultural loops or reinvestments that characterize both iterability and alterity, we will find that postmodernist textuality is one of the elements of a general "return to the Middle Ages" that Umberto Eco observes in present culture.[12]

Postmodernism as medieval? Contemporary textuality as anti-modernist? These are large claims, and they might make some of my colleagues distinctly uncomfortable. Hasn't the death of the author (to say nothing of the death of God) liberated us from the constraints of a theocratic universe and a rigid social and philosophical system, as well as from the claims of the Renaissance and Enlightenment? Wasn't the Middle Ages a period of textual certitudes, or at least of hope for such certitudes? Is not the history of medieval textuality (from Isidore's *Etymologiae* with its agenda for a transparent and universal link between text and meaning[13] to Scholasticism and the similarly universalist agenda of

---

11. This is a dense scenario and cannot be articulated fully here. My contention is that, paradoxically, both the rationalism of the Enlightenment and the uncanny criticism of deconstruction argue that philology must, of its very nature, be objectivist and positivist. As co-opted by the analytical bibliographers of the Anglo-American school (from Pollard to Greg and Bowers), textual criticism lost most of its critical faculties in order to become an empiricist exemplar of the history of technology. As intellectually ghettoized by the deconstructors, these positivist claims for textual criticism were taken all too seriously, and poststructuralists like de Man failed to perceive that the activities of bibliographers and textuists could not be neatly ignored as pre-hermeneutic. See "The Resistance to Philology" in this volume and Greetham 1997d.

12. See Eco 1986. For the textual historian, it is (in Eco's terminology) the formal shift from a "systematic" textuality to an "additive and compositive" one that best illustrates the conflation of premodern and postmodern aesthetics.

13. See Isidori Hispalensis 1911. Isidore sought to arrange the text of the entire phenomenological universe around the transcendental principle of etymology, by which all of nature could be properly construed if only the (Latin) terms of identity could be made transparent. That is, he used a DOS-based system.

the Encyclopedists to comprehend all phenomena)[14] the most egregious example of a longing for a *grand reçit*? And finally—however uneasy we may now feel about Renaissance subjectivity, Cartesian dialectic, and Enlightenment rationalism—were not all these components of modernity advances over the epistemological aridity, structural insularity, and unthinking authoritarianism of the medieval Christian West? Well, yes and no; or, in Abelard's phrase, *sic et non*.[15]

I do not go so far as to claim that Abelard's *sic et non* is a "negative dialectics" in the mode of Adorno, nor that the fracturing of textuality that was inherent in the method known as *sic et non* is somehow a response to Habermas *avant la lettre*.[16] It is important, however, to remember that Scholastic dialectic presupposed the potential viability (and thus rhetorical authority) of both parts of the evidentiary formula—thesis and antithesis—without the positivist cop-out, or rhetorical failure of nerve, that characterizes both Hegelian and Marxist dialectics. That is, although textual synthesis was indeed the trope under which the Scholastic agenda and medieval textuality as a whole might have operated (specifically, to find the *grand reçit* that would provide a typological unification of pagan classical texts with the revealed truth of Judeo-Christian texts), the fulfillment of these scriptures and their conjoining into a full discourse of textuality were in practice forever deferred. Textual synthesis was forever placed under the graphic mark of *différance*, to be given a totalized, modernist utterance only outside the limitations of human history, *after*

---

14. The Encyclopedist movement as a whole, particularly as it became a populist summa for Scholastic thought, was an attempt to chart the "properties of things," as is suggested by the title of the most populist of all the medieval encyclopedias, Bartholomaeus Anglicus's *De Proprietatibus Rerum*, which was translated into Middle English by John Trevisa at the end of the fourteenth century.

15. The modified nominalism of Abelard's *Sic et Non* (included in Migne 1844–1855: 178) proposes a system of "methodical doubt," confronting 150 theological questions, each both supported and opposed by authority and specific canonical utterance. Although the avowed aim of this dialectic was to subject theological texts to the rigor of logical analysis and resolution (by making the postulates of faith susceptible to scientific rather than contemplative scrutiny), the very arrangement of the contradictory but authoritative texts in opposed pairs created a systemics that phenomenologically emphasized the disjunction over the synthesis.

16. The deeper cynicism of Adorno's *Negative Dialectics* moves the irrational to another stage of development, resisting affirmative thought in any mode.

the full text of history had been "always already written" and compre-
hended typologically. Because the synthesis was (unlike those of Hegel
and Marx) post-historical and post-empirical, the most that the alert tex-
tuist/hermeneuticist/dialectician could look to find was the traces or
signatures of a now-cloudy transparency of meaning: "For now we see
through a glass, darkly; but then face to face" (1 Corinthians 13:11). Windows indeed; and windows that, like those on my screen, paradoxically
only seem to have a transparency of iconic meaning while in fact they hide
the operations of the text.

For the Renaissance—or, in its self-nomination rather than its Enlightenment reinscription, the "Revival of Learning"—these operations
had become stable rather than fluid and fluctuating. As W. Speed Hill
(1996) has observed, for the Revival of Learning, and perhaps particularly
for the Reformation and the Elizabethan religious settlement, scripture
had been stabilized in the sense that its author had already withdrawn
from his work, thereby making the textuality of scripture amenable to human reason. Though not yet simply the clockmaker, God had, in authorial
terms, ceased revising his work, which had thus achieved an ontological
and thus potentially hermeneutic perfection, if only we could approach
it with the right interpretive tools. In Hooker's *Laws of Ecclesiastical Polity,* we are already halfway to the Enlightenment conviction that laws in
general are discoverable and the universe is permanently in place. Far
from sympathizing with and continuing the medieval deferred dialectic
in the Abelardian sense of *sic et non,* Hooker is emblematic of the textuality of empirical transparency, which was to lead to the empiricism (and
the endorsement of a "plain style") of the British Royal Society, and to
the belief that the laws of physics, biology, economics, politics, and even
human nature were as tractable and discoverable through patient and
replicable observation as were the laws of ecclesiastical polity. The constitutionalism of the American and French revolutions, with their inscription of texts that were constructed to cover all the eventualities of social
behavior and governmental prerogative, was as symptomatic of this shift
(within the agenda of modernity) from the *différance,* traces, and negative
dialectics of medieval textuality as were Newton's laws of motion, Adam
Smith's economics, the secure classification of Linnaean taxonomy, and
the political determinism of the Glorious Revolution of 1688.

But how do these historical *données* (the "givens" both of an Enlightenment, progressivist view of human development and of a postmodernist, diffusionist, and nonteleological view) impinge on the reimagining of textuality? Can it really be that, in reveling in the postmodernist breakdown of the *grands reçits* of Christianity, Marxism, Newtonian physics, and the Enlightenment, we have constructed or fallen unwittingly into another, even greater *reçit*—one that does not simply take us out of the Enlightenment project but fulfills a project that preceded modernity?

Again, *sic et non.* There is one recursive characteristic of postmodernist textuality that does reinscribe us firmly within an earlier model, and that is the interrogation of the singularity and ontologically circumscribed nature of *text.* It is a rhetorical trope of the recent historiography of textuality that modernist criticism, despite its apparent denial of the historicized author as a dangerous fallacy, required the unifying cognitive consciousness of authoriality to resolve the tensions, ambiguities, ironies, and so on that motivated the modernist *explication de texte.* Moreover, this formalist concentration on "the text itself" was deeply implicated in the actual graphic (clear-text) construction as well as in the ideology of the great period of modernist editing, which was dominated by Greg-Bowers copy-text theory, and most conspicuous in the monumental editions "sealed" by the MLA's Center for Editions of American Authors and its successor, the Center for (later Committee on) Scholarly Editions. The pristine transparency of those clear-text editions—in which the text itself asserts its logistic and phenomenological superiority over the record of variance embedded in the deliberately invisible, or occluded, apparatus—sought to render culturally impotent the margins of discourse, whether bibliographical or political, and to separate the Platonized *textus* of the "text that never was" from the accreted social detritus that too often accompanied the text proper in this fallen world. The corollary of this segment of recent historiography is that the fractured, fragmentary, versionist, and extratextual editorial enterprise of postmodernism denies the firm structuralist bipolarity between the text itself and its margins. Indeed, the very term *editing,* insofar as it is associated with modernist, Platonist eclecticism, has become something of a slur under postmodernism: McGann argues that Greg-Bowers "critical editing" is an impropriety in its attempt to deny the socialization of text, and he insists that his hypermedia Rossetti Archive is just that, an "archive," not an "edition" (1994); and Randall McLeod (1990) declares that "editions suck. Somebody should tell the editors."[17]

This shift from modernist text to postmodernist text is more or less that between the two main strands of the etymological *text:* from the *textus* to the *textile.* If this is so, and if postmodernism celebrates the continual weaving of text and its dispersal over the entire field of human activity and its traces, then I contend that, in this aspect of reimagined textuality, we have indeed become medievalists again and have cast off the securities of the modernist distinction between text and margin.

In this reimagined universe of textuality, postmodernism collapses the text itself and its accoutrements, for it is no longer possible to discern exactly where "text" ends and "commentary" begins.[18] The irony of this seepage between *textus* and *textile* is that, eventually, there is no *outside,* since "text" becomes inclusive of all its variants and its belated critiques: "Il n'y a pas dehors de texte." Such a territorial impasse can be seen by modernist textuists as a counsel of despair[19] that makes editing (especially in the sense of "cutting" or "pruning" or "cleaning")[20] no longer possible. Exactly: we cannot prune or cut or clean because we can no

---

17. See also Hershel Parker's case (1987) against the singular modality of formalist, modernist editing; and Derek Pearsall's brief (1985, 1994) against the modern critical edition as a betrayal of medieval textuality; but see also Patterson's defense (1985) of the modernist (and specifically New Critical) ideology and methods of the Kane-Donaldson edition of the B version of *Piers Plowman.* For the alternative, German, school of genetic rather than eclectic or idealist editing, see Bornstein, Gabler, and Pierce 1996.

18. See Hill 1997 for an account of the layering of commentary (which then becomes text for the next commentary).

19. See Lee Patterson's claim (1985: 60) that, because there can be no clear distinction between external and internal evidence, editing is inevitably "circular." See also Howard-Hill's modernist dissatisfaction (1988) with McKenzie 1986, and his critique (1991) of McGann's social textual criticism. Howard-Hill's objections arise mostly because the enlarged view of text proposed by both McKenzie and McGann does not easily admit of a secure boundary to text.

20. See Kenney 1974 for an account of humanist/Enlightenment/modern metaphors of *cleansing* and *restoring,* esp. 21–25. The popular usage of *editing* to mean "trimming" or "removing of offensive material" (as in a movie that is "edited for television") may reverse the moral imperative of humanist editing (the omitted parts of the text are not seen as corruptions of an authorial text but as potential corruptions to the current cultural response), but both rationales depend on some means of adjudicating between the detritus and the "proper" form of the text.

longer be sure what initial/ideal/originary shape we are seeking to reveal in hacking at the raw marble of text, by gradually removing all that is extraneous to its pure form. And so, if both Michelangelo's formula for a text in the plastic arts (simply to remove from the block everything that is extraneous to the sculpture that resides within it, by "hacking," *per forza di levare,* with a claw chisel) and the "passionate" formula of Stephen Dedalus ("If a man hacking in fury at a block of wood . . . make there an image of a cow, is that image a work of art? If not, why not?" 1964: 214) for separating text from textile are called in doubt by the lack of a self-delimiting outside, a firm edge or boundary to the patterns discoverable, then what Tanselle has described (1986: 18n39) as a bibliography that "moves outside books and . . . becomes a pattern of life" is, by default, the only possible medium for full textual analysis.[21]

As medieval textuists from Isidore to Abelard to Aquinas might say, "So what?" Of course, mundane texts can have no perceptible edges to us, because we cannot stand sufficiently outside them; we cannot get a purchase on their always already written strands of meaning. The medieval concept of text is always already written and universal because its author, God, stands outside the constraints of time (the Crucifixion is thus *always* happening, before and after as well as during the actual historicized event), and also because the total narrative that is the creation on both syntagmatic and paradigmatic axes must cohere, but it can do so only beyond our ability to observe the totality of that coherence. Fortunately for us dull sublunary textuists, the author has been gracious enough to sign his work—indeed, to embed "signatures" in the book of creation in a fully bibliographical sense.[22] That is, the signatures serve to demarcate gatherings of text, *sequentia* or quires or quaternions or *collectanea* or *florilegia* (depending on the semantics of bibliographical *formula,* i.e., "little form"). The medieval book—with its spatial ambiguities and collocations between text and margin, and its linear inconclusiveness (the

---

21. There is doubtless an irony in Tanselle's having set up an inclusive agenda of co-option (i.e., Greg-Bowers as a unified field theory to encompass all textual phenomena) only to have that model of inclusivity as a trope raised to an even higher level of experience, that is, the "pattern of life."

22. See Gellrich 1985 for a poststructuralist account of the doctrine of signatures; he cites, for example, Hugh of St. Victor's concept of "universal history [as] a book of three stages . . . (*lex naturalis; lex scripta; tempus gratiae*)" with "all of nature [as] God's script—the Book of nature" (34).

seeming adventitious binding of "separate" works into a single, but often temporary, bibliographical unit)—is difficult, even impossible, to decode using modernist principles of external unity and singularity of utterance. Just so, the universal (i.e., medieval) text of phenomena will be susceptible to analysis only with tools other than those promoted by modernism and its tropes (tension, paradox, irony, and so on, all resolvable under the singularity of the "well-wrought urn").

There is already some sign that modernist scruples about the propriety of textual evidence are being challenged. As I have written elsewhere ("History" in 1999b), the influence of *annaliste* history on both New Historicism and *l'histoire du livre* has promoted an explosion of the bibliographical phenomena of textual evidence, often to the discomfort of those to whom the intrinsic/extrinsic, internal/external, textual/nontextual dialectic is an important epistemological tool—indeed, a precision instrument for textual surgery.[23] Make this tool blunt or its practitioners indecisive, and we have lost far more in particularity and local knowledge than we can possibly have gained in contemplating the whole world.[24] But when D. F. McKenzie (1986: 31–32) uses landscape as a "text" for bibliographical construal, or when McGann (1990: 13–14) uses "Reagan's Farewell" as an exemplary "text" on "how to read a book," or when Joseph Grigely (1995b: 11–50) uses the human body as a "text" to comment on eclecticism and idealism—all are being eminently postmodern in breaking down the *grand récit* of modernist textuality. And they are being eminently medieval as well. Landscape, politics, and the body—these are all perfectly susceptible to textual analysis according to a medieval hermeneutic of textuality; indeed, it would be impious to declare that they are "nontextual" and thus not part of either (or both) the *textus* and/ or the *textile*.[25]

---

23. See the various attempts by Tanselle (esp. 1981a) to incorporate *l'histoire du livre* into the *Weltanschauung* of Greg-Bowers eclecticism.

24. I use "local knowledge" in Paul Oskar Kristeller's sense (1987) of textual criticism as having only local and specific validity rather than general and theoretical validity.

25. See Gellrich (1985: 35), who discusses "the inevitability of the 'idea of the Book' in the Middle Ages as soon as a signifying system—words in Scripture, things in nature—became a metaphor for divinity: the entire preexistent 'totality' of God's plan was potential in the signifying means."

There are, of course, enormous differences in rationale and expectations between medieval and postmodernist discourses of textuality. Although both might look for Derridean "traces," and both would accept *différance* as a necessary hermeneutic and phenomenological condition, they would do so for very different reasons. I hope I am not seen as merely playing into the romance of postmodernism by linking its textuality to the medieval. The return to the Middle Ages that Eco describes is not a nostalgic yearning for a lost immediacy that both Marx and the Victorian medievalists (Morris, Tennyson, Rossetti) mourned. Even though much of the hypertextual manifestation of postmodernist textuality (Dungeons and Dragons leading to MOOs and numerous "medieval" video games)[26] seems to carry some freight of nostalgia, and even though there have been acute attempts to link the bibliographical phenomena of hypertext to medieval habits of reading, my argument differs from these critiques (Sanders 1996, deriving from Bolter 1991). Although my brief in this chapter is to provide a historical and conceptual frame for any reimagining of textuality, it does not really matter to me whether we accept Eco's cultural diagnosis; and, therefore, it does not really matter whether we might eventually imagine the line from humanism to the Enlightenment to modernity as a "middle" age of cultural variance away from the normative phenomena of the premodern and the postmodern, although there are good bibliographical grounds for doing so.[27] As a (quondam) medievalist, I might feel some delicious cultural schadenfreude to see the Renaissance, the Enlightenment, and modernity (all those movements that conspired to degrade and devalue the premodern as an unfortunate episode, a "middle" age that we must overleap and get beyond) lose their status as the fulfillment of the textual scriptures and be reduced to a back-formed "middle" ages. But though the symmetry of premodern and postmodern is obviously seductive, my exposition of textuality does

---

26. See Turkle 1995, esp. 11–14, "Living in the MUD." It is a cultural commonplace to observe that a large segment of popular computer games and software feature consciously "medieval" characters and ethics, derived out of the arcade video games of an earlier decade and before that from the fantasy genre of pulp fiction.

27. Increasingly, historians of bibliography are beginning to see the modern period and its documentary characteristics as an editorially convenient but chronologically atypical transitional era between the medieval and the postmodern. See Greetham 1992c, esp. 74–75; and Reiman 1997.

not depend on such seductions. In fact, I might just as easily draw my evidence against modernist textuality from the uncanny Pergamanians of the classical period, or from the cultural dispersal of manuscript transmission described by Love (1993), Marotti (1993a), McKenzie (1990), and others.

My point is rather that there will always be the opportunity, even the necessity, for a battle of the books between "modernists" and "pre/postmodernists" and what they represent about textual authority, variance, resolution, and teleology, just as there have been almost continuous battles between *antiqui* and *moderni.* Despite the increasingly convoluted rearguard actions of scholars like Tanselle to hold onto the modern and its textual protocols, we have moved through an epistemic shift in which the values prized by modernist textuality, and especially modernist editing, either are regarded with suspicion or are deemed inimical to currently favored means of textual production. Just as Mark Twain claimed that New York and religion could not cohabit (because those living in the close quarters of urban life were not susceptible to superstition), so it may have been phenomenologically and practically easier for modernist textuality to thrive in the period of the printed book, and it may now be more difficult for this same textuality to inhabit electronic hypertext.[28] Perhaps: except that postmodernist textuality can certainly be seen in various bibliographical artifacts of the printed book, from Sterne's *Tristram Shandy* to Derrida's *Glas;* and I have already demonstrated how modernist principles of coherence and control can be just as present (maybe, given the technical complexity, even more so) in hypermedia textual reproduction as in the print codex. Indeed, the masculinist, phallocentric, positivist features of hypertext and hypermedia may be even more dangerous to feminist, fluid, postmodernist textuality precisely because the controls and constraints are hidden—by those opaque Windows.[29] We may *think*

---

28. Such cohabitation or confluence of form and function may, moreover, be a liability. McGann (1996) claims that it was the precise "fit" of the print medium of the critical edition with that of its subject—the literary text—that prevented such editions from achieving the necessary distance from the subject.

29. Patricia Cockram, a former graduate student at the City University of New York, produced a hypermedia archive of Pound's Cantos, in which she demonstrated the "fascistic," "totalitarian" aspects of hypertext, especially in its appearing to provide fluidity of movement (the trains do run on time) while constraining narrative and expression through preconstructed but barely visible hyperlinks.

that we are doing postmodern textuality at the very moment that we are being done by modernism, just as the *moderni* of one cultural moment are the *antiqui* of another.

There is no way out of this double bind, nor should there be. When the previously unthinkable becomes the *donnée* of the current moment, it is in a sense still (or equally) unthinkable, for it has now been fully consumed and digested by its cultural practitioners in what Jauss (1974, esp. 18–19) called "culinary reading," unexamined because normative, and therefore invisible. This is, after all, Althusser's prescription (1971) for an ideology: it should be internalized to the point that it becomes invisible. I do not believe that postmodernist textuality has yet been so fully consumed that it has disappeared from view, or from interrogation. Indeed, the very publication of the collection in which an earlier version of this chapter appeared suggests that current textuality has not achieved the sort of invisibility that characterized the high modernism of the CEAA and CSE editions in the 1960s and 1970s. Eventually, however, the critical indeterminacies that animate this book will probably be resolved into textual *données,* and we will need another medievalization, another redrawing of the lines of descent and argument and critical filiation. It is only through the invocation of some middle ages that we keep ourselves modern.

TWELVE

The Telephone Directory and Dr. Seuss: Scholarly Editing after *Feist v. Rural Telephone*

The poet, described in *ideal* perfection, brings the whole soul of man into activity.... He diffuses a tone and spirit of unity, that blends, and (as it were) *fuses* each into each, by that synthetic and magical power, to which we have exclusively appropriated the name of imagination.

SAMUEL TAYLOR COLERIDGE

As the poete seith ...

JOHN TREVISA

Oh, the thinks you can think, if only you try!

DR. SEUSS

One of the more provocative sessions during my stint on the Committee on Scholarly Editions (CSE), sponsored by the Modern Language Association of America, was a presentation by intellectual-property lawyers concerning the likely effects on scholarly editing of the Supreme Court's unanimous 1991 *Feist* decision. The *Feist* decision held that the white pages of a telephone directory were not protectable under current copyright law because the mere use of an external system of organization, in this case the alphabet, did not manifest a genuinely "creative" or "original" contribution to human knowledge. Brushing aside an earlier argument for protectability based on the "sweat of the brow" of the compiler,[1] the Court in 1991 held that labor in and of itself was insufficient to warrant the ownership of the results of this work. If the labors of the researcher produced only "historical fact," such as the names of individuals in a town in their alphabetical order, then such "fact" was not protectable. One cannot copyright the fact that the Spanish Armada set sail in 1588 or that William the Conqueror defeated Harold at the Battle of Hastings in 1066. Only if the intervention of the scholar brought about a new "synthesis" or "unity," to co-opt the language of Coleridge, something that was uniquely the property of an individual consciousness acting upon the data, would the resulting text fall under copyright protection.[2]

---

1. See *Jeweler's Circular Publishing Co.*, 281 F., at 88:

> The right to copyright a book upon which one has expended labor in its preparation does not depend upon whether the materials which he has collected consist or not of matters which are *publici juris*, or whether such materials show literary skill *or originality*, either in thought or in language, or anything more than industrious collection. The man who goes through the streets of a town and puts down the names of each of the inhabitants, with their occupations and their street number, acquires material of which he is the author. (Quoted by Sandra Day O'Connor, in *Feist* 353–54; emphasis O'Connor's)

Justice O'Connor found that this "sweat of the brow" doctrine had "numerous flaws, the most glaring being that it extended copyright protection in a compilation beyond selection and arrangement—the compiler's original contributions—to the facts themselves.... 'Sweat of the brow' courts therefore eschewed the most fundamental axiom of copyright law—that no-one may copyright facts or ideas." Justice O'Connor went on to cite *Miller v. Universal City Studios, Inc.*, 650 F.2d, at 372 ("the law is clear that facts are not entitled [to copyright] protection"); and *International News Service v. Associated Press*, 248 U.S. 215 (1918), at 234, which "rejected ... the notion that copyright in an article extended to the factual information it contained": "The news element—the information respecting current events contained in the literary production—is not the creation of the writer, but is a report of matters that ordinarily are *publici juris*; it is the history of the day" (*Feist* 353–54).

2. Justice O'Connor noted (*Feist* 355) that in the 1976 Copyright Act, "Congress dropped the [1909] reference to 'all the writings of an author' and replaced it with the phrase 'original works of authorship'" (a more Coleridgean formulation). She emphasized that the 1976 act had specifically omitted compilation in and of itself as protectable in favor of an originary form for the collection of data: "It defines a 'compilation' in the copyright sense as 'a work formed by the collection and assembly of preexisting materials or of data that are selected, coordinated, or arranged in such a way that the resulting work as a whole constitutes an original work of authorship'" (¶ 101, quoted in *Feist* 356). "It is not enough for copyright purposes that an author collects and assembles facts.... [A] compilation, like any other work, is copyrightable only if it satisfies the originality requirement" (357).

The copyright lawyers who briefed the Committee on Scholarly Editions initially offered a gloomy prognostication concerning the possible effects of *Feist* on scholarly editions, while emphasizing that no subsequent litigation had yet established a clear formula for adjudicating the relevance of *Feist* to scholarly editions.[3] But it seemed possible that the most common type of CSE-approved edition—a "clear text" with pages of text physically separated from pages containing various apparatuses and tables that sustained its readings[4]—would in practice be much more susceptible to a form of piracy such as that described in *Feist* and to duplication than would an "inclusive text" edition, in which the editor littered the page with the record of variants, deletions, interlineations, and so on (i.e., with the record of "professional judgment and expertise").[5] This was for two reasons.

---

3. Since then, *CCC Information Services v. MacLean Hunter Market Reports* (1994) has reversed a *Feist*-based decision by a district court which had found that no infringement of copyright occurred when CCC entered data from MacLean Hunter's *Red Book* compilation of predicted used-car prices into its computer database. For its reversal of the lower court's decision, the appeals court accepted the argument that the "valuation figures given in the *Red Book* are not historical market prices, quotations, or averages; nor are they derived by mathematical formulas from available statistics. They represent, rather, the MacLean editors' predictions, based on a wide variety of informational sources and their professional judgment" (*Federal Reporter* 44, 3rd ser., 63). Noting that even a reader's own interpretation of the predictions was specifically demanded in the introductory text of the *Red Book* (63–64), the appeals court claimed that "[t]he thrust of the Supreme Court's ruling in *Feist* was not to erect a high barrier of originality requirement. It was rather to specify, rejecting the strain of lower court rulings that sought to base protection on the 'sweat of the brow,' that some originality is essential to protection of authorship, and that the protection afforded extends only to those original elements" (66). In arguing that "[t]he district court was simply mistaken in its conclusion that the *Red Book* valuations were, like the telephone numbers in *Feist*, pre-existing facts that had merely been discovered by the *Red Book* editors" (67), the appeals court emphasized that the data did not exist outside the "edition" published by MacLean Hunter and that "professional judgment and expertise" were at the heart of the compilation.

4. Such editions include the University Press of Virginia edition of *The Works of Stephen Crane*, ed. Fredson Bowers; *The Centenary Edition of the Works of Nathaniel Hawthorne*, ed. Fredson Bowers; *A Selected Edition of W. D. Howells*, ed. Edwin H. Cady et al.; *The Writings of Herman Melville*, ed. Harrison Hayford, G. Thomas Tanselle, and Hershel Parker; and *The Mark Twain Papers*, ed. Frederick Anderson et al. See also the CEAA's *Statement of Editorial Principles and Procedures*, rev. ed., together with the update included in Barnard, O'Keefe, and Unsworth 2006. Many CEAA editions are discussed in Tanselle 1975 and in Greetham 1995b.

5. The best-known inclusive text editions are the genetic texts produced under Franco-German auspices. For a survey of these, see Hay 1987. Genetic editions of Anglo-American texts

First, a clear text would, quite simply, be easier to photocopy (as had happened with the white pages in *Feist*) and to distribute without its accompanying textual data.[6] Ironically, this separate (but legal) publication had always been one of the rationales for the clear-text editions of CSE and its earlier incarnation, the Center for Editions of American Authors (CEAA): the results of the editorial "sweat of the brow" could be made available to the reading public in two forms, a scholarly edition containing all the evidence and a reading text for wider distribution. Many of the Library of America volumes had taken their texts from CEAA-approved scholarly editions. As has been frequently noted, the Library of America volumes thus fulfilled Edmund Wilson's agenda for a Pléiade-like series of American canonical texts blissfully free from what he and Lewis Mumford had labeled the "barbed wire" of editorial sigla placed between an author and his/her text in a typical inclusive text, like the von Frank edition of Emerson's *Sermons* (1999).

Second, because a clear text banished all signs of editorial intervention to a separate location in the book (sometimes, especially in medieval texts published by the Early English Text Society, to a separate volume, often published many years after the "text" volume), there was no direct evidence on the textual page either for the editorial "sweat of the brow" or, more important, for the editorial construction of a "new synthesis" that was a genuinely creative addition to the sum of human knowledge. By adopting what E. Talbot Donaldson has called the editorial "death-wish"—to disappear into the woodwork of the apparatus and "leave not

---

include *The Cornell Wordsworth*, ed. Stephen Parrish et al.; *The Cornell Yeats*, ed. Richard J. Finneran et al.; and the Harvard edition of the *Journals and Miscellaneous Notebooks of Ralph Waldo Emerson*, ed. William H. Gilman et al. Also, see von Frank (1987) for an account of the editorial principles in genetic editing (especially for Emerson), together with the collection by Deppman, Ferrer, and Groden (2004); and Myerson 1995 for a survey of the mixed fortunes of genetic editing of American fiction.

6. Recent developments in copying have made clear texts even more open to co-option. Relatively inexpensive scanners with optical character recognition (OCR) programs are capable of entering text into an electronic file and reproducing it in a different font and layout to obscure its bibliographical origins. In practical and legal terms, it would be much more difficult to prove piracy of an OCR'd text than of a photocopied text. Optical collators could not do it; it would require manual collation even to establish lexical similarity. The copier might, of course, introduce occasional "errors" or "variants" into scanned text to differentiate it from the "original." A similar problem occurs in establishing provenance and original form in the digital scanning of broadcast music (see Sanjek 1992).

a rack behind"—clear-text editors of the CEAA/CSE school had constructed what could be arguably regarded as "historical fact," an author's actual intentions rather than a visually demonstrable critical *fusing* of the *imagination* (Coleridge again) of the editor with that of the writer.

Several ironies appear in this situation. For example, the more an edition, especially a clear-text edition, claims "definitiveness" and "historical fact" for its text, the more like the white pages it becomes and the less protectable.[7] On the other hand, the more an edition openly avows its speculative, personal, and critical nature, even its own failure to achieve definitiveness—especially if this critical component is visually interwoven or fused with the text rather than separated from it—the less like the white pages it becomes and the more protectable. Put another way, the sort of positivism for which nineteenth-century philology frequently strove[8] pushed textual scholarship and editing conceptually, procedurally, and legally closer to the nonprotectable and fragmentary "useful knowledge" of science rather than to the protectable and organic "creative originality" of literature. Such a contiguity, if still insisted upon by present-day editors, might place scholarly editions in the common marketplace of ideas, valuable in themselves but not covered by copyright protection.

How did we get into this mess? Whom can we blame? And how do we protect our labors from improper co-option? The full answers to these questions—involving theories of authoriality, organicism, and epistemology from the Middle Ages to the present—lie outside the compass of this short chapter, but I hope to suggest a speculative orientation toward these issues that might help in clarifying the intellectual and social history and set scholarly editing in a more defensible position relative to the technological and legal developments sure to occur in the future. Consider just these few *exempla:*

1 Inexpensive optical scanners can now convert a text to an electronic file, which can then, by a few keystrokes or clicks on a mouse, be formatted in a typeface and page layout that obscures its origin from immediate

7. For an account of the social, academic, epistemological, and legal liabilities attendant on claims for definitiveness and scientific positivism in scholarly editing, see the chapter "The Resistance to Philology" in this volume.

8. See the "Phenomenology" and "Intention" chapters of Greetham 1999b for a historical account of the struggle between an interpretive hermeneutic phenomenology for textual scholarship versus a faith in transcendental phenomenology.

recognition, in a way that simple photocopying could not achieve (see n. 6).

2 The designers of an entrance to a warehouse in New York City won a legal decision preventing the Helmsley-Spear company from moving their site-specific installation while any of the three artists was still alive. This occurred only two years after Richard Serra lost his suit to prevent the federal government from similarly moving his site-specific *Tilted Arc* to a location other than the one for which it was designed. However, the sculptors' victory was temporary, for, on appeal, the "owners" of the commodified installation won the right to dismantle it.

3 The digital sampling that began with rap and hip-hop has moved into many other forms of popular music, so that "recordings can be constructed wholecloth from samples to create a new aesthetic" (Sanjek 1992: 614); for example, the drumming on a 1971 James Brown recording has been sampled and transmogrified in later work by many other artists. The legal status of such sampling reached a new level of complexity when DJ Girl Talk, for example, made "musical collages" out of as many as three hundred short samples on the album *Feed the Animals* (released online at www.illegalart.net in June 2008; see Levine 2008).[9]

4 MGM successfully sued to prevent the BBC from using the title *Lady Chatterley's Lover* for a television adaptation of the Lawrence novel, on the grounds that this particular formulation had been purchased by MGM for all movie and television versions. The program therefore had to be broadcast as *Lady Chatterley,* thus changing the subject of Lawrence's work. However, when Warner Brothers similarly sued the Marx Brothers to prevent the use of the word "Casablanca" in the title of the movie *A Night in Casablanca,* the Marx Brothers counter-sued against Warner's use of "Brothers" in its corporate title. Both suits were eventually dropped. Presumably, there were similar constraints involved in the titling of the two films based on the Lawrence novel, both of which abandoned the "Lover" and made "Lady Chatterley" the subject.

Admittedly, there is an air of unreality or irony in the use of the name "Wimbledon" being owned in the United States by the British Lawn Tennis Association, thereby preventing British Rail from issuing a series of commemorative posters with the word prominently displayed, just as there is an irony in the unsuccessful suit by the Los Angeles Dodgers to prevent a Brooklyn bar from continuing to use the name "Brooklyn

9. Sanjek (1992: 613) records that the performance of Clyde Stubblefield, percussionist for James Brown from 1965 to 1971, on the 1971 "Funky Drummer" has been appropriated by Sinead O'Connor, Fine Young Cannibals, Big Daddy Kane, Good Girls, Grace Jones, Mantronix, Michel'le, Seduction, Todd Terry Project, Alyson Williams, and Public Enemy.

Dodgers," even though the Los Angeles "owners" had never made use of the name and had made no plans to do so. These rearguard attempts to constrain language and representation might seem truly absurd, but they testify to a significant cultural momentum for copyright protection, often in the face of increased technical facility for invading such protection. Mark Rose (1993) catches this historical and conceptual irony when he notes:

> Copyright developed as a consequence of printing technology's ability to produce large numbers of copies of a text quickly and cheaply. But present-day technology makes it virtually impossible to prevent people from making copies of almost any text—printed, musical, cinematic, computerized—rapidly and at a negligible cost. (142)

Rose's response to the seemingly logical question, "Why, then, don't we abandon copyright as an archaic and cumbersome system of cultural regulation?" is that "copyright is deeply rooted in our conception of ourselves as individuals with at least a modest grade of singularity, some degree of personality" (ibid.). This is, I think, an appropriate epistemological answer, for we come to "know" ourselves in part by being able to constitute a body of acts that cumulatively define a reflexive self-awareness. It is a philosophical *donnée* that, from at least Descartes to the adherents of analytical philosophy, one of the central problems in the ontology of the subject has been to describe and define the evidence for the existence of the self, which is a necessary emblem of Enlightenment, Romantic, and post-Romantic theories of the individual. Put coarsely, the question is whether we can achieve a sense of an "I," a first-person identity, that is demonstrably different in kind from all other subjects.

This issue lies, I believe, at the heart of both copyright theory and a theory and practice of authoriality as manifest in Anglo-American scholarly editing. In wrestling with the concept of this "I," Robert Nozick asks (1981: 72), "Do I know myself as the possessor of some property? Is there any such property P so my knowing that the individual who has P also has Q also guarantees that I know that Q applies to me?"[10] In linking

---

10. Nozick specifically excludes from this "property" the property of "being the producer of this spoken token" or "being the thinker of these words," for in both cases the agency would not be sufficient to establish identity. As he puts it, "[f]or a person X to reflexively self-refer is not merely for X to use a term that actually refers to X; this omits as internal to

the concepts of unification and synthesis (a central core of Romantic copyright theory) to this reflexive self-awareness, Nozick argues that if we consider A_0 as an act (say, a "collected works" of an "author") which "brings together $A_1, \ldots, An$, and A_0 itself," then "A_0 is (partially) a reflexively self-referring act: the act of synthesizing $A_1, \ldots, An$, and this very act itself A_0 [our edition] unites these acts together as parts or components or things arising from the same entity E" (1981: 89). While Nozick admits that there will be other methods of unification that are not dependent on the doer or agent (our author as creator and thus protectable commodity), it is convenient to think that E "thus synthesized, is the doer of the acts, including A_0."

It is here that my identification of A_0 as a scholarly edition of the works of that "singularity" we call an author runs into trouble in copyright theory. Nozick's formula works only if "E exists independently [i.e., as historical fact], and A_0 [the scholarly edition] is merely a demarcation, a drawing of a boundary, around the preexisting entity E which was there all the time and, among other things, performed the act of demarcating itself" (1981: 89), in other words, E is the alphabet and A_0 the white pages. If all we have done in constructing a collected works that serves to represent the singular act of cognition that ought to be the proof for an authorial identity is to "demarcate" that which preexisted the edition, then the edition is not creative or original but is again a matter of the representation (A_0) of E, which, as we have already seen, already incorporates A_0 as part of its singularity. Now, this would be a nice conceit if we want to claim that we are passive and objective fulfillers of authorial intention and that our own productive, or self-reflexive, role is limited to the automatic sorting of data that together constitute the entity E. But if we are therefore

---

the act of referring that it is himself to which it refers" (1981: 72). This necessity for a collapse of the reflexive and the identity (illustrated by Nozick through the dramatically ironic statements of Oedipus about "himself") means that, say, it is not simply enough for Wordsworth to have declared that it is unprecedented in a poetic oeuvre for "a man to have talked so much about himself," for this utterance about "I" must be confirmed by a property other than the act of enunciation itself. In what Joyce (1964: 214) calls the lyric mode of the first person, the collapse of reflection and identity might be taken for granted ("I feel," "I love," etc.), but in the second-person (epical or fictional) mode, and especially in the third-person (dramatic) mode of utterance, the gap between reflection and identity becomes too uncomfortably large for any firm correspondence. For further investigation of the editorial and textual implications of this phenomenological gap, see the "Ontology" chapter of Greetham 1999b, esp. 29–31.

as editors reduced to sorters of the mail sent by other people, then our agency is severely circumscribed in copyright theory, and the productions of that agency—our scholarly editions—are left vulnerable, as historical fact, to copying and redistribution on the open market.

There is a way around this impasse, a way that gives further prominence to the Romantic figure of unity and organicism already promoted in the Coleridge epigraph. Following Fichte's argument that the self consists in its "positing" of itself and even more so in its "positing" of itself "positing" itself down the *mise-en-abyme*, Nozick suggests that we can extricate ourselves from the reciprocal hazards of demarcation and merging of identities by presuming that the entity E only comes to exist "in the act A_0 of synthesis." The problem for traditional scholarly editors is that this conceptual leap, itself a product of circular reasoning since we can argue for the existence of E only through the agency of A_0, demands both enormous hubris (you can have access to E only through the acts $A_1, \ldots,$ An, I have assembled as A_0) and at the same time paradoxically undercuts the claim to definitiveness or historical determinedness because of the cognitive circularity. As Nozick astutely asks: "Can the rabbit be pulled out of the rabbit?" (1981: 89).

If both rabbits are singularities and both involve cognitive acts of self-reflection, then, yes, the rabbit that is our text needs neither a magician nor a hat. The evidentiary problem, and the one that affects the status of the text in current copyright litigation, is how we may demonstrate that the two rabbits are really one and share the same property P.

A brief answer to this further conundrum is that we cannot so demonstrate. If the property P of rabbit 1 (the author's entity E) is argued by the editor to have the same DNA makeup as rabbit 2 (the scholarly edition) drawn from it, then the proof resides in the preexistence of the entity E, the form from which the clone of rabbit 2 is created. However, that lands us back in the problem of historical fact and the role of the editor as mere clerical sorter, the very role from which we have been trying to escape. If rabbit 2 is not derivative of rabbit 1 but coterminous and cosubstantial, then we have only the twin self-reflexivity of the two as evidence for E—another version of circular argument. Nozick recognizes the dilemma or polylemma in admitting that a "theory of the self arising in an act of self-synthesis seems bizarre if not incoherent" (1981: 89). If it is incoherent, then what hope can we have for demonstrating the property of unity or organicism that is the primary means for establishing the legal basis for protectability of the works that together make up the entity E and/or its embodiment in the collected edition A_0? According to Nozick, we are left with the dubious proposition that the self may be a "Fichtetious object" (ibid.).

What if it is? What if the self that underwrites both Romantic copyright theory and the rationale for the collected works edition is a product of Fichte's concept of the self as "positing itself"? And what if the self both as entity and as synthesis is indeed fictitious? Within literature as a mode of utterance, this is no more than what Plato was saying in the *Republic* and *Ion:* because "poetry" (i.e., "making" or "fiction") is at best only a simulacrum (the immediate medium) of a simulacrum (the physical referent) of a simulacrum (the idea of that referent), then the A_0 that constitutes both the artistic work and its representation (in, say, an edition) is a result of a series of reflexive positings, one upon another, caught in Grendel's highly Berkeleyan formula that, as "author" of the "discourse" that is his life, "I observe myself observing what I observe" (Gardner 1971: 29).

For Berkeley's theory of metaphysics and epistemology, this particular form of the *mise-en-abyme* could be arrested by the assurance that God, as originary originator, was observing everybody observing themselves. With the existence of an unmoved first mover, the fiction of a life and its works could at least put off the ontological problem by passing the epistemological buck back to an entity E that, by its very definition, must not only preexist independently but also secure for secondary and tertiary creations (lives, books) a logistical ground that did not yet discover itself as part of circular reasoning. Vicarious creation, even of fiction, is nonetheless creation, although the best it might manage would be the simulacrum, or the neoclassical conceit of *imitatio,* even if only at the level of rhetoric and sorting ("What oft was thought, but ne'er so well express'd").

As Mark Rose demonstrates, the Popean formula for the singularity of fiction came as almost a rearguard action in a period which, parallel to the growth of authorial sanction for the property of literature, saw John Dennis, Edward Young, Samuel Johnson, and many others arguing for originality as the property P of literature by which the author might be known. This would be the exact opposite of Pope's evocation of "the idea of the poet as the reproducer of traditional truths" (Rose 1993: 6).[11]

---

11. Rose (1993) cites, for example, Dennis on Milton's originality as the basis for his importance as a poet; Young's claim that "in every work of genius, somewhat of an original

The confluence of originality and the growing identity of the literary author as "proprietor" over the work was not therefore simply a matter of Locke's argument that the labors of the mind, as they produce identifiable works, should be analogous with real estate and the ownership of land. This argument, as I have already shown, has been rendered moot by the *Feist* decision in which labor in and of itself does not produce proprietorship. Yes, there was property in the traditional sense of ownership of a commodity, but this was in large part confirmed and sustained by a growing recognition that the Berkeleyan cognitive model could not fully account for acts of creation, whether imitative or original, in a mechanistic universe in which all proof for the existence of an unmoved prime mover must perforce reside in the artifactual status of the creation itself, for the creator was no longer moved to intervene in the creation with direct evidence for his existence.[12] As Matthew Arnold recorded in "The Function of Criticism at the Present Time" and "The Study of Poetry," the dominant clockmaker image for the creator was thus to put enormous cultural and philosophical pressure on the secular inheritor of the creationist myth: the literary artist. If poetry had replaced religion as the source of beliefs and morals (an idea that would presumably have horrified Plato), then the originator of poetry in a mechanistic universe from which the creator had retired had a vastly enlarged prerogative and responsibility. Clearly, it was only fair that this new cultural burden produce some benefit for the burdened poet. As Defoe had put it, following Locke's arguments about literary property, "'Twould be unaccountably severe, to make a Man answerable for the Miscarriages of a thing which he shall not reap the benefit of if well perform'd" (quoted in Rose 1993: 35). Having just emerged from the stocks for the potentially bad social effects of his ironic *Shortest Way with the Dissenters,* Defoe was particularly sensitive to the "severity" whereby the law would not secure authors' rights of

---

spirit should at least be attempted. . . . Originals only have true life, and differ as much from the best imitations as men from the most animated pictures of them" ("On Lyric Poetry," quoted in Rose 1993: 414); and Johnson's assumption, in the *Lives of the English Poets,* that "[t]he highest praise of genius is original invention."

12. See Hill 1996 concerning Hooker's assumption that, by the late sixteenth century, the age of direct intervention was long past and that the laws of ecclesiastical polity must be empirically worked out.

ownership in their books but would "pretend to punish" authors for the social "miscarriage" of their works. Defoe's argument on the reciprocity of responsibility and benefit anticipated Foucault's claim that "discourses are objects of appropriation" and that "ownership" of literary discourses "has always been subject to what one might call penal appropriation. Texts, books, and discourses really [began] to have authors ... to the extent that their authors became subject to punishment, that is, to the extent that discourses could be transgressive" (1984: 108). "Responsibility" was very much a double-edged weapon, and when the failure of religion in the nineteenth century put literary creators at the center of Arnold's new map of responsibility, it was perhaps inevitable that the Romantic theory of organicism and unity should be co-opted to secure further social rights as well as obligations. Of course, in a postmodernist climate in which, according to Lyotard, all the "master narratives" of modernism have failed (including literature),[13] then the claims of literary authors to extend and enlarge their prerogative when their social responsibility has declined may be a sophistry that is more concerned with self-aggrandizement than with Defoe's claim that benefit and punishment should be reciprocal. This suspicion remains even in the grossly drawn circumstances surrounding, say, the fatwa against Salman Rushdie for *The Satanic Verses,* where Defoe's formula came back to haunt the creator with a vengeance, in this case a literal vengeance.

My citing a narrative of responsibility from Locke and Defoe to Arnold, Lyotard, and Rushdie severely compromises the metaphysical arguments upon which Nozick relies for his definition of the self-reflexive self as an entity. The possible relationships among P, Q, E, and A_0 in their various formulations will work only if Defoe's and Arnold's reciprocal arguments have already been established as the epistemological norm. But as Foucault, Rose, Feather, de Grazia, and various others have recorded, the concept of property (in and of a work) on which copyright rests is by no means a universal. It has depended on a capitalist commodification of labor (and, at least, in Anglo-American jurisprudence, the corollary that

---

13. Lyotard 1984: xiii, 37. For an examination of the editorial implications of Lyotard's argument, see "Textual Theory and the Territorial Metaphor" in Greetham 1999b; also, for a consideration of the hermeneutic function of editorial emendation, annotation, and glossing under such a postmodernist dispensation, see Greetham 1997e.

the products of that labor could be alienated, that is, sold as commodities),[14] together with the Romantic enlargement of the originary as the mark of creation. Both of these concepts are epistemic disjunctions in the Foucauldian sense,[15] and both occurred in specific cultural contexts at particular moments. As epistemic disjunctions, the concepts did not necessarily evolve in a natural or predictable discourse of cause and effect. While it is possible, from the vantage point of *Feist* and all that it means, to regard Locke and Defoe and Coleridge and Arnold as way stations in the consistent evolution of an idea that we now find entirely natural,[16] the work of A. J. Minnis, Tim William Machan, Anne Middleton, and various other medievalists should be sufficient to demonstrate that Defoe's argument in favor of the reciprocity of labor and responsibility is distinctly a mark of a modern sensibility and that Nozick's models for the self-reflexive self must be similarly adjudicated as a post-humanist (and perhaps even post-Enlightenment) phenomenon. Moreover, the digitization of contemporary culture might (despite Rose's assurances that subject formation is still central to our definition of existence) engender a further technological epistemic disjunction that will be as significant for the dissolution of the Enlightenment myth of creation as the invention of printing was for its construction. If Bakhtin (1986) was right, many years ago, in suggesting that our discourses consist of "various degrees of otherness or varying degrees of 'our-own-ness'" (89), interweaved in a pattern that cannot be unraveled, then the doctrine of originality and property on which both copyright theory and Nozick's models depend

---

14. Obviously, this is unlike Continental copyright legislation, which typically recognizes the moral and permanent *droits d'auteur* beyond the period of formal copyright and even after the work of the author has been alienated and commodified by sale to another property owner. According to Serra, it was the omission of this clause in the much-delayed signing of the Berne Convention by the United States that allowed his *Tilted Arc* to be moved and in effect "destroyed." For an account of the implications of the *Tilted Arc* case on textual theory, see Grigely 1995a: 56–65. Of late, there has been a legal/proprietary shift, whereby more and more British (and even some U.S.) publications now assert the "moral rights" of the author, doubtless as a result of European Union legislation.

15. See Foucault 1972b for the textual significance of the epistemic disjunction; and see the "History" chapter of Greetham 1999b (esp. "Archaeologies of the Past and Future," 95–97).

16. On the concept of the natural rights of copyright ownership, see Rose 1993: 5–6, 69.

might turn out to be only a brief (two- or three-hundred-year) blip in the ongoing negotiations among author, work, text, and audience.

Here, we must return to Foucault, and to a questionable generic distinction he makes in setting out the demarcation that Nozick sees as one of the functions of the text constituting the series beginning with A_0. It is a distinction which, as we shall see, has major implications for the problems of copyright. Recognizing that the "author function does not affect all discourses in a universal and constant way," Foucault argues that in the Middle Ages literary texts "were accepted, put into circulation, and valorized without any question about the identity of their author; their anonymity caused no difficulties since their ancientness, whether real or imagined, was regarded as a sufficient guarantee of their status" (1984: 109). Foucault here conflates two types of medieval discourse: first, "anonymous" vernacular and contemporary "literature" (from which such writers as Chaucer and Hoccleve were trying to escape), by setting up a textual condition (A_0), either bibliographically or rhetorically, that could sustain their authoriality;[17] and, second, the inherited writings of the classical *auctores,* whose wisdom was indeed confirmed by their age (and later, in neoclassical theory, by their closeness to nature), but whose names were attached to texts as a mark of authority. I recall being perplexed, as a neophyte editor trying to subdue the text of Trevisa's *De Proprietatibus Rerum,* by the frequent allusions to a seemingly anonymous classical source in validating the findings of the late medieval encyclopedia. The formula "as the poete seith" stumped me—until I realized that this oblique construction was not a confirmation of anonymity but quite the opposite. In a sense, the trope was an anticipation of the generic "poet" of Coleridge's later formulation, that is, anyone who is a real poet will know this or have these attributes. But more significantly for the medieval concept of tradition and authority, "the poete" was *the* poet,

---

17. That is, Chaucer seems to have relied on rhetoric (the "naming" of himself as author within his poems and the frequent recitation, by characters created for those poems, of a canon of utterance [A_0] that is demonstrably "Chaucerian"). But Chaucer does not seem to have tried to construct a bibliographical collected works, as Hoccleve did (in his own hand, for he was a professional scribe) in the early fifteenth century. Note that the coding of the name of the writer *within* the text is not only a late medieval phenomenon; in vernacular texts, it goes back at least as far as Cynewulf's runic inscription of the letters of his name as part of the poetic utterance of the text.

namely Virgil, the textual ground for vernacular authority, as Dante demonstrated in *The Divine Comedy*. So Foucault is right about the category of anonymity but wrong about its implementation.

The categories get further confused when Foucault turns to other forms of medieval discourse. He writes:

> [T]hose texts that we would now call scientific ... were accepted in the Middle Ages, and accepted as "true," only when marked with the name of their author. "Hippocrates said," "Pliny recounts," were not really formulas of an argument based on authority; they were the markers inserted in discourses that were supposed to be received as statements of demonstrated truth. (1984: 109)

Developing the history of this dichotomy between literature and science, Foucault then argues that the conditions of the two types of "Entity" were reversed in the seventeenth and eighteenth centuries:

> Scientific discourses began to be received for themselves, in the anonymity of an established or always redemonstrable truth. ... The author function faded away, and the inventor's name served only to christen a theorem, proposition, [etc.]. By the same token, literary discourses came to be accepted only when endowed with the author function. We now ask of each poetic or fictional text: From where does it come, who wrote it, when, and under what circumstances, or beginning with what design? (ibid.)

This is a fair statement of the Enlightenment construction of the relation between E and A_0, as we have already seen, and it matches Foucault's earlier prescription for the punitive aspects of the author function: authors became proprietors of their works only when they could also be punished for their effects.

The cultural significance of the "plain style" espoused by the discourse of the Royal Society was indeed that there should be no traces of E in A_0 and therefore in $A_1, \ldots, An$, for to include them there would betray the "redemonstrable" empiricism of a scientific regimen that operated outside or beyond the previously vicarious creative role of the natural philosopher. That is, with the gradual withdrawal of the clockmaker God from his handiwork in a mechanistic universe, the laws of nature could be stabilized and thus discoverable, for the creator would no longer intervene in the operation of these laws by, for example, parting the waves of the Red Sea. It is no accident that the historically parallel movement from the divine right of a monarchic ruler (as "vicar" of the creator) toward constitutionalism observed the same epistemic shift in politics. The Glorious Revolution of 1688 (whereby nominal heads of state could be selected according to social necessity) was in large part underwritten by the empiricist credo of the Royal Society, just as the American and French revolutions (and, more important, their constitutions) depended on a Newtonian empiricism that could account for the laws of motion, just as constitutionalism could account for the laws of behavior.

For our purposes as editors of the works of the originary and independent selves we call authors, the most pressing of these potentially discoverable laws of nature and behavior is the recognition of the evidence necessary to sustain the authorial "I" that is the motivation for our editions. In a sense, we are all engaged in playing a version of Turing's Test (or "Imitation Game") for intelligence, where an observer assumes that the black box he/she is "talking" to is "a highly plausible candidate for the role of 'thinker.'" That is, we have assumed, or perhaps hoped, that there is an "I" in the black box of the documents we have sorted, and that the natural features of this speaking authorial voice will be clarified in the process of our editing. We are looking for the covert laws of personality that are presumably enshrined (albeit in a corrupted form) in the overt evidence of the document. To this extent, we may have become practitioners of the science of editing, if by "science" we accept Douglas Hofstadter's argument that the Turing Test is an emblem of the "idea that covert mechanisms can be deeply probed and eventually revealed merely by means of watching overt behavior ... [a] premise [that] lies at the very heart of modern science" (1995: 482).[18] He makes this claim for the Turing

---

18. Hofstadter uses the example of ultrasound scanning of the fetus to argue that "any boundary between 'direct observation' and 'inference' is a subjective matter" (1995: 488); that is, we have become culturally conditioned to believe we actually "see" the fetus, whereas it is only the existence of fast computer hardware capable of reconstituting the scattered sound waves that allows the apparent but not real direct observation. I have some problems with this formulation, for even spectacles are a type of hardware that allows us to think we are observing directly, but is the mere bending of light waves through the lenses of spectacles (rather than the visual reconstitution of sound waves) dependent on cultural conditioning? Perhaps. Hofstadter's main point—that taking the phenomenological reconstitution for the "real" thing breaks down the barrier between direct observation and inference—is still an apt figure for an editor's phenomenological reconstitution of an authorial text.

Test (a claim that exactly replicates Nozick's concern for discovering the E that binds $A_1, \ldots, An$ together to produce the A_0 that is the empirical evidence for thought) by noting that Turing's "conversations" with the black box that might have intelligence are symptomatic of the scientific breaking down of the boundary between "direct observation" and "inference": "[t]he main idea of interacting with a cognitive model over a long period of time is simply to allow its full range of behaviors to become gradually visible, and thereby to allow its innermost mechanisms to be revealed" (ibid.). We assume no less in our decades-long observation of and interaction with the black box of authorial texts, hoping for the revelation that Hofstadter regards as quintessentially scientific.

The cultural and epistemological problem both with Hofstadter's formula for modern science and with Foucault's for medieval science is that both formulas misstate the role of the author function in the growth of empiricism, misstatements that have immediate ramifications for the interpretation of the *Feist* decision and for contemporary copyright theory.

To return to Trevisa and his scientific encyclopedia: just as in the case of the ubiquitous anonymity seemingly typical of the authorizing "poete" in the text of *De Proprietatibus Rerum,* so I and my colleagues had to put a modern name to such collocations as "the philosophre" and "the physicien" (respectively, Aristotle and Constantinus Africanus). Again, the power of the authorizer of the discourse was so great that he could reside behind the generic classification—just like Coleridge's "poet." But this did not mean that the name was effaced or deemed of no value— quite the contrary. Thus Foucault's distinction between scientific and poetic discourses in terms of their authorizing voice, from medieval to modern, does not hold up in the text of one of the most popular and accessible of cultural documents. In Trevisa's encyclopedia, the unnamed names of poet, philosopher, and physician bear equally the status and responsibility of the authorizer.

Similarly, while Hofstadter concedes that the recognition of the supposed "boundary" between direct observation and inference is "subjective" (1995: 488), he does not admit the same subjectivity into the initiator of the conversations held with the black box in the Turing Test. Thus, he can promote the "subtlety of the probes" (490) which the test offers, but in linking this subtlety with the distance testing performed by astronomers and physicists,[19] he is primarily concerned with showing that "the fundamental mechanisms of thought . . . all the way down to where the essence of thinking really takes place" (491) can be plotted empirically by a neutral observer standing outside the act of the creation of the evidence for "essence" or "fundamentals."[20]

This characterization of science obviously accords well with Foucault's prescription for the "disappearance" of the authorizing authority in Enlightenment scientific discourse, but it runs up against Nozick's model for testing the self-reflexivity necessary to recognize "thinking." Nozick's critique of the latent Cartesianism of such formulations as Hofstadter's is that "Descartes can only reach 'thinking is going on' and not 'I think,' at least not with an independently existing I (even if its nature is to think)" (1981: 93). Because Hofstadter's interpretation of the Turing Test can postulate only that "thinking is going on" and not that "I think," it therefore lacks the E that, according to Nozick (and Coleridge) is the sine qua non of thought.

Dr. Seuss sums up this conflict nicely in his book *Oh, the Thinks You Can Think (If Only You Try)*. The "thinks" that Dr. Seuss conjures up are "things unimagined yet in prose or rime," and include "BLOOGS blowing by," "snuvs and their gloves," and "Schlopp. Schlopp. Beautiful schlopp. Beautiful schlopp with a cherry on top." These "unnatural" objects constructed by the synthesizing power of the poet's imagination were great favorites of both my children, not only because of their typically Seussian rhetoric (which could, in a different universe, correspond merely with Pope's "What oft was thought, but ne'er so well express'd"), but also because they challenge the protocols that Hofstadter's faith in the black box and behavioral analysis promotes. Putting it bluntly: no black box

---

19.   As astronomers and physicists know, external behavior far removed in location and scale from its sources, if scrutinized carefully, can be phenomenally revelatory of mechanisms; likewise, cognitive scientists should appreciate the analogous fact about behavior of the mind. In short, the Turing Test, if exploited properly, can be used to probe mental mechanisms at arbitrary levels of depth and subtlety. (Hofstadter 1995: 490)

20.   On the forensic significance of the creation of bibliographical evidence and its role in the cognitive models for authority, see the chapter "Textual Forensics" in the current volume.

could think these Seussian "thinks" because they fall outside the conceptual parameters established by the various "laws" of rhetoric Hofstadter lists.[21]

This may seem a very conservative position to take these days, but I think it responds better to such quantum concepts as the uncertainty principle dependent on the phenomenology of observation and the observer than does the Enlightenment Cartesianism of Foucault or the confident empiricism of Hofstadter. I will concede that it is the Foucauldian model that has been enshrined in Romantic and post-Romantic copyright legislation, but (perhaps paradoxically) it is with Wordsworth, and specifically with his influence over the drafting of the United Kingdom's 1842 Copyright Act, that, as Vanden Bossche has shown,[22] Romanticism allied with capitalism to produce (eventually) Justice Sandra Day O'Connor's decision in *Feist.* It was the argument made in the 1842 act that turned the author into a national treasure—thereby perhaps further embodying the U.S. Constitution's insistence that it is in the national interest to "encourage the arts and sciences." But Wordsworth's great contribution to the intellectual property debate—as Vanden Bossche demonstrates—is that the 1842 act made a distinction between these two components of the national interest.

The implications for textual editing of the Coleridgean definition of the poet's synthesizing imagination have been explored by McGann, Rajan,[23] and others, but I find the intellectual-property ramifications, and

---

21. These laws include "timing data," "throwaway counterfactuals," "throwaway analogies," "levels of abstraction of word choices," "word frequencies," "types of errors," and "word flavors" (Hofstadter 1995: 489–90). Such cognitive models for rhetorical strategies would probably include or embrace most idiolects but could have problems in mapping Dr. Seuss, James Joyce, and other non-normative writers. See my discussion of the function of such corrective grammars in textual editing in Greetham 1999b, esp. 159–63.

22. Vanden Bossche argues that "[u]nderlying the emphasis on the author's moral integrity is the assumption that the author of a literary work possesses an integrated or unified personality" (1994: 61), i.e., Nozick's E or entity.

23. See, for example, McGann 1983, esp. 102–103, citing Shelley: "'When composition begins, inspiration is already on the decline, and the most glorious poetry that has ever been communicated to the world is probably a feeble shadow of the original conception of the Poet'" ("Defence of Poetry," in Shelley 1966: 294); also, from a very different perspective, see Rajan 1988. See also my analysis of this "Romantic ideology" for textual editing in Greetham 1999b, esp. "Hermeneutics and Intention: The 'Standard' History" (167–78) and "Rajan's Rival History" (179–84).

their exemplification in *Feist* and elsewhere in current Anglo-American copyright law just as compelling as the effects upon theories of creativity and socialization. Indeed, as is the cultural norm in such cases, it is the legal and punitive embodiment of cognitive theory that fully socializes the critical argument, usually slightly after the event. That *Feist* is still a "Romantic" decision in a period of critical poststructuralism and post-modernism may therefore just be further indication of this chronological gap. I will offer a few speculations at the end of this chapter on where a poststructuralist intellectual-property principle might take us. For the moment, I will stay with Wordsworth and Coleridge and what they have wrought.

For the fortunes of textual criticism and scholarly editing, the most significant taxonomy of utterance adumbrated by the 1842 act is the wedge placed between the cognitive and protectable faculties of the "arts" and "sciences." The 1842 act declares not only that the artist is a national resource requiring investment by the nation (a principle rejected by right-wing Republicans in their desire to eliminate the National Endowment for the Humanities and the National Endowment for the Arts) but also that the artist, as the exerciser of an organicizing imagination, is of a different order from the scientist, who works with divisible and fragmentable pieces of "useful knowledge" and does not bring a brooding dove-like conception to the construction of the new, totalizing, self-referential, and internally coherent whole that is the poem and the protectable work.[24] Now, from a post-Newtonian and post-empiricist position, it is easy for us to argue against this dichotomy. Did it not require a brooding imagination to postulate relativity or quantum theory just as much as in the creation of a literary work? Do not such miraculously provocative concepts

---

24. Vanden Bossche sees this division very much in the terms of the *Feist* distinction between original, copyrightable organicism and the mere collation of preexistent facts:

> The author of useful works could be compared to other laborers who work on existing raw material supplied by the employer's capital. Such an author compiled books by cutting and pasting as well as reducing existing materials on a given subject. But the author of imaginative literature . . . produced the matter itself: "The man who acquires wealth, must acquire it, in great measure, by abstracting it . . . from the hoards of others; for men cannot all grow rich together. The author on the contrary, takes from none; no one loses by his gain, his productions are created by him, and are therefore additions to the general wealth of the world." ("The Copy-right Law," in *Monthly Review*; quoted in Vanden Bossche 1994: 56)

as Schrödinger's cat (which can be both dead and alive depending on the perspective of the observer) require a revolutionary investment in the nonverifiability of the consistently empirical? Did not Watson and Crick's rejection of earlier models for DNA, because they were not "beautiful" (unlike the aesthetically pleasing double helix), depend upon a phenomenology of critical response quite as human and even individual as the search for apt poetic form? Is not the obsession with a unified field theory perhaps the most pervasively Romantic, organicist, totalizing quest of all? Well, yes, but the science of Wordsworth's "useful knowledge" was only an empiricist, mechanistic, and divisible property, not the sort of imaginative property that, because it is whole and organic and the product of a brooding national treasure, therefore becomes protectable. To Wordsworth and the framers of the 1842 act, the sort of thinking that is going on in the useful knowledge of science is like the Enlightenment thinking that Hofstadter postulates: thought without agency or motivation, as per the Cartesian dichotomy, and thought that therefore can float free of its putative originator, who becomes like the clockmaker creator of the mechanistic universe, separate from and no longer responsible for the predictable working-out of the creation. But for Wordsworth, as for Dr. Seuss, thinking of a genuinely synthetic, creative mode requires active agency: Dr. Seuss demands not only a "you" to do the thinking but also a motivation for thought ("if only you try"), and this "you" (the protectable "poet") is again a Romantic construction. Thus the 1842 act (and its Seussian elaboration) may be described as an early, pre-*Feist* confrontation with the distinction between the white pages and the yellow pages of the telephone directory. That is, Hofstadter's thinking can produce the white pages without agency, precisely because its graphic and lexical content is predetermined by the codification of an external, non-synthesizing, and non-creative entablature—the alphabet. Of course, the alphabet is itself creative or poetic in that it is not merely a force or law of nature, but the cultural conditioning that accompanies its imbrication in society makes it appear natural, and we no longer have to imagine the original poet's fusing of elements to produce the template of ABC. On the other hand, the yellow pages (and, apparently, a manual of automobile prices) does demand either, or both, Nozick's "I" and Seuss's "you," so that while it may contain useful knowledge, it does not embody it as a creative construct. Or thus, at least, the court cases *Feist* and *MacLean Hunter* seem to declare.

I hold, therefore, that scholarly editors in the post-*Feist* period desiring to hold onto their intellectual property should resist the allurements of external structure, laws of nature, science, and facts, in favor of criticism and speculation. By the still-dominant Wordsworthian formula, facts are not protectable, and it is imagination (and perhaps creative misprision) that separates an intellectual property from a raw datum. Note that even Dr. Seuss's motivation ("if only you try") is thus not sufficient argument, as a version of the now-rejected sweat of the brow, for intellectual protection. The all-too-human trying and sweat are helpful in current copyright jurisprudence only if they produce one of Seuss's "thinks," a new construction and definition for knowledge, not knowledge or fact themselves. Despite what textual critics from Japan to Germany tell us,[25] a non-Seussian science will not serve us as the epistemological paradigm for our work; only poetry and "thinks" can claim that position. We must thus all become poets and thinkers, even when we write the collaborative poetry of a scholarly edition.

Thus, I *think* it is striking that, even when referring to collaboration, that authorial grail for the Stillinger-McGann-Pizer-Gaskell apostasy against the "myth of solitary genius," current copyright legislation describes collaborative composition and proprietorship in terms designed to out-Wordsworth Wordsworth's insistence on the organic whole: "A compilation is a work formed by the collection and assembling of preexisting materials or of data that are selected, coordinated, or arranged in such a way that the resulting work as a whole constitutes an original work of authorship" (Copyright Act 1976: sec. 101). Collaboration by this formula is simply another Romanticized embodiment of organicism and nothing like the divisible useful knowledge that should have distinguished it from the "solitary genius" of a truly poetic, synthesizing imagination. As Nozick poses the question, confronting the classic Kantian example

---

25. See the chapter "Textual Forensics" on the struggle between the "scientific," Galilean model for textual scholarship versus the "venatic lore" of hermeneutic analysis, including the references to the various attempts by twentieth-century textualists (Yamashita, Maas, Timpanaro) to emphasize the Galilean over the venatic.

of imagining that each word of the sentence "I wonder how things can be unified" is conceived and spoken serially by a different conceiver and speaker: "What makes one mind one, rather than a composite of different entities? ... the problem is thrown back to the unity of what does the unifying. (How can a purported unifier, which is not itself unified, produce unity?)" (Nozick 1981: 94, 95). To put the arithmetic in fairly crude terms: to Wordsworth and the Copyright Act of 1842, two imaginations are not twice as poetic (and protectable) as one; they are probably only half as poetic—despite any inferences to be drawn from Wordsworth's own "collaboration" with Coleridge. But in current law, synthesis can operate at a secondary or metalevel of composition and loses neither its intuitive and organicist credentials nor its protectability as a result of the cumulative effort.

I am not certain whether this account is a historically retrograde or conceptually adventurous prescription for action, but measured against several aspects of our current culture's preference for the original, the solitary, and the socially unsullied against the collaborative and the cumulative, it may be that any copyright legislation is swimming upstream. Consider the premium on restored, "director's cut," original versions of such movies (a medium that is probably the most exemplary for collaboration) as *Lawrence of Arabia* and *Blade Runner;* or, consider the pro and con arguments over the restoration of the Sistine Chapel frescoes as fulfilling or masking original and singular artistic intention; or consider that, when I inquired of the New York Shakespeare Festival whether any of the plays in its Shakespeare Marathon had been listed as "by William Shakespeare and someone else," the press office was horrified at the suggestion: the capital invested in Shakespeare might decline in value if, say, *Macbeth* were marketed as a play by William Shakespeare *and* Thomas Middleton (the preferred attribution in the Oxford Shakespeare and, of course, in the Oxford Middleton). So brood we must and bring forth progeny by parthenogenesis. Editors can brood too, especially if such brooding is tied to a Lockean capitalistic investment. While I do not necessarily subscribe to Alvin Kernan's conspiracy theory of the attempted renewal of copyright in such authors as D. H. Lawrence and James Joyce, and I do not wax quite as outraged as he does against "the loitering heirs of dead authors" (1990: 106) handily continuing to pick up profits from the sales of works that might otherwise be in the public domain, I cannot resist the suspicion that the impending lapse of copyright for, say, Lawrence was not wholly absent from the decision of Cambridge University Press to bring out a new, "authoritative" edition, which set the copyright clock ticking anew. Cambridge argued that its editorial intervention (ironically, by the standards of *Feist*, to restore authorial, original, historical intention) was sufficient to generate a series of new works (for which, read organic wholes) which were protectable *de novo*. The problem with this argument vis-à-vis *Feist* is that the Cambridge editions are clear text, not inclusive text. Does this mean that they are like the white pages or like an automobile pricing manual? While I hesitate to be responsible for encouraging an infringement of the asserted intellectual properties of such an august institution as the Cambridge University Press, I have to acknowledge that the primary way of testing the inviolability of these new/old Cambridge texts would be to take one to a photocopying store, reproduce it like the white pages in *Feist*, and wait for Cambridge to jump.

How the courts might react to Cambridge's jump is yet to be determined. While I have spent most of this very hurried view of copyright stressing the continuity and evolution of intellectual-property legislation, this apparently natural state of intellectual property must be put into its broadest historical context. Copyright is, in the millennial history of authoriality, a comparatively new idea, given particular force and momentum by the capitalist and Romantic revolutions and still enshrined in such decisions as *Feist*. Whether it will survive an increasingly electronic environment for dissemination and whether it will be able to deal with the cracks appearing in our cultural reconfiguration of authoriality remains to be seen.

Let me suggest a couple of emblems for this problem. During an early stage of the protracted Malcolm-Masson suit over the accuracy of quotations attributed to Jeffrey Masson in the *New Yorker*, and before being reversed by the Supreme Court, a lower court found for Janet Malcolm by declaring that it was not the verbal accuracy of the quotations that was at issue but whether Masson *might* have made such remarks as Malcolm attributed to him,[26] a deconstructive, anti-historicist ruling that

---

26. *Masson v. New Yorker Magazine,* 895 F.2d 1535 (9th Cir. 1989). See the commentary by de Grazia (1992) concerning quotation marks:

> [T]he Court overlooked the grammatical distinction that quotation marks function to sustain: the distinction between direct quotation and indirect quotation. . . . The district court's decision suggests that statements within quotation marks need not

put the links among utterance, authoriality, and proprietorship severely in jeopardy.

And, as I understand, in the interactive version of J. David Bolter's *Writing Space,* there is a tantalizing copyright notice. The "author" of the text grants permission for any "reader" to play in the text by making revisions and additions, creating new links and structural tags, but does not grant permission to issue the resultant work independently. So far, so good. But the copyright notice then goes on to warn the reader that any part of the text might already have been created as the result of such manipulation by a previous reader, including the part containing this very copyright notice! The *mise-en-abyme* yawns before us.

Despite such deconstructive play, by the courts or by authors, the lure of authoriality and intellectual property is difficult to resist. When I first presented an early draft of parts of this essay at an MLA convention, I brought with me what was then a strange exhibit. I told the conferees that I had encountered a copyright notice pushing in the opposite direction from hypertextual conflation and authorial ambiguity. Given the (then) differences between Anglo-American and Continental copyright law regarding *droit d'auteur,* the copyright notice in J. M. Roberts's *History of the World* (1995) was startling for the time. After all the conventional signs such as © and various publication notices (thirteen in all) came this brief advice: "The moral right of the author has been asserted." I confessed to not understanding the full cultural import of this bizarre statement of assertion at the time. Anglo-American intellectual property law had not usually embodied the sort of *droit d'auteur* of Continental copyright legislation, whereby a permanent "moral right" of the author not to have his or her work disfigured or misrepresented was enshrined, even after the lapse of formal copyright. The Anglo-American tradition had, via Locke, been much more concerned with the capitalist commodification of the work, its salability, and its alienability.[27] The Serra and Helmsley-

---

reproduce what was said word for word in order to be constitutionally protected as free speech.... According to this ruling, quotation marks no longer set off words a person said from words a person might have said. (546–47)

27. Since then, presumably as a result of the United Kingdom having adopted European Union copyright legislation, there has been a noticeable increase in the assertions of moral rights in British publications, and even in some American ones.

Spear warehouse cases cited earlier are powerful demonstrations of this capitalistic view of alienable rights. Anglo-American commodification did not recognize the moral rights of the author/artist. As Ted Turner put it when arguing against those who wanted to prevent him from "colorizing" his collection of black-and-white movies: "When I last looked, they belonged to me." What practical effects Roberts hoped to obtain by his assertion of author's moral rights over his *History of the World* within the Anglo-American tradition was unclear then, but with the proliferation of claims of moral rights Roberts might now seem to have been in the vanguard. But that he even made the assertion, which was then derived from a different, non-Anglo-American cultural and legal tradition, demonstrates once more just how contingent, conditioned, and local our attitudes toward copyright remain. Intellectual property is not a force of nature; it is a right asserted and worked for. If scholarly editors wish to retain their property now that "sweat of the brow" has been cast aside, we would do well to continue to align ourselves with the hermeneutic, interpretive community rather than risk our work's being downgraded to the unprotectable status of scientific useful knowledge.

Epilogue:
The Limits of Contamination

After all this contamination, the reader deserves a pause—and a clarification. We began with the assumption that contamination had a bad name. In the days of the search for the pure, the unsullied, and the originary, clearly anything that interfered with the transmission of this Platonized ideal was suspect. It is therefore no surprise that the language of traditional textual criticism was characterized by images of cleansing, scouring, purging, and even, as Joseph Grigely (1995b) has pointed out, racial eugenics. Grigely specifically links the Greg-Bowers eclectic system of restoring the "ideal" text with Clorox and Hitler, in that all three sought to decontaminate the racial/textual stock and to remove "impurities" that had crept into the otherwise unsullied body of textual/racial identity. Such fear of the mixing of states, of miscegenation biological, textual, or cultural, can unfortunately still be found on the fringes of our political climate, as when some supporters of John McCain and Sarah Palin claimed that Barack Obama was unacceptable, un-American, not because he was black, but rather because he represented the contamination of one race by another. Ricky Thompson, a pipe fitter from Alabama, was quoted by Adam Nossiter in the *New York Times* as claiming, "[Obama's] neither-nor. . . . He's other. It's in the Bible. Come as one. Don't create other breeds." And Glenn Reynolds, a textile worker from Virginia, similarly claimed that "God taught the children of Israel not to intermarry. You should be proud of what you are, and not intermarry" (quoted in Nossiter 2008).

Of course, it is easy to respond to this sort of prejudice by pointing out that not only are Messrs. Thompson and Reynolds unlikely to be examples of a "pure" breeding stock, but (as is dealt with in the chapter "Phylum-Tree-Rhizome") the genealogical model often cited by textual critics is upside down, for sexual reproduction (presumably responsible for both Thompson and Reynolds) is emblematic of the mixing of states—male and female. Neither texts nor humans come into being by parthenogenesis.

Nonetheless, the sort of suspicion of contamination represented and exploited by McCain-Palin cannot simply be ignored. Contamination clearly threatens a cozy sense of identity even in a mongrel country like the United States, and it is hardly surprising that it does still have a bad name, and not just among textual critics. I hope that by now it is also not surprising that one of the main purposes of this book has been to rehabilitate both the concept and the actual term *contamination,* and I recognize that this polemical purpose does therefore strain at the conventional meanings of *contamination* in this attempt to focus on its "pleasures."

When I began to circulate various parts of the book among colleagues whose judgment I respected, I found (not unexpectedly) that the chief demurral was that "contamination" was being made to do more work, to cover more territory, than they were used to or happy with. This was a perfectly proper observation, as was the suggestion by my colleague Gerhard Joseph that a less loaded, more familiar term like "intertextuality" might make readers more comfortable. Well, yes, *if* my intention were indeed to make readers comfortable and if I could co-opt the seemingly more neutral "intertextuality" (or "influence" or "citation" or a host of other alternatives).

The problem with this suggestion was two-fold: first, "intertextuality" (and the cultural/ideological baggage it brings with it) is almost as suspect as "contamination," perhaps even more so, in that my spell-checker flagged "intertextuality" as an "improper" usage for which no suggestions are available in the thesaurus, whereas "contamination" escaped without being flagged. Introduced by Julia Kristeva in the late 1960s, in her account of "The Semiotic and the Symbolic" in *Revolution in Poetic Language* (1984), "intertextuality" was indeed a useful way of describing how "no text, much as it might appear so, is original and unique-in-itself; rather it is a tissue of inevitable, and to an extent unwitting, references to and quotations from other texts" (Allen 2000: n.p.). It is perhaps ironic (given the later adoption of "intertextuality" as a commonplace of literary theory) that Kristeva herself preferred the term *transposition*[1] (derived from Freud), since "*inter-textuality* . . . has often been understood in the banal sense of 'study of sources'" (1984: 59–60). As she noted: "we prefer the term *transposition* because it specifies that the new passage from one signifying system to another demands a new articulation of the thetic— of enunciative and denotative positionality" (60). But no matter how limited Kristeva intended the concept of *transposition* to be (and no matter how she wished to differentiate it from intertextuality), as is now widely recognized the critical reach of "intertextuality" has been extended to a point where it is "impossibly freighted with meanings and uses" (Allen 2000: n.p.), although the fact that a conventional computer spell-checker does not recognize the term suggests that it is still primarily an example of critical jargon associated with a specific period of (French) poststructuralist theory. The second problem with Kristevan usage is that the Freudian implications of "transposition" (and the suspicion of "intertextuality" as the banal "study of sources") does limit Kristeva's concept (whatever its precise terminology) to unconscious rather than deliberate co-option.[2]

Thus, the substitution of "intertextuality" for "contamination" would, ironically, be both too general (and now meaningless) and too specific, in that it would exclude some of the more provocative examples in this book—both those in which intentional allusion is being made and those that raise an even more challenging question, where a difference in cultural meaning can depend upon whether the allusion is deliberate or not. In what I regard as some of the most critical examples in this book, it may be impossible to establish with any certainty whether the contamination is intended (and therefore banal) or seditious (and therefore transpositional).[3] And in such cases, the possibility not only of differing authorial types of co-option but also of differing attitudes toward the apparent

---

1. The entry for "inter-textuality" [*sic*] in the index of Kristeva's book simply refers the reader to "transposition."

2. Allen (2000: n.p.) pronounces that "intertextuality" "should not be . . . used to refer to *conscious influence* [or] to *intentional allusion*."

3. See the examples of the Shostakovich quotation from *The Lone Ranger* (or not), the Berg quotation from a Bach chorale (or not), and St. Paul's (mis)citation of himself—and God (or not).

embedding of one text in another[4] clearly enriches the critical history, although making it more ambiguous.

Kristevan transposition/intertextuality are not the only contenders for an alternative terminology to describe the multiple examples in various media covered in this book. While the influence (transposition?) of Bakhtin is not specifically cited by Kristeva in her account of intertextuality, it has become accepted that the lurking presence of the dialogism of Bakhtin is difficult to ignore. Consider, for example, this quotation from a late work on speech acts:

> The sentence as a unit of language, like the word, has no author. Like the word, it belongs to *nobody*. . . . Our speech, that is, all our utterances (including creative works) is filled with others' words, [with] varying degrees of awareness and detachment. . . . However monological the utterance may be . . . it cannot but be, in some measure, a response to what has already been said. . . . The utterance is filled with *dialogic overtones*. (Bakhtin 1986: 83–84, 89, 92)

Are not these "dialogic overtones" Kristeva's transposition in a linguistic rather than psychologistic model? Maybe they could even be intertextual, except that, if we adopt Kristeva's demurral, since Bakhtin's *overtones* are unavoidable and inherent in all speech (even creative works), then they can hardly be "banal . . . sources."

And so it continues as we plumb the thesaurus. *Influence*? Possibly, but then we would need some sort of Bloomian *anxiety* to cover the insidious interventions that form large parts of this study. *Iterability*? Useful in the shifting definitions of text/work (see Grigely 1991), but too specifically associated with poststructuralism and Derrida (*Limited Inc.*). *Heteroglossia*? Back to Bakhtin. *Interpolation*? Too mechanical and too easily testable. *Conflation*? Often confused with *contamination,* but requiring a different model of agency and uptake. None of these will quite do the extra "work" that I have asked of *contamination,* and none will provide the various sorts of pleasure that I believe the reader/listener/observer can derive from contaminated texts. I recognize that this last phrase may be an unavoidable tautology, for if *texts* are textile, woven, interlaced, then

---

4. When I cited the Berg disavowal to the distinguished musicologist Leo Treitler, in a team-taught seminar, Treitler's response was refreshingly dismissive: "He was lying."

it is the admixture of the disparate, the variously colored threads, that creates the successful and pleasurable pattern. And this may just be a more neutral, less polemical, more politic (or polite) way of naming what happens in the texts discussed here.

But given that this book does not aim for neutrality (or even politeness), I am not convinced that "the patterns in the text," "the weaving of the text," and so on would convey the sense of aggression, infiltration, even defilement, at which the accounts of "truthiness" or "faith v. fact" aim. And while I hope it is by now not necessary to take refuge in mere philology, the attestations for *contamination* in the *OED* do provide a wide enough range of technical, formal, and moral possibilities.[5] My main objection to the philological way is that it is both too hesitant and too formalistic (and I think not sufficiently distinct from *conflation*). What we need is a combination of the formal with a suspicion of Hall's morality. If *contamination* is to work harder, we must demand something more active, more invasive than the philologists will give us.

And the limits? Given that "intertextuality" is both too broad and too banal; given that "dialogic overtones" are too ubiquitous, it may be that "contamination" will provide us with at least the possibility of choice, and thus of criticism. There will, one hopes, be limits on both of these activities. A choice must be made from culturally plausible responses to the contaminated text, and the criticism must take account of both the new integrity of the contamination and the elements from which it could be made. Within these limits, I would not want to question the propriety of our various pleasures. Berg may indeed have been lying about Bach, but we can derive as much delight from his misrepresentations as from his ignorance.

---

5. So, we fully expect Bishop Hall's fulmination: "What was he that accused marriage . . . of contamination with carnal concupiscence" (1b; 1620); but the philological entries (1d) provide a much wider range, from Strong (1888): "By 'contamination' I understand the process by which synonymous forms of expression force themselves simultaneously into consciousness, so that neither of the two makes its influence felt simply and purely: a new form arises in which elements of the one mingle with elements of the other"; to Sturtevant's (1947) claim: "Momentary hesitation between two possible linguistic responses is extremely common, and not infrequently it leads to a mingling of the two. [One instance is] . . . *ruvershoes* (*rubbers overshoes*). We call this process contamination."

Works Cited and Consulted

Abailard [Abelard], Peter. 1976. *Sic et Non: A Critical Edition*, ed. Blanche B. Boyer and Richard McKeon. Chicago: University of Chicago Press.

Adams, Robert. 1992. "Editing *Piers Plowman B:* The Imperative of an Intermittently Critical Edition." *Studies in Bibliography* 45: 31–68.

Adorno, Theodor. 1992. *Negative Dialectics*, trans. E. B. Ashton. New York: Continuum.

Allen, Graham. 2000. "Intertextuality." www.litencyc.com/php/stopics .php?rec=true&UID=1229.

———. 2005. *Intertextuality*. London: Routledge.

Allott, Miriam, ed. 1970. *The Poems of John Keats*. London: Longman; and New York: Norton.

Althusser, Louis. 1971. "Ideology and Ideological State Apparatuses (Notes toward an Investigation)." In *Lenin and Philosophy and Other Essays*, trans. Ben Brewster. New York: Monthly Review.

Amory, Hugh. 1984. "Physical Bibliography, Cultural History, and the Disappearance of the Book." *Papers of the Bibliographical Society of America* 78: 341–48.

Andrews, William L. 1997. "Editing 'Minority' Texts." In *The Margins of the Text*, ed. D. C. Greetham. Ann Arbor: University of Michigan Press.

Angier, Natalie. 2008. "Who Is the Walrus?" *New York Times* 20 May. Science section: 1. www.nytimes.com/2008/05/20/science/20walrus .html?_r=1&scp=1&sq=Natalie%20Angier%20Who%20Is%20the%20 Walrus&st=cse&oref=slogin.

Annals of the Fine Arts. 1820. (Jan.). London.

Anti-Ballistic Missile Treaty. 1986. Moscow, 26 May. www.state.gov/www/ global/arms/treaties/abm/abm2.html (withdrawal by United States, 23 Mar. 1983, 31 Dec. 2001).

Appiah, Kwame Anthony, and Henry Louis Gates, eds. 1997. *Dictionary of Global Culture.* New York: Knopf.

Arango, Tim. 2008. "I Got the News Instantaneously, Oh Boy." *New York Times* 14 Sept.: WK3.

Arnold, Bruce. 1992. *The Scandal of "Ulysses": The Sensational Life of a Twentieth-Century Masterpiece.* New York: St. Martin's.

Arnold, Matthew. 1960–1977. "The Function of Criticism at the Present Time" and "The Study of Poetry." In *The Complete Prose Works,* ed. R. H. Super. Ann Arbor: University of Michigan Press.

Austin, J. L. 1975. *How to Do Things with Words,* ed. J. O. Urmson and Marina Sbisa. 2nd ed. Cambridge, Mass.: Harvard University Press.

Bach, Johann Sebastian. *Cantata No. 20: Es Ist Genug.* BWV 82. Based on Johann Rudolf Ahle, "Es Ist Genug" (1662, Zahn 7173).

Baker, Nicholson. 1997. "Discards." In his *The Size of Thoughts: Essays and Other Lumber.* New York: Vintage.

———. 2001. *Double Fold: Libraries and the Assault on Paper.* New York: Vintage.

Baker, William, and Kenneth Womack, comps. 2000. *Twentieth-Century Bibliography and Textual Criticism: An Annotated Bibliography.* Westport, Conn.: Greenwood.

Bakhtin, Mikhail. 1986. "The Problem of Speech Genres." In *Speech Genres and Other Late Essays,* trans. Vern W. McGee, ed. Caryl Emerson and Michael Holquist. Austin: University of Texas Press.

Bale, John. 1548. *Illustrium majoris brittaniae scriptorum summarium.* Wesel, Germany: Van den Staten.

Band, Jonathan. 2006. *The Google Library Project: The Copyright Debate.* Chicago: American Library Association, Office for Information Technology Policy.

Barker, Nicholas. 1990. "Textual Forgery." In *Fake? The Art of Deception,* ed. Mark Jones. Berkeley: University of California Press.

Barlow, Wm. P., Jr. 1996. "Bibliography and Bibliophily." *Papers of the Bibliographical Society of America* 90: 139–50.

Barnard, John, ed. 1988. *John Keats: The Complete Poems.* 3rd ed. London: Penguin.

Barnard, Lou, Katherine O'Brien O'Keefe, and John Unsworth, eds. 2006. *Electronic Textual Editing.* New York: MLA.

Barney, Stephen, ed. 1991. *Annotation and Its Texts.* Oxford: Oxford University Press.

Barron, James. 1988. "In a Word, No, No, No." *New York Times* 20 Aug.: A24.

Barthes, Roland. 1972. "Myth Today." In *Mythologies,* trans. Annette Lavers. New York: Noonday.

———. 1974. *S/Z: An Essay*, trans. Richard Miller. New York: Noonday.

———. 1975. *The Pleasure of the Text*, trans. Richard Miller. New York: Hill and Wang.

———. 1977. "From Work to Text." In *Image Music Text*, trans. Stephen Heath, 155–64. New York: Hill and Wang.

Basile, Michael. 1994. "A Semiotic Analysis of the Texts of *Romeo and Juliet*." Ph.D. diss., City University of New York Graduate School.

Bate, Jonathan, and Sonia Massai. 1997. "Adaptation as Edition." In *The Margins of the Text*, ed. D. C. Greetham. Ann Arbor: University of Michigan Press.

Bate, Walter Jackson. 1982. *Harvard Magazine*, Sept.–Oct.

Bateson, F. W. 1961. "Modern Bibliography and the Literary Artifact." In *English Studies Today*, ed. Georges A. Bonnard, 67–77. 2nd ed. Bern: Francke.

Baudrillard, Jean. 1995. *Simulacra and Simulation*, trans. Sheila Faria Glaser. Ann Arbor: University of Michigan Press.

Baugh, Albert C., ed. 1963. *Chaucer's Major Poetry*. Englewood Cliffs, N.J.: Prentice-Hall.

Beardsley, Monroe. 1978. "Languages of Art and Art Criticism." *Erkenntnis* 12: 95–118.

Beaumarchais, Pierre-Augustin Caron de. 1784. *Le Marriage de Figaro*. 27 Apr., Odéon. Paris: Rualt.

———. 1792–1794. *La Mère coupable ou L'Autre Tartuffe*. 26 June, Théâtre du Marais. Paris: Silvestre.

Beckett, Samuel. 1967. *Stories and Texts for Nothing*. New York: Grove.

Bédier, Joseph. 1928. "La tradition manuscrite du *Lai de l'ombre:* Réflections sur l'art d'éditer les anciens textes." *Romania* 54: 161–96, 321–56. Rpt. as pamphlet, Paris, 1929.

Benjamin, Walter. 1968. "The Work of Art in the Age of Mechanical Reproduction." In *Illuminations: Essays and Reflections*, trans. Harry Zohn, ed. Hannah Arendt. New York: Schocken.

Benson, Larry, ed. 1987. *The Riverside Chaucer*. Boston: Houghton Mifflin.

Beowulf. MS Cotton Vitellius a.xv. British Library, London.

Berg, Alban. 1936. Violin Concerto: "To the Memory of an Angel." 19 Apr., Palau de la Música Catalana, Barcelona.

———. 1979. *Lulu*, ed. Friedrich Cerha. Théâtre National de l'Opéra de Paris. Pierre Boulez, cond.; Patrice Chéreau, dir.

Berger, Thomas L. 1993. "The New Historicism and the Editing of English Renaissance Texts." In *New Ways of Looking at Old Texts: Papers of the Renaissance English Text Society, 1985–1991*, ed. W. Speed Hill, 195–97. Binghamton, N.Y.: Medieval and Renaissance Texts and Studies/Renaissance English Text Society.

Bernstein, Charles. 2006. "Making Audio Visible: The Lessons of Visual Language for the Textualization of Sound." *Text* 16: 277–92.

Bibliographical Society of Australia and New Zealand Bulletin. 1970–. Bibliographical Society of Australia and New Zealand.

Bidwell, John. 1992. "The Study of Paper as Evidence, Artefact, and Commodity." In *The Book Encompassed,* ed. Peter Hobley Davison, 69–82. Cambridge: Cambridge University Press.

Bland, Mark. 1996. "'Invisible Dangers': Censorship and the Subversion of Authority in Early Modern England." *Papers of the Bibliographical Society of America* 90: 151–94.

———. 1998. "The Appearance of the Text in Early Modern England." *Text* 11: 91–154.

Blatner, David. 1997. *The Joy of Pi.* London: Allen Lane/Penguin.

Blecua, Alberto. 1983. *Manual de crítica textual.* Madrid: Castalia.

———. 1995. "Medieval Castilian Texts and Their Editions." In *Scholarly Editing: A Guide to Research,* ed. D. C. Greetham. New York: MLA.

Bloch, Howard, and Stephen G. Nichols, eds. 1996. *Medievalism and the Modernist Temper.* Baltimore, Md.: Johns Hopkins University Press.

Bloom, Harold. 1979. "The Breaking of Form." Rpt. in Bloom et al., *Deconstruction and Criticism.* New York: Continuum, 2004.

Bloom, Julie. 2008. "Sydney Orchestra Admits to Fakery." *New York Times* 30 Aug.: A20.

Bloomfield, Josephine. 1994. "Diminished by Kindness: Frederick Klaeber's Rewriting of Wealtheow." *Journal of English and Germanic Philology* 93.2: 183–203.

Blum, Rudolf. 1991. *Kallimachos: The Alexandrian Library and the Origins of Bibliography,* trans. Hans H. Welisch. Madison: University of Wisconsin Press.

Bolter, Jay David. 1991. Writing Space: The Computer, Hypertext, and the History of Writing. Hillsdale, N.J.: Erlbaum.

Book History. 1998–. Society for the History of Authorship, Reading and Publishing. www.sharpweb.org/bookhist.html.

Bornstein, George. 1999. Review of Greetham, *Textual Transgressions: Essays toward the Construction of a Biobibliography* (New York: Garland, 1998). *Analytical and Enumerative Bibliography* 10: 166–69.

———. 2001. *Material Modernism: The Politics of the Page.* Cambridge: Cambridge University Press.

Bornstein, George, ed. 1991. *Representing Modernist Texts: Editing as Interpretation.* Ann Arbor: University of Michigan Press.

Bornstein, George, Hans Walter Gabler, and Gillian Borland Pierce, eds. 1996. *Contemporary German Editorial Theory*. Ann Arbor: University of Michigan Press.

Bornstein, George, and Ralph G. Williams, eds. 1993. *Palimpsest: Editorial Theory in the Humanities*. Ann Arbor: University of Michigan Press.

Bowers, Fredson. 1948–1949. "Running-Title Evidence for Determining Half-Sheet Imposition." *Studies in Bibliography* 1: 199–202.

———. 1949–1950. "Bibliographical Evidence from the Printer's Measure." *Studies in Bibliography* 2: 153–67.

———. 1959. *Textual and Literary Criticism*. Cambridge: Cambridge University Press.

———. 1964a. *Bibliography and Textual Criticism*. Oxford: Clarendon.

———. 1964b. "Some Principles for Scholarly Editions of Nineteenth-Century American Authors." *Studies in Bibliography* 17: 223–28.

———. 1970. "Textual Criticism." In *The Aims and Methods of Scholarship in the Modern Languages and Literatures*, ed. James Thorpe. New York: MLA.

———. 1975. *Essays in Bibliography, Text, and Editing*. Charlottesville: University Press of Virginia.

———. 1978. "Greg's 'Rationale of Copy-Text' Revisited." *Studies in Bibliography* 31: 90–161.

———. 1987. "Mixed Texts and Multiple Authority." *Text* 3: 63–90.

———. 1988. "Unfinished Business." *Text* 4: 1–12.

———. 1992. "Notes on Theory and Practice in Editing Texts." In *The Book Encompassed*, ed. Peter Davison, 244–57. Cambridge: Cambridge University Press.

———. 1994. "Why Apparatus?" *Text* 6: 11–19.

Boydston, Jo Ann, ed. 1969–1972. *The Early Works, 1882–1898. By John Dewey*. 5 vols. Carbondale: Southern Illinois University Press.

———. 1976–1983. *The Middle Works, 1899–1924. By John Dewey*. 15 vols. Carbondale: Southern Illinois University Press (1976–1980, vols. 1–10; 1982–1983, vols. 11–15).

———. 1981–1990. *The Later Works, 1925–1953. By John Dewey*. 17 vols. Carbondale: Southern Illinois University Press.

———. 1991a. "The Collected Works of John Dewey and the CEAA/CSE: A Case History." *Papers of the Bibliographical Society of America* 85: 119–44.

———. 1991b. "In Praise of Apparatus." *Text* 5: 1–14.

Boyle, James, ed. 2003. *The Public Domain: Collected Papers*. Durham, N.C.: Duke University Press/Center for the Public Domain.

———. 2008. *The Public Domain: Enclosing the Commons of the Mind.* New Haven, Conn.: Yale University Press.

Boyle, Leonard P. 1988. "'Epistulae Venerunt Parum Dulces': The Place of Codicology in the Editing of Medieval Latin Texts." In *Editing and Editors: A Retrospect,* ed. Richard Landon. New York: AMS.

Brack, O M, Jr., and Warner Barnes, eds. 1969. *Bibliography and Textual Criticism: English and American Literature 1700 to the Present.* Chicago: University of Chicago Press.

Braunmuller, A. R. 1993. "Work, Document, and Miscellany: A Response to Professors de Grazia and Marotti." In *New Ways of Looking at Old Texts: Papers of the Renaissance English Text Society, 1985–1991,* ed. W. Speed Hill, 223–27. Binghamton, N.Y.: Medieval and Renaissance Texts and Studies/ Renaissance English Text Society.

Brewer, Charlotte. 1991. "Authorial vs. Scribal Writing in *Piers Plowman.*" In *Medieval Literature: Texts and Interpretation,* ed. Tim William Machan, 59–89. Binghamton, N.Y.: Medieval and Renaissance Texts and Studies.

Brewer, Charlotte, and A. G. Rigg, eds. 1983. *Piers Plowman: The Z Version.* Toronto: Pontifical Institute of Medieval Studies.

Britten, Benjamin. 1953. *Gloriana.* Covent Garden, London.

Britten, Benjamin, E. M. Forster, and Eric Crozier. 1988. *Billy Budd.* Paris: Erato; and London: Boosey & Hawkes (original four-act version, 1951).

Broude, Ronald. 1991. "When Accidentals Are Substantive: Applying Methods of Textual Criticism to Scholarly Editions of Music." *Text* 5: 105–20.

Brown, John Seely, and Paul Duguid. 2002. *The Social Life of Information.* Cambridge, Mass.: Harvard Business School Press.

Browne, Malcolm. 1995. "Two Groups of Physicists Produce Matter That Einstein Postulated." *New York Times* 14 July: A1.

Bruccoli, Matthew J., ed. 1991. *The Great Gatsby.* In *The Cambridge Edition of the Works of F. Scott Fitzgerald.* Cambridge: Cambridge University Press.

Bryant, John. 2007. "Witness and Access: The Uses of the Fluid Text." *Textual Cultures: Texts, Contexts, Interpretation* 2.1: 16–42.

Buckley, Christopher. 1995. "Doing the McNamara." *New Yorker* 22 May: 100.

Bull, George. 1996. *Michelangelo: A Biography.* New York: St. Martin's.

Bulwer Lytton, Edward George. 1830. *Paul Clifford.* London: Routledge, 1874 (Knebworth edition); electronic text at http://books.google.com/ books?id=XJACAAAAQAAJ&dq=Bulwer+Lytton+Paul+Clifford&pg =PP1&ots=f8sa8dZG0-&sig=saMMfAx8rroAkgQ9SXfzhx5dPHU&hl =en&sa=X&oi=book_result&resnum=1&ct=result#PPP1,M1. London: Chapman and Hall, 1877; electronic text at http://books.google.com/ books?hl=en&id=4jEEAAAAQAAJ&dq=Bulwer+Lytton+Paul+Clifford &printsec=frontcover&source=web&ots=20PPsrcvh9&sig=poyFQI3Tu

U5pyxMD5Gnl_dgPRQY&sa=X&oi=book_result&resnum=2&ct=resu
lt#PPR4,M1.

Buonarroti, Michelangelo. *Lettere/contratti CDLXII*, no. 32; *Carteggio*, vol. 4,
MLXXXII, both quoted in George Bull, *Michelangelo: A Biography*. New
York: St. Martin's, 1996.

Burger, Konrad. 1892–1913. *Monumenta Germaniæ et Italiæ typographica*. Berlin: Reichsdruckerei.

Burns, John F., and Elaine Schiolino. 2008. "No One Convicted of Terror Plot
to Bomb Planes." *New York Times* 9 Sept.: A1, A14.

Burrow, J. A. 1982. "Autobiographical Poetry in the Middle Ages: The Case of
Thomas Hoccleve." *Proceedings of the British Academy* 63: 389–412.

———. 1984. "Hoccleve's Series: Experience and Books." In *Fifteenth-Century
Studies: Recent Essays*, ed. R. F. Yeager, 259–73. Hamden, Conn.: Archon.

Bush, Douglas, ed. 1959. *John Keats: Selected Poems and Letters*. Boston:
Houghton Mifflin.

Bushell, Sally. 2007. "Textual Process and the Denial of Origins." *Textual Cultures: Texts, Contexts, Interpretation* 2.2: 100–117.

Butchko, Mark. 2005. *Lord of the Rings Trailer Spoof*. www.youtube.com/
watch?v=ajZflZMXEpM&feature=related.

Byrne, Sister Lavinia. 1999. *Woman at the Altar*. Collegeville, Minn.: Liturgical, 1993. Rpt., New York: Continuum.

Canfora, Luciano. 1987. *The Vanished Library: A Wonder of the Ancient World*,
trans. Martin Ryle. Berkeley: University of California Press.

Carruthers, Mary. 1990. *The Book of Memory: A Study of Memory in Medieval
Culture*. Cambridge: Cambridge University Press.

Carter, Harry, and Herbert Davis, eds. 1962. *Mechanick Exercises on the Whole
Art of Printing. By Joseph Moxon* (1683–1684). 2nd ed. Oxford: Oxford
University Press.

Carter, John, and Graham Pollard. 1934. *An Enquiry into the Nature of Certain
Nineteenth-Century Pamphlets*. London: Constable. 2nd ed. Ed. Nicholas
Barker and John Collins. London: Scolar, 1983.

Casson, Lionel. 2001. *Libraries in the Ancient World*. New Haven, Conn.: Yale
University Press.

Casti, John L. 1995. *Complexification: Explaining a Paradoxical World through
the Science of Surprise*. New York: Harper.

Caws, Mary Ann. 1986. "The Conception of Engendering: The Erotics of Editing." In *The Poetics of Gender*, ed. Nancy K. Miller. New York: Columbia
University Press.

CCC Information Services, Inc. v. MacLean Hunter Market Reports, Inc.
1994. U.S. Court of Appeals, Second Circuit, No. 1312, Docket 93-7687, 5
Dec.

Center for Editions of American Authors. 1972. *Statement of Editorial Principles and Procedures*. Rev. ed. New York: MLA.

Center for/Committee on Scholarly Editions. 1977. *An Introductory Statement*. New York: MLA.

———. 1991. *Guidelines*. Rev. ed. New York: MLA. Rpt. in *Electronic Textual Editing*, ed. Lou Barnard, Katherine O'Brien O'Keefe, and John Unsworth. New York: MLA, 2006.

Cerha, Friedrich. 1979. "The Third Act of Alban Berg's *Lulu*," trans. Paul Griffiths. Pierre Boulez, cond. Deutsche Grammaphon: 9–10.

Cerquiglini, Bernard. 1989. *Éloge de la variante: Histoire critique de la philologie*. Paris: Seuil. Translated as *In Praise of the Variant: A Critical History of Philology*, trans. Betsy Wing. Baltimore, Md.: Johns Hopkins University Press, 1999.

Chadwick, Henry. 1993. "To Be or Not to Be." *Times Literary Supplement* 24 Dec.

Chambers, Suzanna. 1998. "Pope Bans British Nun's Book about Women Priests." *Independent on Sunday* 9 Aug.: 9.

Chandler, James K., Arnold I. Davidson, and Harry D. Harootunian, eds. 1993. *Questions of Evidence*. Chicago: University of Chicago Press.

Channell, David F. 1991. *The Valid Machine: A Study of Technology and Organic Life*. New York: Oxford University Press.

Chartier, Roger. 1994. "Libraries without Walls." In *The Order of Books: Readers, Authors, and Libraries in Europe between the Fourteenth and Eighteenth Centuries*, trans. Lydia G. Cochrane. Stanford, Calif.: Stanford University Press.

———. 2005. "Crossing Borders in Early Modern Europe: Sociology of Texts and Literature," trans. Maurice Elton. *Book History* 8: 37–50.

Christianson, C. Paul. 1989. "Evidence for the Study of London's Late Medieval Manuscript Book Trade." In *Book Production and Publishing in Britain, 1375–1475*, ed. Jeremy Griffiths and Derek Pearsall. Cambridge: Cambridge University Press.

Cixous, Hélène. 1991. *"Coming to Writing" and Other Essays*. Cambridge, Mass.: Harvard University Press.

Cockram, Patricia. 1999. "Ezra Pound's Italian Cantos: Collapse and Recall." Ph.D. diss., City University of New York Graduate Center. CD-ROM.

Cohen, Noam. 2008. "Link by Link." *New York Times* 1 Sept.: C3.

Cohen, Philip, ed. 1991. *Devils and Angels: Textual Editing and Literary Theory*. Charlottesville: University Press of Virginia.

———. 1997. *Texts and Textuality: Textual Instability, Theory, and Interpretation*. New York: Garland.

Colbert, Stephen. 2005–. *The Colbert Report*. Comedy Central.

Coleridge, Samuel Taylor. 1983. "Biographia Literaria." In *Collected Works of Samuel Taylor Coleridge,* ed. James Engell and W. Jackson Bate. Princeton, N.J.: Princeton University Press.

Cook, Don L. 1981. "The Short, Happy Thesis of G. Thomas Tanselle." *Newsletter of the Association for Documentary Editing* 3.1: 1–4.

Cook, Elizabeth, ed. 1990. *John Keats*. Oxford: Oxford University Press.

Cooke, Deryck. 1968. *An Introduction to "Der Ring des Nibelungen."* London: Decca Records.

Coppola, Francis Ford, dir. 1972. *The Godfather*. Paramount.

———. 1979. *Apocalypse Now*. Zoetrope.

Copyright Act. 1976. 17 U.S.C. sec. 101.

"The Copy-right Law." 1838. *Monthly Review* 145: 52–63.

Corigliano, John, and William Hoffman. 1991. *The Ghosts of Versailles*. Metropolitan Opera, New York.

Cosgrove, Peter W. 1991. "Undermining the Text: Edward Gibbon, Alexander Pope, and the Anti-Authenticating Footnote." In *Annotation and Its Texts,* ed. Stephen Barney. Oxford: Oxford University Press.

Crane, Elaine Forman. 1988. "Gender Consciousness in Editing: The Diary of Elizabeth Drinker." *Text* 4: 375–84.

Culler, Jonathan. 1982. "Reading as a Woman." In Culler, *On Deconstruction: Theory and Practice after Structuralism*. Ithaca, N.Y.: Cornell University Press.

———. 1990. "Antifoundational Philology." In *On Philology,* ed. Jan Ziolkowski. University Park: Pennsylvania State University Press.

Dane, Joseph A. 2003. *The Myth of Print Culture: Essays on Evidence, Textuality, and Bibliographical Method*. Toronto: University of Toronto Press.

Danziger, Marlies K., and Wendell Stacy Johnson, eds. 1968. *A Poetry Anthology*. New York: Random House.

Davidson, Donald. 1978. "What Metaphors Mean." *Critical Inquiry* 5: 31–47.

Davies, Peter Maxwell. 1969. *St. Thomas Wake: Foxtrot for Orchestra on a Pavan by John Bull*. Peter Maxwell Davies, cond. BBC Philharmonic Orchestra. MaxOpusMusic.

———. 1972. *Taverner*. Covent Garden, London.

———. 1987. *Resurrection*. Darmstadt Stadtstheater, 18 Sept.

Davison, Peter. 1977. "The Selection and Presentation of Bibliographical Evidence." *Analytical and Enumerative Bibliography* 1: 101–36.

Davison, Peter, ed. 1992. *The Book Encompassed: Studies in Twentieth-Century Bibliography*. Cambridge: Cambridge University Press.

Dearing, Vinton. 1974. *Principles and Practice of Textual Analysis.* Berkeley: University of California Press.

Deforest, Peter. 1983. *Forensic Science: An Introduction to Criminalistics.* New York: McGraw-Hill.

de Grazia, Margreta. 1992. "Sanctioning Voice: Quotation Marks, the Abolition of Torture, and the Fifth Amendment." In *Intellectual Property and the Construction of Authorship,* special issue of *Cardozo Arts & Entertainment Law Journal* 10: 545–66.

de Tienne, André. 1996. "Selecting Alterations for the Apparatus of a Critical Edition." *Text* 9: 33–62.

Delany, Paul. 1979. "Letters of the Artist as a Young Man." *New York Times Book Review,* 9 Sept.: 44. Review of *The Letters of D. H. Lawrence,* vol. 1, ed. James T. Boulton. Cambridge: Cambridge University Press.

Deleuze, Gilles. 1968. *Difference and Repetition,* trans. Paul Patton. New York: Columbia University Press.

Deleuze, Gilles, and Félix Guattari. 1987. *A Thousand Plateaus,* vol. 2 of *Capitalism and Schizophrenia,* trans. Brian Massumi. Minneapolis: University of Minnesota Press.

DeLillo, Don. 1997. *Underworld.* New York: Scribner, 1997.

de Man, Paul. 1979. *Allegories of Reading: Figural Language in Rousseau, Nietzsche, Rilke, and Proust.* New Haven, Conn.: Yale University Press.

———. 1986a. "The Resistance to Theory." In de Man, *The Resistance to Theory.* Minneapolis: University of Minnesota Press.

———. 1986b. "The Return to Philology." In de Man, *The Resistance to Theory.* Minneapolis: University of Minnesota Press.

Deppman, Jed, Daniel Ferrer, and Michael Groden, eds. 2004. *Genetic Criticism: Texts and Avant-textes.* Philadelphia: University of Pennsylvania Press.

Derrida, Jacques. 1979. "Living On/Border Lines," trans. James Hulbert. Rpt. in Harold Bloom et al., *Deconstruction and Criticism.* New York: Continuum, 2004.

———. 1988. *Limited Inc.,* trans. Samuel Weber and Jeffrey Mehlman. Evanston, Ill.: Northwestern University Press.

———. 1991. "This Is Not an Oral Footnote." In *Annotation and Its Texts,* ed. Stephen Barney. New York: Oxford University Press.

———. 1996. *Archive Fever: A Freudian Impression,* trans. Eric Prenowitz. Chicago: University of Chicago Press.

Dery, Mark. 1992. "Cyberculture." *South Atlantic Quarterly* 91.3 (Summer): 501–24.

DeSalvo, Louise A. 1979. "Sorting, Sequencing, and Dating the Drafts of Virginia Woolf's *The Voyage Out.*" *Bulletin of the New York Public Library* 82 (Autumn).

DeSalvo, Louise A., ed. 1982. *Melymbrosia: An Early Version of "The Voyage Out."* New York: New York Public Library.

Dinnage, Rosemary. 1979. "Dodgson's Passion." *New York Review of Books* 16 Apr.: 10. Review of *The Letters of Lewis Carroll,* ed. Morton N. Cohen. Oxford: Oxford University Press, 1979.

Disclosure. 1994. Barry Levinson, dir. Warner Bros.

Documentary Editing. 1979–.

Dodgson, Charles Lutwidge [Lewis Carroll]. 1871. "The Walrus and the Carpenter." In Lewis Carroll, *Through the Looking Glass and What Alice Found There.* London: Macmillan.

———. 1876. *The Hunting of the Snark.* London: Macmillan.

Donaldson, E. Talbot. 1970. "The Psychology of Editors of Middle English Texts." In Donaldson, *Speaking of Chaucer.* New York: Norton.

Donaldson, E. Talbot, ed. 1962. *The Norton Anthology of English Literature.* New York: Norton.

Dooley, Allan C. 1992. *Author and Printer in Victorian England.* Charlottesville: University Press of Virginia.

Dreyfus, John. 1996. "The Kelmscott Press." In *William Morris,* ed. Lynda Parry. London: Philip Wilson/Victoria and Albert Museum.

Drinker, Elizabeth. 1889. *Extracts from the Journal of Elizabeth Drinker,* ed. Henry D. Biddle. Philadelphia: Lippincott.

Drucker, Johanna. 2006. "Graphical Readings and the Visual Aesthetics of Textuality." *Text* 16: 267–76.

Dryden, John. 1700. *Fables Ancient and Modern.* London: Tonson.

Duff, Gordon E. 1886, 1970. *Early English Printing . . . Facsimiles of All Types Used in England during the XV Century.* London: Kegan Paul; and New York: Franklin.

Duggan, Hoyt N. 1993. "The Electronic *Piers Plowman B*: A New Diplomatic-Critical Edition." *Æstel* 1: 55–75.

———. 1994. The *"Piers Plowman" Electronic Archive.* http://jefferson.village .virginia.edu/seenet/piers/archivegoals.htm

Eastman, Arthur M., et al., eds. 1970. *The Norton Anthology of Poetry.* New York: Norton.

Eaves, Morris. 1994. "Why Don't They Leave It Alone? Speculations on the Authority of Audience in Editorial Theory." In *Cultural Artifacts and the Production of Meaning: The Page, the Image, and the Body,* ed. Margaret

J. M. Ezell and Katherine O'Brien O'Keefe. Ann Arbor: University of Michigan Press.

Ecdotica. 2004–. Alma Mater Studiorum. Università di Bologna/Centro para la Edición de los Clásicos Españoles.

Echard, Siân, and Stephen Partridge, eds. 2004. *The Book Unbound: Editing and Reading Medieval Manuscripts and Texts.* Toronto: University of Toronto Press.

Eco, Umberto. 1983. *The Name of the Rose,* trans. William Weaver. New York: Harcourt Brace Jovanovich.

———. 1986. *Travels in Hyperreality,* trans. William Weaver. New York: Harcourt Brace.

Eco, Umberto, et al. 1973. *Il nouvo medioevo.* Milan: Bompiani.

Edwards, A. S. G. 1995. "Middle English Literature." In *Scholarly Editing: A Guide to Research,* ed. D. C. Greetham. New York: MLA.

Eggert, Paul. 1994. "Document and Text: The 'Life' of a Literary Work and the Capacities of Editing." *Text* 7: 1–24.

———. 1998. "The Work Unravelled." *Text* 11: 41–60.

Eggert, Paul, and Margaret Sankey, eds. 1997. *The Editorial Gaze: Mediating Texts in Literature and the Arts.* New York: Garland.

Encyclopaedia Britannica. 1998–. CD-ROM.

Epstein, Joseph. 1993. "Too Relevant by Half." Review of *The Columbia Dictionary of Quotations,* ed. Robert Andrews. *Times Literary Supplement* 10 Dec.: 9.

Erasmus, Desiderius. 1516. *Novum Instrumentum omne.* Basel: Frobel.

Erdman, David V. 1966. "The Signature of Style." In *Evidence for Authorship: Essays on Problems of Attribution,* ed. David V. Erdman and Ephim G. Fogel. Ithaca, N.Y.: Cornell University Press.

Erdman, David V., and Ephim G. Fogel, eds. 1966. *Evidence for Authorship: Essays on Problems of Attribution.* Ithaca, N.Y.: Cornell University Press.

Ess, Charles. 1994. "The Political Computer: Hypertext, Democracy, and Habermas." In *Hyper/Text/Theory,* ed. George Landow. Baltimore, Md.: Johns Hopkins University Press.

Fabricius, Johann. 1697. *Bibliotheca latina.* Venice, Italy: S. Coleti.

———. 1705–1726. *Bibliotheca græca.* Hamburg, Germany: C. Leibzeit.

———. 1713. *Bibliotheca antiquaria.* Hamburg, Germany: C. Leibzeit.

———. 1734–1736. *Bibliotheca latinæ mediæ et infimæ æetis.* Hamburg, Germany: C. Leibzeit.

Fantham, Elaine. 1989. *The Cambridge History of Literary Criticism: Classical Criticism.* Cambridge: Cambridge University Press.

Faulkner, Peter. 1980. *Against the Age: An Introduction to William Morris.* Boston: Allen, Unwin.

Faulkner, William. 1986. *Absalom, Absalom! The Corrected Text,* ed. Noel Polk. New York: Random House.

Feather, John. 1986. *A Dictionary of Book History.* New York: Oxford University Press.

———. 1992. "From Rights in Copies to Copyright: The Recognition of Authors' Rights in English Law and Practice in the Sixteenth and Seventeenth Centuries." In *Intellectual Property and the Construction of Authorship,* special issue of *Cardozo Arts & Entertainment Law Journal* 10: 455–76.

Feist Publications, Inc. v. Rural Telephone Service Co., Inc. 499 U.S. 340 (1991), No. 89-1909. 27 Mar. http://caselaw.lp.findlaw.com/scripts/getcase. pl?court=us&vol=499&invol=340.

Ferguson, Alfred R., et al., eds. 1971–. *The Collected Works of Ralph Waldo Emerson.* Cambridge, Mass.: Belknap.

Fineman, Joel. 1989. "The History of the Anecdote: Fiction and Fiction." In *The New Historicism,* ed. H. Aram Veeser. New York: Routledge.

Finneran, Richard J., ed. 1996. *The Literary Text in the Digital Age.* Ann Arbor: University of Michigan Press.

Finneran, Richard J., et al., eds. 1982–. *The Cornell Yeats.* Ithaca, N.Y.: Cornell University Press.

Firestone, David. 1993. "While Barbie Talks Tough, G.I. Joe Goes Shopping." *New York Times* 31 Dec.

Fish, Stanley. 1980. "Interpreting the Variorum." In Fish, *Is There a Text in This Class? The Authority of Interpretive Communities.* Cambridge, Mass.: Harvard University Press.

———. 1989a. "Being Interdisciplinary Is So Very Hard to Do." *Profession* 89: 15–22.

———. 1989b. *Doing What Comes Naturally: Change, Rhetoric, and the Practice of Theory in Literary and Legal Studies.* Durham, N.C.: Duke University Press.

———. 1995. "Rhetoric." In *Critical Terms for Literary Study,* ed. Frank Lentricchia and Thomas McLaughlin. 2nd ed. Chicago: University of Chicago Press.

Fisher, John H., ed. 1977. *The Complete Poetry and Prose of Geoffrey Chaucer.* New York: Holt, Rinehart.

Fleischman, Suzanne. 1990. "Philology, Linguistics, and the Discourse of the Medieval Text." *Speculum* 65: 19–37.

Foley, John Miles. 1984. "Editing Oral Epic Texts: Theory and Practice." *Text* 1: 75–94, 107–16.

———. 1995. "Folk Literature." In *Scholarly Editing: A Guide to Research,* ed. D. C. Greetham. New York: MLA.

Ford, J. Massyngberde, ed. 1975. *The Anchor Bible*. Garden City, N.Y.: Doubleday.

Foucault, Michel. 1972a. *The Archeology of Knowledge and the Discourse on Language,* trans. A. M. Sheridan Smith. New York: Pantheon.

———. 1972b. "Change and Transformation." In Foucault, *The Archeology of Knowledge and the Discourse on Language,* trans. A. M. Sheridan Smith. New York: Pantheon.

———. 1980. *Power/Knowledge,* ed. Colin Gordon. New York: Pantheon.

———. 1984. "What Is an Author?" trans. Josue V. Harari. In *Textual Strategies: Perspectives in Post-Structuralist Criticism,* ed. Josue V. Harari. Ithaca, N.Y.: Cornell University Press, 1979. Rpt. in Paul Rabinowitz, ed., *The Foucault Reader.* New York: Pantheon (citations in the text to this edition).

———. 1990. *The History of Sexuality,* trans. Robert Hurley. New York: Random House/Vintage.

Foulet, Alfred, and Mary B. Speer. 1979. *On Editing Old French Texts.* Lawrence: Regents Press of Kansas.

Fowler, David C. 1977. "A New Edition of the B Text of *Piers Plowman.*" *Yearbook of English Studies* 1: 23–42.

Fowles, John. 1969. *The French Lieutenant's Woman.* Boston: Little, Brown.

———. 1985. *A Maggot.* Boston: Little, Brown.

Fraistat, Neil, and Steven E. Jones. 2002. "Immersive Textuality: The Editing of Virtual Spaces." *Text* 15: 69–82.

Frank, Anne. 1989. *The Diary of Anne Frank: The Critical Edition.* Garden City, N.Y.: Doubleday.

———. 1992. *Diary of a Young Girl: The Definitive Edition.* Garden City, N.Y.: Doubleday.

Frantzen, Allen J. 1991. *The Desire for Origins: New Language, Old English, and Teaching the Tradition.* New Brunswick, N.J.: Rutgers University Press.

Frese, Dolores Warwick, and Katherine O'Brien O'Keeffe, eds. 1997. *The Book and the Body.* Notre Dame, Ind.: University of Notre Dame Press.

Freud, Sigmund. 1965. *The Psychopathology of Everyday Life,* trans. Alan Tyson, ed. James Strachey. New York: Norton.

Friedman, Albert B., ed. 1956. *The Viking Book of Folk-Ballads of the English-Speaking World.* New York: Viking.

Froula, Christine. 1986. "Out of the Chrysalis: Female Initiation and Female Authority in Virginia Woolf's *The Voyage Out.*" *Tulsa Studies in Women's Literature* 5.1 (Spring): 63–90.

Frow, John. 2007. "The Practice of Value." *Textual Cultures: Texts, Contexts, Interpretation* 2.2: 61–76.

Frye, Northrop. 1957. *Anatomy of Criticism: Four Essays.* Princeton, N.J.: Princeton University Press.

Fugmann, Nicole. 1997. "Contemporary Editorial Theory and the Transvaluation of Postmodern Critique." *Text* 10: 15–30.

Furness, H. H., ed. 1966. *The Tempest: New Variorum.* New York: Dover.

Gabler, Hans Walter. 1984. "The Synchrony and Diachrony of Texts: Practice and Theory of the Critical Edition of James Joyce's *Ulysses.*" *Text* 1: 305–26.

———. 1985. "A Response to John Kidd: 'Errors of Execution in the 1984 *Ulysses.*'" Paper presented at the Society for Textual Scholarship conference, 26 Apr. Rpt. in *Studies in the Novel: A Special Issue on Editing "Ulysses"* 22 (Summer 1990): 250–56.

———. 1987. "The Text as Process and the Problem of Intentionality." *Text* 3: 107–116.

———. 1991. "Unsought Encounters." In *Devils and Angels: Textual Editing and Literary Theory,* ed. Philip Cohen. Charlottesville: University Press of Virginia.

———. 1993. "What *Ulysses* Requires." *Papers of the Bibliographical Society of America* 87: 187–248.

Gardner, John. 1971. *Grendel.* New York: Knopf.

———. 1976. *October Light.* New York: Knopf.

Gaskell, Philip. 1972, 1985. *A New Introduction to Bibliography.* Oxford: Oxford University Press.

———. 1978. *From Writer to Reader: Studies in Editorial Method.* Oxford: Clarendon.

Gaskell, Philip, and Clive Hart. 1989. *"Ulysses": A Review of Three Texts: Proposals for Alterations in the Texts of 1922, 1961, and 1984.* Gerrards Cross, England: Colin Smythe.

Gaumer, M. C. 1971. "John Trevisa's Translation of the *De Proprietatibus Rerum* of Bartholomaeus Anglicus: An Edition of the Plimpton Manuscript." Ph.D. diss., University of Washington.

Geertz, Clifford. 1973. *The Interpretation of Cultures.* New York: Basic.

———. 1983. *Local Knowledge: Further Essays in Interpretive Anthropology.* New York: Basic.

Gell-Mann, Murray. 1994. *The Quark and the Jaguar: Adventures in the Simple and the Complex.* New York: Freeman.

Gellrich, Jesse M. 1985. *The Idea of the Book in the Middle Ages: Language Theory, Mythology, and Fiction.* Ithaca, N.Y.: Cornell University Press.

Gesner, Konrad. 1545. *Bibliotheca universalis.* Zurich: Froschauer. Rpt., Osnabruck: Zeller, 1966.

Ginzburg, Carlo. 1986. *Clues, Myths, and the Historical Method,* trans. John Tedeschi and Anne C. Tedeschi. Baltimore, Md.: Johns Hopkins University Press.

Glaberson, William. 2008. "Evidence Faulted in Detainee Case: Court Rejects Finding of 'Enemy Combatant.'" *New York Times* 1 July: A1.

Glavin, John. 1988. "Bulgakov's Lizard and the Problem of the Playwright's Authority." *Text* 4: 385–406.

Goldberg, Jonathan. 1990. *Writing Matter: From the Hands of the English Renaissance.* Stanford, Calif.: Stanford University Press.

———. 1997. "Under the Covers with Caliban." In *The Margins of the Text,* ed. D. C. Greetham. Ann Arbor: University of Michigan Press.

Goldstein, Paul. 2003. *Copyright's Highway: From Gutenberg to the Celestial Jukebox.* Stanford, Calif.: Stanford University Press.

Goodheart, Eugene. 1991. "Censorship and Self-Censorship in the Fiction of D. H. Lawrence." In *Representing Modernist Texts: Editing as Interpretation,* ed. George Bornstein. Ann Arbor: University of Michigan Press.

Goodman, Nelson. 1969. *Languages of Art: An Approach to a Theory of Symbols.* Indianapolis, Ind.: Bobbs-Merrill.

———. 1984. *Of Mind and Other Matters.* Cambridge, Mass.: Harvard University Press.

Google Books Library Project. http://books.google.com/googlebooks/library.html.

Google Library Partners. http://books.google.com/googlebooks/partners.html.

Gore, Al. 2007. *The Assault on Reason.* London: Penguin.

Gossett, Philip. 1995. "Knowing the Score: Italian Opera as Work and Play." Society for Textual Scholarship Presidential Address, 1993. *Text* 8: 1–24.

———. 2006. *Divas and Scholars: Performing Italian Opera.* Chicago: University of Chicago Press.

Gossett, Suzanne. 1996. "Why Should a Woman Edit a Man?" *Text* 9: 111–18.

Gould, Stephen Jay. 1996. "Triumph of the Root-Heads." *Natural History* 105: 10–17.

Gove, Philip B., ed. 1961. *Webster's Third New International Dictionary of the English Language, Unabridged.* Springfield, Mass.: Merriam-Webster.

Gracia, Jorge J. E. 1995. *A Theory of Textuality.* Albany: State University of New York Press.

———. 2000. *The Metaphysics of Texts: Ontological Status, Identity, Author, and Audience.* Albany: State University of New York Press.

Graff, Gerald. 1992. "The Scholar in Society." In *Introduction to Scholarship in Modern Languages and Literatures,* ed. Joseph Gibaldi. 2nd ed. New York: MLA.

Grafton, Anthony. 1990. *Forgers and Critics: Creativity and Duplicity in Western Scholarship*. Princeton, N.J.: Princeton University Press.

———. 1997a. "Is the History of Reading a Marginal Enterprise? Guillaume Budé and His Books." *Papers of the Bibliographical Society of America* 91: 139–58.

———. 1997b. *The Footnote: A Curious History*. Cambridge, Mass.: Harvard University Press.

———. 2009. *Worlds Made by Words: Scholarship and Community in the Modern West*. Cambridge, Mass.: Harvard University Press.

Greenberg, Clement. 1980a. "Modern and Postmodern." *Arts Magazine* 54: 64–66.

———. 1980b. *The Notion of the "Post-modern."* Sydney, Australia: Bloxham.

Greetham, David. 1975. *On the Properties of Things: John Trevisa's Translation of Bartholomaeus Anglicus' De Proprietatibus Rerum (XV)*. 2 vols. Oxford: Clarendon. Vol. 3, 1989.

———. 1981. "The Concept of Nature in Bartholomaeus Anglicus." *Journal of the History of Ideas* 41: 663–77.

———. 1984. "Models for the Textual Transmission of Translation: The Case of John Trevisa." *Studies in Bibliography* 37: 131–55.

———. 1985. "Normalisation of Accidentals in Middle English Texts: The Paradox of Thomas Hoccleve." *Studies in Bibliography* 38: 120–50.

———. 1987a. "Challenges of Theory and Practice in the Editing of Hoccleve's *Regement of Princes*." In *Manuscripts and Texts: Editorial Problems in Later Middle English Literature*, ed. Derek Pearsall. Cambridge: Boydell and Brewer.

———. 1987b. "A Suspicion of Texts." *Thesis* 2.1: 18–25.

———. 1988. "The Place of Fredson Bowers in Mediaeval Editing." *Papers of the Bibliographical Society of America* 82: 53–69.

———. 1989. "Self-Referential Artifacts: Hoccleve's Persona as a Literary Device." *Modern Philology* 86: 242–51.

———. 1991a. "The Manifestation and Accommodation of Theory in Textual Editing." In *Devils and Angels: Textual Editing and Literary Theory*, ed. Philip Cohen. Charlottesville: University Press of Virginia.

———. 1991b. "[Textual] Criticism and Deconstruction." *Studies in Bibliography* 44: 1–30.

———. 1992a. "Enlarging the Text." *Review* 14: 1–33.

———. 1992b. "Textual Scholarship." In *Introduction to Scholarship in Modern Languages and Literatures*, ed. Joseph Gibaldi. 2nd ed. New York: MLA.

———. 1992c. *Textual Scholarship: An Introduction*. New York: Garland.

———. 1993a. "Contemporary Editorial Theory: From Modernism to Post-Modernism." In *Palimpsest: Editorial Theory in the Humanities*, ed. George

Bornstein and Ralph G. Williams. Ann Arbor: University of Michigan Press.

———. 1993b. *Review of The Book Encompassed: Studies in Twentieth-Century Bibliography,* ed. Peter Davison. *Analytical and Enumerative Bibliography,* new ser., 7: 216–22.

———. 1994. "'Copy/Right,©' or 'How to Do Things with Searle and Derrida.'" Paper presented at conference on Literary Theory and the Practice of Editing, Liverpool, July 1993, and Canberra, Apr. 1994.

———. 1995a. "Getting Personal/Going Public." Review of Donald H. Reiman, *The Study of Modern Manuscripts: Public, Confidential, and Private.* Baltimore, Md.: Johns Hopkins University Press, 1993. *Review* 7: 225–52.

———. 1995b. "If That Was Then, Is This Now?" *Studies in the Novel* 27: 427–50.

———. 1996a. "Parallel Texts." *Text* 9: 408–29.

———. 1996b. "Phylum-Tree-Rhizome." In *Reading from the Margins: Textual Studies, Chaucer, and Medieval Literature,* ed. Seth Lerer. San Marino, Calif.: Huntington Library Press.

———. 1996c. "Rights to Copy." Rpt. in Greetham, *Textual Transgressions: Essays toward the Construction of a Biobibliography.* New York: Garland, 1998.

———. 1996d. "The Telephone Directory and Dr. Seuss: Scholarly Editing after *Feist v. Rural Telephone.*" In *Editing the Literary Imagination,* ed. Tom Quirk, special issue of *Studies in the Literary Imagination* 29: 53–74.

———. 1996e. "Textual Forensics." *PMLA* 111 (Jan.): 32–51.

———. 1997a. "Copy/Right." Rpt. in Greetham, *Textual Transgressions: Essays toward the Construction of a Biobibliography.* New York: Garland, 1998.

———. 1997b. "Slips and Errors in Textual Criticism." Rpt. in Greetham, *Textual Transgressions: Essays toward the Construction of a Biobibliography.* New York: Garland, 1998.

———. 1997c. "Textual Imperialism and Post-Colonial Bibliography." Rpt. in Greetham, *Textual Transgressions: Essays toward the Construction of a Biobibliography.* New York: Garland, 1998.

———. 1997d. "Resistance to Philology." In *The Margins of the Text,* ed. D. C. Greetham. Ann Arbor: University of Michigan Press.

———. 1997e. "Postduction: 'Glosynge is a glorious thyng, certayn.'" In *A Guide to Editing Middle English,* ed. Douglas Moffat and Vincent McCarren. Ann Arbor: University of Michigan Press.

———. 1997f. "Reading in and around *Piers Plowman.*" In *Text and Textuality,* ed. Philip Cohen. New York: Garland.

———. 1997g. "Resistance to Philology" and "Uncanny Texts and the Science of Textuality." Papers presented at Symposium on Rationality, Trinity College, Hartford, Conn., Apr.

———. 1997h. """"What Does It Matter Who Is Speaking,' Someone Said, 'What Does It Matter Who Is Speaking'?"'" In *The Editorial Gaze,* ed. Paul Eggert and Margaret Sanger. New York: Garland.

———. 1998. *Textual Transgressions: Essays toward the Construction of a Biobibliography.* New York: Garland.

———. 1999a. "This Page Left Intnetionally Blank." *Review* 21: 221–56.

———. 1999b. *Theories of the Text.* Oxford: Oxford University Press.

———. 2002. "Contamination and/of Resistance." In *Never Would Birds' Song Be the Same: Essays on Early Modern and Modern Poetry in Honor of John Hollander,* ed. Jennifer Levin. New Haven, Conn.: Yale University Press/ Beinecke Library.

———. 2004a. "Against Millennialism: First and Last Words from the Cross." Society for Textual Scholarship Presidential Address, New York, Apr. 1999. *Text* 16: 1–53.

———. 2004b. "The Function of [Textual] Criticism at the Present Time." In *Voice, Text, and Hypertext at the Millennium,* ed. Raimonda Modiano, Leroy Searle, and Peter L. Shillingsburg. Seattle: University of Washington Press.

———. 2008. "Uncoupled; or, How I Lost My Author(s)." *Textual Cultures* 3.1: 44–55.

———. 2010. "Editing the Novel." In *The Blackwell Encyclopaedia of the Novel,* ed. Peter Logan. Oxford: Blackwell.

———. Forthcoming. ™*Copyright©.*

Greetham, David, ed. 1995. *Scholarly Editing: A Guide to Research.* New York: MLA.

———. 1997. *The Margins of the Text.* Ann Arbor: University of Michigan Press.

Greetham, David, and Alex Greetham. 2008. "Teenage Textualities." Paper presented at Society for Textual Scholarship conference, Boston Editorial Institute, Mar.

Greg, W. W. 1927. *The Calculus of Variants: An Essay on Textual Criticism.* Oxford: Clarendon.

———. 1939–1959. *Bibliography of the English Printed Drama to the Restoration.* London: Bibliographical Society.

———. 1950–1951. "The Rationale of Copy-Text." *Studies in Bibliography* 3: 19–36.

———. 1966. *Collected Papers,* ed. J. C. Maxwell. Oxford: Clarendon.

Grier, James. 1996. *The Critical Editing of Music: History, Method, and Practice.* Cambridge: Cambridge University Press.

Griffith, Virgil. 2008. *WikiScanner.* http://wikiscanner.virgil.gr.

Grigely, Joseph. 1991. "The Textual Event." In *Devils and Angels: Textual Editing and Literary Theory,* ed. Philip Cohen. Charlottesville: University Press of Virginia. Rpt. in Grigely, *Textualterity: Art, Theory, and Textual Criticism.* Ann Arbor: University of Michigan Press, 1995.

———. 1995a. *Textualterity: Art, Theory, and Textual Criticism.* Ann Arbor: University of Michigan Press.

———. 1995b. "Textual Eugenics." In Grigely, *Textualterity: Art, Theory, and Textual Criticism.* Ann Arbor: University of Michigan Press.

Gross, John. 1979. "The Wars of D. H. Lawrence." *New York Review of Books* 27 Sept.: 17. Review of *The Letters of D. H. Lawrence,* vol. 1, ed. James T. Boulton. Cambridge: Cambridge University Press, 1979.

Gross, John G. 1990. *The Rhetoric of Science.* Cambridge, Mass.: Harvard University Press.

Gutjahr, Paul C., and Megan L. Benton, eds. 2001. *Illuminating Letters: Typography and Literary Interpretation.* Boston: University of Massachusetts Press.

Haack, Susan. 1993. *Evidence and Enquiry: Towards Reconstruction in Epistemology.* Oxford: Blackwell.

———. 1996. *Deviant Logic, Fuzzy Logic: Beyond the Formalism.* Chicago: University of Chicago Press.

Habermas, Jürgen. 1970. "Toward a Theory of Communicative Competence." In *Patterns of Communicative Behavior,* ed. Hans Dreitzel. New York: Macmillan.

———. 1975. *Legitimation Crisis,* trans. Thomas McCarthy. Boston: Beacon.

———. 1984. *Theory of Communicative Action,* vol. 1, *Reason and the Rationalization of Society,* trans. Thomas McCarthy. Boston: Beacon.

———. 1987. *The Philosophical Discourse of Modernity,* trans. Frederick Lawrence. Cambridge, Mass.: MIT Press.

Haebler, Konrad. 1905–1924. *Typenrepertorium der Wiegendrucke.* 6 vols. Leipzig: Haupt.

Hanna, Ralph, III. 1991. "Annotation as Social Practice." In *Annotation and Its Texts,* ed. Stephen Barney. Oxford: Oxford University Press.

———. 1993. "Annotating *Piers Plowman.*" *Text* 6: 153–63.

Haraway, Donna. 1991. *Simians, Cyborgs and Women: The Reinvention of Nature.* New York: Routledge.

Harris, Kate. 1989. "Patrons, Buyers and Owners: The Evidence for Ownership, and the Role of Book Owners in Book Production and the Book

Trade." In *Book Production and Publishing in Britain, 1375–1475,* ed. Jeremy Griffiths and Derek Pearsall. Cambridge: Cambridge University Press.

Hay, Louis. 1987. "Genetic Editing, Past and Future: A Few Reflexions by a User." *Text* 3: 117–34.

———. 1988. "Does Text Exist?" *Studies in Bibliography* 41: 64–76.

Hayford, Harrison, Hershel Parker, and G. Thomas Tanselle, eds. 1968. *Typee: A Peep at Polynesian Life. By Herman Melville.* Evanston, Ill.: Northwestern University Press.

Hayles, N. Katherine. 2002. *Writing Machines.* Cambridge, Mass.: MIT Press.

———. 2005. *My Mother Was a Computer: Digital Subjects and Literary Texts.* Chicago: University of Chicago Press.

———. 2008. *Electronic Literature: New Horizons for the Literary.* Notre Dame, Ind.: University of Notre Dame Press.

Heffernan, Virginia. 2008. "Pixels at an Exhibition: Art, Mystery and the Meaning of YouTube." *New York Times Magazine* 18 May: 20. www .nytimes.com/2008/05/18/magazine/18wwln-medium-t.html?scp=1&sq= Virginia%20Heffernan%20Pixels%20at%20an%20Exhibition&st=cse.

Heiatt, A. Kent, and Constance Heiatt, eds. 1964. *Chaucer: Canterbury Tales.* New York: Benton.

Heim, Michael. 1993. *The Metaphysics of Virtual Reality.* New York: Oxford University Press.

Heine, Elizabeth. 1979. "The Earlier *Voyage Out:* Virginia Woolf's First Novel." *Bulletin of the New York Public Library* 8.2 (Autumn).

Hellinga, Lotte. 1998. "A Meditation on the Variety in Scale and Context in the Modern Study of the Early Printed Heritage." *Papers of the Bibliographical Society of America* 92: 401–26.

Higdon, David Leon. 2002. "The Concordance: Mere Index or Needful Census?" *Text* 15: 51–68.

Hill, Archibald. 1950–1951. "Some Postulates for Distributional Study of Texts." *Studies in Bibliography* 3: 63–95.

Hill, W. Speed. 1978. "The Calculus of Error; or, Confessions of a General Editor." *Modern Philology* 75: 247–60.

———. 1996. "Text as Scripture, Scripture as Text: The Case of Richard Hooker." *Text* 9: 93–110.

———. 1997. "Commentary on Commentary on Commentary." In *The Margins of the Text,* ed. D. C. Greetham. Ann Arbor: University of Michigan Press.

———. 2006. "From 'an Age of Editing' to a 'Paradigm Shift': An Editorial Retrospect." Society for Textual Scholarship Presidential Address, 2003. *Text* 16: 33–48.

Hinman, Charlton, ed. 1968. *The Norton Facsimile: The Shakespeare First Folio.* New York: Norton.

Hirsch, E. D. 1967. *Validity in Interpretation.* New Haven, Conn.: Yale University Press.

———. 1998. *Cultural Literacy: What Every American Needs to Know.* Rev. ed. New York: Vintage.

Hispalensis, Isidori. 1911. *Episcopi etymologiarum sive originum libri XX,* ed. W. M. Lindsay. Oxford: Clarendon.

Hitchcock, Alfred, dir. 1950. *Stage Fright.* Warner Bros.

Hjort, G. 1926. "The Good and Bad Quartos of *Romeo and Juliet* and *Love's Labour's Lost.*" *Modern Language Review* 21.2: 140–46.

Hockey, Susan. 2000. *Electronic Texts in the Humanities.* Oxford: Oxford University Press.

Hofstadter, Douglas. 1995. "On Computers, Creativity, Credit, Brain Mechanisms, and the Turing Test." In Hofstadter, *Fluid Concepts and Creative Analogies: Computer Models of the Fundamental Mechanisms of Thought.* New York: Basic.

Holderness, Graham, and Bryan Loughrey, eds. 1993. *The Tragicall Historie of Hamlet Prince of Denmark. By William Shakespeare.* Hemel Hempstead, England: Harvester Wheatsheaf.

Holtrop, J. W. 1857–1868. *Monuments typographiques des Pays-Bas au quinzième siècle.* 24 vols. Paris: Nijhoff.

Holzer, Jenny. 2008. *Projections.* Massachusetts Museum of Contemporary Art, North Adams.

Hooker, Richard. 1978–1998. *Folger Library Edition of the Works of Richard Hooker,* ed. W. Speed Hill et al. Cambridge, Mass.: Harvard University Press, 1978–1990; Binghamton, N.Y.: Medieval and Renaissance Texts and Studies, 1993–1998.

Horgan, John. 1994. "Trends in Physics: Particle Physics." *Scientific American* (Feb.): 97–99, 102–106.

Horkheimer, Max, and Theodor W. Adorno. 2002. *Dialectic of Enlightenment,* trans. Edmund Jephcott. Stanford, Calif.: Stanford University Press.

Housman, A. E. 1921. "The Application of Thought to Textual Criticism." *Proceedings of the Classical Association* 18: 67–84. Rpt. in *Selected Prose,* ed. John Carter. Cambridge: Cambridge University Press, 1961; in *Collected Poems and Selected Prose,* ed. Christopher Ricks. London: Allen Lane, 1988.

Howard-Hill, Trevor H. 1988. Review of D. F. McKenzie, *Bibliography and the Sociology of Texts* (1986). *Library,* 6th ser., 10: 151–58.

———. 1991. "Theory and Praxis in the Social Approach to Editing." *Text* 5: 31–46.

Hoyt, Clark. 2008. "When to Quote Those Potty Mouths." *New York Times* 13 July. http://www.nytimes.com/2008/07/13/opinion/13pubed.html?scp=2 0&sq=the+public+editor&st=nyt.

Hudson, Anne. 1977. "Middle English." In *Editing Medieval Texts: English, French, and Latin Written in England,* ed. A. G. Rigg. New York: Garland.

Hunt, Lynn, ed. 1989. *The New Cultural History.* Berkeley: University of California Press.

Hurlebusch, Klaus. 2000. "Understanding the Author's Compositional Method: Prolegomenon to a Hermeneutics of Genetic Writing." *Text* 13: 55–101.

Hussey, Maurice, ed. 1966. *The Merchant's Prologue and Tale.* Cambridge: Cambridge University Press.

Hutcheon, Linda. 1991. *A Theory of Parody: The Teachings of Twentieth-Century Art Forms.* New York: Routledge.

Intellectual Property and the Construction of Authorship. 1992. Special issue of *Cardozo Arts & Entertainment Law Journal* 10.

Irigary, Luce. 1985. *This Sex Which Is Not One,* trans. Catherine Porter. Ithaca, N.Y.: Cornell University Press.

Itzkoff, Dave. 2009a. "Did Shakespeare Write This? Computer Says Yes." *Arts Beat.* http://artsbeat.blogs.nytimes.com/2009/10/12/did-shakespeare-write-this-play-computer-says-yes/?scp=1&sq=Shakespeare%20 Edward%20III&st=cse.

———. 2009b. "No Doubt Sues Maker of Guitar Hero Games." *New York Times* 6 Nov.: C5.

Jackson, Heather. 2001. *Marginalia: Readers Writing in Texts.* New Haven, Conn.: Yale University Press.

Jackson, Michael. 1991. *Black or White.* MJJ Productions.

James, Jamie. 1994. "Classical Music: A Model T Fuels a Masterpiece." *New York Times* 20 Mar. http://query.nytimes.com/gst/fullpage.html?res=9D 0DE1D7103DF933A15750C0A962958260&sec=&spon=&&scp=12&sq=B erg%20Violin%20Concerto&st=cse.

Jameson, Fredric. 1991. *Postmodernism; or, The Cultural Logic of Late Capitalism.* Durham, N.C.: Duke University Press.

Jauss, Hans Robert. 1974. "Literary History as a Challenge to Literary Theory." In *New Directions in Literary History,* ed. Ralph Cohen. Baltimore, Md.: Johns Hopkins University Press.

Jenkins, Henry. 2006. *Convergence Culture: Where Old and New Media Collide.* New York. New York University Press.

Jerome, Saint. 1516, 1969. *Biblia Sacra iuxta Vulgatem Versionem,* ed. R. Weber et al. 2 vols. Stuttgart: Würtembergissche Bibelanstalt.

Jeweler, Robin. 2005. *The Google Book Search Project: Is Online Indexing a Fair Use under Copyright Law?* Congressional Research Service, Library of Congress. Order Code RS22356.

Johns, Adrian. 1998. *The Nature of the Book: Print and Knowledge in the Making.* Chicago: University of Chicago Press.

Johnson, George. 1996. "New Family Tree Is Constructed for Indo-European." *New York Times* 2 Jan.: B15.

Jones, Mark, ed. 1990. *Fake? The Art of Deception.* Berkeley: University of California Press.

Jones, Steven A. 2007. *The Meaning of Video Games: Gaming and Textual Strategies.* New York: Routledge.

Joseph, Gerhard. 1992. *Tennyson and the Text: The Weaver's Shuttle.* Cambridge: Cambridge University Press.

———. 1996. "Text versus Hypertext: Seeing the Victorian Object as in Itself It Really Is." Paper presented at MLA conference, Chicago. In *Knowing the Past: Victorian Literature and Culture,* ed. Suzy Anger. Ithaca, N.Y.: Cornell University Press, 2001.

———. 2009. "Re: Contamination." E-mail message. 27 Sept.

Joyce, James. 1964. *A Portrait of the Artist as a Young Man,* ed. Chester G. Anderson. New York: Viking.

———. 1984. *Ulysses: A Critical and Synoptic Edition,* ed. Hans Walter Gabler, with Wolfhard Steppe and Claus Melchior. New York: Garland.

———. 1986. *Ulysses: Corrected Text,* ed. Hans Walter Gabler. New York: Random House.

Kallberg, Jeffrey. 1990. "Are Variants a Problem? 'Composer's Intentions' in Editing Chopin." *Chopin Studies* 4: 257–67.

Kane, George. 1985. "The 'Z Version' of *Piers Plowman.*" *Speculum* 60: 910–30.

Kane, George, ed. 1960. *Piers Plowman: The A Version.* London: Athlone.

Kane, George, and E. Talbot Donaldson, eds. 1975. *Piers Plowman: The B Version.* London: Athlone.

Kastan, David Scott. 2001. *Shakespeare and the Book.* Cambridge: Cambridge University Press.

Kelemen, Erick, ed. 2009. *Textual Editing and Criticism: An Introduction.* New York: Norton.

Kenney, E. J. 1974. *The Classical Text: Aspects of Editing in the Age of the Printed Book.* Berkeley: University of California Press.

Kernan, Alvin. 1990. *The Death of Literature.* New Haven, Conn.: Yale University Press.

Kidd, John. 1985. "Errors of Execution in the 1984 *Ulysses*." Paper presented at Society for Textual Scholarship conference, New York City, 26 Apr. Rpt. in *Studies in the Novel* 22 (1990): 243–49.

———. 1988a. "An Inquiry into *Ulysses: The Corrected Text*." Papers of the Bibliographical Society of America 82.4: 411–584.

———. 1988b. "The Scandal of *Ulysses*." *New York Review of Books* 30 June: 32–39.

Kiernan, Kevin. 1996. *Beowulf and the Beowulf Manuscript*. Rev. ed. Ann Arbor: University of Michigan Press.

Kiernan, Kevin, ed. *The Electronic Beowulf*. www.uky.edu/?kiernan/BL/kportico.html.

Kimmelman, Burt. 1996. *The Poetics of Authorship in the Later Middle Ages: The Emergence of the Modern Literary Persona*. New York: Lang.

Kirkpatrick, David D. 2004. "A Call to 'Win This Culture War.'" *New York Times* 1 Sept. www.nytimes.com/2004/09/01/politics/campaign/01faith.html?scp=1&sq=Kirkpatrick,%20David%20Win%20This%20Culture%20War&st=cse.

Kirschenbaum, Matthew G. 2002. "Editing the Interface: Textual Studies and First Generation Electronic Objects." *Text* 14: 15–52.

———. 2008. *Mechanisms: New Media and the Forensic Imagination*. Cambridge, Mass.: MIT Press.

Kjørup, Søren. 1978. "Pictorial Speech Acts." *Erkenntnis* 12: 55–71.

Kline, Mary-Jo. 2008. *A Guide to Documentary Editing*. 3rd ed. Charlottesville: University Press of Virginia.

Knott, T. A., and David C. Fowler, eds. 1952. *Piers the Plowman: A Critical Edition of the A Version*. Baltimore, Md.: Johns Hopkins University Press.

Knowles, Richard. 1994. "Variorum Commentary." *Text* 6: 35–47.

Koepsell, David R. 2000. *The Ontology of Cyberspace: Law, Philosophy, and the Future of Intellectual Property*. Chicago: Open Court.

Kolb, David. 1994. "Socrates in the Labyrinth." In *Hyper/Text/Theory*, ed. George Landow. Baltimore, Md.: Johns Hopkins University Press.

Kozinn, Allan. 2008. "A Dark and Stormy Night, Played for All Its Drama." *New York Times* 20 May: E1. www.nytimes.com/2008/05/20/arts/music/20gerg.html?scp=2&sq=Allan%20Kozinn%20A%20Dark%20and%20Stormy%20Night&st=cse.

Kristeller, Paul Oskar. 1984. "The Lachmann Method: Merits and Limitations." *Text* 1: 11–20.

———. 1987. "Textual Scholarship and General Theories of History and Literature." *Text* 3: 1–9.

Kristeva, Julia. 1984. *Revolution in Poetic Language,* trans. Margaret Waller. New York: Columbia University Press.

Kugel, James L. 1997. *The Bible as It Was.* Cambridge, Mass.: Harvard University Press.

Kuhn, Thomas. 1970. *The Structure of Scientific Revolutions.* 2nd ed. Chicago: University of Chicago Press.

Kulenkampff, Jens. 1981. "Music Considered as a Way of Worldmaking." *Journal of Aesthetics and Art Criticism* 39: 254–58.

Landow, George. 1992, 1993, 2006. *Hypertext: The Convergence of Contemporary Critical Theory and Technology* (retitled in 2006 *Hypertext 3.0: Critical Theory and New Media in an Age of Globalization*). Baltimore, Md.: Johns Hopkins University Press.

Lanham, Richard. 1976. *The Motives of Eloquence.* New Haven, Conn.: Yale University Press.

———. 1989. "Convergent Pressures: Social, Technological, Theoretical." In *The Future of Doctoral Studies in English,* ed. Andrea Lunsford, Helene Moglen, and James F. Slevin. New York: MLA.

Latour, Bruno. 1987. *Science in Action: How to Follow Scientists and Engineers through Society.* Cambridge, Mass.: Harvard University Press.

———. 1999. *Pandora's Hope: Essays on the Reality of Scientific Studies.* Cambridge, Mass.: Harvard University Press.

Latour, Bruno, and Stephen Woolger. 1986. *Laboratory Life: The Construction of Scientific Facts.* Princeton, N.J.: Princeton University Press.

Lauter, Paul, ed. 1997. *Heath Anthology of American Literature.* 3rd ed. 2 vols. Boston: Houghton Mifflin.

Lavagnino, John. 1995. "Reading, Scholarship, and Hypertext Editions." *Text* 8: 109–24.

Lawler, Traugott. 1991. "Medieval Annotation: The Example of the Commentaries on Walter Map's *Dissuasio Valerii.*" In *Annotation and Its Texts,* ed. Stephen Barney. Oxford: Oxford University Press.

Lawrence, D. H. 1960. *Lady Chatterley's Lover.* Harmondsworth, England: Penguin.

Leader, Zachary. 1996. *Revision and Romantic Authorship.* Oxford: Oxford University Press.

Leff, Gordon. 1958. *Medieval Thought: St. Augustine to Ockham.* Harmondsworth, England: Penguin.

Leland, John. 1549. *The Laboryouse Journey and Serche of J. Leylande for Englandes Antiquities, Given of Hym as a Newe Gyfte to Kinge Henry the VIII.* London: J. Bale.

————. 1774. *Joannis Lelandi antiquarii De rebvs britannicis collectanea*. London: White.

Lennon, John. 1967. "I Am the Walrus." *Magical Mystery Tour*. Parlophone. http://en.wikipedia.org/wiki/I_Am_the_Walrus.

Lennon, John, and Paul McCartney. 1967. "A Day in the Life." *Sgt. Pepper's Lonely Hearts Club Band*. EMI.

Lerer, Seth 1991. "Medievalist Mayhem." *Times Literary Supplement* 4 Jan.: 17. Review of Malcolm Godden, *The Making of Piers Plowman* (1990).

————. 1996. *Literary History and the Challenge of Philology: The Legacy of Erich Auerbach*. Stanford, Calif.: Stanford University Press.

————. 2002. *Error and the Academic Self: The Scholarly Imagination, Medieval to Modern*. New York: Columbia University Press.

Lernout, Geert. 2002. "Genetic Criticism and Philology." *Text* 14: 53–76.

Lesk, Michael. 2005. *Understanding Digital Libraries*. 2nd ed. Amsterdam: Elsevier/Morgan Kaufmann.

Lessig, Lawrence. 1999. *Code and Other Laws of Cyberspace*. New York: Basic.

————. 2001. *The Future of Ideas: The Fate of the Commons in a Connected World*. New York: Random House.

————. 2008. *Remix: Making Art and Commerce Thrive in the Hybrid Economy*. New York: Penguin.

Levine, Robert. 2008. "Steal This Hook? D.J. Skirts Copyright Law." *New York Times* 7 Aug.: B1–5.

Levinson, Paul. 1997. *The Soft Edge: A Natural History and Future of the Information Revolution*. New York: Routledge.

Levy, Clifford J. 2008. "Russia Prevailed on the Ground, but Not in the Media." *New York Times* 22 Aug.: A9.

Levy, David M. 2001. *Scrolling Forward: Making Sense of Documents in the Digital Age*. New York: Arcade.

Library of America. 1982–. www.loa.org.

The Library: Transactions of the Bibliographical Society. 1892–. Bibliographical Society (London). www.bibsoc.org.uk/index.htm.

Listener. 1967. 28 Sept., 386/2.

Litman, Jessica. 2001. *Digital Copyright*. Amherst, N.Y.: Prometheus.

Lixačev, Dmitrij Sergeevič. 1983. *Tekstologija russkoj literatury X–XVII vekov*. Leningrad: Nauka.

Love, Harold. 1993. *Scribal Publication in Seventeenth-Century England*. Oxford: Clarendon.

Lucretius, Titus Carus [Titi Lucreti Cari]. 1947. *Titi Lucreti Cari De Rerum Natura Libri Sex*. 3 vols. Oxford: Oxford University Press.

Lyall, Sarah. 1994. "In *Catch-22* Sequel, Heller Brings Back Yossarian, Milo, et al." *New York Times* 16 Feb.: C13.

Lyotard, Jean-François. 1984. *The Postmodern Condition: A Report on Knowledge,* trans. Geoff Bennington and Brian Massumi. Minneapolis: University of Minnesota Press.

Maas, Paul. 1927. *Textkritik.* Leipzig: Teubner. Rev. ed., Leipzig: Teubner, 1950; 3rd ed., Leipzig, Germany: Teubner, 1956.

———. 1958. *Textual Criticism,* trans. Barbara Flower. Oxford: Clarendon.

Mabillon, Jean. 1709. *De re diplomatica libri sex in quibus quidquid ad veterum instrumentorum antiquitatem, materiam, scripturam et stilum: quidquid ad sigilla, monogrammata, subscriptiones ac notas chronologicas; quidquid inde ad antiquariam, historicam, forensemque disciplinam pertinet, explicatur et illustratur.* 2nd ed. Paris: Robustel.

Machan, Tim William. 1994. *Textual Criticism and Middle English Texts.* Charlottesville: University Press of Virginia.

———. 1995. "Speght's Works and the Invention of Chaucer." *Text* 8: 145–70.

MacLean, Gerald. 1987a. "An Edition of Poems on the Restoration." *Restoration* 11: 117–21.

———. 1987b. "What Is a Restoration Poem? Editing a Discourse, Not an Author." *Text* 3: 319–46.

———. 1995. "Literacy, Class, and Gender in Restoration England." *Text* 7: 177–95.

———. 1997. "What's Class Got to Do with It?" In *The Margins of the Text,* ed. D. C. Greetham. Ann Arbor: University of Michigan Press.

MacLean, Gerald, ed. 1999–2004. *The Return of the King: An Anthology of English Poems Commemorating the Stuart Restoration, 1660.* E-Text Center, Alderman Library. University of Virginia.

Maguire, Lauri E., and Thomas L. Berger, eds. 1998. *Textual Formations and Reformations.* Cranbury, N.J.: Associated University Presses.

Mahaffey, Vicki. 1991. "Intentional Error: The Paradox of Editing Joyce's *Ulysses.*" In *Representing Modernist Texts: Editing as Interpretation,* ed. George Bornstein. Ann Arbor: University of Michigan Press.

Mailloux, Steven. 1990. "Interpretation." In *Critical Terms for Literary Study,* ed. Frank Lentricchia and Thomas McLaughlin. Chicago: University of Chicago Press. 2nd ed., Chicago: University of Chicago Press, 1995.

Manjoo, Farhad. 2008. *True Enough: Learning to Live in a Post-Fact Society.* Hoboken, N.J.: Wiley.

Manly, J. M., and Edith Rickert. 1940. *The Text of the Canterbury Tales.* 8 vols. Chicago: University of Chicago Press. Ed. Roy Vance Ramsey. Lewiston, N.Y.: Mellen, 1994.

Marcum, Deanna B. 1998. "We Can't Save Everything." *New York Times* 6 July: A15.

Marotti, Arthur. 1993a. "Malleable and Fixed Texts: Manuscript and Printed Miscellanies and the Transmission of Lyric Poetry in the English Renaissance." In *New Ways of Looking at Old Texts: Papers of the Renaissance English Text Society,* ed. W. Speed Hill. Binghamton, N.Y.: Renaissance English Text Society/Medieval and Renaissance Texts and Studies.

———. 1993b. "Manuscript, Print, and the English Renaissance Lyric." In *New Ways of Looking at Old Texts: Papers of the Renaissance English Text Society,* ed. W. Speed Hill. Binghamton, N.Y.: Renaissance English Text Society/Medieval and Renaissance Texts and Studies.

Martin, Richard. 1981. "On Some Aesthetic Relations." *Journal of Aesthetics and Art Criticism* 39: 275–77.

Masters, Alexander. 1997. "An Irrational Number." Review of David Blatner, *The Joy of Pi.* London: Allen Lane/Penguin, 1997. *Times Literary Supplement* 12 Dec.: 28.

Mathijsen, Marita. 2002. "The Concept of Authorisation." *Text* 14: 77–90.

The Matrix. 1999. Andy Wachowski and Larry Wachowski, dirs. Warner Bros.

Max, D. T. 2006. "The Injustice Collector: Is James Joyce's Grandson Suppressing Scholarship?" *New Yorker* 19 June.

Mays, J. C. C. 1995. "Editing Coleridge in the Historicized Present." *Text* 8: 217–38.

McCauley, Kym. 2000. "Genealogy, History and Hypermedia Authorship." *Electronic Journal of Australian and New Zealand History.* http://www.jcu.edu.au/aff/history/conferences/virtual/mccauley.htm.

McGann, Jerome J. 1983. *A Critique of Modern Textual Criticism.* Chicago: University of Chicago Press. Rpt., Charlottesville: University Press of Virginia, 1992.

———. 1984. "Shall These Bones Live?" *Text* 1: 21–40.

———. 1985. "The Monks and the Giants: Textual and Bibliographical Studies and the Interpretation of Literary Works." In *Textual Criticism and Literary Interpretation,* ed. Jerome J. McGann. Chicago: University of Chicago Press.

———. 1990. "How to Read a Book." In *New Directions in Textual Studies,* ed. Dave Oliphant and Robin Bradford. Austin: University of Texas Press/Harry Ransom Humanities Research Center.

———. 1991a. "Theory, Literary Pragmatics, and the Editorial Horizon." Rpt. in McGann, *The Textual Condition.* Princeton, N.J.: Princeton University Press.

———. 1991b. "What Is Critical Editing?" *Text* 5: 15–30. Rpt. in McGann, *The Textual Condition*. Princeton, N.J.: Princeton University Press.

———. 1992. "Revision, Rewriting, Rereading; or, 'An Error [Not] in *The Ambassadors.*'" *American Literature* 64: 95–110.

———. 1993a. *Black Riders: The Visible Language of Modernism*. Princeton, N.J.: Princeton University Press.

———. 1993b. "The Case of *The Ambassadors* and the Textual Condition." In *Palimpsest: Editorial Theory in the Humanities*, ed. George Bornstein and Ralph G. Williams. Ann Arbor: University of Michigan Press.

———. 1993c. "Literature, Meaning, and the Discontinuity of Fact." *Modern Language Quarterly* 54: 165–69.

———. 1994. "The Complete Writings and Pictures of Dante Gabriel Rossetti: A Hypermedia Research Archive." *Text* 7: 95–105.

———. 1996. "The Rationale of HyperText." *Text* 9: 11–32.

———. 1997. "The Rationale of Hypertext." In *Electronic Text: Investigations in the Method and Theory of Computerized Textuality*, ed. Kathryn Sutherland. Oxford: Clarendon.

———. 1998. "Hideous Progeny, Rough Beasts: Editing as a Theoretical Pursuit." Society for Textual Scholarship Presidential Address, 1997. *Text* 11: 1–16.

———. 2001. *Radiant Textuality: Literature after the World Wide Web*. New York: Palgrave Macmillan.

———. 2002. "The Gutenberg Variations." *Text* 14: 1–14.

———. 2006. "From Text to Work: Digital Tools and the Emergence of the Social Text." *Text* 16: 49–62.

McGann, Jerome J., ed. *The Complete Writings and Pictures of Dante Gabriel Rossetti: A Hypermedia Archive*. www.rossettiarchive.org.

McGillivray, Murray. 1994a. "Creative Anachronism: Marx's Problem with Homer, Gadamer's Discussion of 'the Classical,' and Our Understanding of Older Literature." *New Literary History* 25: 399–413.

———. 1994b. "Towards a Post-Critical Edition: Theory, Hypertext, and the Presentation of Middle English Works." *Text* 7: 175–200.

McKenzie, D. F. 1969. "Printers of the Mind: Some Notes on Bibliographical Theories and Printing-House Practices." *Studies in Bibliography* 22: 1–75.

———. 1986. *Bibliography and the Sociology of Texts: The Panizzi Lectures*. London: British Library.

———. 1990. "Speech—Manuscript—Print." In *New Directions in Textual Studies*, ed. Dave Oliphant and Robin Bradford. Austin: University of Texas Press/Harry Ransom Humanities Research Center.

———. 1992. "The History of the Book." In *The Book Encompassed: Studies in Twentieth-Century Bibliography*, ed. Peter Davison. Cambridge: Cambridge University Press.

———. 1996. E-mail message. 7 June.

McLaverty, James. 1984a. "The Concept of Authorial Intention in Textual Criticism." *Library*, 6th ser., 6 (June): 121–38.

———. 1984b. "The Mode of Existence of Literary Works of Art: The Case of the Dunciad Variorum." *Studies in Bibliography* 37: 82–105.

———. 1991. "Issues of Identity and Utterance: An Intentionalist Response to 'Textual Instability.'" In *Devils and Angels: Textual Editing and Literary Theory*, ed. Philip Cohen. Charlottesville: University Press of Virginia.

McLeod, Randall. 1990. "From 'Tranceformations in the Text of *Orlando Furioso*.'" In *New Directions in Textual Studies*, ed. Dave Oliphant and Robin Bradford. Austin: University of Texas Press/Harry Ransom Humanities Research Center.

———. 1991. "Information on Information." *Text* 5: 240–81.

———. 1979. "Avail of Print." St. Louis Conference on Manuscript Studies.

McLeod, Randall, ed. 1994. *Crisis in Editing: Texts of the English Renaissance*. New York: AMS.

McLuhan, Marshall. 1965. *The Gutenberg Galaxy: The Making of Typographic Man*. Toronto: University of Toronto Press.

McNamara, Robert S., with Brian VanDeMark. 1995. *In Retrospect: The Tragedy and Lessons of Vietnam*. New York: Random House.

Meltzer, Françoise. 1994. *Hot Property: The Stakes and Claims of Literary Originality*. Chicago: University of Chicago Press.

Melville, Herman. 1988. *Moby-Dick; or, The Whale*. In *The Writings of Herman Melville*, ed. Harrison Hayford, G. Thomas Tanselle, and Hershel Parker. Chicago: Northwestern University Press/Newberry Library.

Mendelson, Edward. 1987. "The Fading Coal vs. the Gothic Cathedral; or, What to Do about an Author Both Forgetful and Deceased." *Text* 3: 409–16.

Merrell, Floyd. 1998. *Simplicity and Complexity: Pondering Literature, Science, and Painting*. Ann Arbor: University of Michigan Press.

Metzger, Bruce. 1992. *The Text of the New Testament: Its Transmission, Corruption, and Restoration*. 3rd ed. New York: Oxford University Press.

———. 1996. "Some Curious Bibles." Society for Textual Scholarship Presidential Address, 1995. *Text* 9: 1–10.

Meyer, Ann R. 1994. "Shakespeare's Art and the Texts of *King Lear*." *Studies in Bibliography* 47: 128–46.

Michaels, David. 2008. *Doubt Is Their Product: How Industry's Assault on Science Threatens Your Health.* Oxford: Oxford University Press.

Middleton, Anne. 1990. "Life in the Margins; or, What's an Annotator to Do?" In *New Directions in Textual Studies,* ed. Dave Oliphant and Robin Bradford. Austin: Harry Ransom Humanities Research Center/University of Texas Press.

Middleton, Thomas. 2007. *Complete Works,* ed. Gary Taylor et al. Oxford: Clarendon.

Migne, Jacques-Paul, ed. 1844–1855. *Patrologia Latina.* Paris: Garnier. http:// pld.chadwyck.com.

Miller, J. Hillis. 1979. "The Critic as Host." Rpt. in Harold Bloom et al., *Deconstruction and Criticism.* New York: Continuum, 2004.

———. 1986. "The Triumph of Theory, the Resistance to Reading, and the Question of the Material Base." MLA Presidential Address. *PMLA* 102: 281–91.

Miller, Judith, and Michael R. Gordon. 2002. "U.S. Says Hussein Intensifies Quest for A-Bomb Parts." *New York Times* 8 Sept. http://www .nytimes.com/2002/09/08/international/middleeast/08IRAQ. html?scp=9&sq=Judith%20Miller%20Weapons%20of%20Mass%20 Destruction&st=cse.

Miller, Mark Crispin. 1989. *Boxed In: The Culture of TV.* Evanston, Ill.: Northwestern University Press.

Miller, Nancy K. 1991. *Getting Personal: Feminist Occasions and Other Autobiographical Acts.* New York: Routledge.

Miller, Sarah Bryan. 1998. "When a Look Back Is a Step Forward." *New York Times* 12 July: AR14.

Minnis, A. J. 1988. *Medieval Theory of Authorship: Scholastic Attitudes in the Later Middle Ages.* Aldershot, England: Scolar.

Minnis, A. J., and Charlotte Brewer, eds. 1992. *Crux and Controversy in Middle English Textual Criticism.* Cambridge: Brewer.

Mitchell, W. J. T. 1986. *Iconology: Image, Text, Ideology.* Chicago: University of Chicago Press.

Mitchener, R. W. 1951. "Wynkyn de Worde's Use of the Plimpton Manuscript of *De Proprietatibus Rerum.*" *Library,* 5th ser., 6: 7–18.

Moffat, Douglas, and Vincent McCarren, eds. 1997. *A Guide to Editing Middle English.* Ann Arbor: University of Michigan Press.

Monumenta Germaniae historica inde ab anno Christi quingentesimo usque ad annum millesimum et quingentesimum. 1840–. Hanover: Impensis Bibliopolii Hahniani.

Moorman, Charles. 1975. *Editing the Middle English Manuscript.* Jackson: University Press of Mississippi.

Morris, William. 1898, 1969. *A Note by William Morris on His Aims in Founding the Kelmscott Press.* N.p.: published by author.

Morton, Herbert C. 1994. *The Story of Webster's Third: Philip Gove's Controversial Dictionary and Its Critics.* Cambridge: Cambridge University Press.

Mosser, Daniel W. 1994. "Reading and Editing *The Canterbury Tales:* Past, Present, and Future(?)." *Text* 7: 201–32.

Moulthrop, Stuart. 1994. "Rhizome and Resistance." In *Hyper/Text/Theory,* ed. George P. Landow. Baltimore, Md.: Johns Hopkins University Press.

Mozart, Wolfgang Amadeus. 1786. *Le Nozze di Figaro.* Burgtheater, Vienna.

Mumford, Lewis. 1968. "Emerson behind Barbed Wire." *New York Review of Books* 18 Jan.: 3–5.

The Muppet Movie. 1979. James Frawley, dir. Henson Associates/Incorporated Television Company/Associated Fill Distributors.

Murray, K. M. Elisabeth. 1977. *Caught in the Web of Words: James Murray and the Oxford English Dictionary.* New Haven, Conn.: Yale University Press.

Murry, John Middleton, ed. 1949. *The Poems and Verses of John Keats.* New York: Macmillan.

Mussorgsky, Modest. 1867. *Night on Bald Mountain,* arr. N. Rimsky-Korsakov, 1881.

———. 1874. *Pictures at an Exhibition,* arr. N. Rimsky-Korsakov, 1886; arr. M. Ravel, 1922.

Myerson, Joel. 1995. "Colonial and Nineteenth-Century American Literature." In *Scholarly Editing: A Guide to Research,* ed. D. C. Greetham. New York: MLA.

Naso, Publius Ovidius. 2001. *Metamorphoses,* trans. Horace Gregory. New York: Signet.

National Treasure. 2004. Jon Turteltaub, dir. Walt Disney Pictures.

Naudé, Gabriel. 1627. *Avis pour dresser une bibliothèque.* Paris: Tarya.

Needham, Paul. 1979. *Twelve Centuries of Bookbinding: 400–1600.* New York: Pierpont Morgan Library.

Negroponte, Nicholas. 1995. *Being Digital.* New York: Knopf.

Neilson, Allan, and Thomas A. Knott, eds. 1934. *Webster's New International Dictionary.* 2nd ed. Springfield, Mass.: Merriam-Webster.

New Literary History. 1979. 10.2: "Medieval Literature and Contemporary Theory."

Nichols, Stephen. 1990. "Introduction: Philology in a Manuscript Culture." *Speculum* 65: 1–10.

Night at the Museum. 2006. Sean Levy, dir. Twentieth Century–Fox.

Nisus Writer Pro. 2008. Version 1.2. www.nisus.com/pro.

Nossiter, Adam. 2008. "For Some, Uncertainty Starts at Racial Identity." *New York Times* 14 Oct. www.nytimes.com/2008/10/15/us/politics/15biracial .html?scp=1&sq=Adam%20Nossiter%20Barack%20Obama&st=cse.

Nozick, Robert. 1981. *Philosophical Explanations*. Cambridge, Mass.: Belknap.

O'Connell, Pamela Li Calzi. 1999. "Time in a Bottle." *New York Times* 22 Apr.: G1.

O'Keefe, Katherine O'Brien, and Sarah Larratt Keefer, eds. 1998. *New Approaches to Editing Old English Verse*. Cambridge: Brewer.

Olivier, Laurence, dir. 1948. *Hamlet by William Shakespeare*. Rank/Two Cities.

Orgel, Stephen. 1996. "The Status of Evidence: A Roundtable." *PMLA* 111: 21–32.

Ostler, Nicholas. 2007. *Ad Infinitum: A Biography of Latin*. New York: Walker.

Overbye, Dennis. 2009. "Giant Particle Collider Struggles." *New York Times* 4 Aug. http://www.nytimes.com/2009/08/04/science/space/04collide .html?_r=1.

Oxford Dictionary of Quotations. 2004. "Opening Lines," ed. Elizabeth Knowles. Oxford: Oxford University Press.

Oxford English Dictionary. 1933. Ed. James Murray et al. Oxford: Oxford University Press.

———. 1989. 2nd ed. Ed. J. A. Simpson and E. S. C. Weiner. Oxford: Oxford University Press.

———. 1994–. CD-ROM. Oxford: Oxford University Press. Version 3.0, 2003.

Palin, Sarah. 2008. "Sarah Louise Heath Palin." http://en.wikipedia.org/wiki/ Sarah_Palin.

Papers of the Bibliographical Society of America. 1906–. www.bibsocamer .org.

Papers of the Bibliographical Society of Canada/Cahiers de la Société bibliographique du Canada. 1962–. www.library.utoronto.ca/bsc.

Parker, Hershel. 1984. *Flawed Texts and Verbal Icons: Literary Authority in American Fiction*. Evanston, Ill.: Northwestern University Press.

———. 1987. "'The Text Itself—Whatever That Is.'" *Text* 3: 47–54.

Parkes, M[alcolm] B. 1993. *Pause and Effect: An Introduction to the History of Punctuation in the West*. Berkeley: University of California Press.

Parrish, Stephen, gen. ed. 1975–. *The Cornell Wordsworth*. Ithaca, N.Y.: Cornell University Press.

Patterson, Lee. 1985. "The Logic of Textual Criticism and the Way of Genius: The Kane-Donaldson *Piers Plowman* in Historical Perspective." In *Tex-*

tual Criticism and Literary Interpretation, ed. Jerome J. McGann. Chicago: University of Chicago Press.

Patterson, Lyman Ray. 1968. *Copyright in Historical Perspective*. Nashville, Tenn.: Vanderbilt University Press.

Patterson, Lyman Ray, and Stanley W. Lindberg. 1991. *The Nature of Copyright: A Law of Users' Rights*. Athens: University of Georgia Press.

Pear, Robert. 2008. "Health Database Was Set Up to Ignore 'Abortion.'" *New York Times* 5 Apr. www.nytimes.com/2008/04/05/us/05popline.html?_r=1&sq=Johns%20Hopkins%20Abortion&st=cse&adxnnl=1&oref=slogin&scp=1&adxnnlx=1221238970-m7hHsspia366hGjkvZwX/Q

Pearl. MS Cotton Nero a.x. British Library, London.

Pearsall, Derek. 1985. "Editing Medieval Texts: Some Developments and Some Problems." In *Textual Criticism and Literary Interpretation*, ed. Jerome J. McGann. Chicago: University of Chicago Press.

———. 1994. "Theory and Practice in Middle English Editing." *Text* 7: 107–26.

Pearsall, Derek, and R. A. Cooper. 1988. "The Gawain Poems: A Statistical Approach to the Question of Common Authorship." *Review of English Studies*, n.s., 39: 365–85.

Peck, Jeffrey M. 1996. "'In the Beginning Was the Word': Germany and the Origins of German Studies." In *Medievalism and the Modernist Temper*, ed. R. Howard Bloch and Stephen G. Nichols. Baltimore, Md.: Johns Hopkins University Press.

Percy, Thomas. 1765. *Reliques of Ancient English Poetry*. London.

Perelman, Michael. 2002. *Steal This Book: Intellectual Property Rights and the Corporate Confiscation of Creativity*. New York: Palgrave.

Perloff, Marjorie. 2006. "Facturing Out Faktura: The Plight of Visual Text." *Text* 16: 249–66.

Peterson, William S. 1984. *A Bibliography of the Kelmscott Press*. Oxford: Oxford University Press.

Phelps, Deirdre C. 1994. "The Edition as Art Form in Textual and Interpretive Criticism." *Text* 7: 61–75.

———. 1996. "Where's the Book? The Text in the Development of Literary Sociology." *Text* 9: 63–92.

Piers Plowman Archive. 1995–. Ed. Hoyt N. Duggan et al. Ann Arbor: University of Michigan Press.

Pits, John. 1619. *Relationum historicarum de rebus anglicis, tomus primus quatuor partes complectens, quorum elenehum pagina sequens indicat*. Paris: Thierry/Cramoisy.

Pizer, Donald. 1971. "On the Editing of Modern American Texts." *Bulletin of the New York Public Library* 75: 147–53.

———. 1985. "Self-Censorship and Textual Editing." In *Textual Criticism and Literary Interpretation,* ed. Jerome J. McGann. Chicago: University of Chicago Press.

Plachta, Bodo. 1999. "In Between the 'Royal Way' of Philology and 'Occult Science': Some Remarks about German Discussion of Text Constitution in the Last Ten Years." *Text* 12: 31–48.

Pogrebin, Robin. 1998. "The Multi in Cultural Troubles Anthologies." *New York Times* 25 July: A15, A17.

Polk, Noel. 1991. "Where the Comma Goes." In *Representing Modernist Texts: Editing as Interpretation,* ed. George Bornstein. Ann Arbor: University of Michigan Press.

Polastron, Lucien X. 2008. *Books on Fire: The Destruction of Libraries throughout History.* Rochester, N.Y.: Inner Traditions.

Power, Carla. 2000. "A British Nun's Rebellion." *Newsweek* 24 Jan.

Pollard, Alfred W., and J. Dover Wilson. 1919. "The 'stolne surreptitious' Shakesperian [*sic*] Texts." *Times Literary Supplement* 14 Aug.: 434.

Portela, Manuel. 2002. "Untranslations and Transcreations." *Text* 15: 305–22.

Porter, Cole. 1934. "I Get a Kick Out of You." *Anything Goes.* Alvin Theatre, New York, 21 Nov.

———. 1989. *Anything Goes.* London Symphony Orchestra. John McGlinn, cond. EMI.

Pratt, Robert A., ed. 1974. *The Tales of Canterbury.* Boston, Mass.: Houghton Mifflin.

Proctor, Robert. 1898–1903. *An Index to the Early Printed Books in the British Museum: From the Invention of Printing to the Year 1500. With Notes of Those in the Bodleian Library.* London: Kegan Paul. Rpt., London: Holland, 1960.

Propp, Vladimir. 1989. "Fairy Tale Transformations," trans. Ladislaw Matejka and Krystyna Pomorska. In *The Critical Tradition: Classic Texts and Contemporary Trends,* ed. David H. Richter. New York: St. Martin's.

Pugliatti, Paola. 1998. "Textual Perspectives in Italy: From Pasquali's Historicism to the Challenge of 'Variantistica' (and Beyond)." *Text* 11: 155–88.

Quartermain, Peter. 1996. "Undoing the Book." *Text* 9: 119–34.

Quentin, Dom Henri. 1926. *Essai de critique textuelle.* Paris: Picard.

Radin, Grace. 1977. "'Two Enormous Chunks': Episodes Excluded during the Final Revisions of *The Years.*" *Bulletin of the New York Public Library* 80 (Winter).

———. 1981. *Virginia Woolf's "The Years": The Evolution of a Novel.* Knoxville: University of Tennessee Press.

Rainey, Lawrence. 1993. "Cultural Authority and the Crisis of Editorial Theory." Paper presented at the Society for Textual Scholarship conference,
New York City, 17 Apr.

Rainman. 1988. Barry Levinson, dir. United Artists.

Rajan, Tilottama. 1988. "Is There a Romantic Ideology? Some Thoughts on
Schleiermacher's Hermeneutic and Textual Criticism." *Text* 4: 57–76.

Random House Dictionary of the English Language. 1987. 2nd ed. New York:
Random House.

Reiman, Donald H. 1984. "The Four Ages of Editing and the English Roman-
tics." *Text* 1: 231–55.

———. 1987. "'Versioning': The Presentation of Multiple Texts." In Reiman,
Romantic Texts and Contexts. Columbia: University of Missouri Press.

———. 1993. *The Study of Modern Manuscripts: Public, Confidential, and Private.* Baltimore, Md.: Johns Hopkins University Press.

———. 1997. "A Happy Medium: Books between 1475 and 1975." Paper presented at the Society for Textual Scholarship conference, New York, Apr.

———. 2006. "A Great Society." Society for Textual Scholarship Presidential
Address, 2005. *Textual Cultures: Texts, Contexts, Interpretation* 1.1: 75–87.

Rerum Britannicorum medii aevi scriptores. 1858–1891. London: Rolls.

Rerum gallicarum et francicarum scriptores. 1783–1904. Paris.

The Return of the King. 2003. Peter Jackson, dir. New Line Cinema.

Rich, Frank. 2006. *The Greatest Story Ever Sold: The Decline and Fall of Truth
from 9/11 to Katrina.* London: Penguin.

Ricks, Thomas E. 2006. *Fiasco: The American Military Adventure in Iraq.* London: Penguin.

Robbe-Grillet, Alain. 1958. *The Voyeur,* trans. Richard Howard. New York:
Grove.

Roberts, J. M. 1995. *The Penguin History of the World.* Harmondsworth, England: Penguin.

Roberts, Paul. 1989. *The Role of Forensic Science Evidence in Criminal Proceedings.* London: HMSO.

Robinson, Fred C. 1994. *The Editing of Old English.* Cambridge: Blackwell.

Robinson, Jenefer. 1978. "Two Theories of Representation." *Erkenntnis* 12:
27–53.

Robinson, Peter M. W. 1994. "Collation, Textual Criticism, Publication, and
the Computer." *Text* 7: 77–94.

———. 2006. "*The Canterbury Tales* and Other Medieval Texts." In *Electronic
Textual Editing,* ed. Lou Barnard, Katherine O'Brien O'Keefe, and John
Unsworth. New York: MLA.

Rocky. 1976. John D. Alvidsen, dir. Chartoff-Winkler/United Artists.

Rollison, Damian Judge. 2002. "The Poem on the Page: Graphical Prosody in Postmodern American Poetry." *Text* 15: 291–304.

Rorty, Richard. 1982. "Nineteenth-Century Idealism and Twentieth-Century Textualism." In Rorty, *Consequences of Pragmatism.* Minneapolis: University of Minnesota Press.

———. 1989. *Contingency, Irony and Solidarity.* Cambridge: Cambridge University Press.

Rose, Mark. 1993. *Authors and Owners: The Invention of Copyright.* Cambridge, Mass.: Harvard University Press.

Rosenberg, Edgar. 1981. "Last Words on *Great Expectations:* A Textual Brief on the Six Endings." *Dickens Studies Annual* 9: 87–116.

Rosenblum, Ron. 2008. *The Shakespeare Wars: Clashing Scholars, Public Fiascos, Palace Coups.* New York: Random House.

Ross, Charles L., and Dennis Jackson, eds. 1995. *Editing D. H. Lawrence: New Versions of a Modern Author.* Ann Arbor: University of Michigan Press.

Rossini, Gioachino. 1816. *Il Barbiere di Siviglia.* Teatro Argentina, Rome.

Rosten, Leo. 1968. *The Joys of Yiddish.* New York: McGraw-Hill.

Rothenberg, Jerome, and Steven Clay, eds. 2000. *A Book of the Book: Some Works and Projections about the Book and Writing.* New York: Granary.

Rothstein, Edward. 1996. "Technology: If Life on the Web Is Postmodern, Maybe Foucault Really Was a Power Ranger." *New York Times* 1 Apr.: D3.

Rubinstein, E. 1987. "What Is the Text of a Film?" *Text* 3: 417–26.

Rudner, Richard. 1978. "Show or Tell: Incoherence among Symbol Systems." *Erkenntnis* 12: 176–79.

Saferstein, Richard. 1997. *Criminalistics: An Introduction to Forensic Science.* 6th ed. Englewood Cliffs, N.J.: Prentice-Hall.

Salmon, Nicholas. 1996. "The Political Activist." In *William Morris,* ed. Lynda Parry. London: Philip Wilson/Victoria and Albert Museum.

Sanders, Arnold. 1996. "Hypertext, Learning, and Memory: Some Implications from Manuscript Tradition." *Text* 8: 125–44.

Sanjek, David. 1992. "'Don't Have to DJ No More': Sampling and the 'Autonomous' Creator." In *Intellectual Property and the Construction of Authorship,* special issue of *Cardozo Arts & Entertainment Law Journal* 10: 607–24.

Saving Jessica Lynch. 2004. NBC Television, 9 Nov.

Schama, Simon. 1989. *Citizens: A Chronicle of the French Revolution.* New York: Vintage.

———. 1992. *Dead Certainties/Unwarranted Speculations.* New York: Vintage.

Schindler's List. 1993. Steven Spielberg, dir. Universal.

Scholes, Robert. 1992. "Canonicity and Textuality." In *Introduction to Scholarship in Modern Languages and Literatures,* ed. Joseph Gibaldi. 2nd ed. New York: MLA.

Schrøder, Kim Christian. 2007. "Media Discourse Analysis: Researching Cultural Meanings from Inception to Reception." *Textual Cultures: Texts, Contexts, Interpretation* 2.2: 77–99.

Schwab, Richard N., et al. 1983. "Cyclotron Analysis of the Ink in the Forty-Two Line Bible." *Papers of the Bibliographical Society of America* 11: 285–315.

———. 1986. "Ink Patterns in the Gutenberg New Testament: The Proton Milliprobe Analysis of the Lilly Library Copy." *Papers of the Bibliographical Society of America* 80: 305–31.

———. 1987. "The Proton Milliprobe Ink Analysis of the Harvard B42, Volume II." *Papers of the Bibliographical Society of America* 81: 403–32.

Schwartz, Hillel. 1996. *The Culture of the Copy: Striking Likenesses, Unreasonable Facsimiles.* New York: Zone.

Schwartz, Regina, ed. 1990. *The Book and the Text: The Bible and Literary Theory.* Oxford: Blackwell.

Searle, John. 1977. "Reiterating the Differences." *Glyph* 1: 198–208.

Seary, Peter. 1990. *Lewis Theobald and the Editing of Shakespeare.* Oxford: Clarendon.

Serra, Richard. 1991. "Art and Censorship." *Critical Inquiry* 17: 514–81.

Seuss, Dr. 1975. *Oh, the Thinks You Can Think (If Only You Try).* New York: Random House.

Shailor, Barbara A. 1988. *The Medieval Book.* New Haven, Conn.: Beinecke Rare Book and Manuscript Library. Rpt., Toronto: University of Toronto Press, in association with Medieval Academy of America, 1991.

Shakespeare, William. 1602, 1623. *Hamlet,* ed. T. J. B. Spencer. New York: Viking/Penguin.

———. 1723–1725, 1728. *Works,* ed. Alexander Pope. London.

———. 1740. *Works,* ed. Lewis Theobald. London.

———. 1765, 1768. *Works,* ed. Samuel Johnson. London.

——— 1977 *As You Like It,* ed. Richard Knowles. New York: MLA.

———. 1984–. *New Cambridge Shakespeare,* ed. Philip Brockbank et al. Cambridge: Cambridge University Press.

———. 1986. *The Complete Works,* ed. Stanley Wells and Gary Taylor. Oxford: Clarendon.

———. 1992–. *New Folger Library Shakespeare,* ed. Barbara W. Mowatt and Paul Werstine. New York: Simon and Schuster.

———. 1996–. *Arden Shakespeare*. 3rd ser. Ed. Ann Thompson et al. London: Routledge.

———. 2002. *A Synoptic "Hamlet": A Critical-Synoptic Edition of the Second Quarto and First Folio Texts of "Hamlet,"* ed. Jesús Tronch-Pérez. Valencia: Sociedad Española de Estudios Renacentistas Ingleses.

Shaw, David. 1972. "A Sampling Theory for Bibliographical Research." *Library,* 5th ser., 27: 310–19.

———. 1992. *"La bibliologie* in France." In *The Book Encompassed: Studies in Twentieth-Century Bibliography,* ed. Peter Davison. Cambridge: Cambridge University Press.

Shelley, Percy Bysshe. 1954. "Defence of Poetry." In *Shelley's Prose,* rev. ed., ed. David Lee Clark. Albuquerque: University of New Mexico Press, 1966.

Sherbo, Arthur. 1966. "The Uses and Abuses of Internal Evidence." In *Evidence for Authorship: Essays on Problems of Attribution,* ed. David Erdman and Ephim G. Fogel. Ithaca, N.Y.: Cornell University Press.

Shillingsburg, Peter L. 1993. "Textual Variants, Performance Variants, and Concept of Work." *Editio* 7: 221–34.

———. 1996. *Scholarly Editing in the Computer Age: Theory and Practice.* 3rd ed. Athens: University of Georgia Press.

———. 1997. *Resisting Texts: Authority and Submission in Constructions of Meaning.* Ann Arbor: University of Michigan Press.

———. 1999. "Editing Determinate Material Texts." *Text* 12: 59–72.

———. 2006. *From Gutenberg to Google: Electronic Representations of Literary Texts.* Cambridge: Cambridge University Press.

The Shining. 1980. Stanley Kubrick, dir. Hawk Films/Warner Bros.

Shostakovich, Dmitri. 1972. *Symphony No. 15 in A Major, Op. 141.* All-Union Radio and Television Orchestra. Maxim Shostakovich, cond. 8 Jan.

Sibelius, Jan. 1903–1905. *Violin Concerto in D Major, Op. 47.* Original (1903–1904) version and final (1905) version. Leonidas Kavakos, violin. Lahti Symphony Orchestra/Osmo Vänskä. BIS/Conifer CD500.

Silver, Brenda R. 1991. "Textual Criticism as Feminist Practice; or, Who's Afraid of Virginia Woolf: Part II." In *Representing Modernist Texts: Editing as Interpretation,* ed. George Bornstein. Ann Arbor: University of Michigan Press.

———. 1997. "Whose Room of Orlando's Own? The Politics of Adaptation." In *The Margins of the Text,* ed. D. C. Greetham. Ann Arbor: University of Michigan Press.

Sinatra, Frank. 1959. "I Get a Kick Out of You." *Frank Sinatra with the Red Norvo Quintet Live in Australia.* Blue Note, 1997.

Sir Gawain and the Green Knight. MS Cotton Nero a.x. British Library, London.

Siskin, Clifford. 2007. "Textual Culture in the History of the Real." *Textual Cultures: Texts, Contexts, Interpretation* 2.2: 118–30.

Sisson, C. H. 1979. "Pound among the Pedants." *Times Literary Supplement* 20 May: 616. Review of *Collected Early Poems of Ezra Pound,* ed. Michael John King. London: Faber, 1979.

Slevin, James F., with Steve Woolgar. 1986. *Laboratory Life: The Construction of Scientific Facts.* Princeton, N.J.: Princeton University Press.

Small, Ian. 1991. "The Editor as Annotator as Ideal Reader." In *The Theory and Practice of Text-Editing,* ed. Ian Small and Marcus Walsh. Cambridge: Cambridge University Press.

Smith, Martha Nell. 2007. "The Human Touch, Software of the Highest Order: Revisiting Editing as Interpretation." *Textual Cultures: Texts, Contexts, Interpretation* 2.1: 1–15.

Sonn, William. 2006. *Paradigms Lost: The Life and Deaths of the Printed Word.* Lanham, Md.: Scarecrow.

Sonnenberg, Hubert von, et al., eds. 1995. *Rembrandt. Not Rembrandt: Aspects of Connoisseurship.* New York: Metropolitan Museum of Art.

Souter, David. 1994. Supreme Court of the United States, 510 U.S. 569; *Luther R. Campbell aka Luke Skywalker et al. v. Acuff-Rose Music, Inc.,* on a writ of a certiorari to the U.S. Court of Appeals for the Sixth Circuit. 7 Mar. http://caselaw.lp.findlaw.com/scripts/getcase.pl?navby=case&court=us&vol=510&page=569.

space coyote. 2008. *Deviant Art.* http://spacecoyote.deviantart.com/art/John-Calvin-and-Thomas-Hobbes-68330601.

Spenser, Edmund. 1609. *Two Cantos of Mvtabilitie.* London: H.L. for Matthew Lownes.

Sprinchorn, Evert. 1994. "Shakespeare's Bad Quarto." *Times Literary Supplement* 21 Jan.: 15.

Stevenson, Allan. 1962. "Paper as Bibliographical Evidence." *Library,* 5th ser., 17: 285–315.

Stillinger, Jack, ed. 1967. *Twentieth-Century Interpretations of Keats's Odes.* Englewood Cliffs, N.J.: Prentice-Hall.

———. 1978. *The Poems of John Keats.* Cambridge, Mass.: Belknap.

———. 1991. *Multiple Authorship and the Myth of Solitary Genius.* New York: Oxford University Press.

———. 1994. *Coleridge and Textual Instability: The Multiple Versions of the Major Poems.* New York: Oxford University Press.

Stoppard, Tom. 1968. *Rosencrantz and Guildenstern Are Dead.* New York: Grove.

———. 1997. *The Invention of Love.* London: Faber.

Strauss, Richard. 1911. *Der Rosenkavalier.* Königlisches Opernhaus, Dresden.

Suskind, Ron. 2008. *The Way of the World: A Story of Truth and Hope in an Age of Extremism.* New York: Harper.

Sutherland, John. 1988. "Publishing History: A Hole at the Centre of Literary Sociology." *Critical Inquiry* 14: 575–89.

Sutherland, Kathryn. 1998. "Revised Relations? Material Text, Immaterial Text, and the Electronic Environment." *Text* 11: 17–40.

Syme, Holger Schott. 2007. "The Look of Speech." *Textual Cultures: Texts, Contexts, Interpretation* 2.2: 34–60.

Tanner, Thomas. 1748. *Catalogi codicum manuscriptorum Bibliothecae Bodleiana.* Oxford: Bodleian Library.

Tanselle, G. Thomas. 1968. "The Use of Type Damage as Evidence in Bibliographical Description." *Library*, 5th ser., 23: 328–51.

———. 1972. "Some Principles for Editorial Apparatus." *Studies in Bibliography* 25: 41–88.

———. 1974. "Bibliography and Science." *Studies in Bibliography* 27: 55–89. Rpt. in *Selected Studies in Bibliography*, ed. G. Thomas Tanselle. Charlottesville: University Press of Virginia, 1979.

———. 1975. "Problems and Accomplishments in the Editing of the Novel." *Studies in the Novel* 7: 323–60.

———. 1976. "The Editorial Problem of Authorial Final Intention." *Studies in Bibliography* 29: 167–211.

———. 1978. "The Editing of Historical Documents." *Studies in Bibliography* 31: 1–56.

———. 1979. "External Fact as an Editorial Problem." *Studies in Bibliography* 32: 1–47.

———. 1980. "The Concept of Ideal Copy." *Studies in Bibliography* 33: 18–53.

———. 1981a. "From Bibliography to *Histoire Totale:* The History of Books as a Field of Study." *Times Literary Supplement* 5 June: 647–49. Rpt. as *The History of Books as a Field of Study: Second Hanes Lecture.* Chapel Hill: Hanes Foundation/University of North Carolina Press, 1981.

———. 1981b. "Recent Editorial Discussions and the Central Questions of Editing." *Studies in Bibliography* 34: 23–65.

———. 1981c. "Textual Scholarship." In *Introduction to Scholarship in Modern Languages and Literatures,* ed. Joseph Gibaldi. New York: MLA.

———. 1983. "Classical, Biblical, and Medieval Textual Criticism and Modern Editing." *Studies in Bibliography* 36: 21–68.

———. 1986. "Historicism and Critical Editing." *Studies in Bibliography* 39: 1–46.

———. 1988. *Textual Criticism since Greg: A Chronicle 1950–1985.* Charlottesville: University Press of Virginia.

———. 1989. *A Rationale of Textual Criticism.* Philadelphia: University of Pennsylvania Press.

———. 1990a. "Textual Criticism and Deconstruction." *Studies in Bibliography* 43: 1–33.

———. 1990b. *Textual Criticism and Scholarly Editing.* Charlottesville: University Press of Virginia.

———. 1990c. "Texts of Documents and Texts of Works." In his *Textual Criticism and Scholarly Editing.* Charlottesville: University Press of Virginia.

———. 1994. "Editing without a Copy-Text." *Studies in Bibliography* 47: 1–22.

———. 1995a. "Critical Editions, Hypertexts, and Genetic Criticism." *Romanic Review* 86: 581–93.

———. 1995b. "Printing History and Other History." *Studies in Bibliography* 48: 269–89.

———. 1996a. " Reflections on Scholarly Editing." *Raritan* 16.2: 52–64.

———. 1996b. "Textual Instability and Editorial Idealisms." *Studies in Bibliography* 49: 1–60.

———. 1998. *Literature and Artifacts.* Charlottesville: University Press of Virginia.

———. 2001. "Textual Criticism at the Millennium." *Studies in Bibliography* 54: 1–80.

———. 2006. "The Textual Criticism of Visual and Aural Works." *Studies in Bibliography* 57: 1–37.

Tanselle, G. Thomas, ed. 1979. *Selected Studies in Bibliography.* Charlottesville: University Press of Virginia.

Tarrant, R. J. 1995. "Classical Latin Literature." In *Scholarly Editing: A Guide to Research,* ed. D. C. Greetham. New York: MLA.

Tate, Nahum. 1681. *The History of King Lear, Acted at the Duke's Theatre. Reviv'd with Alterations.* By N. Tate. London: E. Flesher.

———. 1976. *The History of King Lear,* ed. James Black. London: Edward Arnold.

Taylor, Gary. 1987. "Revising Shakespeare." *Text* 3: 285–304.

———. 1988. "The Rhetoric of Textual Criticism." *Text* 4: 39–56.

———. 1993. "The Renaissance and the End of Editing." In *Palimpsest: Editorial Theory in the Humanities,* ed. George Bornstein and Ralph G. Williams. Ann Arbor: University of Michigan Press.

———. 1994. "The Rhetoric of Reception." In *Crisis in Editing: The Texts of the English Renaissance,* ed. Randall McLeod. New York: AMS.

Taylor, Gary, and John Lavagnino, eds. 2007. *Thomas Middleton: The Collected Works.* Oxford: Clarendon.

Taylor, Gary, and Michael Warren, eds. 1988. *The Division of the Kingdoms: Shakespeare's Two Versions of "King Lear."* Oxford: Oxford University Press.

Taylor, Mark C., and Esa Saarinen. 1994. *Imagologies: Media Philosophy.* London: Routledge.

Taylor, Robert. 1981. "Editorial Practices—An Historian's View." *Newsletter of the Association for Documentary Editing* 3.1: 4–8.

Terminator 2: Judgment Day. 1991. James Cameron, dir. Tristar.

Text: Transactions of the Society for Textual Scholarship. 1984–. Society for Textual Scholarship. (Beginning with vol. 9, *Text: An Interdisciplinary Annual of Textual Studies*)

Theweleit, Klaus. 1987. *Male Fantasies.* Oxford: Oxford University Press.

Thierer, Adam, and Clyde Wayne Crews Jr., eds. 2002. *Copyfights: The Future of Intellectual Property in the Information Age.* Washington, D.C.: Cato Institute.

Thompson, Ann. 1997. "Feminist Theory and the Editing of Shakespeare: *The Taming of the Shrew* Revisited." In *The Margins of the Text,* ed. D. C. Greetham. Ann Arbor: University of Michigan Press.

Thompson, E. P. 1955, 1977. *William Morris: Romantic to Revolutionary.* New York: Monthly Review Press, and London: Lawrence and Wishart. Rpt., New York: Pantheon, 1977.

Thompson, John. 1991. "Textual Instability and the Late Medieval Reputation of Some Middle English Literature." *Text* 5: 175–94.

Thorpe, James. 1972. *Principles of Textual Criticism.* San Marino, Calif.: Huntington Library.

Timmons, Heather. 2008. "Vogue's Fashion Photos Spark Debate in India." *New York Times* 1 Sept.: C1, C5.

Timpanaro, Sebastiano. 1976. *The Freudian Slip: Psychoanalysis and Textual Criticism,* trans. Kate Soper. London: Verso.

Tinkle, Theresa. 1998. "The Wife of Bath's Textual/Sexual Lives." In *The Iconic Page in Manuscript, PRINT, and Digital Culture,* ed. George Bornstein and Theresa Tinkle. Ann Arbor: University of Michigan Press.

Tougaw, Jason, ed. 1993. "Selections from *Teleny* (attrib. Oscar Wilde)." Seminar paper, City University of New York Graduate School.

Toulmin, Stephen. 1990. *Cosmopolis: The Hidden Agenda of Modernity.* Chicago: University of Chicago Press.

Trachsler, Richard. 2006. "How to Do Things with Manuscripts: From Humanist Practice to Recent Textual Criticism." *Textual Cultures: Texts, Contexts, Interpretation* 1.1: 5–28.

Trapp, J. B., ed. 1973. *The Oxford Anthology of English Literature.* Oxford: Oxford University Press.

Travis, Trysh. 2000. "What We Talk About When We Talk About the *New Yorker.*" *Book History* 3: 253–85.

Treitler, Leo. 1992. "The Politics of Reception: Tailoring the Present as Fulfillment of a Desired Past." *Journal of the Royal Musicological Association* 116: 280–98.

———. 1993. "History and Ontology." *Journal of Aesthetics and Art Criticism* 51.3: 483–97.

———. 1995. "Text and Performance in Music and Literature." Doctoral seminar, City University of New York Graduate Center.

Trevisa, John. n.d. *De Proprietatibus Rerum.* MS Plimpton 263, Columbia University Library, New York.

———. 1495(?). *De Proprietatibus Rerum,* ed. Wynkyn de Worde. Westminster: Wynkyn de Worde.

———. 1975. *Trevisa's Translation of "Bartholomaeus Anglicus De Proprietatibus Rerum,"* ed. M. C. Seymour et al. Oxford: Clarendon.

Tribble, Evelyn B. 1993. *Margins and Marginality: The Printed Page in Early Modern England.* Charlottesville: University Press of Virginia.

———. 1997. "'Like a Looking-Glas in the Frame': From the Marginal Note to the Footnote." In *The Margins of the Text,* ed. D. C. Greetham. Ann Arbor: University of Michigan Press.

Trible, Phyllis. 1997. "What God Meant to Say . . ." Review of James L. Kugel, *The Bible as It Was* (1997). *New York Times Book Review* 21 Dec.: 8.

Turkle, Sherry. 1984. *The Second Self: Computers and the Human Spirit.* New York: Simon and Schuster.

———. 1995. *Life on the Screen: Identity in the Age of the Internet.* New York: Simon and Schuster.

Turner, Robert K., Jr. 1966. "Reappearing Types as Bibliographical Evidence." *Studies in Bibliography* 19: 198–209.

Urkowitz, Steven. 1980. *Shakespeare's Revision of "King Lear."* Princeton, N.J.: Princeton University Press.

———. 1986. "'Well Said, Old Mole': Burying Three *Hamlets,* in Modern Editions." In *Shakespeare Study Today,* ed. Georgiana Ziegler. New York: AMS.

Urmson, J. O. 1976. "The Performing Arts." *Contemporary British Philosophy,* 4th ser., 239–52.

Utz, Richard. 1998. "Speaking of Medievalism: An Interview with Leslie J. Workman." In *Medievalism in the Modern World: Essays in Honor of Leslie J. Workman,* ed. Richard Utz and Tom Shippey. Turnhout: Brepols.

Vaidhyanathan, Siva. 2001. *Copyrights and Copywrongs: The Rise of Intellectual Property and How It Threatens Creativity.* New York: New York University Press.

Valdes, Mario. 1992. World-Making: The Literary Truth-Claim and the Interpretation of Texts. Toronto: University of Toronto Press.

Valla, Lorenzo. 1440. *Constitutum Constantini/On the Donation of Constantine.* Rpt., trans. G. W. Bowersock. Cambridge, Mass.: I Tatti Renaissance Library/Harvard University Press, 2007.

Vanden Bossche, Chris R. 1994. "The Value of Literature: Representations of Print Culture in the Copyright Debate of 1837–1842." *Victorian Studies* 23: 41–68.

Vandendorpe, Christian. 2009. *From Papyrus to Hypertext: Toward the Universal Digital Library,* trans. Phyllis Aronoff and Howard Scott. Urbana: University of Illinois Press.

Van Doren, Charles. 1991. *A History of Knowledge.* New York: Birch Lane.

Varvaro, Alberto. 1999. "The 'New Philology' from an Italian Perspective." *Text* 12: 49–58.

Vendler, Helen. 1983. *The Odes of John Keats.* Cambridge, Mass.: Belknap.

Vickers, Brian. 1993. "Hamlet by Dogberry: A Perverse Reading of the Bad Quarto." *Times Literary Supplement* 24 Dec.: 5–6. Review of Graham Holderness and Bryan Loughrey's edition of *Hamlet* Q1 in the Shakespearean Originals series. The editors respond in *TLS* 4 Feb. 1994: 14.

———. 1994. *Appropriating Shakespeare: Contemporary Critical Quarrels.* New Haven, Conn.: Yale University Press.

Vinaver, Eugène. 1930. "Principles of Textual Emendation." In *Studies in French Language and Medieval Literature Presented to Professor M. K. Pope.* Manchester: University of Manchester Press. Rpt. in *Literary and Historical Editing,* ed. George L. Vogt and John Bush Jones. Lawrence: University of Kansas Libraries, 1981.

Vinaver, Eugène, ed. 1967. *The Works of Sir Thomas Malory.* 2nd ed. Oxford: Clarendon.

Vliet, H. T. M. van. 2006. "Compositional History as a Key to Textual Interpretation." *Text* 16: 67–78.

von Frank, Albert, Jr. 1987. "Genetic versus Clear Texts: Reading and Writing Emerson." *Documentary Editing* (Dec.): 5–9.

von Frank, Albert, Jr., ed. 1999. *The Complete Sermons of Ralph Waldo Emerson.* 4 vols. Columbia: University of Missouri Press.

Wagner, Richard. 1845. *Tannhäuser.* Dresden Hoftheater, Dresden. Opéra Paris, 1861.

Walton, Kendall. 1988. "The Presentation and Portrayal of Sound Patterns." In *Human Agency: Language, Duty, and Value,* ed. J. Dancy, J. Moravcsik, and C. C. W. Taylor. Stanford, Calif.: Stanford University Press.

WALL-E. 2008. Andrew Stanton, dir. Pixar.

Warren, Michael. 1990. "The Theatricalization of Text: Beckett, Jonson, Shakespeare." In *New Directions in Textual Studies,* ed. Dave Oliphant and Robin Bradford. Austin: Harry Ransom Humanities Research Center/ University of Texas Press.

Warren, Michael, ed. 1989. *The Complete King Lear, 1608–1623.* Berkeley: University of California Press.

Wedekind, Frank. 1895. *Erdgeist (Earth Spirit).* Munich: A. Langen.

———. 1904. *Die Büchse der Pandora (Pandora's Box).* Berlin: B. Cassirer.

———. 1993. *The First Lulu,* trans. Eric Bentley. New York: Applause.

Weiss, Adrian. 1988. "Reproductions of Early Dramatic Texts as a Source of Bibliographical Evidence." *Text* 4: 237–68.

Weissman, Stephen. 1995. "What Use Is Bibliography?" *Papers of the Bibliographical Society of America* 89: 133–48.

Weitzman, Michael. 1985. "The Analysis of Open Traditions." *Studies in Bibliography* 38: 82–120.

Wellek, René, and Alvaro Ribeiro, eds. 1979. *Evidence in Literary Scholarship: Essays in Memory of James Marshall Osborn.* Oxford: Clarendon.

Wellek, René, and Austin Warren. 1956. *Theory of Literature.* 3rd ed. New York: Harcourt Brace.

Wells, Stanley. 2006. *Shakespeare & Co.: Christopher Marlowe, Thomas Dekker, Ben Jonson, Thomas Middleton, John Fletcher, & the Other Players in His Story.* New York: Vintage.

Wells, Stanley, et al., eds. 1987. *William Shakespeare: A Textual Companion.* Oxford: Clarendon.

Werner, Marta. 1995. *Emily Dickinson's Open Folios: Scenes of Reading, Surfaces of Writing.* Ann Arbor: University of Michigan Press.

West, James L. W., III. 1989. "Editorial Theory and the Act of Submission." *Papers of the Bibliographical Society of America* 83: 169–85.

———. 1994a. "Fair Copy, Authorial Intention, and 'Versioning.'" *Text* 7: 81–89.

———. 1994b. "Novelist's Champion Vows to Keep the Flame Burning." *Chronicle of Higher Education* 2 Nov.: A11–13.

———. 1995. "The Scholarly Editor as Biographer." In *Editing Novels and Novelists, Now,* special issue of *Studies in the Novel* 27: 295–303.

Widmer, Ted. 2008. "Looking for Liberty." *New York Times* 4 July: A19.

Wilde, Oscar (attrib.). 1893. *Teleny; or, The Reverse of the Medal,* ed. Leonard Smithers. Paris(?): Erotika Biblion, 1934; Paris: Olympia, 1958; San Francisco, Calif.: Gay Sunshine, 1984; n.p.: BadBoy, 1992.

Williams, William P., and Craig S. Abbott. 1999. *An Introduction to Bibliography and Textual Studies.* 3rd ed. New York: MLA.

Willinsky, John. 1994. *Empire of Words: The Reign of the OED.* Princeton, N.J.: Princeton University Press.

———. 2006. *The Access Principle: The Case for Open Access to Research and Scholarship.* Cambridge, Mass.: MIT Press.

Willis, James. 1972. *Latin Textual Criticism.* Urbana: University of Illinois Press.

Wilson, Edmund. 1968. "The Fruits of the MLA." *New York Review of Books* 26 Sept.: 7–10; 10 Oct.: 6+. Rpt. as pamphlet, New York: New York Review of Books, 1968.

Wilson, J. Dover, ed. 1962. *Love's Labour's Lost. By William Shakespeare.* 2nd ed. Cambridge: Cambridge University Press.

Wollheim, Richard. 1972. "On an Alleged Inconsistency in Collingwood's Aesthetic." In *Critical Essays on the Philosophy of R. G. Collingwood,* ed. Michael Krausz. Oxford: Clarendon. Rpt. in *On Art and the Mind: Essays and Lectures.* London: Allen Lane, 1973.

Womack, Kenneth. 1998. "Editing the Beatles: Addressing the Roles of Authority and Editorial Theory in the Creation of Popular Music's Most Valuable Canon." *Text* 11: 189–205.

Woodring, Carl, and James Shapiro, eds. 1995. *Columbia Anthology of British Poetry.* New York: Columbia University Press.

WordPerfect 8.0. 1997. Automatic spell-checker. Ottawa, Canada: Corel.

Worthen, John. 1994. "Checking for Fact-Checkers." *Times Literary Supplement* 1 Jan.: 11–12.

Wynne-Davies, Marion, ed. 1992. *The Tales of the Clerk and the Wife of Bath. By Geoffrey Chaucer.* London: Routledge.

Yamashita, Hiroshi. 1995. "Fredson Bowers and the Editing of Modern Japanese Literature." *Text* 8: 85–100.

Zaknic, Ivan. 1983. *Pompidou Centre.* Paris: Flammarion.

Zeffirelli, Franco, dir. 1968. *Romeo and Juliet.* Paramount.

Zeller, Hans. 1975. "A New Approach to the Critical Constitution of Literary Texts." *Studies in Bibliography* 28: 231–64.

General Index

Index of Topics

DAVID GREETHAM is Distinguished Professor of English, Interactive Technology and Pedagogy, and Medieval Studies at the City University of New York Graduate Center. He founded the interdisciplinary Society for Textual Scholarship, is a past president of the society, and was co-editor of the initial volumes of its journal, *Text*. His books include *Textual Scholarship: An Introduction*, *Textual Transgressions*, and *Theories of the Text*, and he edited *The Margins of the Text* and *Scholarly Editing*. He has published in *PMLA*, *Modern Philology*, *Journal of the History of Ideas*, *Studies in Bibliography*, and *Papers of the Bibliographical Society of America*. He is currently working on the theory of copyright as it affects textual studies and on the concept of the unfinished work.